# East End Chronicles

# ED GLINERT

# East End Chronicles

ALLEN LANE
*an imprint of*
PENGUIN BOOKS

*To the memory of Harold Forman Levy*

ALLEN LANE

Published by the Penguin Group
Penguin Books Ltd, 80 Strand, London WC2R ORL, England
Penguin Group (USA) Inc., 375 Hudson Street, New York, New York 10014, USA
Penguin Group (Canada), 10 Alcorn Avenue, Toronto, Ontario, Canada M4V 3B2
(a division of Pearson Penguin Canada Inc.)
Penguin Ireland, 25 St Stephen's Green, Dublin 2, Ireland (a division of Penguin Books Ltd)
Penguin Group (Australia), 250 Camberwell Road,
Camberwell, Victoria 3124, Australia (a division of Pearson Australia Group Pty Ltd)
Penguin Books India Pvt Ltd, 11 Community Centre,
Panchsheel Park, New Delhi – 110 017, India
Penguin Group (NZ), cnr Airborne and Rosedale Roads, Albany,
Auckland 1310, New Zealand (a division of Pearson New Zealand Ltd)
Penguin Books (South Africa) (Pty) Ltd, 24 Sturdee Avenue,
Rosebank 2196, South Africa

Penguin Books Ltd, Registered Offices: 80 Strand, London WC2R ORL, England

www.penguin.com

First published 2005
1

Copyright © Ed Glinert, 2005

The moral right of the author has been asserted

Set in 10.5/14 pt Linotype Sabon
Typeset by Palimpsest Book Production Limited, Polmont, Stirlingshire
Printed in Great Britain by Clays Ltd, St Ives plc

A CIP catalogue record for this book is available from the British Library

ISBN 0-713-99774-5

# Contents

| | | |
|---|---|---:|
| | *Foreword* | vii |
| 1 | A Vast Shocking City | 1 |
| 2 | Building the New Jerusalem | 5 |
| 3 | Docks, Dockers and River Pirates | 15 |
| 4 | The Silk Weavers of Spitalfields | 40 |
| 5 | Ratcliff Highway: Murder and Mayhem | 53 |
| 6 | Mystics and Myth-makers | 71 |
| 7 | The Mysteries of the Orient | 99 |
| 8 | The Jewish Ghetto | 117 |
| 9 | In Darkest London and the Way Out | 148 |
| 10 | Riot and Revolution | 177 |
| 11 | The Unlucky Isle of Dogs | 213 |
| 12 | Blitz and Bombs | 226 |
| 13 | Dark Ages | 243 |
| 14 | Rebirth? | 287 |
| | *Acknowledgements* | 298 |
| | *Bibliography* | 299 |
| | *Index* | 302 |

# *Foreword*

The East End is a bizarre world with its own codes, rules and symbols. Its history rests oddly alongside that of London, the capital, tourist magnet, seat of government and royalty.

It is a history of strangeness and savagery, of mystery and mayhem. The strangeness and mystery derive from the location of Tower Hill, a rare stretch of high ground in this mostly flat, featureless area on the north bank of the Thames. Tower Hill is located at the point where the western stretches of the East End give way to the City of London. To the ancient tribes of London the hill was holy. In the first century AD the Roman invaders honoured Tower Hill's hallowed status and left the land by the hill as 'sacred territory', where no development could take place.

The medieval church adapted this tradition, filling the 'sacred territory' with a ring of monasteries. These included Holy Trinity Aldgate, where the East End's first documented murder took place in the early sixteenth century, and which was later, in 1888, the site where Jack the Ripper killed one of his victims.

After London was burnt out by the 1666 Fire, those charged with rebuilding the capital, led by Christopher Wren and powered by the intellectual might of the Royal Society, looked east. They secretly wanted to rebuild London as the New Jerusalem, capital of a Protestant world free of Popery, as befitting a city which had embraced Christianity centuries before it conquered Rome. Wren and his team were unable to fulfil all their ambitions owing to the impenetrable bureaucracy surrounding ownership of the land and the prohibitive cost of demolishing what remained of the capital. Few of the master architect's grand schemes – for instance the building of wide, spacious boulevards and piazzas to replace the narrow winding lanes of the old City – came to pass. But Wren's overriding aim – to convert London into the world's greatest city – was realized.

One factor hitherto overlooked (or unobserved) by historians is that the new London Wren created was calculated systematically rather than arbitrarily. The mathematics he and assistants such as Nicholas Hawksmoor chose in siting their major buildings came not from empirical science but from the Old Testament and the sacred geometry of the Kabbalah. It was this arcane religious philosophy that gave the East End its first planned estate: Wellclose Square, a haven for intellectuals, bohemians and free-thinkers, and the setting for considerable philosophical and religious intrigue over the next 300 years.

The savagery and mayhem derive from the proximity of the river, which has brought to London a continuous wave of penniless, fearful immigrants. Their arrival has usually been greeted with hostility from the natives, themselves mostly descendants from earlier immigrants.

The Chinese who came in the mid nineteenth century were mostly left unharmed, probably because Londoners wanted their opium. Jewish refugees who arrived in the East End after the 1881 pogroms in eastern Europe faced not only the usual impoverishment, over-crowding and physical attacks from xenophobic locals, but humiliation from their own religious brethren. The Jewish Board of Guardians wrote to their counterparts in eastern Europe pleading with them 'to place a barrier to the flow of foreigners, to persuade these voyagers not to venture to come to a land they know nothing about. It is better that they live a life of sorrow in their native place than bear the shame of famine and perish in a strange land.'

The river gave rise to its own idiosyncratic type of crime: pilfering from the vessels bringing produce to London, led by teams of exotically named gangs – Heavy Horsemen, Lumpers, Dredgermen, Mudlarks, Monkey Suckers. Entire neighbourhoods raised on robbery. This sort of crime was toughed out by the building of the docks, which fronted the East End for over 150 years and became the main source of industry. Casual local crime dropped but was replaced by casual local employment; fitful, brutal and appallingly paid.

The river brought to east London thousands of excitable sailors looking for relief after months aboard ship. Fuelled by cheap alcohol, whoring and sin, they turned this part of London into a dystopia of debauchery.

Unlike other parts of London the East End offered almost no buffers of wealth or comfort, little in the way of suburban safety or petit-bourgeois gentility to dampen the gloom. The riches passing through the docks and being created in the factories failed to trickle down to the locale. Perhaps some of this explains the intensity of East End violence, manifested most horribly in the Ratcliff Highway murders of 1811 and by Jack the Ripper nearly eighty years later. It may also explain why the East End gangs – the Old Nichol, the Bessarabians, the Krays – have always been among London's most feared.

*East End Chronicles* brings together more than 400 years of such stories, the horror and awful excitement, the devilment and the danger: from the Black Death and the Plague to the Fire, the rebuilding of London according to religious rite, the East End as a starting point for overseas exploration, the growth of trade dominated by the ruthless East India Company; silk weaving in Spitalfields, Wellclose Square as a centre of mystical intrigue, the rise of Chinatown, the Ratcliff Highway murders, the Jack the Ripper murders of 1888, the Jewish Ghetto, the poverty of the gentile ghetto, the philanthropists and their hopelessly optimistic social cures, the music hall, Jewish anarchists, the early days of the Labour Party and the Communist Party, the British Union of Fascists, Second World War devastation, dead-end estates, the Krays, the National Front, Banglatown, eastern mysticism, Canary Wharf and the Brick Lane industry.

Lastly let me clarify some misconceptions over what constitutes the East End. The term has become ubiquitous in recent years and has come to be misused in describing anywhere lying roughly between St Paul's Cathedral and the North Sea. Residents of suburban towns located a short drive from Romford Market or the Lakeside shopping centre in Thurrock lovingly refer to their manor as 'the East End'. Sports commentators on BBC radio excitedly welcome listeners to West Ham United's Boleyn ground in Upton Park 'in the heart of the East End'. Pilots bringing their planes to land at London City Airport welcome passengers to London's 'famous East End'. Of course none of those places is in the East End, even though all are to the east of central London.

So where is the East End? The East End is the four-mile-wide territory east of the City of London leading up to the river Lea, a natural and obvious eastern boundary. The other traditional boundaries are equally formidable: another powerful natural and obvious river boundary – the Thames – to the south, and the thick woodland long prettified into Victoria Park to the north.

This is *not* the East End: Dalston and Hackney. They are in east London but not in the East End. This is also *not* the East End: Canning Town, East Ham, Ilford, Leyton, Leytonstone, Romford, Silvertown, Stratford, Wanstead and West Ham. Historically they are in Essex. In 1965 they were sucked into Greater London and are now part of the capital's overspill that threatens to take over the entire south-east, but they are not part of the East End.

This *is* the East End: Bethnal Green, Blackwall, Bow, Bromley-by-Bow, Cubitt Town, Globe Town, Limehouse, Mile End, Millwall, Old Ford, Poplar, Ratcliff, Shadwell, Spitalfields, Stepney, Wapping, Whitechapel. Now read on . . .

# I

# A Vast Shocking City

They came from afar to marvel at the horrors of London's ugly *alter ego*, to damn the rotting underbelly of the teeming metropolis. It was 'a vast shocking city, an evil plexus of slums that hide human creeping things, where filthy men and women live on gin, where collars and clean shirts are decencies unknown, where every citizen wears a black eye', according to Arthur Morrison's 1894 work *Tales of Mean Streets*. Its inhabitants were 'almost as removed from Christian influences as savages in the wilds of Africa [living in] the hell of poverty which like one enormous, black, motionless, giant kraken lurks in silence encircling with its mighty tentacles the life and wealth of the City and of the West End', claimed the *Daily Telegraph*. The American writer Jack London could find

no more dreary spectacle on this earth. The color of life is gray and drab. Everything is helpless, hopeless, unrelieved, and dirty. Bath-tubs are a thing totally unknown, as mythical as the ambrosia of the gods. The people themselves are dirty, while any attempt at cleanliness becomes howling farce, when it is not pitiful and tragic. Strange, vagrant odors come drifting along the greasy wind, and the rain, when it falls, is more like grease than water from heaven. The very cobblestones are scummed with grease.

This was the East End: Victorian hell hole, horrific afterbirth of the Industrial Revolution.

Although other parts of London suffered equal decline during the capital's fierce early nineteenth-century growth – there was little difference between the depravities of Stepney and, say, Saffron Hill; between the horrors of Whitechapel and Walworth – the East End offered almost no buffers of wealth or comfort and little in the way of suburban safety or petit-bourgeois gentility to lighten the gloom.

The riches passing through the docks and being created in the factories failed to trickle down to the locality, leaving much of the district teetering on the edge of social disaster. The term 'East Ender' became a description of someone unfortunate, someone to be pitied, ignored or avoided: 'dwarfs and hunchbacks, creatures bent double, crooked and bandy and rickety babes, listless emaciated middle-aged women who looked as though they supported nature on a diet of Lucifer matches and gin', wrote the leader writer of the *Daily Telegraph*, overcome with the loathsomeness of the area.

Disease has long been a great leveller in the East End. Even though most of London succumbed when the Black Death, the Bubonic Plague and cholera hit the capital, these epidemics always arrived first and hit worst in the East End.

Crime has been the great local growth industry. It is not that wrongdoing here is more violent, immoral and degenerate than elsewhere in London, but simply that the area always spawns criminals that capture the imagination – Spring-heeled Jack, the Ratcliff Highway murderer (or, more probably, murderers) and Jack the Ripper; three outbreaks of the cruellest violence and not one satisfactory conviction found for any of them. The East End villains of the twentieth century were more conspicuous but equally nasty: the Bessarabians, who terrorized the Edwardian era Jewish ghetto, and the Kray twins, who imposed their own martial law on the area in the 1950s and 1960s, fiercely loyal to those who complied, swiftly brutal to those who did not.

Sometimes the criminals have simply responded to the authorities' irresponsibility. On 30 April 1517 the canon of the Hospital of the Blessed Virgin Mary Without Bishopsgate delivered a sermon that aroused such xenophobic feelings that a mob of apprentices went on the rampage, attacking the homes of Flemings, Italians and French, until they were scattered by the Duke of Norfolk and 2,000 soldiers. The event was soon dubbed 'Evil May Day', and twelve apprentices were hanged and quartered for their involvement, their body parts left to rot on various gates around London.

The East End has long been prone to political manipulation by fiery orators with convincing answers – the poll-tax rebels of 1381; the Kent insurgent Jack Cade the following century; a group of odd-looking, noisy Russians assembled at the Jewish socialist club on the corner of Fulbourne Street and Whitechapel Road in 1907 who went on to stage bloody revolution in their own country ten years later; and black-clad, baton-swishing fascists who attacked the local Jewish population in the 1930s.

Alongside the squalor, disease, crime and proto-revolution there has been one other force which, more than anything else, has contributed to the strangeness of the East End: religious manipulation. The area has long been prone to spiritual and mystical excess. Local ancient British tribes, who believed Tower Hill was holy, buried inside it the skull of Bran, a Celtic god king whose head was said to possess magical powers and had remained alive after his death. It was interred facing France to ward off invaders but it failed to repel the Romans. Nevertheless the Romans adapted the legend into their own tradition of leaving the eastern end of their cities as sacred territory, where no development could take place, and built their fortifications, baths and basilicas further west in what is now the City of London.

When the Normans took over the country in the eleventh century they built what is still East London's greatest landmark – the Tower – by the ancient tribes' sacred hill. Those who ran the Tower later adapted the Bran legend, stocking the building with ravens ('bran' in Welsh), whose presence symbolically ensures the safety of the kingdom.

When the Black Death hit the East End in 1348 it was the Pope, Clement VI, not local physicians, who devised an imaginative antidote. He sent to London a group of 120 holy men, who walked through the East End, their faces hidden, chanting paternosters and Ave Marias. When they arrived at Stepney Green they stopped marching, stripped to the waist and formed a large circle. Their leaders, who were carrying banners of purple velvet and gold cloth, passed around a number of heavy leather scourges tipped with metal studs, and while the master of the holy men prayed for God's mercy those who had been given the scourges began beating other members of the group until the blood flowed freely. They repeated this ceremony twice during the day and once at night for thirty-three and a half days, regardless of the occasional death. The Black Death subsequently abated, but probably not because of such strange rituals.

The medieval east London landscape was dominated by religious institutions. They colonized the border between the East End and the City, building a line of monasteries – St Katharine's Hospital, Minories, Eastminster and Holy Trinity Aldgate – on the Romans' sacred ground. It was at Holy Trinity in 1530 that the first of many unusual and disturbing East End murders took place, when Brother Martin, a Holy Trinity monk, stabbed to death a woman praying at the high altar, and then killed himself. By what is probably an astonishing coincidence Jack the Ripper killed Catherine Eddowes on the same spot, now Mitre Square, in 1888.

But the East End is full of such twists of fate. Violence and mystery gathering at evil corners, people acting in unusual ways, believing and doing things they would not believe or do elsewhere.

# 2

# Building the New Jerusalem

The year 1665 was bound to be a bad one. A comet had passed over the capital the previous December, a sign that God was not happy with London's behaviour. And with it came the Bubonic Plague, a punishment outlined in the Old Testament Book of Chronicles, experts explained, whereby the Lord smote 'the people, children, wives and all goods [causing] great sickness by disease'. As the Plague spread through the East End, Whitechapel Road filled with wagons, carts and coaches taking the wealthy to safety. Sentries were stationed at the boundaries of the district to turn back the poor, as they were considered to be carriers of the disease.

Victims often didn't wait to die. Wrapped in blankets and rugs they threw themselves into burial pits like the one in St Botolph's churchyard, Aldgate, at the edge of the East End. Those who stayed at home to die were sealed up inside, a red cross painted on the door to warn off visitors and a guard standing outside to make sure they did not escape. Some broke free, however, and fled, infecting all those they encountered. But most victims stayed put, for fleeing would be an attempt to escape God's will and God would surely hunt down the fugitive, they feared.

As the Plague raged, so the harbingers of doom raved. One man paced the streets of Whitechapel crying out like Jonah: 'Yet forty days, and Nineveh shall be overthrown!' A Stepney resident, Solomon Eagle, one of a group of Quakers known for holding fasting contests with Anglican priests and stripping in churchyards to prove their true piety, strode through the area naked, a pan of burning charcoal on his head, proclaiming awful warnings. A man wearing nothing other than a pair of underpants, which he wrapped around his head, was seen throughout the East End wailing: 'O! the Great and the Dreadful God!' Outside a house in Mile End a crowd gathered as a woman pointed to the sky, claiming she could see a white angel brandishing a fiery sword, warning those who could not see the vision that God's anger had been aroused and that 'dreadful judgments were approaching'.

On 2 September the Lord Mayor ordered that fires should be lit in various streets, courtyards and alleyways, and kept alight for three days to purify the air, as Hippocrates of Athens had ordered during a fifth-century plague. As the months moved into winter the plague did recede, but it was not the fires, nor the severe frost, that curtailed the epidemic, but the sating of *Rattus rattus* (the black rat) and *Ceratophyllus fasciatus* (the black rat's flea) which after their mass feast had left 6,583 dead in Stepney and 3,855 dead in Whitechapel.

## THE YEAR OF THE BEAST

If 1665 was always going to be a difficult year, then 1666 was bound to be worse. The year contained the number 666 – the number of the Beast of the Book of Revelation. Many forecast that London would therefore be ravaged by the fiery lake which, according to the same book, 'burneth the fearful and unbelieving, the abominable, the murders, the whoremongers, sorcerers, idolaters and liars'.

Two well-known books of the time predicted that the city would burn. Daniel Baker, in *A Certaine Warning for a Naked Heart*, explained how London would be destroyed by a 'consuming fire', while Walter Gostelo in *The Coming of God in Mercy, in Vengeance, Beginning with Fire, to Convert or Consume all this so Sinful City* boasted: 'If fire make not ashes of the City, and thy bones also, conclude me a liar for ever.' And sure enough, on 2 September 1666, exactly a year after the Lord Mayor had ordered Londoners to light fires to burn out the Plague, a greater fire – the Great Fire of London – broke out and destroyed much of the capital.

The Fire began in the bakery of Thomas Farriner on Pudding Lane, just north of London Bridge. It scared few at first, and it looked as if the blaze would soon fizzle out. But a strong wind fanned the flames and when some hay in the yard of the nearby Star Inn caught alight the fire spread south to Thames Street, where the warehouses stored sugar and oil. Once these buildings began to burn it wasn't long before the tightly packed wooden houses close by were on fire and London was burning down.

The Fire raged for a week, destroying 13,200 properties, 400 streets, eighty-seven churches and fifteen of the city's twenty-six wards. Remarkably only nine people died from the flames (Farriner, the baker, survived, but his wife and child perished), mostly because, as with the Plague, people fled, the wealthy to the fields west of London (Mayfair) or the countryside beyond, the poor to the east.

Before Londoners could plan rebuilding the city they wanted explanations for the disaster and blame apportioned. London, everyone agreed, had been punished for being a city of greed. Surely the course of the fire – from *Pudding* Lane in the east to *Pie* Corner, Smithfield, in the north-west – proved this? Consequently a fat gilt cherub was placed on the corner of the building at Pie Corner to warn future Londoners to curb their desires.

London had also been punished for being a city of sin. Catholics could count more than a hundred years' worth of transgressions, dating back to Henry VIII, who in 1530 had defied the Pope over his marriage to Catherine of Aragon, had broken the ties that bound the English Church to Rome and had dissolved the monasteries and abbeys. They could point to the sins of Oliver Cromwell and the Parliamentarians, who had ordered the execution of the 'holy' king, Charles I, he who had lived a life of devotion and had 'suffered martyrdom in defence of the most holy religion'. They could also draw up a list of current sins – 'the prodigious ingratitude, burning lusts, dissolute court, profane and abominable lives' – which the mostly Protestant population had indulged in.

And for Protestants there was an alternative list of sins that a different God had punished in the Fire of London. There were the sins of the corrupt Romish monasteries and abbeys, who had perverted the ancient religion and accumulated vast treasure houses of wealth, owning one-quarter of all the cultivated land in England while indulging in simony, landlordism, fecundity and hypocrisy. They remembered the sins of the Catholic queen, Mary Tudor, who had ordered some

300 Protestants to be prosecuted for heresy in the 1550s and had watched them burn at Smithfield from the window of the St Bartholomew-the-Great Gatehouse while feasting on chicken and red wine. They also blamed Catholic agitators looking to overthrow the government. Had not James, Duke of York, the king's brother, whose faith was wavering dangerously towards Rome, been seen gloating near the flames?

Both Catholics and Protestants did not just cite divine sources as being responsible for the flames. Many suspected members of the Royal Society, the learned group formed in 1645 to promote mathematics and engineering, such was the swiftness with which Christopher Wren and John Evelyn, both leading members of the Society, produced plans to rebuild the burnt-out city. And both sides suspected republicans looking to restore the Commonwealth that had briefly replaced the monarchy from 1649 to 1660.

As the embers died down, the king, Charles II – himself not entirely free of suspicion, for some thought he had caused the Fire in revenge for the execution of his father – publicly put the blame on foreigners. He told a crowd in Moorfields that 'divers strangers, Dutch and French, were during the Fire apprehended upon suspicion that they contributed mischievously to it'. This led to vigilantes indiscriminately attacking European nationals. Surprisingly, it also produced a breakthrough.

Word spread that Robert Hubert, a French silversmith, allegedly an agent of the French king, had started the Fire under the Pope's orders. Hubert was arrested in east London and admitted that he had journeyed from Sweden to London, moored his boat near the Tower and gone to Pudding Lane where, using a long pole, he had carefully placed a fireball through the window of Farriner's house. Hubert boasted of twenty-three co-conspirators, but his confession was shown to be false; there was no window at Farriner's bakery and no ship had sailed into east London from Sweden on the day he claimed to have arrived.

Nevertheless Hubert was a convenient scapegoat, and he was hanged at Tyburn for starting the Fire. Alongside him an effigy of the Pope, its head filled with live cats, was set alight. As the flames rose the cats screamed in torment, but it looked as if the 'Pope', rather than the animals, who could not be seen, was being burnt alive, to whoops of delight from the large crowd.

## BUILDING THE NEW JERUSALEM

Realizing that the closely packed houses of the City had contributed to the spread of the Fire, Charles II amended laws passed during Elizabeth's reign so that new houses could be built in and around London. The capital would have to spread eastwards, for south of the river lay mostly swamp and builders lacked the technical expertise to tame the morass, to the north were farms, and to the west the land was too expensive to accommodate the arrival of large numbers of people.

On 8 February 1667 the king appointed Christopher Wren Surveyor General and principal architect in charge of rebuilding London. Wren engaged fellow Royal Society members to help him. Among them were the polymath scientist Robert Hooke, the diarist, landscape gardener and architecture expert John Evelyn, and the Danish sculptor and architect Caius Gabriel Cibber.

Their first major construction was the Monument, an imposing Doric column of Portland stone, built on Fish Street Hill, just north of London Bridge, to commemorate the Fire. Standing 202 feet high and set 202 feet from Farriner's Pudding Lane bakery, where the blaze had started, it is positioned so that an observer looking east in the morning and west in the afternoon on the day of the summer solstice can see the sun sitting directly on top of the flaming urn of gilt bronze that crowns its top. On the Monument's base Cibber, enjoying daytime parole from debtors' prison, designed a relief depicting a female figure (London) grieving in front of burning buildings to recall the fallen Jerusalem from Lamentations 'sitting solitary as a widow [that] weepeth sore in the night, her tears on her cheeks'. On the pedestal an inscription, since removed, blamed the Fire on the 'treachery and malice of the Popish faction, in order to the effecting their horrid plot for the extirpating the Protestant religion and English liberties, and to introduce Popery and Heresy'. And just in case anyone had not fully received the message, another inscription by Farriner's bakery explained how 'here by permission of heaven hell broke loose upon this Protestant City from the malicious hearts of barbarous Papists . . .'

Wren and his team wanted to rebuild London on a grid system, with wide spacious boulevards centring on St Paul's replacing the antiquated medieval city of twisting, winding lanes and rickety over-hanging houses. New public buildings would be in stone and houses in red brick; timber was banned. The philosophy behind the new London appeared to be cloaked in the cold logic of Renaissance architecture and scientific reason. But behind the façade of the stream-lined modern city Wren and his associates looked beyond contemporary styles to ancient texts on geometry and architecture, to the 'sacred' measurements of the Bible, whose translation into English was still a novelty, to Freemasonry and to the Kabbalah, the mystical accompaniment to the Old Testament, handed down from generation to generation until it was transcribed after the break-up of the kingdom of Israel.

That scientists, mathematicians and men of reason possessed an agenda rich with religious and mystical arcana should not be a surprise. Science told them what, but didn't tell them why. That members of the Royal Society were involved with Freemasonry should not be considered strange, for this was not the Masonry of a secret club engaged in bizarre rituals, but a movement reaching back centuries before the birth of Christ, whose members had been instrumental in devising fundamental architectural and geometric measurements, and had been responsible for preserving that knowledge during the Dark Ages.

For Wren and his colleagues, who understood that Christianity had arrived in England probably as early as the first century AD, long before it reached Rome, London would be the capital of a Christian world free of Papist rule. It would be the New Jerusalem long envisaged by the enlightened and promised by the king's father, Charles I, in a 1620 sermon: 'For Here hath the Lord ordained the thrones of David, for judgement: and the charre of Moyses, for instruction, this Church, your Son indeed, others are but Synagogues, this your Jerusalem, the mother to them all.' It was a theme later adopted by, among others, William Blake, whose epic poem *Jerusalem* casts London as the holy city: 'We builded Jerusalem as a City & a Temple.'

Their inspiration was the Old Testament prophet Zechariah. Had he not predicted the English Civil War ('and they shall lay hold every one on the hand of his neighbour, and his hand shall rise up against the hand of his neighbour')? Had he not foretold the Plague ('their flesh shall consume away while they stand upon their feet, and their eyes shall consume away in their holes, and their tongue shall consume away in their mouth')? It was Zechariah who had been passed a message from God explaining that the rebuilt Jerusalem (that is, London) needed no walls, for He would protect it from flames by acting as a 'wall of fire round about . . . the glory in the midst of her'. It was Zechariah who had met the Lord Himself. The Lord was disguised as an architect – the Great Architect – the one deity of Masonic lore: 'I lifted up mine eyes again, and looked, and behold there was a man with a measuring line in his hand. Then said I, "Whither goest thou?" And he said unto me, "To measure Jerusalem, to see what is the breadth thereof, and what is the length thereof."'

With this in mind, Wren and his colleagues began measuring out a plan for rebuilding London. First they turned to the Kabbalah, from which they appropriated the Tree of Life, an interlocking pattern of ten connecting spheres representing the ten heavenly bodies and symbolizing wisdom, which they adopted not only for St Paul's, whose floor-plan is based on the Tree of Life, but for London itself. These holy arrangements would ensure that the city would be indestructible, would be protected by divine power from other disasters such as the Fire. Around St Paul's there would be ten important civic or religious buildings, at locations determined by 'sacred geometry'. In some cases these positions had already been decided by earlier architects.

One such was the church of St Dunstan in the West on Fleet Street, which stands only a few yards short of where the Fire of London ceased to burn. Another was the church of St Dunstan in the East, near the Tower, its body so sturdy it withstood the flames of the Fire. To decide on their lengths and distances, Wren and his associates turned to the Old Testament Book of Numbers which instructs how 'ye shall measure from without the city on the east side two thousand cubits, and on the south side two thousand cubits, and on the west side two thousand cubits, and on the north side two thousand cubits, and the city shall be in the midst'.

Such was the importance of the length 2,000 cubits (about two-thirds of a mile), the distance from Jerusalem to the Mount of Olives and the furthest a Jew is allowed to travel on the Sabbath: 'Up to the hill by Hebron, seat of giants old/No journey of a Sabbath Day, and loaded so', as Milton wrote in *Samson Agonistes*, published in 1671, around the time when London was being rebuilt.

It was a distance London's ancient builders had already set for both the western boundary of the city, Temple Bar, which is 2,000 cubits from the western end of St Paul's, and for the eastern boundary of the city, St Dunstan in the East, which is 2,000 cubits from the eastern end of the cathedral.

Wren's team positioned the apex of their Kabbalah-inspired London a further 2,000 cubits to the east, beyond the Tower of London, on the site of an ancient well used by the medieval abbey of St Mary Graces, which was believed to possess healing powers and which stood on the sacred territory east of the city the Romans had left vacant during their time in London. Here the rebuilders of London created a square – Marine Square – later renamed Wellclose Square as the first planned residential estate in east London. Smart houses were set around a railed-off grassed area containing a church paid for by the Danish king Christian V and built by the Danish architect Caius Gabriel Cibber, the designer of the relief on the Monument, aided by Nicholas Hawksmoor, an assistant to Wren. This elegant format can still be seen throughout London – Myddelton Square near the Angel is a typical example – but has practically disappeared from the East End.

Thanks to a charter drawn up by Henry IV in 1442 and redrawn by James II in 1688, the land was freed from the jurisdiction of all but the Lord Chancellor – that is, it was freed from the everyday powers of the City, the County of Middlesex and the Sheriff. It meant that the residents could enjoy special privileges: they would be exempt from jury service at the assizes and pay less tax than their neighbours.

St Katharine's, the next neighbourhood to the west, was run under a similar system. But whereas it descended into lawlessness and chaos due to its proximity to the docks bringing immigrants and renegade sailors into London, Marine/Wellclose Square became a haven of gentility, its handsome, well-appointed villas attracting an impressive population to the previously undeveloped east. At first there were shipmasters and Scandinavian timber merchants, who came to London to capitalize on the boom in house-building in the wake of the Fire. Later there were professionals and intellectuals – in particular two of the eighteenth-century's most illustrious figures: the Kabbalist *extraordinaire* Chaim Jacob Samuel Falk, known as the *Ba'al Shem* of London, and the scientist-cum-theologian Emanuel Swedenborg, who made this obscure corner of London a centre of mystical intrigue (see Chapter 6).

Nicholas Hawksmoor also set his own churches according to the same 'sacred' measurements: St George's-in-the-East stands 2,000 cubits from the Roman wall, Christ Church Spitalfields 2,000 cubits from Marine/Wellclose Square, and St Mary Woolnoth (by the modern-day Bank tube station) 2,000 cubits from Christ Church.

Wren and his associates were unable to complete much of their planned reborn city. The costs were too high and impenetrable bureaucracy surrounded the ownership of the burnt plots. The only other East End estate created in the style of Marine/Wellclose Square was Princes Square, a short distance to the east, developed in 1729 by John Prince, a speculative builder, and featuring a Swedish church. Like Wellclose Square it also survives – ravaged, despoiled, windswept, overlooked by crumbling tower blocks, wrapped in despondency, the church long gone.

By the early eighteenth century the East End fitted into what were mostly natural boundaries: the broad sweep of the Thames to the south; the walled city to the west; Hackney Marsh to the north; and the fast-flowing river Lea, originally navigable as far as Hertfordshire, to the east.

Within, the communities acquired their own distinctive identity. Bethnal Green, at the north-west corner of the East End, lost its rural isolation when it was colonized by weavers working in the Spitalfields silk industry. Their cottages were packed together too closely and the area became a byword for urban deprivation. Bow, to the east, abutting the Lea, was still mostly farmland, although the calico-printing and scarlet-dyeing that took place here by the river dissuaded middle-class settlers. To the south were Limehouse and

Poplar, rural and marshy, but with a small lime-burning industry. On the river nearby, Ratcliff and Blackwall had their burgeoning shipbuilding yards.

The most populous East End community was Whitechapel, which grew around the old Roman route from London to Colchester. At its centre was the church of St Mary Matfellon (destroyed in the Second World War, the land now known as Altab Ali Park). The name 'Matfellon' is a corruption of Mary *matri et filio* (mother and son), and its parishioners were bound by ancient custom to march in solemn procession to St Paul's Cathedral every Pentecost with charitable offerings.

The heart of an East End that grew apace after the Fire was Stepney. Here the parish church, St Dunstan and All Saints, the oldest surviving place of worship in the East End, predates the Norman Conquest. Its saint, Dunstan, a native of Glastonbury, who became Bishop of London in the tenth century, was supposedly tempted from his metal workshop by the devil. He responded by picking up a pair of tongs and tweaking the devil's nose, a story depicted in the carving above the west door. In 1540 the vicar, William Jerome, was burnt alive for preaching a sermon denying the merit of infant baptism. St Dunstan later became known as the Church of the High Seas, thanks to its largely seafaring congregation ('He who sails on the wide sea/Is a parishioner of Stepney') and the requirement that every baby baptized at sea had to be registered there. By then the East End's waterside position had made the area the centre of the fastest growing industry in London – river-borne trade, the key to the growth of the British Empire.

# 3

# Docks, Dockers and River Pirates

Energy made London the world's greatest port. Energy to trade and open new trade routes. Energy to tame the river and make it work for those transporting goods. Energy to tame the sea and make it work for the merchant adventurer. Energy to build bigger, better boats that could bring more goods back to London. Energy to construct more accurate compasses and chronometers. Energy to make London the world's busiest port from 1800 to 1970.

No city had ever witnessed such dynamic riverside activity. At its peak tens of thousands of dockers, stevedores, samplers, boiler-smiths, customs officers, cargo superintendents, yardmasters, winch-men, lightermen and lumpers worked the tens of thousands of ships bringing the world's produce to London's seven sets of docks – four in the East End – which covered 720 acres and 35 miles of quayside servicing the most vibrant empire the world had ever known.

London was a port from its earliest days. By the time the Normans arrived locally in the eleventh century the waterfront was alive and bustling. But as the quantity of goods arriving in the capital by boat increased, the early port, based at Queenhithe, near St Paul's Cathedral, became unmanageable. Trade was forced to move further east, away from central London, for neither the merchants nor the inhabitants of the city wanted their part of the Thames congested with boats awaiting custom clearance or the chaos, noise and industry of boat-building.

By the sixteenth century the East End's waterfront had taken dramatic shape. At its western end was the formidable outline of the Tower. Alongside, moving east, was the jumble of houses by St Katharine's, the mills of Wapping, the wharves of Shadwell, Ratcliff

Stairs, where epic journeys across the oceans often began, and the barge-building yards of Limehouse. Then the land swerved southwards to form the western side of the undeveloped peninsula of Stepney Marsh (the Isle of Dogs), and where the eastern end of this peninsula met the River Lea there was Blackwall, the best site in London for boat-building, offering easy access from the river to the timber of the Forest of Middlesex.

## AROUND THE WORLD FROM RATCLIFF AND BLACKWALL

Spurred on by the voyages of the Portuguese explorer Bartolomeu Dias, who sailed south along the coast of Africa and found out that the water at the Equator didn't boil, as feared, and enthused by the prospect of riches and immortality, sixteenth-century seafarers left Ratcliff and Blackwall to explore the furthest reaches of the globe. The first of these great expeditions was led by Sir Hugh Willoughby, whose party of three ships departed from the East End on 10 May 1553. Willoughby went in search of the North-east Passage, an accessible route north of Russia leading to China, which would allow him to participate in the lucrative spice trade without going through Constantinople, at that time closed off to the West.

Willoughby had no prior nautical experience – he was chosen mostly for his leadership qualities – and as his ships prepared to round the Scandinavian North Cape they were overcome by a storm and became separated from one another. Willoughby crossed the Barents Sea, off Siberia, returned to Scandinavia, but later became trapped in the ice, where he and his men froze to death, not being found by Russian fishermen until a year later.

His deputy, Richard Chancellor, pilot general of the small fleet, fared better. He journeyed on alone into the Russian White Sea and travelled to Moscow, where he met Ivan the Terrible, a serendipitous event that resulted in the formation of the Muscovy Company to boost trade between London and Russia. Willoughby's men never realized that there is no North-east Passage.

Other explorers prepared to find the North-*west* Passage to the

Orient. Their inspiration was Humphrey Gilbert, half-brother of Walter Ralegh and an East End resident. In 1576 Gilbert published a paper, 'Discourse of a Discoverie for a new passage to Cataia', which promoted the idea of sailing north of America, rounding what he believed to be an island, the Atlantis of Plato, to reach Cataia (or Cathay) – China. Martin Frobisher was the first explorer to take up Gilbert's recommendation. He left Ratcliff Cross with thirty-five men on 7 June 1576, first making a stop at Friesland in the Netherlands, where he stranded a group of convicts, after which the crew of one ship, the *Michael*, deserted. Frobisher continued alone in the *Gabriel*, its navigation aided by the crash course in geometry that John Dee, the so-called black magician of Mortlake, had given him.

When the ship approached two large bodies of land in northern Canada, Frobisher explained to the men that the northern one was Asia and the southern America; in reality they had simply neared the 150-mile bay leading into two parts of Baffin Island. The party landed. They clashed with the Eskimos and seized one native whom they brought back to the East End where he died from a cold shortly after arriving. Frobisher also brought back a huge black rock which he was mistakenly convinced contained gold. He set up the Cathay Company, journeyed back to Baffin Island (*not* Cathay), and left with another 200 tons of ore. Like the first rock it turned out to be worthless. Undaunted, Frobisher returned west with fifteen ships and built a colony in the Arctic wastes, sending home more of the ore, which continued to fail to yield any gold. Gilbert, meanwhile, met a tragic end. Leaving Newfoundland in 1583, his crew spotted a sea monster which one of them described as 'a lion with glaring eyes'. It was probably a giant squid, and it sank the ship, as Gilbert emotionally told the men: 'We are as near to heaven by sea as by land.'

Henry, Prince of Wales, and his entourage went to St Katharine's Dock near the Tower of London on 17 April 1610 to wave off another expedition. This one was led by Henry Hudson, who was aiming to succeed where Frobisher had failed by finding the North-west Passage to China. Hudson's crew spent much time bickering and carping. The salted meat was too salty. The hard biscuits too hard. When first mate Robert Juet jeered sarcastically at Hudson's desire to see Java by Candlemas, the captain's nerves snapped and he ordered the mate to be tried for mutiny. Hudson's party did make one important discovery: the great bay at the north-east of Canada, since named after him. Relations on board continued to deteriorate, however, and the following June most of the crew mutinied, setting Hudson adrift on a small boat with his son and seven loyal sailors. They were never seen again.

The greatest explorer associated with the East End was an eighteenth-century figure, the Yorkshireman James Cook, who married a local girl, Elizabeth Betts, in 1762, and moved first to Shadwell and later to Mile End. That decade his regular schedule was to sail to Newfoundland in April, where he would remain surveying the land until October, and return in the winter to the East End, where he spent his time drawing up charts and maps. The crew on Cook's ships lived on salt meat, biscuit, beer and sauerkraut, which was taken to stave off the ever-present maritime threat of scurvy, caused by lack of vitamin C.

Cook earned his place in history with his voyages to the Pacific, beginning in 1768, on which he and his crew saw wonders never before witnessed by Westerners – waterspouts, tornadoes, the ash volcanoes of Vanuatu – observed the passage of the planet Venus, which helped astronomers measure the distance of the earth from the sun, and searched for the supposed 'great southern continent', which turned out to be inhospitable frozen Antarctica.

In 1776 Cook was chief astronomer on a voyage arranged to find the elusive North-west Passage north of Canada but he too failed, unaware that as with the eastern route there is no accessible passage. Back in the Pacific in 1778, Cook went a shore on Hawaii and was greeted as a Polynesian god, but when his party returned a few months later the natives were not so friendly. He was attacked and stabbed to death, probably as part of the ritual death of the Hawaiian year-god, Lono. Cook's crew identified the corpse only from the scars on his hands, which he had received when a powder-horn had exploded on one of his earlier trips.

# SLAVE SHIPS, THE PRESS GANG AND RIVER PIRATES

At the same time as the first wave of explorers was leaving the East End to investigate uncharted territories, London was becoming the largest slaving port in Britain. The slave trade met the British public's insatiable demand for sugar. Slaves were captured in west Africa and taken to the American sugar plantations in tightly packed ships with no sanitation or ventilation, obliged to survive on the most meagre rations.

Smallpox on board was rife, and victims were often thrown overboard to make conditions more bearable for the non-sufferers, which was fine for the captain, as he would be compensated through the insurance. Occasionally the slaves revolted and seized the ship, but they would then find they were incapable of steering it successfully. Or they would place a curse on the ship's water. Wapping-born slave master John Newton, who later disowned his support for slavery and wrote the hymn 'Amazing Grace' in penitence, described these curses in his diary of voyages as 'country fetishes which they had the credulity to suppose must inevitably kill all who drank of it'.

Going to sea was 'akin to being in prison, with the added danger of drowning', claimed Dr Johnson, which probably explains why there were never enough volunteers for maritime life. The authorities redressed this in the sixteenth century by introducing the impress service, better known as the press gang. Gangers roamed the countryside and towns looking for potential sailors, receiving up to ten shillings for each man they pressed. Once a man had been seized he was offered a choice, if he was lucky: he could either sign up as a volunteer, and receive advance payment and other benefits (debts of less than £20 were wiped off) or remain as an unwilling crew member, receiving nothing.

England had a lax recruitment regime compared with some countries. The Admiralty issued exemption cards to those with important jobs – the clergy, physicians. Nevertheless there were misunderstandings. One East End legend tells of how the Lord Chancellor, carrying the Great Seal of England in a carpet bag, was kidnapped by a press gang while drunkenly crossing Tower Hill one night and sent to sea. He was not released until three months later when he was discovered scraping the mizzen-mast on board a frigate in the Toulon fleet.

Sometimes the river was treated to the arrival of an even nastier type of villain than the press-ganger – a real pirate of the high seas. Those captured and brought to London were taken to Marshalsea prison in Southwark and then led on a cart by the Admiralty Marshal, seated on a horse and carrying a silver oar, to Execution Dock in Wapping. There they were hanged until three tides had washed over them, *pour encourager les autres*. When the victim had finished making his last speech the cart on which he was standing would be driven away, leaving him hanging. The most notorious felons were covered with tar before the ceremony began.

Of the thousands who met their end at Wapping in this way, Captain (William) Kidd is the most famous. Kidd was a mercenary who struck the ship's gunner with an iron bucket, fracturing his skull, when his crew were on the verge of mutiny. He was sent for execution in May 1701. In his final speech he warned all ship-masters to learn from his fate. When the men holding the line attached to Kidd's neck rode off, the rope snapped and Kidd fell to the ground still alive. He was hoisted up again and this time the rope held and the hanging was successful.

Convict hulks were moored on the Thames near the marshes at the edge of the East End in the eighteenth century. On board were felons bound for Australia who lived in foul conditions and ate monotonous meals of ox cheek, pease and biscuits that had mould growing on both sides. They often succumbed to diseases such as typhoid and dysentery, which spread quickly through the brackish water. Those who fell ill rarely received treatment, and were made to lie on bare floorboards in iron chains.

As maritime trade in London increased so riverside crime rose. The greater the quantity of goods arriving at the port's quays, the more ingenious means the various gangs of thieves adopted to remove them, using what the magistrate Patrick Colquhon succinctly described as 'acts of peculation, fraud, embezzlement, pillage and depredation'. The most simple and effective thievery was to go in a large armed group to rob the ship during the day. But it was often more useful to cut the vessel from its mooring by daylight and follow it as it drifted downstream before staging the robbery by moonlight. It was also safer to abandon plans of devil-may-care assault, battery and robbery, and plan clever scams instead.

By the late eighteenth century all manner of colourfully named groups were indulging in some form of river piracy. Dredgermen trawled the Thames bed for loose coal. Heavy horsemen specialized in pilfering coffee, sugar and ginger. They wore abnormally wide trousers to conceal the long narrow bags attached to their thighs in which they secreted their pickings. Light horsemen were legitimate workers who would pay for any breakages, ensuring that as many packages as possible were broken so that they could be patched up and ransacked later without any sign that they had been tampered with. Lumpers threw stolen objects into the river that could be retrieved at low tide by the mudlarks, who sifted through the soggy banks. Scuffle hunters scavenged on the quays, toshers stole the copper from the bottom of ships and monkey suckers would drill a hole in a barrel of rum, insert a tube and suck, quickly, transferring the hose to a bottle once the liquid was flowing and stopping up the barrel when it had all been removed. Often the monkey suckers used boys, who would not be as keen to drink the alcohol, but would likely be overcome by the fumes of the raw spirit.

And all the time these dubious characters would be on the look-out for the Pantomime Police – security men dressed in outlandish garb who were employed by the traders to prevent pilfering.

## THE WINDS OF TRADE

Spain and Portugal, the two most powerful sixteenth-century maritime powers, had a loose agreement that they could freely exploit any new territories they found: Spain had free run in America; Portugal, to the routes around the Cape of Africa. England reluctantly accepted this impasse while it remained confident that new, unexplored routes could be found north of Asia and America. But when Francis Drake defeated the Spanish Armada in 1588 the English merchant adventurers' impatience got the better of them. They urged Queen Elizabeth to grant permission to set up a new company to exploit the huge Indian market. Their reward was a charter for what became the East India Company, the most powerful commercial concern in British history.

The first East India entrepreneurs and seafarers mostly lived in

Stepney and Ratcliff, and the company was based at Blackwall, where it opened shipbuilding yards to construct its East Indiamen vessels. Because plying the spice routes from the Isle of Dogs to the East Indies was a risky business, the East Indiamen were armed as warships for protection against (other) pirates and the rival Dutch. Only two in every three ships made it through to the Orient, often with only half the crew they started with, the others perishing through scurvy, execution for attempted mutiny or battle.

Of the early East India explorers the most fearless was Nathaniel Courthorpe, who led an expedition from East London to the tiny island of Poolaroone, near Sumatra, with a crew who lived on a diet of mostly rats, ox hides and sawdust. Their anthem went: 'Our beef and pork is very scant,/I'm sure of weight, one half it want/Our bread is black, and maggots in it crawl/That's all the fresh meat we are fed withal.'

Courthorpe and his team went in search of nutmeg, a valuable spice used in soaps and perfume, which cost a halfpenny for ten pounds weight (the natives wouldn't take the tweed cloth on offer) and which they sold at a profit of 32,000 per cent, the booty divided among the shareholders. Early primitive capitalism. Courthorpe held the island for five years, but when the Dutch murdered him a deal was done: the Europeans took Poolaroone, the British the Dutch north American colony of New Amsterdam – that later became Manhattan.

## THE DOCKS

During the eighteenth century the volume of trade being handled on the London riverside grew to unforeseen levels. The antiquated legal quays and sufferance wharves, where customs officials cleared goods arriving into the capital, could no longer cope. Merchants were becoming increasingly exasperated with the long delays and the lack of warehouse space. Valuable cargoes were being piled on the quay, tempting miscreants.

To try to tackle these barely controllable levels of crime, a force of river police was set up, and an office for the 'Marine Police Establishment' duly opened at Wapping New Stairs in July 1798, but this was hardly enough to protect the 13,444 ships and vessels that used the river that year. A better solution was found through a 1799 act that allowed a new body, the West India Dock Company, to build a vast, secure, enclosed dock, surrounded by high walls and tall warehouses, at the north-west corner of the Isle of Dogs.

West India Dock, two parallel stretches of water occupying over 164 acres, was opened on 21 August 1802 by the prime minister, William Pitt. A large model of a West Indiaman ship made of stone and copper greeted visitors above the simple arch and pediment at its western entrance. The West India Company was granted a twenty-one-year monopoly for importing sugar, rum and coffee, and was able to capitalize quickly on a number of new technological and scientific breakthroughs made possible by James Watt's invention of the steam engine. This led to an explosion of industry based on coal-driven machinery and saw huge quantities of coal shipped to London on a new kind of vessel, the steamship.

It wasn't long before other companies sought to join the West India. Merchants formed a company to build another set of docks in Wapping in 1805. Known prosaically as London Docks they soon smelled of wine, spices, oakum, wool and hides, which were stored in huge on-site warehouses where they could be inspected before being released. Below the docks was the company's *pièce de résistance*: voluminous vaults occupying labyrinthine stretches of brick under-croft, the walls black with fungus, where hundreds of thousands of bottles and barrels were stored in dark, dank conditions, guarded by men smelling of old claret and pontificating about Madeiras and sherries 'fine as a sovereign and sparkling as the sun'. Only the most upstanding workers, who would not be tempted by the bibulous amounts of alcohol surrounding them, could be employed to look after this treasure trove. But occasionally a renegade would slip through, and one worker who was overcome by his proximity to 60,000 large casks of brandy prised open a sample, thrust his head into the aperture, and choked and died . . . before he even had a chance to sup.

Then came East India Dock, 'a place of savagely masculine charac-ter', according to Thomas Burke, which was built in 1806 on the eastern, Blackwall, side of the Isle of Dogs. Behind the venture was local entrepreneur Robert Wigram, originally a surgeon's mate for the East India Company, who moved on to supplying medicines to ships. After buying shares in the East Indiamen vessels he made what was a fortune for the time – half a million pounds – which he mostly invested in Meux's Brewery.

East India Dock handled tea. It employed a well-trained, well-paid paramilitary workforce to look after vessels such as the *Cutty Sark*, the finest of the great tea clippers, which now stands in dry dock on the opposite bank at Greenwich, and to ensure that those who unloaded ships further downstream, transferring the cargoes to lighters that were emptied at East India, desisted from 'idleness and peculation'.

There were no dockside warehouses here, so goods were taken under armed guard along the grand, newly built highway, Commercial Road, to the company's Cutler Street warehouses, off Petticoat Lane. Such measures ensured there would be little crime. Or put it this way: in the three years before the company built the docks 210 chests of tea were stolen. In the next three years none was stolen; thieves had to make do with stuffing handfuls of loose tea into their pockets instead.

Crime might have declined but incompetence did not, and in 1827, after years of bureaucratic mismanagement, the East India Dock Company lost its monopoly. The warehouses were sold off to the newly formed St Katharine's Dock Company. The original East India Company later endured an ignominious end. The British government abolished its monopoly following the 1858 Indian Mutiny and it collapsed.

The construction of St Katharine's Dock on land to the immediate east of the Tower in the 1820s was more controversial than any of the other dock-building programmes. The area had a history stretching back to 1148 when a religious institution, the Hospital of St Katharine, was founded here by Matilda, wife of King Stephen, as a memorial to the death of her two sons. Unusually for a religious house St Katharine's allowed the sisters equality with the brothers. In 1442 St Katharine's became a Royal Peculiar, a body directly answerable to the Crown, so when the monasteries were bloodily dissolved in the 1530s St Katharine's royal links saved it from abolition.

Time then slowed down in St Katharine's cloistered walks. Its cobbled quadrangles, Tudor wooden buildings and Gothic arches set in a warren of alleyways sporting whimsical names – Dark Entry, Cat's Hole, Shovel Alley, Rookery, Money Bag Alley, Cherubim Court, Pillory Lane – remained a bizarre sight in the ever-changing East End. The unusual terms of ownership of the land meant that the neighbourhood was beyond the powers of the town aldermen and county sheriff, and free from many everyday laws. But despite its quaint appearance, St Katharine's came to house levels of infamy and villainy that made even the East End shudder. It was overrun by prostitutes, vagabonds and those seeking sanctuary from crimes committed in the outside world, who lived here in barely disguised anarchy. It also attracted numerous foreigners, who after arriving in London at the nearby docks found that commercial restrictions banned them from trading in the city. When slavery was abolished in 1782 many of those freed came to St Katharine's, and by the beginning of the nineteenth century the neighbourhood was home to more than 11,000 people living in cramped overcrowded houses.

Initial opposition to the plans to demolish St Katharine's was fierce. One local clergyman complained that there was as much need for a new dock here as there was for one at the foot of Ludgate Hill, while the *Gentleman's Magazine* wondered if some future company petitioning Parliament might appropriate St Paul's Cathedral for a pawnbroker's warehouse. Such was the strength of opinion that the St Katharine's bill was withdrawn in April 1824, prompting celebration in both the shabby tenements of the old precinct and the boardrooms of the West India and East India companies. But when the powerful interests behind the scheme regrouped, the master and chapter of the hospital were too timid in their opposition. This time they lost their case. It took one month – November 1825 – to wipe out 650 years of history. The residents were evicted without compensation, turned on to the streets to find shelter where they could. At least the hospital received £125,000 for the land and distress, and £36,000 towards new premises in Regent's Park.

The new St Katharine's Dock may not have been particularly welcomed but at least it was expertly constructed. The great road and canal builder Thomas Telford created three large basins surrounded by elegant yellow brick warehouses whose arches, set above the water line, allowed goods to be swung from boats through the open windows. The dock specialized in luxury goods: perfume, wine, silver, ostrich feathers, china, tortoiseshell, oriental carpets, live turtles for turtle soup (a Victorian delicacy) and the ivory of not just African elephants but long extinct mammoths, whose remains had recently been unearthed in Siberia.

What smells this collection exuded! The fumes of the rum, the stench of the hides, the bitter fragrance of the coffee and the noxiousness of the sulphur were barely tempered by the exotic songs of the sailors, the hammer blows of the coopers and the clanking of the cranes. One entire floor of St Katharine's was dedicated to shells sorted, weighed and valued by neat little men with neat clipped moustaches and even neater bowler hats who swarmed into the docks every morning from the newly built suburban estates of Ilford and Walthamstow. There was also an unusual security force: 300 cats chosen for their rat-catching ability, and, working alongside the cats, ratcatchers, human not feline, who were paid £1 for ridding newly arrived ships of vermin and a 2d bonus for each rat they caught alive.

Riverside security along the 2,000 acres of docklands and 700 acres of water remained intense. The companies employed men armed with muskets, pistols and swords to ward off potential miscreants, but there were always too many villains – and they came in all manner of guises. Dock workers would leave the site, their pockets bulging with a surreptitious bottle of Jamaica rum, a roll of copper or a bundle of cigars. One time, a team of robbers distracted a shipmaster, broke into his office and emptied an entire barrel of sugar, transferring the contents into bags and passing them out through the window. By the time the shipmaster returned to his desk the barrel was empty, the only clue to the sugar's disappearance the open window.

A man leaving the docks was stopped by a policeman, who remarked, 'You feel rather lumpy, my man.' To which the man replied, 'That's my lunch.' 'Lunch!' exclaimed the constable. 'Just step in here a minute.' A quick search uncovered a couple of bottles of brandy hidden in the man's clothing.

A limping man coming out of the gate was apprehended by an officer, who remained unconvinced by the man's protestations of lameness. He made him undress and found a leg of mutton strapped to the man's leg. Having been in the deep chill, the meat had frozen on to him. And three 'dockers' exiting a gate with uncertain motion turned out to be two men and a pig's carcass dressed in shabby suit and battered hat.

By the mid-1830s the monopolies enjoyed by the first docks had run out. With the growth of free trade the docks companies feared they would soon be put out of business by the new breed of self-made tycoons; men such as Samuel Morton Peto, the railway contractor and Liberal MP. Indeed it was Peto who built the new ultra-modern Victoria Dock, downriver of the East End in Plaistow Marshes. Alongside he set 200 acres aside for foreign cattle that could graze by the Thames before being slaughtered. Strangely no cattle ever arrived, but Victoria Dock did have a telegraph service that enabled managers to keep track of the movement of steamships, access to a fast railway (with the early docks there was no room for proper rail links) and jetties that projected into the water rather than straight quay walls.

Victoria Dock was so successful that by 1860 it was receiving double the amount of shipping that was going to London Docks, 70 per cent more than the East and West India Docks, and four times that of St Katharine's. Things might not have been economically fair, as far as the sated old-style dock companies were concerned, but this was the era of great economic expansion, the golden age of British imperialism and commerce, when the country controlled more than half the world's total tonnage of shipping. Such growth depended on unbridled capitalism.

By 1875 the Victoria Dock Company owned London Docks and St Katharine's Docks, and it celebrated its increased might by building another new dock east of the East End – Royal Albert Dock. A mile and three-quarters long, 27 feet deep, with 16,500 feet of quays and able to take vessels of 12,000 tons, Royal Albert Dock opened in June 1880 as the world's largest.

But the original dock companies were not beaten yet. The East and West India Dock Company hired agents to survey the land further downriver, conducting their work amid the utmost secrecy, lest any competitors usurp them. The following decade it opened new docks at Tilbury – bigger, better and deeper than anything that had gone before, and nearly 20 miles closer to the sea than the Victoria and

Albert. Vessels would be able to enter Tilbury's 56 acres of water no matter how unfavourable the tidal conditions. Goods could then be unloaded on to the trains of the London, Tilbury and Southend Railway Company, which would speed to an immense new depot built in the centre of the East End, just off Commercial Road.

Everything was set for the triumph of Tilbury. But there were construction problems, and in 1884 the contractors were ejected from the site. Then came another setback. The London and St Katharine's Docks Company cheekily enlarged Albert's entrance to the proposed dimensions of Tilbury. Even though the new Tilbury Docks opened on time in April 1886 they remained almost empty, with only one regular customer, after four months. Within two years Tilbury's owner, the East and West India Company, was in administration.

## THE DOCKERS

Once the first deep-water docks opened in 1802, the medieval porterage brotherhoods lost the monopoly they had enjoyed since the Middle Ages for unloading vessels bringing goods into London. These brotherhoods had performed all the waterside work. The ticket porters dealt with American cargoes; the Billingsgate porters unloaded dry goods such as corn, coal and salt; the tacklehouse porters weighed goods; and the companies' porters handled trade with Europe. Because of their monopoly the brotherhoods were not popular, and when they opposed the building of the new docks they received little sympathy, either from the public or from the City Corporation who licensed them. They were doomed, and they knew it.

Work at the new deep-water docks needed a new type of labourer – the docker. Originally there were 900 of them, employed from six in the morning till six at night in summer and from sunrise to sunset in the winter to move goods on and off the ships. Dress rules were strict. Dockers could wear only 'Stockings and Breeches'; no 'Frocks, Trowsers [sic], Jemmies, Pouches or Bags' were allowed.

By the mid nineteenth century there were more than 10,000 dockers in East London. The height of ambition for many an East End youth was to be made a permanent dock labourer at twenty-one and still be working at seventy, at which point he would be pensioned off on 10s a week (won after the 1889 strike), provided he could show a work record with 'fifty years of undetected crime'.

Dockers were engaged in the most arduous work to be found anywhere in the capital. For instance, those who moved the wheels round were little more than walking human cranes, spending most of the day inside a wooden drum, 16 feet in diameter, which they trod round some forty times an hour in lifting ton weights. Deal porters carried piles of planks over slippery shaking bridges on their shoulders, which after a few months developed a callosity that enabled them to take the weight but did little for their physique. Sugarmen carried sacks of sugar through North Quay, which became known as the 'blood hole' because of the amount of blood that was spilled from the men's hands due to the friction of the sugar sacks rubbing against the innumerable particles caught between their fingers. Losing the top of a finger that had been caught in the bight of the rope was an occupational hazard.

The dockers formed themselves into an elaborate hierarchy. At the top were the stevedores (a word derived from the Spanish *estibador* – packer), who loaded the goods that left London from the export docks in Poplar. Their work demanded special skills, for cargo had to be placed in the hold so that the ship's weight balanced and the loads could be taken off easily at the other end. The stevedores' work and conditions were mostly insufferable, despite their elevated status and pay: no special clothing or protection from the weather, lunch on a plate tied up with a handkerchief brought by a relative.

Below the stevedores came interminable levels of skilled workers – cornporters, dealporters, coopers, riggers, 'gentlemen dockers', who dealt with the ships in the short-stay docks, tallymen, who arranged sets of cargoes for export, warehousemen, pilers, baulkers and blenders. At the bottom of the heap, reviled by all the other waterside workers, were the ordinary dockers. Even here there was a clear divide between the regulars and the casuals, on whom the regulars looked down scornfully. And, even among the casuals, noses would be turned up at the poor unfortunates unloading phosphates, asbestos or lampblack, a fine type of pure carbon produced by the incomplete combustion of organic compounds. Touching the lampblack produced a shiny black pigment that remained on the skin for two weeks, an unfortunate residue of the work not helped by the one communal bucket of water the men had to share at the end of the working day. Of course these dockers soon found skivvies more miserable than they: those who worked the deep-freeze ships, who needed to wear sacking on their feet to stave off frostbite, and those who unloaded the horns of African animals, knowing that the opening of the boxes would release insects with a venomous bite . . .

The dockers were paid by the hour (5d by the 1880s), usually in pubs owned by the docks companies, which meant that the wages barely left the premises. But then dock labouring was thirsty work. The coal-whippers and coal-backers who lifted the fuel from the hold of a ship and carried it in sacks on their backs spent at least 12s of their £1 weekly income on beer and spirits. When Henry Mayhew, the campaigning journalist and founder of *Punch*, carried out his investigation into the working and drinking habits of the dockers, he interviewed a basket-man, a part-time scholar of Greek and Latin, who explained why the men drank prodigious quantities: 'What renders it necessary to have three pints of beer in winter and two pots in summer is the coal dust arising from the work, which occasions great thirst.' When the man contracted breathing problems, caused by the coal dust, his doctor recommended him to drink six or seven pints a day and two extra pints of porter as a stimulus. Tea was not an alternative, for there was little opportunity to boil water, and clean water was almost unknown. As the engineer Ralph Dodd outlined in an early nineteenth-century report: 'Thames water being kept in wooden vessels becomes putrid after a few months and produces a disagreeable smell.'

It was not easy to get a regular job at the docks. In fact, unless you were a member of a docks family, it was nigh on impossible. But when a boat needed unloading, casuals were taken on for a few days. One day 3,000 men might be wanted; the next day 200. Those who were hired were taken on through a befuddling system – the 'Call On' – a frenzied, public free-for-all which continued until the docks closed down, at which the foreman would take his pick from the hundreds of labourers gathered outside the main dock gates looking for work.

When the Call On began the men would rush towards the foreman, shouting his name, calling out their own names, scuffling with each other to gain ground. Some would triumph by a look or a wink, others would scream and scream but remain ignored. The foreman would throw down brass tickets, and anybody catching one would be guaranteed work. But picking up a ticket was something only the meanest fighter could guarantee. And all the while the foreman would stand to one side, hands on hips, laughing uproariously at the chaos he had caused.

The foremen always had a list of men known as the 'royals', who were guaranteed work. Many thought they could get on that list by standing a foreman a few drinks in his local the night before work was due to start. Indeed, once word had got round that a ship was due in, the pubs around Wapping High Street and East India Dock Road would be bursting with hopefuls anxiously trying to impress the docks foremen. Men went to extraordinary lengths to get on that list. They would even follow the foreman home and cut his grass – without asking or being asked. But the best way to get your name on was to become a member of the families from the Watney Street area who wielded tyrannical power. This status prevailed over all favours and bribes, for blood was thicker even than a pint of mild and bitter.

## A NEW DOCKSIDE COMMUNITY – WAPPING

A strange name, Wapping. It may have come from Waeppa, who was a Saxon chieftain, so that Wapping meant 'the people of Waeppa', or it may have come from the antiquated word wapol – bubble or foam.

Wapping, which occupies a U-shaped peninsula to the east of the Tower, has always been an isolated area. Nobody can get to it easily by car or bus and in rail terms it is stuck out on the East London tube line. It was mostly marshland, regularly flooded by the Thames, until the late sixteenth century, when it was drained by Cornelius Vanderdelf, a Dutchman, who built a wall that stretched a mile to Shadwell. There the marshes gave way to a rich meadowland of gardens, orchards and fields that were popular with hunters; in July 1629 Charles I chased a stag all the way from Wanstead to Wapping, capturing it by the water.

But Wapping on the Woze (Wapping in the drain), as it was then known, didn't remain rural for long. In the mid seventeenth century industry arrived in the shape of a chemical works where alum could be extracted from urine, causing a noisome and evil air. Until the sewers were improved in the late nineteenth century, the alum works' odours were rivalled by those of the open ditch cut through the land which emptied into the Thames, especially at the outlet. For those who could stand the stink there was the added pleasure of being able to watch pirates being hanged at Execution Dock. Understandably this dissuaded many from settling locally, and meant that Wapping never attracted much of a respectable population.

Discharged sailors, often the worse for drink, and slave traders filled the area's main stretch, Wapping High Street, staying in filthy lodging houses, where they slept propped up by their sea chests once they had been thrown out of the brothels. The High Street shops were laden with maritime gear: quadrants and bright brass sextants; chronometers and huge mariner's compasses; enormous boots and oilskin caps; tinned meat, biscuits and other groceries suitable only for those who would be away at sea for a few weeks. Every other building was a pub. The most notorious of these was the Red Cow (now the Town of Ramsgate), where convicts awaiting deportation to Australia were chained in the cellars. It was here that the notorious Judge Jeffreys, known as the Hanging Judge after sentencing 320 people to the gallows, went for one last drink on English soil in 1688 when fleeing arrest during a purge of pro-Catholic figures hostile to the new Protestant king, William III. Jeffreys entered the Red Cow dressed as a woman but, despite his disguise, was soon recognized by a scrivener he had previously sentenced. He was surrounded by a mob that stopped him boarding the collier he was going to take to Hamburg and took him to the Tower to answer to the king instead.

Further east along Wapping High Street was the Devil's Tavern, built c. 1520 and still standing, its name changed in 1777 to Prospect of Whitby, in honour of a Whitby-registered ship moored on the Thames outside. It has since served Charles Dickens, the painter Turner and the dictionary compiler Samuel Johnson; indeed it was in Wapping in 1767 that Dr Johnson was introduced into Freemasonry, joining the Dundee Lodge and celebrating with a party that consumed 'bowls of steaming punch, bottles of wine, rum, Hollands, brandy, sugar, lemons, nutmegs and glasses, and for the smokers screws of tobacco and pipe lights'.

Much of Wapping was dug up in 1800 to build London Docks. Architect Daniel Alexander used some of the flavour of his earlier commission, Dartmoor prison, for the bleak and formidable brick warehouses, with their tiny windows, which filled the High Street, shutting out the river and light in canyons that terrified the unwary visitor, joined to each other by catwalks slung high above the street. By an opening at the water's edge – Pierhead – handsome Regency houses, of a type usually found in Kensington, were built for the dock masters. River users looking at Wapping from the Thames would have seen 'a mighty mass of brick and smoke and shipping/Dirty and dusky, but as wide as eye/Could reach, with here and there a sail just skipping/In sight then lost amidst the forestry of masts', as Lord Byron described it in *Don Juan* (1821). On land passers-by turning a street corner might have suddenly come face to face with a ship which seemed to have fallen from the sky into the centre of Wapping but was merely moving slowly along the inlet that connected the Thames to the docks.

A life of casual irregular work, casual regular violence and bad pay supplemented by the meagre wages women could glean from menial local jobs and whatever could be pilfered from the goods being handled at the water's edge, made for mean, poor and wretched waterside communities throughout the East End, but particularly in Wapping.

The area's mad, haphazard, violent growth attracted the leading social commentators of the day to marvel at the filth and degradation. David Bartlett, researching *London by Day and Night* in the early 1850s, was so upset at what he described as 'one of the dirtiest places in London . . . full of low houses, ignorant people, obnoxious scents' that he fled along the Thames Tunnel to Rotherhithe. Henry Mayhew, founder of *Punch* and chronicler of the poor, asked his guide to take him to one of the largest lodging-houses in the neighbourhood, and was led through a narrow passage into a small room on the ground floor in which sat 'thirty of the most wretched objects I ever beheld' – shoeless, coatless, shirtless – from whom came 'so rank and foul a stench I was sickened with a moment's inhalation of the foetid atmosphere'. The landlord accosted Mayhew and accused him of being a spy sent by the Secretary of State to check on the number of people living in the property before chasing him out.

Watts Phillips, author of *The Wild Tribes of London* (1855), blamed Wapping's problems on the Irish, who had moved here to unload colliers bringing coal from Newcastle, and whose number was aggravated during the potato famine of the 1840s, which saw hundreds of thousands flee the country: 'They all had the same wild features of false ingenuity, restlessness, misery, and mockery. They lived in squalor and unreason, in falsity and drunken violence as the ready-made nucleus of degradation and disorder.'

The Irish were hated by the native East Ender almost as much as policemen, not merely because they were Irish, but because they were Catholic, and the Irish press returned the sentiment. 'We are sick of the blatant howl with which shallow, half-educated English scribblers keep up about the wonderful attributes of the "Anglo-Saxon",' railed the nationalist paper *The Irish Liberator* on 14 November 1863: 'Everything great and noble in the world is attributed to this imaginary race; every evil in the world to the inferiority of all other peoples who do not come within the magic circle,' noting the irony that 'at this very hour, the preponderance of blood and race in London itself, is, beyond all question, Celtic'.

## THE 1889 DOCK STRIKE

Trade unions were not legalized until 1871, but the dockers had always been quick to withdraw their labour. Wages were meagre, conditions barely humane, work irregular. Men were hired not just by the day, or even half a day, but by the hour. Spurred on by the success of the East End match girls' strike in 1888, the dock workers demanded an increase in pay of 1d an hour to 6d – 'the docker's tanner'. They also wanted improved working conditions, Call Ons reduced to two a day and a guarantee of at least four hours' work a day.

A row over the unloading of a ship, the *Lady Armstrong*, at West India Dock on 14 August 1889 sparked off a strike. The dockers successfully persuaded the stevedores and other groups of dock workers to join in, and by 22 August some 20,000 men were out. The docks were paralysed and the strike committee, based at the Wade's Arms public house on Jeremiah Street, Poplar, led a series of well-organized marches to the City on which the men carried poles topped with rotting fish heads – what they claimed was their main diet. With no earnings the dockers were unable to pay the rent and they slung a banner across Hungerford Street, off Commercial Road, warning rent collectors: 'As we are on strike landlords need not call', while another, on nearby Star Street, erected by local women proclaimed:

> Our husbands are on strike; for the wives it is not honey,
> And we all think it is right not to pay the landlord's money,
> Everyone is on strike, so landlords do not be offended;
> The rent that's due we'll pay you when the strike is ended.

Soon, workers in other industries – rope-making, printing, chemicals, biscuit-making – had downed tools in support. By the third week 130,000 men were on strike. Who would fall first: the workers through hunger, or the dock owners through pressure from the shipping companies? A boost for the strikers came from an unexpected source – Australia – where supporters had raised £30,423 15s. From these funds 100,000 food tickets, each worth one shilling – enough to sustain a family for a day – were issued.

On 5 September, with the strike in its fourth week, the Lord Mayor of London set up a committee to solve the dispute. It included Cardinal Manning, Primate of England, who took charge, winning respect from the largely Irish Catholic workforce, charming the trade union leaders and bringing pressure on the dock directors, who gradually conceded terms and agreed on a settlement acceptable to the strike leaders.

The dockers returned to work on Monday 16 September after a triumphant procession along Commercial Road and a rally in Hyde Park. They were now earning sixpence – the hitherto elusive 'docker's tanner'. Their endeavours inspired a new song, 'The Red Flag', set to the tune of 'The White Cockade', which was adopted by the Labour Party as its anthem.

Their triumphs were shortlived. The owners regrouped, forming the Shipping Federation to stamp out strike action and unionism, and manning three ships with blacklegs to be transported to wherever there might be a strike. But the dock owners weren't sure how to maintain London's status as the world's greatest port. Their desperation for unbridled competition might have made London rich, but it had also saddled the Thames with bureaucratic confusion: too many docks of the wrong size in the wrong place. Dock charges were excessive, rail communication was decrepit, and rival cities such as Liverpool, Antwerp and Rotterdam were taking some of London's trade.

In 1909 the government came up with what seemed a solution to economic decline. It set up a new body, the Port of London Authority (PLA), to take control of the docks and quays from the estuary mouth to Teddington, south-west London, where the Thames loses its tidal properties. But even the PLA could not prevent more industrial action. In 1912 a strike over the location of the Call On broke the summer calm. Innumerable rallies were held on Tower Hill, and during one of these the union leader Ben Tillett instructed the crowd: 'Now repeat after me, O God, strike Lord Devonport dead', to which the massed dockers responded in song: 'He shall die! He shall die! He shall die tiddly-i-ti-ti-ti-ti-ti-ti-ti!', as in the new Billy Merson music hall number 'The Spaniard That Blighted My Life', later popularized by Al Jolson. But the strike leaders failed to win national support, and the men were told that the Call On would still take place inside the gates. When strike-breakers were then given jobs at the expense of strikers the reputation of the dockers' union crashed.

## BEVIN, BOMBS, BOOM AND BUST

The outbreak of the First World War meant more work for the docks; the number of dockers soared from the usual 4,500 to more than 8,000. Ships awaiting clearance crowded the Thames at Gravesend, where the sea gives way to the river, and dockside warehouses bulged with imported goods. But when the Germans introduced submarines into their armoury, and American supplies for British troops were diverted to French ports, the boom ended. By 1918 the tonnage of goods using London's docks had slipped to half the pre-war levels.

It was at this time that the dockers gained their greatest champion,

Ernest Bevin. A bluff West Countryman, Bevin began his working life selling ginger beer from a cart, and fifty years later was foreign secretary. In 1919, as national dockers' organizer, he led a campaign to secure the dockers' wages of 16s a day for a 44-hour week, and two years later became leader of the newly established Transport and General Workers' Union, formed from the merger of thirty different unions. The TGWU was known as 'the Whites', on account of the colour of its membership cards, and its only rival was the older National Amalgamated Stevedores' and Dockers' Union – 'the Blues'. Rivalry between the two sects was so fierce that marriages between 'white' and 'blue' families was discouraged.

Bevin's bluster and repertoire of fighting talk masked a moderate, reformist political line, and his efforts to quell revolutionary political activity were recognized in 1940 when the prime minister, Winston Churchill, invited him to become minister of labour in the coalition government, even though Bevin was not then an MP. When Labour took power after the 1945 general election, Bevin became foreign secretary, a role for which he was particularly ill-suited, as captured by these remarks to his Soviet counterpart, Vyacheslav Molotov, in 1947:

Now, Mr Molotov, what is it that you want? What are you after? Do you want to get Austria behind your Iron Curtain? You can't do that. Do you want Turkey and the Straits? You can't have them. Do you want Korea? You can't have that. You are putting your neck out too far, and one day you will have it chopped off.

By 1939 London's docks had reached their greatest size and were being served by a seemingly endless retinue of vessels: Dutch steamers, red-sailed barges, Irish Guinness boats, Cunard liners, Australian grain carriers . . . But that September the Second World War broke out. A year later, on the sunny Saturday afternoon of 7 September 1940, 300 German planes blitzed the docks with bombs. By evening the warehouses and their stores of paint, rum, pepper and flour were alight. In the blaze a vat of brown sugar liquefied on the Thames and a huge containment of rubber exuded such noxious black smoke no one could approach it for days. Four hundred and thirty people were killed that night, 400 the next.

The worst attack came on 10 September when St Katharine's Dock went up in flames in what was probably England's worst ever fire, one that destroyed all the dock warehouses and left a sheet of hardened wax on the water. Nevertheless the docks remained in use, even if much shipping was diverted, and in the winter of 1943 the East India Import Dock was pumped dry so that the ground could be used to construct the floating ports (Mulberry harbours) used by Allied troops for the D-Day landing in Normandy. A third of the dock warehouses and half the storage space were destroyed in the war. It took ten years to repair the damage, but much of St Katharine's Dock had been so badly hit it was left unrestored.

For a while there was no shortage of trade. In the early 1960s the total volume of goods handled by the Port of London broke new records. But trading patterns were changing. Where London had been the centre of trade during the days of the British Empire, drawing in raw materials and exporting manufactured goods in exchange, long-standing trading partners such as Australia were now taking over, and continental ports like Rotterdam, unburdened with the Victorian infrastructure of the London docks, were able to capitalize on the recent creation of a European trading zone.

Rotterdam and other newer ports were also able to make full use of containerization – new technology in which cargoes such as oil, wine, grain and sugar arrived in containers 7 feet high and were moved on to the dockside by fork-lift trucks, or piped directly from ships to refineries – while London dockers continued quaintly to unload cargoes from ships to lighters, from lighters to the quayside and from the quayside to sheds. Many jobs were lost through containerization and the number of strikes increased due to the dockers' frustration with new technology – sophistication rather than slog, streamlining rather than mass labour.

Alongside containerization came another new system that cut out work previously done by hundreds of dockers – roll-on/roll-off ferries. Loads could now travel across Europe on lorries that were taken across the Channel and driven off at the other end. With no need for quayside unpacking or even storage, the revamped industry boomed at Felixstowe and Immingham, new docks situated away from the capital and nearer to Europe. The traditional dock faced extinction and the traditional docker with it. In 1967 the Call On was at last abolished. Now, under the Dock Labour Scheme, dockers could not be sacked except for misconduct. Yet that same year East India Dock closed, and a year later, around the time that the dockers staged a spontaneous march in support of the anti-immigration Tory politician Enoch Powell under banners proclaiming 'Send Them Back', London Docks and St Katharine's followed East India into oblivion.

Some London docks staged a brief revival. Millwall Docks were modernized in the 1970s and equipped with new sheds specially designed for fork-lift trucks, but a trade slump persuaded the Port of London Authority that Millwall could not be made profitable, and in 1979, by which time the number of London dockers had dropped in twelve years from 23,000 to 8,800, it too closed.

In 1981 the 200-year-old battle between the employers and dockers, over how to run the docks, hire the men and devolve the work, ended with neither side winning, for that year the last of London's docks closed.

# 4

# The Silk Weavers of Spitalfields

Immigration has long shaped the East End. The Belgae, who came to the area from Flanders in the first century BC, were followed by the Romans (in AD 43), Saxons (fifth century), Danes (ninth century), Normans (1060s) and Flemish (fourteenth century). The latter opened dye-works alongside the River Lea, bringing to London new methods for working textiles. This set a pattern that exists to this day, whereby foreigners possessing skills undeveloped by Londoners arrive in the capital to res-cue a stagnant local economy. In this way the Flemish were followed by Frankish calico-printers, French gardeners, Belgian brewers (in 1499 Henry VII licensed John Merchant from Flanders to export '50 tuns of Ale called Berre') and some with more esoteric skills. When Henry VIII needed an executioner to behead his queen, Anne Boleyn, on Tower Green in 1536 he was obliged to hire a Frenchman, as there was no native executioner able to manipulate a sword so dextrously.

After the 1572 Massacre of St Bartholomew in France, a murderous attack on Protestants led by the king, Charles IX, many French silk workers fled to London. In France they had been known as *réformés* – they were members of the Reformed Church John Calvin had set up in 1550 – but in England they became known as Huguenots, a word derived from the German *eidgenosse* or confederate.

When the authorities prevented the Huguenots settling in the City, citing their lack of support for the Church of England, the newcomers went east, colonizing the nearest available land, around the ruins of St Mary Spital, once a flourishing priory and hospital, which had become known as the Spital Fields. It was clearly defined territory. To the west was Bishopsgate, the Roman road leading from the City towards Hertfordshire. To the east lay a narrow track which led past the brick kilns (what is now Brick Lane). To the north were the fields of Shoreditch and Bethnal Green, and to the south an archery and crossbow training ground which Henry VIII had granted to the Fraternity of the Artillery (now covered by Artillery Lane).

Alongside these archery butts was an enclosed piece of ground, Tasel Close, named after the prickly teazles plant, where the silk workers treated their cloth. In the centre of the Spital Fields, by the ruins of the sacked priory, stood the St Mary Spital Cross, setting for the Easter Spital sermons attended, until the execution of Charles I, by the Lord Mayor, aldermen and sheriffs robed in violet gowns. Here, every summer, was held the Spitalfields Fair where, according to an anonymous poet, astrologers and mountebanks tried 'In one poore day to vent their foolerie;/Whereupon resolved to constitute a faire;/In Spittlefields, exposing each man's ware/To public view.'

When James I took the English throne in 1603 he boosted the silk trade by planting mulberry trees to rear silkworms, following in a royal tradition established by the Chinese Emperor Hwang-ti around the year 2650 BC. Unfortunately, he mistakenly introduced the black mulberry; the silkworm flourishes on the white mulberry. In 1629 James's successor, Charles I, incorporated one branch of the silk workers, the throwsters, which meant that no one could join the industry without serving an apprenticeship of seven years. Spitalfields gained another boost in 1682, when Charles II granted the neighbourhood a charter for a market to sell 'flesh, fowl and roots', a market that still exists today in an altered form.

Not all the Huguenots lived in Spitalfields. Christopher Mountjoy, a Huguenot wig-maker, resided in what is now the Barbican in 1604 with his actor-playwright tenant, William Shakespeare. And not all Spitalfields inhabitants were engaged in the silk industry. The most famous local resident in the seventeenth century was the apothecary Nicholas Culpepper, author of *The Complete Herbal*, billed as an 'astrologo-physical discourse of common herbs of the nation; containing a complete Method or Practice of Physic whereby a Man may preserve his Body in Health, or cure himself when sick'. The book was an unlikely bestseller and provided Londoners with a welcome relief from the absurd medicines of the time, made mostly from dead insects and birds, and administered in compulsory Latin.

By the end of Charles II's reign in 1685 more than 20,000 East Enders were engaged in the silk trade. Then came more drama in France. That year, the French king overturned the Edict of Nantes, legislation enacted to protect the rights of Protestants following the Massacre of St Bartholomew, and carnage ensued. Across France churches were destroyed, and bibles and hymn books burned. Although emigration was outlawed, some 13,000 Huguenots, including many silk weavers, fled the cities of Tours and Lyon, leaving their possessions behind. They hid in boats under bales of merchandise, and journeyed to East London, an attractive destination given the capital's renunciation of Rome.

Watching the Protestant persecution in France was the English ambassador, Sir Henry Savile, who wrote to the Secretary of State, urging the government to pass laws quickly to naturalize the French refugees. The government complied. William III guaranteed the Huguenots' right of worship, issuing a proclamation granting them 'all privileges and immunities for the liberty and free exercise of their trade and craft . . . to render their living here comfortable and easy to them'. When the French government realized that some of its most industrious people were leaving the country, it dropped its hostile policy and tried to entice the Huguenots back. But it was too late.

## 'WE ARE SHADOWS'

Silkmaking Spitalfields style was intricate and ordered work. Before weaving could begin, the raw silk, which was imported from the continent in skeins, needed to be throwsted – twisted into thread. The weaving itself involved winding or quilling, pulling the warp on the loom beam and passing the shuttle through the warp. The throwsting, winding and quilling required skill, but as for passing the shuttle through the warp, it was said that an able person who had never seen a loom would be able to figure out the nature of the task within an hour without any help.

The Spitalfields Huguenots manufactured fabrics that were in everyday demand, such as lustrings, made of glossy silk cloth, and alamodes, a soft light silk used for shawls, its name a corruption of *à la mode*. They also made velvets, a Chinese invention and at that time an Italian speciality, which were used for hangings. For designs the master weavers either created their own or used freelancers, of whom Anna Maria Garthwaite, who lived in Spitalfields at 2 Princes (now Princelet) Street, became the most celebrated. Examples of her work are stored at London's Victoria and Albert Museum.

Spitalfields fabrics were in great demand, but the fashions of the day were quite rigid. Gentlemen wore wigs which fell on both sides of the face, the drooping ends enclosed at the back in a silk bag, and were often the first thing snatched by street robbers. They also wore long waistcoats, shirts of fine white linen with a lace frill, and cravats. For women, small laced aprons were popular, as were flowered petticoats, a conspicuously high head-dress and a lace cap which stood on the head. Perhaps the purpose of the strange headgear was to avert attention from the face, which women anointed with wash-balls made of lead, rice and flour.

The Spitalfields silk and velvet industry, which previously had only fitfully taken root, flowered after 1685. 'The Huguenots labour truthfully,' a local cleric noted, 'they live sparingly. They are good examples of labour, travail, faith and patience. The towns in which they live are happy; for God doth follow them with His blessing.' The Huguenots prospered not only as silk weavers but also as glass blowers, jewellers, silversmiths, gunsmiths, engravers and locksmiths. They assimilated quickly for, even if native East Enders found them strange, at least, like them, the Huguenots hated the Pope.

The Huguenot population soon divided itself into well-demarcated enclaves. The weavers, who comprised the majority of the local silk workers, lived in cramped cottages on what were then still semi-rural lanes – Fleur de Lys Street, Greenwood Alley, Sweet Apple Court. As the industry grew so the weavers' cottages spread further out, to Brick Lane and Bethnal Green.

The artisans lived in new houses on Elder Street and Wilkes Street, many of which survive, working at the top of the house in attics whose windows, known as 'long lights', occupied the entire length of the property. They filled these attics with looms and spinning-wheels that clanged and shook the room, and made the long scarlet drops of the fuchsias, which lined the window ledges in small pots, swing gently backwards and forwards.

The merchants lived in more spacious properties built on Spitalfields' most impressive turning, Church Street (now Fournier Street), which survives as a quintessential stretch of Georgian London. At No. 2 is the Minister's House, a rare Nicholas Hawksmoor-designed domestic property (as opposed to church). No. 4, which Marmaduke Smith, a local carpenter, built for himself in 1726, incorporates England's first mahogany staircase, its brackets carved with ears of wheat and scallop shells (the pilgrim badge of St James, an eighteenth-century 'welcome' symbol). At No. 14 is Howard House, another generously proportioned property, whose handsome staircase features exactly one hundred stairs. Here the silk used for Queen Victoria's coronation gown was woven. Behind the houses on the southern side the gardens were filled with vines, and mulberry and fig trees, few of which survive in an area where spare land has long been at a premium. The centrepiece of Huguenot Spitalfields was Spital Square, with its luxurious houses, only one of which remains – the 1740-built No. 37, until recently home to the Georgian Society and the Society for the Protection of Ancient Buildings.

Spitalfields, which lay beyond the powers of the City of London next door, was run as the Liberty of Norton Folgate. It had two charity schools, its own courthouse, almshouses, nightwatchmen and a daily rubbish collection. Its culture was the most sophisticated and advanced in Georgian London. The first gold medal winner at the Royal Academy of Arts, John Bacon Junior, was a Spitalfields resident. (The area has retained its links with art, in particular the avant-garde, being a recent home to Gilbert and George, Tracey Emin, Chris Ofili and Rachael Whiteread.) There were societies for music, recitation, history and horticulture. At well-attended mathematics lectures locals discussed exacting theorems, such as whether an equation of the form $x^3 + x = 1$ can be solved philosophically, given that $x^3$ is a cube, but $x$ a line, and that a three-dimensional shape cannot be added to a one-dimensional object.

The Huguenots formed mutual benefit societies to protect themselves in times of sickness. They worked and socialized together. The master weavers and artisans used the same churches, attended the same clubs, shopped for fruit and vegetables at Spitalfields market, and on Club Row traded the goldfinches, chaffinches and greenfinches they kept in small aviaries in the roofs of their cottages. They planted many flowers and introduced to the natives new dishes such as oxtail, which London butchers had previously thrown away. They also pioneered a taste for the hitherto unknown combination of fried fish with pieces of fried potato, reinvented in Manchester in the nineteenth century as 'fish and chips'.

Because so many foreigners who bear no allegiance to the Church of England have settled in Spitalfields over the centuries, the area has long been a centre of nonconformism. A small group of Baptists moved from Holland to Spitalfields in 1612. Their leader, Thomas Helwys, soon irked the established Church with his tract *A Short Declaration of the Mystery of Iniquity*, which begged James I not to impose laws against the consciences of his subjects. 'The King is a mortal man and not God, therefore hath no power over the mortal soul of his subjects to make laws and ordinances for them and to set spiritual Lords over them,' Helwys wrote. This, the first statement of absolute religious liberty written in English, landed Helwys in Newgate prison, where he died in 1616.

The Huguenots built eight French Protestant churches locally between 1687 and 1703. A rare surviving example stands on the corner of Brick Lane and Fournier Street. In the nineteenth century it was converted from a church into a synagogue. It is now a mosque, the Jamme Masjid, on which the sundial inscribed by Huguenots *umbra sumus* – 'We are shadows' – remains in place.

By the end of the seventeenth century the authorities were so alarmed about the rise of non-Anglican denominations in east London that they commissioned Nicholas Hawksmoor, assistant to Christopher Wren and an equally imaginative architect, to build a new church in the heart of Spitalfields, at what is now the junction of Fournier Street and Commercial Street, 'to keep off filth Nastiness & Brutes'.

Inspired by the earliest Christian churches, those which by this time were ruins in the sands of the Levant, Hawksmoor created the epic Christ Church Spitalfields, its immensity and grandeur impressing generations of Londoners. Christ Church fitted the requirements of the 1711 Fifty New Churches Act in that it was made of 'Stone and other proper Materials' with a spire that soared high above the weavers' houses and could be seen from afar. But even it couldn't transform the religious convictions of the local Irish. In February 1735 the *Gentleman's Magazine* related a story of how mass, which was then illegal, was being held in front of nearly a hundred people, 'most of them miserably poor and ragged', in a garret visible from Christ Church. When parish officials launched a raid, the infidels made off quickly through a trap door, the only means of access and escape, to avoid arrest.

Within a couple of generations the Huguenots lost much of their outward ethnic trappings: French Protestant churches were converted to English Protestant churches; family names were anglicized – Lenoir became Black, Blanc White, Bonenfant Goodchild, de la Neuve Maison Newhouse. One local pastor complained of the 'growing aversion of the young for the language of fathers, from whom they almost seemed ashamed to be descended'.

Yet behind the brocade curtains on Elder Street and Norton Folgate the old customs persisted for a few generations: a rule that French was always spoken on weekends; the French manner to serve the Sunday supper salads garnished with burnet, chervil and dandelion; the Bible open at Ezekiel 16: '*Ainsi tu fus parée d'or et d'argent, et tu fus vêtue de fin lin, de soie et d'étoffes brodées. La fleur de farine, le miel et l'huile, furent ta nourriture. Tu étais d'une beauté accomplie, digne de la royauté*' ('Thus wast thou decked with gold and silver; and thy raiment was of fine linen, and *silk*, and broidered work; thou didst eat fine flour, and honey, and oil: and thou wast exceedingly beautiful, and thou didst prosper into a kingdom').

## THE SPITALFIELDS RIOTS

The manufacture of silk, one of the capital's few industries, was considered to be of national importance, worthy of protection from foreign competition. In 1692 Parliament set high protective duties on silks imported from France and India, but the number of imports brought into London by the East India Company continued to grow, and local manufacturers panicked. They denounced rival calicoes as 'worthless, scandalous, unprofitable sort of goods embraced by a luxuriant humour among the women, prompted by the art and fraud of the drapers and the East India Company to whom alone they are profitable'. Some went as far as physically attacking passers-by who wore rival materials, tearing the clothes off their backs. Another target was Irish silk workers believed to be taking lower wages.

In 1699 Spitalfields silk weavers stormed nearby East India House to protest against cheap imports, and the following year the government banned imports of dyed and printed cloth. For a while this legislation protected the industry, and by the time of the Hanoverian accession to the throne in 1714 Spitalfields silks were worth £700,000 more than in 1688 when wrought silks were first imported from the old country.

By then Spitalfields silks, with their distinctive floral motifs, were rated as highly as those made in France; they were being spoken of alongside Lucca velvets and Honiton lace. But the industry still faced other problems – fluctuations in fashion and the uncertain passage of ships arriving from abroad with the raw silk – and wages were never high enough for the journeyman weaver to save up for periods of unemployment.

The Seven Years War (1756–63) between England and France over control of North America blocked the importing of French silk fabrics and further boosted the Spitalfields industry. But French goods were still being smuggled in and they began to flood the English market once the war had ended.

Again the silk weavers complained to Parliament. Again the Commons complied, drafting a bill to exclude foreign silks, but the House of Lords rejected the proposals. Several thousand weavers took to the streets, marching through Spitalfields 'in riotous manner', according to the *Gentleman's Magazine*, and 'broke open the house of one of their masters, destroyed his looms, and cut a great quantity of silk to pieces'. The rioters then put his effigy into a cart, placed a halter about the neck, an executioner on one side and a coffin on the other, and after drawing the cart through the streets hanged the effigy on a gibbet before burning it to ashes.

The riot leaders went to meet the king, George III, and presented him with a petition explaining how clandestine imports of French silks were impoverishing them. Soon after, the government seized a number of French patterns, ranging in value from 5s to £5 a yard, which French natives were handing around Spitalfields, and passed more legislation to protect the Spitalfields weavers.

In 1768 it became a crime punishable by death to break into a house or shop with the intention of maliciously damaging or destroying silk goods. The law made little difference, for the following year was the most violent yet for Spitalfields. Trouble flared when Lewis Chauvet, a handkerchief manufacturer, cut the rate he paid his workers and forbade them from joining a union. On 17 August weaver rebels raided the homes of his workers, cutting the silk from some fifty looms. Four nights later the gangs returned and cut the silk from a hundred more looms as the sound of cracking pistols rent the night air.

Chauvet offered a £500 reward for information leading to the arrest of those responsible for the damage. For several weeks the people of Spitalfields remained silent, either out of fear of the cutters or because they did not wish to impart information that could send a man to the gallows. However, on 26 September witnesses came forward and accused two Irishmen, John Doyle and John Valline, of being behind the violence. The pair were arrested and charged on the flimsiest evidence with breaking into Chauvet's house, which of course led to more trouble. As members of the weavers' union met at the Dolphin tavern under the dramatic-sounding name 'The Conquering and Bold Defiance', to discuss the defence of their victimized colleagues, some thirty officers, soldiers and magistrates were preparing to raid the tavern and arrest the union organizers. Most of the lawmen melted away *en route* from Covent Garden to the East End, leaving only eight or nine officers to raid the premises. When they ordered the silkmen to surrender, one of the cutters opened fire, killing a soldier. In turn the soldiers shot at the windows of the rooms where the cutters were assembled, killing two of the Dolphin's customers, who were not union members. A third man had his hat destroyed by a bullet that tore through it, just missing his head.

The weavers escaped, fleeing through windows and a trapdoor in the roof, and when the authorities arrived they found only one man left. He was lying ill in bed and had had nothing to do with the trouble. Nevertheless he was charged with murdering a soldier and kept in jail for two and a half weeks before being released due to lack of evidence. The Spitalfields merchants, wanting to make an example of Doyle and Valline, the two Irishmen sentenced to hang, demanded that their execution be moved from the usual place, Tyburn (near the modern-day Marble Arch), to the East End, silkland.

As workmen erected the gallows outside the Salmon and Ball public house on the corner of Bethnal Green Road and Cambridge Heath Road, a mob pelted them with bricks, tiles and stones. When Doyle and Valline were brought to the scaffold, the former proclaimed: 'I John Doyle do hereby declare, as my last dying words in the presence of my Almighty God, that I am as innocent of the fact I am now to die for as the child unborn. Let my blood lie to that wicked man who has purchased it with gold, and them notorious wretches who swore it falsely away.' The crowd needed little further convincing of the injustice they were witnessing and sped to 39 Crispin Street, Spitalfields, home of Chauvet, the master weaver who had instigated the trouble, smashing his windows and damaging furniture.

The violence abated briefly after the passing of the Spitalfields Weavers' Act of 1773. This law ensured that the weavers' wages were decided by the Lord Mayor, Recorder and aldermen, and made it illegal for a master to pay more, or any workman to accept less, than the set rate. Five years later more protective legislation was passed, and in 1792 it was extended to cover those manufacturing mixed goods (made of both silk and worsted). Fashion designers tried to help the weavers by encouraging ladies to wear silk fabrics at balls and assemblies and by equating the wearing of silk with self-respect, but these measures failed to protect Spitalfields. The demand for silk encouraged smuggling from France on an extensive scale and the restrictive wages led to manufacturers undertaking similar work elsewhere and paying less for the same product without breaking the law.

## DESCENT INTO POVERTY

The Spitalfields silk industry began its inevitable decline at the end of the eighteenth century. Parts of the area soon teetered over the edge into impoverishment and decay. When John Wesley, the founder of Methodism, visited Spitalfields in 1777 he found Methodists living in 'such poverty as few can conceive without seeing it'. Around this time the luxurious Fournier Street houses were taken over by firms whose employees lived and worked within, packing silk waste between the floor joists to dampen the noise of the looms.

Violence, usually industrially motivated, continued. On Lady Day 1818 a crowd seized a bullock and used it as a battering ram against a Spitalfields silk-warehouse owner who had upset them. Those inside the premises defended themselves by pouring large pans of boiling water on to their attackers. In 1824 some of the laws that had been protecting the industry were rescinded. Local weavers in their small attic workshops found themselves unable to compete with the large factories filled with power looms that were being built in the North. Many left for Macclesfield or Coventry.

What was killing off their industry was the Industrial Revolution; mechanization replacing handicraft. All types of Spitalfields cloth workers began to suffer. Those working with velvet found the price they received for each velvet coat collar drop during the 1820s as the cloth masters began undercutting each other. If they refused to take a reduced price they would be usurped by those who were more desperate, and if they chose to accept they ended up doing twice the work for the same wages, a fifteen-hour day beginning soon after the 5.45 a.m. toll of the Christ Church bell.

In 1824 the number of looms in Spitalfields stood at 20,000; by 1838 it had halved. Those affected looked for a political solution. Many took solace in the People's Charter, a list of political reforms drawn up by the London Working Men's Association. The Charter horrified the establishment, for the Chartists supported universal suffrage (for men only), the removal of the stipulation that Members of Parliament had to be property owners, secret ballots and annual general elections.

Arguments over the Charter, and whether constitutional change could encourage social improvement, were heard nightly in Spitalfields pubs. Locals believed that the decline of the Spitalfields weaving industry was directly related to the weavers' lack of representation in the House of Commons. One well-attended speech ended: 'It is our firm conviction that if affairs continue as at present the fate of the working man must be pauperism, crime or death.' An air of doom began to hang over the place. It may have been a time of enormous prosperity within the British economy, but in Spitalfields, where the silk-weaving industry had practically collapsed, there was despondency and gloom.

The grand merchants' houses of Fournier Street and Elder Street were broken up into flats and labourers and market porters moved in. The weavers' cottages, never the most appealing properties, became slums, leading the poet Matthew Arnold to note in 'Sonnet on East London' that 'Twas August and the fierce sun overhead/Smote on the squalid streets of Bethnal Green/And the pale weaver, through his windows, seen/In Spitalfields, looked thrice dispirited.'

David Bartlett, an American who explored Spitalfields in 1852, noted how

you traverse street after street, and see nothing but the most disgusting, the most beseeching poverty. There are thousands of men and women there who never have known what plenty is, what pure joy is, but are herded together, thieves, prostitutes, robbers and working-men, in frightful masses. You meet beggars at every step; at night the streets are crowded with wretched women.

James Cantlie, who gave a lecture entitled 'Degeneration Amongst Londoners' locally, was even more damning. He described the Spitalfields weavers as a 'stunted, puny race, who become prematurely old, whose grave and sorrowful countenances betray a body and mind at variance with natural habiliments. They are more machines than active livers, and, on the face of it, it is improbable that out of such a class a healthy person could spring.'

Despite the publicity given to Spitalfields' plight, conditions continued to deteriorate. After a treaty was signed with France in 1860 allowing foreign silks to enter Britain at a cost lower than that of home-grown fabrics, more weavers left for the factories of the North or even America. The silk workers dwindled to a hundred or so artisans employed by companies that ordered in bulk for special occasions. For instance in 1870 the Vatican scoured the workshops of Europe for craftsmen who could weave a pontifical robe. A suitable silk weaver was found in Spitalfields. How ironic! Had the Catholic authorities in France not ordered their Protestant silk weavers out of the country 200 years previously, they might have found an appropriate artisan without having to cross the Channel.

Some respite came for Spitalfields in 1870, when Benjamin Warner opened a new local textile firm in Hollybush Gardens, off Bethnal Green Road, run along traditional lines. Warner's *vade mecum* was a book of patterns designed by Walloon refugees who had emigrated to Canterbury centuries before. The company withstood competition from the French and won considerable export trade. In 1895 Princess Mary of Teck visited the premises and commissioned them to weave the silk brocade for her wedding dress. But that was the year that Warner's moved to Essex.

By the time the Great War broke out in 1914 there were still forty-six weaving workshops in the East End. However, when George Doree, the area's most skilled velveteer and a Huguenot descendant, died in 1916, silk-weaving in Spitalfields died with him.

# 5

# Ratcliff Highway: Murder and Mayhem

*If once a man indulges himself in murder, very soon he comes to think little of robbing; and from robbing he comes next to drinking and Sabbath-breaking, and from that to incivility and procrastination.*

'Murder Considered as One of the Fine Arts', Thomas de Quincey, 1827

Ratcliff Highway became London's most violent road during the maritime trade boom of the eighteenth century. Blame the clash of sailors of so many different nationalities: German stevedores in light-blue jackets and yellow trousers, Scandinavians in long sea-boots smelling of tallow and turpentine, tigerish-looking Malays smoking cheroots nearly a foot long, Negroes from the Gold Coast and Guinea sporting necklaces of charms and fetishes, Neapolitans wearing images of their guardian saint and weather-beaten men from the bitter Arctic seas.

Alongside these dissolute sailors, Ratcliff Highway drew in all manner of bravos and bullies taking leave on shore after months at sea to drink, fight, gamble, rob and whore in the taverns and the brothels dotted among the tiny cottages, and run down rice and sugar warehouses. Their riotous behaviour and unbridled passions put the fear of God into the land-locked locals. Trouble was always at hand, but occasionally the locals fought back. In 1768 East End coal-heavers decided they could no longer endure wages paid in beer and shabby second-hand goods, and took their frustrations out on the first sailors they could find. They battled with them in Stepney Fields. Several men were killed and the landlord of the Roundabout Tavern was shot, for which crimes seven coal-heavers were later hanged in Sun Tavern Fields. Peace broke out soon after.

Things hadn't always been this bad. Ratcliff Highway, one of London's oldest roads, was originally a Roman Praetorian Way connecting the lake fort Llyndin, near where the Tower of London now stands, with the gravel spur at the red cliff – Ratcliff. During the Middle Ages it was lined with long, straight rows of elm trees. In the mid sixteenth century the waters of a local well that showed traces of sulphur, steel and antimony were bottled and sold. Despite the vaunted virtues of the water the venture flopped, and the solution was taken up by calico printers, who used it to fix their colours.

By the time John Stowe came to write his *Survey of London* of 1598, Ratcliff Highway had degenerated into a dystopia of debauchery, 'a filthy strait passage with alleys of small tenements'. When the Irish arrived in the late eighteenth century to man the expanding local industry locals nicknamed the area 'Knockfergus' – it was even called that on the map Napoleon used when planning an invasion of London.

Ratcliff Highway continued to attract misfortune. In 1794 one of the worst fires in London's history began here, when a kettle of pitch boiled over in a builder's yard and tore through hundreds of wooden houses. It made a change from violence but did nothing for the area's popularity. Indeed the Ratcliff Highway area had so fearsome a reputation that when a new vicar took over around that time at St Paul's, Shadwell, just off the Highway, he was so terrified he used his first sermon to echo the cry from Psalm 120: 'Woe is me, that I sojourn in Mesech, that I dwell in the tents of Kedar'. He kept his luxurious address off the Strand, and travelled back and forth every day for fifty-seven years.

Ratcliff Highway was also home in the nineteenth century to one of London's most famous shops, Jamrach's animal store – household pets and tropical birds at the front of the premises, monkeys, elephants and great cats at the back – the only place in London where a gentleman could send his servant to buy a lion, no questions asked. But even this led to tragedy. One day a tiger escaped from the shop, picked up a small boy by the collar, doubtless with lunch in mind, and made its way through the East End, causing much alarm, until a passer-by prised the boy from the beast's jaws with a crowbar, capturing the animal but striking the boy a fatal blow.

## MURDER OF THE MARRS

Opposite Jamrach's at No. 29, among the slopsellers, gin palaces, sailors' lodging houses, coffee shops and dancing saloons, was a linen draper's. It was run by 24-year-old Timothy Marr, his wife, Celia, their maid and an apprentice. And it was here that one of the most disturbing events in the history of the East End occurred in the early hours of Sunday 8 December 1811. At ten minutes before midnight on Saturday the 7th Timothy Marr sent the maid, Margaret Jewell, to buy oysters fresh from the Whitstable Bay boats moored in the Pool of London.

Saturday was the busiest day of the week, and as barely an hour had passed since the shop had shut the premises were still bursting with worsted cloth, silk and muslin. Despite the late hour and the notoriety of the area, the maid was not afraid to walk Ratcliff Highway and the back streets of Wapping alone, for the boisterous vulgarity of the drunken revellers would itself provide a kind of protection, and their presence was preferable to the emptiness of the streets in the middle of the week when the clunking of booms against bowsprits and the whistling of the wind through the rigging made Wapping the eeriest place in London.

Unable to find any oysters, Margaret Jewell returned to No. 29. As she approached she could see Marr and his boy hard at work through the shop window. So, lured on by the ever present smell of fish and river, she decided to try another stall by the dock wall. This was also shut, and she returned home, having been gone twenty minutes in all. By then the area had quietened down. Some of the pubs were closing. The drunks were staggering off, and footsteps were becoming rarer.

To Jewell's surprise, No. 29 was in darkness. She pulled the bell as the nightwatchman, George Olney, passed by silently on the other side of the street. When there was no answer, nor any sound from within, she pulled at it again, pressing her ear to the door. After what seemed an eternity, the maid heard the soft sound of a footstep on the stair and a cry from the Marrs' baby. Everything was all right; someone was about to answer her. Yet no one came. The maid began to fear that something was amiss. She rang the bell repeatedly and hammered at the door. A man appeared behind her, a drunk. His presence did nothing to settle her nerves, as he brandished a few insults before making off.

Jewell remained outside Marr's shop for half an hour, desperately waiting for a reassuring response from inside, and unable to comprehend why the inhabitants would have left the premises. Olney, the nightwatchman, reappeared, but he worried her all the more when he told her that although he had seen Marr put up the shutters, he had noticed them unfastened a few minutes later, and that on calling out to the owner he had been answered by a strange voice abruptly shouting, 'We know of it.'

Olney and Jewell banged on the door together as the nightwatchman shouted, 'Mr Marr, Mr Marr, Mr MARR!' They woke the next-door neighbour, John Murray, a pawnbroker, who joined the anxious party and offered to go round the back to rouse the household. Murray made his way in, while the maid and the nightwatchman continued to knock and ring in vain at the front, and finding a candle still burning crept upstairs, whispering emphatically outside a shut bedroom door, 'Marr, Marr, your window shutters are not fastened!'

When no one answered, Murray went downstairs. At the bottom he found a grisly explanation of why the occupants were oblivious to the commotion outside. It was the body of James Gowen, the shop boy, lying in a heap, his face beaten in by a number of blows, blood still flowing from his head, his brains scattered around him. Murray edged shakily towards the door. To his horror it was blocked by another body, that of Mrs Marr. She too was dead, her face a mass of blood. Murray stumbled outside and at first incoherently, then more animatedly, shouted to the small crowd outside, 'Murder! Murder! Come and see what murder is here!'

The small party entered and found more corpses. That of Timothy Marr, the shopkeeper, was behind the counter, his face flat on the floor. The body of the three-month-old baby was in its cradle in the basement, its face battered and throat slit so deeply that the head was almost severed from the body. Someone in the crowd went to fetch the watchmen (there was no Metropolitan Police force then). One officer found on the shop counter a clean ripping chisel that the maid did not recognize, and upstairs, on a chair in the main bedroom, a sailor's maul (a kind of mallet) covered with blood and sticky with hairs, its tip broken. At the back of the shop some of the crowd noticed a number of footprints. Presumably they belonged to the murderer or murderers, who must have escaped over public land south of Ratcliff Highway towards London Docks. A neighbour later confirmed that he had heard 'about ten men' running away.

## FALSE LEADS

As Ratcliff Highway awoke to the horror in its midst, the various local crime-fighting bodies – the churchwardens, beadle, unpaid constables, high constables, river police, and overseers and trustees of the parish vestry – launched their investigations. Lacking any systemized means of collating evidence and analysing findings, they made little progress; all the suspects they rounded up for loitering near the Marrs' house had valid alibis. Hordes of sightseers, both local and from afar, came to No. 29 to see the victims' bodies laid out on their beds. Indeed, so great was the number of visitors to the scene of the murders that when an inquest was held at the Jolly Sailors public house opposite the shop the following Tuesday, Ratcliff Highway was left, according to *The Times*, 'almost impassable by the throng of spectators'.

At the inquest the coroner's jury returned a verdict of 'wilful murder against some person or persons unknown'. The public, spurred on by posters offering a £50 reward for information on the crimes, responded in predictable fashion. Some came forward claiming to have important knowledge, but after being questioned turned out to be attention-seekers. Witnesses to and perpetrators of long forgotten crimes confessed to secrets they had preserved for years, none of which was any use to the investigation, but was enough to keep magistrates busy for some time. Those with a grudge against a neighbour, and mindful of the reward, began to finger unlikely culprits. Worse, some believed they dare not talk of the murders for fear of unleashing whatever demon was responsible. A favourite culprit was the 'London Monster', who had terrorized London women the previous century with volleys of abuse and a stab to the buttocks, but had not been seen since 1790.

Four days after the murders, a carpenter called Pugh, who had lent Marr the chisel found at the scene of the crime, was brought in for questioning. Although it was unlikely that the chisel was the murder weapon, given that it was clean when found, Pugh could not explain why Marr had been unable to find it when he had visited the shop a few days previously, but that it had been found near the bodies of the victims. Why had a supposedly lost chisel been discovered in so central a part of the house in between the time Margaret Jewell left to buy oysters and returned to find the household murdered?

Deciding that the carpenter was of excellent character, and lacking any means of forensically testing the chisel, the magistrates left the incident strangely unresolved. Instead they brought in for questioning a girl who had been Mrs Marr's servant for six months before being dismissed for dishonesty. After quarrelling with her mistress, the girl had vowed to kill her. However, the threats turned out to be bluster, and she too was discharged. The authorities became very excited about two suspicious-looking men seen in Piccadilly inquiring about the coach to Plymouth. One of them had dropped a scrap of paper on which was scrawled a barely literate message about how 'The deed is greatly done', but they were never seen again.

Nearly a week after the murders George, the Prince Regent, offered a reward through a notice displayed in the parish which informed the public that as

Mr Marr, Mrs Celia Marr, his wife, Timothy, their infant child, in the cradle and James Gowen, a servant lad [had been] most inhumanly and barbarously murdered, His Royal Highness, [was] pleased to offer a reward of £100 to any of them (except the person or persons who actually perpetrated the said murders) who shall discover his or their accomplice or accomplices therein.

When the notice resulted only in more fruitless developments Aaron Graham, one of the more capable Bow Street magistrates, was called in. Painstakingly, he ran through the various possibilities. It was unlikely that robbery was the motive for these appalling acts, given that £5 was found in the slain Timothy Marr's pockets and the till had been left well stocked. Such violent killings smacked of a personal vendetta, he surmised. Marr's strange behaviour in sending the maid to buy oysters at so late an hour, when it would have been more normal to send out the shop boy, James Gowen, was suspicious. Perhaps Marr had sent her out so that she would not see the arrival of an invited visitor? Perhaps she was lying about her story and had willingly left the premises in advance of a trespasser whose identity she knew? Or maybe these really were random killings carried out by a dangerous and merciless gang.

Then, at last, a breakthrough! A magistrate at the river police headquarters in Wapping, idly admiring the sailor's maul that had been found at the murder scene, wiped off the tangled mass of hair and dried blood on the implement and noticed some partly decipherable initials. They read 'I. P.' or maybe 'J. P.'

## MURDER OF THE WILLIAMSONS

After more than a week had passed, and no one had been caught for the Marr murders, the public assumed that the killer or killers had fled, probably to sea. They were just beginning to put the events of 7 December behind them when murder returned to the Ratcliff Highway area.

This time the scene of tragedy was a public house, the King's Arms, at 81 New Gravel Lane (now Garnet Street), a few hundred yards east of the Marrs' shop. The King's Arms was run by John Williamson, a burly 56-year-old, his wife Elizabeth, their fourteen-year-old granddaughter Kitty and a servant, Bridget Harrington. Every night at eleven Williamson would clear the pub, put up the shutters and pour a draught of beer for the local constable, Anderson, who was usually the last caller. On Thursday 19 December, nearly a fortnight after the murder of the Marrs, Williamson noticed a suspicious-looking man wearing a brown jacket, listening at the door of the premises. He asked Anderson to look out for the individual, and the constable made off along New Gravel Lane.

Returning to the King's Arms soon after to tell Williamson that he had found nobody fitting the description, Anderson came upon a tremendous commotion in the street outside the pub. A small crowd of people was looking up at the first floor, watching Turner, the Williamsons' lodger, frantically making his way out through the window by means of knotted sheets crying, 'Murder! Murder! . . . they are murdering the people in the house!'

As the half-naked Turner dropped to the ground, Anderson rushed into his own house for his truncheon and returned to beat down the door of the King's Arms. Inside he and the crowd that had followed him in found a chilling sight. It was Williamson, sprawled out on the stairs leading to the taproom, his head beaten to a pulp, his throat cut to the bone. Alongside the publican lay an iron bar covered in blood. Nearby lay Williamson's wife, her skull smashed and throat slashed, blood pouring from the wound. The maid, Bridget Harrington, was also dead. She was lying by the hearth, where there were signs that she had been trying to light the fire. Her skull had been smashed with considerably more force than Mrs Williamson's and her throat sliced through as far as the bone. Kitty Stillwell, the sleeping fourteen-year-grand-daughter, had not been touched. A window at the back of the pub was found to be open. There were bloodstains on the sill, and on the ground outside, eight feet below, a footprint was embedded in the clay. Anyone fleeing this way would have needed to climb a muddy slope to escape and their clothes would have clay stains, which are notoriously difficult to wash off.

Throughout Wapping and Shadwell hundreds came out of their doors when they heard the news. Fire-bells were rung and volunteers beat drums. The police launched their biggest dragnet yet, even going as far as to seal off London Bridge. Turner, who had lived in the house for about eight months, was taken in for questioning. He explained stumblingly that, having retired for the night, he had heard a loud bang at the front door and a few minutes later the servant cry, 'We are all murdered!', followed by the sound of two or three blows and Williamson shouting, 'I'm a dead man!'

Paralysed by fear, Turner lay still for a few moments. He then rose, put his ear to the door and, hearing nothing, left the room gingerly. At the top of the stairs he made out the shape of a man about six feet in height, 'dressed in a genteel style, with a long dark loose coat on', rifling Mrs Williamson's pocket. 'I said nothing to him, but ran upstairs,' Turner explained, 'and taking up the sheets from my bed fastened them together and lashed them to the bed-posts. I called to the watchman to give the alarm and hanging out of the front window by the sheets made my way down. The watchman received me in his arms, naked as I was.' The authorities were satisfied that Turner was not the culprit, and had escaped the house in panic as the murderer or murderers were completing their task. They let him go.

The following morning Covent Garden's Bow Street Runners, the nearest thing London then had to a police force, marched along Ratcliff Highway dressed in their blue coats, crimson waistcoats, long leather boots and black hats in a show of strength. By then panic had spread across the East End. Terror was etched on every face; a bolt drawn on every door, a weapon ready in every hand. Wild rumours circulated. Some spoke of how the landlord of the White Rose in Ratcliff Highway would be the next victim. The terrified man rushed round in a fearful state, unsure of whether to meet the adversity head on or flee. The story went round that a publican on City Road had been murdered and that two policemen in Limehouse had been slain while trying to arrest a suspect. Even when the story turned out not to be true the fear refused to wither.

## ARREST AT THE PEAR TREE TAVERN

The Williamsons were buried on Sunday 22 December at St Paul's Church, Shadwell, half a mile east of the church of St George where the Marrs had been buried a week previously. The second funeral service was not as dramatic as the first, for the novelty of burying members of a household slain in cold blood had worn off. However, the even greater rewards which were now on offer for bringing the perpetrators to justice excited the public.

A man reported seeing two people, one short and lame, running up New Gravel Lane towards Ratcliff Highway around the time of the Williamson murders. Another mentioned seeing a tall man in a 'long Flushing coat' outside the King's Arms around the same time. The authorities kept themselves busy, and by Christmas they had more

than twenty suspects in custody. Three were Irishmen: Michael
Harrington, William Austin and William Emery.

Harrington was arrested in Poplar for looking like the man Turner
had seen bending over the prostrate Mrs Williamson. Austin was
taken in for being short and lame, like the man seen running up New
Gravel Lane. Emery was simply guilty of associating with Harrington
and Austin. There was also a gang of seven men who had been
arrested at a house near the Williamsons' pub for having clothes
marked with suspicious stains. They were locked up until the
garments could be examined by a 'chemical gentleman', a rare
instance of scientific procedure being used during this investigation,
but they too had to be freed for lack of credible evidence.

There was also John Williams, a 27-year-old hot-tempered Irishman
who had once sailed with Timothy Marr, the murdered linen draper.
Following a tip-off for which there is no record, he was arrested at the
Pear Tree Tavern, a few hundred yards from the King's Arms, and
remanded at Coldbath Fields prison in Clerkenwell while further investigations were made. Williams was short and lame, and therefore fitted
the description of one of the men spotted outside the King's Arms. He
had even been seen drinking there regularly, including on the night of
the murders, and had not returned to his lodgings until around midnight, arriving with more silver on him than would be expected.

Williams didn't appear to be at all worried about being a suspect.
He freely told the magistrates of his friendship with the murdered
publican and of his movements on the night in question. He had been
out seeking medical help for his wounded leg. The money in his
possession had come from trading clothes at a pawnbroker's.
Witnesses would vouch that he been drinking in any one of a number
of pubs around the time that Williamson and his family were killed.

Although there was no solid case against Williams, the authorities
were desperate to make sense of the drama, desperate to retain as
many suspects as possible in the hope that something would turn up.
And on Christmas Eve it did. The landlord of the Pear Tree Tavern
where Williams was staying identified the initials on the maul found
at the scene of the Marrs' murders as belonging to a John Peterson, a
German sailor, who had left his tools at the Pear Tree before going
back to sea. John Williams now became chief suspect, and was

brought for trial, which began with barely a delay on Christmas Eve in a candlelit court.

In those days trials were bereft of impartiality. The court's function was purely to allow magistrates to determine whether there was enough evidence to proceed and to decide whether there should be a trial by jury. Any evidence, no matter how trifling, could be submitted, particularly if it was likely to incriminate the accused, who would not be represented or present for much of the time to hear the evidence against him.

When Williams was brought into the court the crowd marvelled at his hair, which was of the 'most extraordinary and vivid colour, viz., bright yellow, something between an orange and lemon colour', according to Thomas De Quincey. When Williams tried to speak he was silenced and sent back to Coldbath Fields prison.

Witnesses were then called. William Rice, the eleven-year-old son of the woman who washed John Williams's clothes, examined the maul in front of the court and revealed how the one with the broken tip found at the Marrs' shop was one which he and his friends had played with at the Pear Tree, where Williams was lodging. Mrs Vermilloe, the landlady of the Pear Tree, broke down in court when she saw the maul, but she added that there were 'two or three mauls' in the tool-box and that countless people would have had access to them.

The trial was then adjourned, but the magistrates were not idle on Christmas Day. They again interviewed the Vermilloes. Mr Vermilloe admitted that the iron bar found alongside the murdered Williamson might have come from his tool-chest. He gave the magistrates the name of a man who would testify that Williams had been seen running up New Gravel Lane after the murders. But that would still fail to clear up the mystery about the blood on the sill and the footprint in the clay behind the pub. Would anyone escaping by this route have headed back to New Gravel Lane before making off?

A few new witnesses came forward. Mrs Orr, who lived next to the Pear Tree Tavern, told the court that a week before the Marr murders she was doing the washing late at night when she heard a noise that sounded as if someone was trying to break into the house. She called out and was answered by Williams, who exclaimed, 'I am a robber!' He entered, they began talking, and he gave her a chisel he had found by the window. It was a mad, maverick story and it only clouded things further.

Meanwhile, the authorities in Marlborough, Wiltshire, revealed that they had detained a man who was carrying bloodied torn garments and answered the description of the taller man who had been seen running up New Gravel Lane after the Williamson murders. He had been corresponding with Williams. Perhaps he was the tall man the lodger Turner had seen bending over the victims he had just murdered?

Another Pear Tree tenant was taken into custody. He was a German sailor called Richter, who had been seen drinking at the King's Arms shortly before the Williamson murders. Officers searching his lodgings had found under his bed a pair of damp trousers with mud stains. Richter could not recollect who they belonged to. His answers to other straightforward questions led the magistrates to believe he was withholding information.

Those watching with a dispassionate eye were asking several critical questions. If Williams had picked up a maul he had found in his room at the Pear Tree and taken it to kill the Marrs, then who had killed the Williamsons? Or, assuming that Williams had killed the Williamsons, possible given the suspicion about his behaviour that night, who had killed the Marrs? Perhaps Williams had committed all the murders, but even so he couldn't have been acting alone. And if he had killed the Williamsons, why hadn't Turner identified him?

## JOHN WILLIAMS:
## MURDERER OR MARTYR?

The crowds returned for the trial on 27 December. Perhaps the tall man arrested in Marlborough would vie with Williams as the centre of attention? But it was neither he nor Williams who stole the show. Rather it was the absence of Williams. For at the start of the day a constable announced to the hushed court that the main suspect would not be returning to the witness stand. Williams had hanged himself overnight!

Now surely the case was solved? Williams was guilty. Why else would he commit suicide? After the crowd had recovered from the shock people began to realize the enormity of Williams's untimely demise. By taking his life he had inconvenienced considerable numbers of people. He had robbed the public of a dramatic court case, which would no doubt have culminated in a public hanging. He had cheated the hangman out of the rightful opportunity to keep his body and clothes, not to mention the rope that would have tied him which, given his notoriety, would have fetched at least a shilling. He had deprived Coldbath Fields prison of the fees from visitors who would have paid handsomely to view a brute like him prior to his demise, and he had denied the hard-working toilers of Grub Street the opportunity of earning their due from publishing his confessions.

The trial continued in Williams's absence. Its highlight was the arrival of the man from Marlborough, the Irishman Thomas Cahill. He looked like the man who had been seen running from the Williamsons' pub. When asked where he was on the night of the murders Cahill told magistrates that he had been lodging with a man called Williamson [sic] at 121 Ratcliff Highway. Like much of what he said it was easily proved to be false. It turned out he was lying to cover his desertion from the Irish army.

Eventually, a witness testified that Cahill had been in a pub well removed from the King's Arms on the night of the Williamson murders, and he was released. A further batch of confused witnesses was brought before the court, and at the end of the proceedings Mr Unwin, the coroner, announced the verdict: 'All homicide is murder till the contrary be shown. The law ranks suicide in the worst class of murder, and this is a case of most unqualified self-murder. We consign the body of this self-murderer to that infamy and disgrace which the law has prescribed, and to leave the punishment of his crimes to him that has said "Vengeance is mine, and I will repay."'

Since Williams had committed suicide his body would be dragged through the streets and buried at a crossroads. This was not unusual. People thought that if the spirit of a suicide did wish to haunt its former home the presence of the four roads would confuse it. Nevertheless, as a precaution, a stake was usually driven through the heart to obstruct further the escaping spirit. (That reprisals were feared from a spectral Williams should not be doubted. In 1784 an

Aberystwyth woman who killed herself after poisoning her lodger was buried by the sea to prevent her joining a band of ghosts who were terrorizing a nearby village.) Williams would be cast to the ground at St George's Turnpike, the crossroads of Cannon Street Road and Back Lane (now Cable Street), near the scene of the murders.

On the night of 30 December 1811 three officials – the High Constable of St George's, his deputy and the tax collector – made their way through the City and Clerkenwell to Coldbath Fields prison to pick up Williams's body, which they took back to the East End and deposited at the St George's Watch House by Wellclose Square. There, it was kept overnight in preparation for the ghoulish ceremony.

At 10.30 the next morning, New Year's Eve, the procession left the Watch House. Williams lay almost vertical on a specially constructed cart. His ruddy freshly scrubbed face, with its demonic staring eyes, was exposed for all to see. He was clothed in blue trousers and white open-necked shirt. His left leg was in irons. Alongside him were the right tools: maul and ripping chisel. The procession moved in silence past the tens of thousands of spectators who had left their shops, pubs, houses and work places and were now incredulous, frozen into immobility. It made its way along Ratcliff Highway to No. 29, the Marrs' shop, where the first murders had occurred three weeks previously. There it stopped for ten minutes, presumably to allow Williams's spirit, should it still be present, to reflect on its behaviour. It then headed for Pear Tree Alley and the Pear Tree pub, where Williams had lodged, outside which a cab driver dashed up to the corpse and whipped it across the face three times. The party then headed back to the King's Arms, so that Williams could contemplate his night of brutality at the Williamsons' pub. From there the route took it along Ratcliff Highway and north up Cannon Street Road, coming to a halt at the designated crossroads, where a four-feet-deep hole had been dug deliberately too small to give the corpse as much discomfort as possible.

At the crossroads one of the party turned the body out of the cart and shoved it into the opening, piercing the heart with a long wooden stake to ensure not only that Williams was dead, but that his spirit was truly extinguished. It was at this point that the crowd found its voice, breaking the silence with a thousand cries, oaths and jeers.

When the wailing ceased the clerk in charge of the performance threw in some lime, topped it with earth, and put the paving stones back in place. The show was over. Williams had been cast into the ground whence he came.

The practice of burying a suicide at a crossroads and driving a stake through the heart continued until Parliament abolished it in 1823, although as late as 1882 an English suicide had to be buried at night. Until 1955 Britain jailed those who unsuccessfully attempted suicide.

## KILLERS ON THE LOOSE?

Anyone considering the events could see that there had to be at least one culprit other than Williams. Even the prime minister, Spencer Perceval, noted that all the available evidence pointed in the direction of there being more than one murderer: there were two sets of footprints outside the Marrs' house; there was the tall man the lodger Turner had seen bending over Mrs Williamson. Yet the magistrates had concentrated all their efforts on Williams and had kept him in custody on the flimsiest of grounds: that he might have had access to the maul found at the scene of the Marrs' murders; that he had been seen at the Williamsons' pub just before the latter were murdered; that being short and lame he fitted the description of a man spotted near the scene of the murders; and that he had returned to his lodgings that night late, even though a guilty man would surely have made for the Pear Tree as quickly as possible to establish an alibi.

A week after Williams's suicide, John Harrison, a sail-maker lodging at the Pear Tree Tavern, gave the magistrates a fresh, if tardy, lead. Three weeks previously he had asked Williams to return a borrowed handkerchief. Williams had told Harrison to go to the jacket to get it himself. In doing so his hand had hit upon something 'sharp and metallic'. It was a knife, which Williams said he had bought a few days before. Harrison told the magistrates that he had not seen the knife since. Could this be the weapon used to slice the throats of the victims?

The authorities ordered a search of the Pear Tree, astonishingly for the first time. It yielded nothing. But on 16 January Harrison, looking through some old clothes at the Pear Tree, found a jacket he thought had belonged to Williams. He looked inside, and in a pocket came upon a mass of material thick with dried blood. The premises were searched again, and this time, in a hole in the wall, they discovered the handle of a knife which Harrison matched with that he had found in Williams's pocket a few weeks previously. This was interesting information, but not enough to damn Williams unequivocally: dried blood on the material did not prove murder had taken place and anyone could have placed the knife handle in that hiding hole.

Soon people began debating the very nature of Williams's suicide, something which was not considered important while the mob was baying for blood. This was more interesting than the uncovering of yet more possible murder weapons. How could Williams, five foot nine inches tall, have hanged himself with his own handkerchief from an iron bar positioned six foot two inches above the ground? The post-mortem revealed that his eyes and mouth were open, and it was clear that he had struggled hard. Therefore he must have been struggling with something or someone, for those injuries could not have been self-inflicted.

A prisoner in a nearby cell described how he had heard the sound of chains being violently shaken in Williams's cell at 3 a.m. Another inmate declared that Williams had grappled with an intruder. Before long many were convinced that Williams was himself a victim, killed by a psychopathic warder perhaps, or maybe a deranged inmate, a prisoner revolted at the thought of his alleged crimes, or, more chillingly, the real murderer or murderers who might have been incarcerated in Coldbath Fields prison at the time and were fearful of being identified. Maybe Williams, guilty or not, had been conveniently eliminated in prison, his demise made to look like suicide, which would be an obvious admission of guilt and would bring a quick ending to this most difficult case?

A check of the prison's other inmates yielded no clues. There was however a farcical interlude involving Sylvester Driscoll, a jolly Irishman who had been locked up for no reason other than that he had been lodging near the King's Arms and was Irish. He told how the prison clerk had complained to him that the place was so full he, Driscoll, would have to spend the night in the same cell as John

Williams's corpse, to which he had replied, 'Don't put me there, for I'm sure I'll die in half an hour!'

The authorities never did apprehend anyone else in connection with the Ratcliff Highway murders. A year later, still desperately hoping that something would turn up, they sent special constables to patrol this most lawless of areas with orders to arrest anyone who looked suspicious. The scheme collapsed as there were so many such people around Ratcliff Highway. Meanwhile, the unsatisfactory nature of the police investigations, along with the disturbing conclusion to the events, was crucial in persuading the government to replace its chaotic system of policing, with ill-trained constables and watchmen often working separately on the same investigation. Things moved slowly. It was twenty years before the Metropolitan Police, Britain's first professional force, came into being.

It took time for life in Ratcliff to improve. Forty-four years after the 1811 murders Watts Phillips, in *The Wild Tribes of London*, was still able to describe Ratcliff Highway as 'the head-quarters of unbridled vice and drunken violence – of all that is dirty, disorderly, and debased'. A trip to New Gravel Lane, where the Williamsons were murdered, depressed him further. 'This place is dismal at all times; but on a night like this, and with such a scene around, [it is] mournful and gloomy beyond expression.' By then the King's Arms, home of the Williamsons, had been knocked down during the building of London Docks.

In the 1870s the authorities, wishing to rid Ratcliff Highway of its nefarious reputation, renamed it St George's Street. At the end of the decade Charles Dickens Jnr was able to record some improvement, noting in his *Dictionary of London*, 'Until the last few years Ratcliff Highway was one of the sights of the metropolis and almost unique in Europe as a scene of coarse riot and debauchery.' Yet it was only a partial improvement. The area continued to lag behind the rest of London socially, and even in the 1930s the police still considered it so dangerous that they patrolled it only in pairs after dark.

In 1937 St George's Street became simply 'The Highway'. Wartime bombing in the next decade cleared it of its sinister look – the bombs destroyed even No. 29, where the Marrs were murdered – and what was once the most dangerous road in London is now shorn of character, little more than a dismal arterial route connecting the Isle of Dogs to the City.

In 1911, a hundred years after the murders, workmen laying a mains at the junction where Williams was buried, accidentally dug up his corpse. One criminologist took Williams's arm, while the owner of the nearby Crown and Dolphin public house kept the skull as a souvenir. When the skull was exhibited at the Three Bells pub it was stolen by the French occultist Mina Bergson, who was trying to create a golem, an artificial human being made according to Kabbalist ritual. It was not the first time that the Kabbalist legend of the golem had come to this corner of the East End.

# 6

# Mystics and Myth-makers

London in the late eighteenth century was awash with mystics, myth-makers, gurus, prophets, seers and false messiahs. Prayer houses resounded to unusual readings of the Old and New Testaments. Meeting halls witnessed fresh insights into the mystical body of work known as the Hermetica, volumes of ancient Mediterranean writings mostly lost when the great library of Alexandria burned down. Occupants of suburban villas debated the finer points of the Kabbalah, the philosophical accompaniment to Judaism said to predate the Ten Commandments. Bookshops sold works explaining such age-old alchemical mysteries as the Everburning Lights of Trithemius, the Six Keys of Eudoxus and the phantom alchemical plants of Quersitanus, alongside more prosaic publications like *Harris's List of Covent Garden Ladies*.

In Marylebone, then on the outskirts of London, Joanna Southcott, a Devonshire-born upholsterer who had led a breakaway movement from the Methodists, claimed to be pregnant at the age of sixty-four with the man-child of the Book of Revelations, 'who is to rule all the nations with a rod of iron'. She died soon after, childless. Richard Brothers, another Marylebone resident, claimed to be the Prince of the Hebrews and devised a plan to lead the Jews back to the Holy Land. He was locked in an Islington asylum before he could put his scheme into operation.

## THE *BA'AL SHEM* OF LONDON

At the centre of this web of mysticism and weird religion was the Polish Jew Chaim Jacob Samuel Falk – alchemist, Freemason and

Kabbalist *extraordinaire*. Falk fled to the capital in 1742 after being sentenced to death by burning in Westphalia, Germany, for sorcery and performing miracles. Before long a near impenetrable web of myth surrounded him. He was no mere alchemist, it was alleged, but could transform base metals into gold. He was no ordinary Freemason, but one sworn into the highest mysteries of the organization, the supreme oracle from whom all others sought guidance. He was no mere Kabbalist but a *Ba'al Shem* – a master of the secret names of God.

These were the names with which God had created the world, according to Kabbalist lore. Names which in biblical times the High Priest in the Temple of Solomon uttered during prayers, but which were always drowned out by blasts on the ram's horn so that the congregation would not be able to hear them. Since the destruction of the Jews' last Temple in AD 70 the names had been lost to all but the *cognoscenti*. However, their powers remained undimmed. If they were used correctly wonders magnificent to behold would result; if inappropriately, horrific display of divine wrath would ensue.

Falk arrived in London at Irongate Stairs near the Tower, a spot where, nearly 150 years later, tens of thousands of east European Jewish immigrants would set foot in Britain for the first time. His possessions were few; mostly alchemical equipment such as ash cupels (small bowls made of bone ash in which gold and silver could be refined); crucibles and alembics for subliming, calcining and heating substances to high temperatures; small, wide, shallow vessels known as phials which could be used for holding liquids; a philosopher's egg for manufacturing the 'Philosopher's Stone', the substance that could supposedly transform base metals into gold or silver; and incantation bowls inscribed with spells in the form of spirals to protect against demons.

Falk moved into rooms friends had found for him on Prescot Street, near the Tower, and rented a workshop on London Bridge. This he furnished with talismans, candles and plates of gold. He inscribed on the floor the Seal of Solomon (better known as the Jewish emblem, the Star of David), which he anointed with alum, raisins, dates, cedar and lignum aloes, and mounted on the wall a deer's head containing holy names to ward off fires.

Walking between Prescot Street and London Bridge, Falk would dress, regardless of the weather, and to the astonishment of locals, in what is now considered the familiar garb of Hasidic Jews – *shtreimel* hat made of thirteen sable skins and *bekeshe* satin coat – but was then unknown in London. Every day in 1742 he took the same route from his home to his workshop, heading past the houses of the Tower Liberty, each marked with a hieroglyph or a personal object placed in the window rather than a number, as their inhabitants were mostly illiterate; alongside the raucous sailors' pubs with their bumptious notices warning against smoking, fighting, swearing and spitting; past the slaughterhouses, the blood and innards of the butchered animals clogging the nearby pavements; around Tower Hill, on whose scaffold the traitor Lord Lovatt became the last person to be executed five years later; past the Tower, outside which bored soldiers could be found polishing their bayonets; and alongside the buildings of the Mint at the edge of the Tower, where he had to sidestep the paupers optimistically hoping to profit from their proximity to the home of the English coinage. On clearing Custom House and Billingsgate fish market Falk would arrive at the foot of the bridge by the church of St Magnus Martyr, from where it was a short walk along the bridge to his workshop.

## THE GOLEM

In his alchemical laboratory Falk extracted oils from eggs, wax, amber, sage, cloves and tartar. He conducted experiments using the three heavenly substances of sulphur, mercury and salt, and tried to re-enact the ancient Kabbalistic experiment in which the essence of God, containing the ten stages of primal divine light, appears from the holy vessels. Some of Falk's alchemy had practical applications. He knew how to electroplate a piece of lead or nickel with a thin coating of gold or silver, thereby convincing onlookers that he had changed base into precious metal. He produced a new bezoar, the antidote to poison named after the clumps of undigested food or solid balls of hair which medieval physicians thought protected the stomach. His bezoar was created according to the recipe in Nicholas Culpepper's *Complete Herbal* of 1653 and contained 'pearls prepared, Crab's eyes, red Coral, white Amber Hart's-horn, powder of the black tops of Crab's claws and the skins which vipers have cast off . . . four or five grains of which is excellently good in a fever to be taken in any cordial, for it cheers the heart and vital spirits exceedingly, and makes them impregnable'. Some of Falk's alchemy had more pleasurable benefits, such as the sexual experiments in which he used a respiration technique that could induce an orgasmic trance, elevating the practitioner to the world of spirits and angels.

It was not the tales of alchemy – mystical, practical or sexual – that excited the East End's small Jewish community, but rumours that Falk was using his laboratory to create a golem. A golem is an artificial being made of clay that a Kabbalist creates by whipping himself into a state of ecstasy using rituals and chants. When the master of ceremonies engraves a Hebrew word on the golem's forehead and places under its tongue a piece of paper bearing one of the secret names of God the creation comes to life. Sometimes the creator might engrave the Hebrew word אמת ('emmes' – truth), later disabling the golem by rubbing out the 'א', leaving the word מת ('mes' – death). Sometimes he might engrave a word that nobody but the initiated can read.

Hebrew legend has many stories of golems. The first golem was Adam, the first man, created out of each of the four letters of the known names of God – י, ה, ו, ה – stacked one on top of the other: Yod (י) being the head, Heh (ה) the arms and shoulders, Vav (ו) the spine and sexual organs, and the final Heh the hips and legs. A golem created by Rabbi David Jaffe to perform tasks such as lighting a fire, forbidden to Jews on the Sabbath, burned down an entire town. A clay calf summoned to life by two hungry rabbis 2,000 years ago in Babylon was promptly eaten; while the golem made by Elijah, *Ba'al Shem* of Chelm, went mad and threatened to destroy the world until he removed the divine name from under its tongue. In literature the golem appears as Frankenstein's monster in Mary Shelley's well-known 1818 novel and in Isaac Bashevis Singer's 1982 story entitled, simply, *The Golem*. Unfortunately, despite all expectation, no golem was forthcoming from the *Ba'al Shem*'s London Bridge workshop.

Despite arriving in London with no money, Falk was soon able to trade in his modest Prescot Street apartment and London Bridge laboratory for a villa on Wellclose Square. This was the smartest address in east London, the golden crown of the New Jerusalem developed by Christopher Wren and other members of the Royal Society after the Fire of London, which they positioned according to biblical and Masonic measurements.

Inside, Falk built his own private synagogue where he indulged in fantastic ceremonies. There he would sit, his factotum Zevi Hirsch Kalish claimed, 'illuminated by a little round lamp placed on the table, with seven wax candles around it, the scabbard of the holy sword standing opposite, a black hide spread on the floor [alongside] a large sheet of his drawings and the naked sword standing before the entrance to the enclosure'. Kalish described how after Falk once stayed in his room for six weeks without meat or drink ten disciples entered and found him seated on a throne 'arrayed like an angel of heaven in Ezekiel's vision, his appearance like burning coals of fire and the appearance of lamps, diademed with a golden mitre, a golden chain round his neck reaching to his waist from which a great silver star was pendent and holy names engraved'.

Over the years the legends associated with Falk's stay in the East End grew ever more bizarre. One story claimed that Falk, by reciting a Hebrew incantation, adding letters, altering combinations, substituting numerical equivalents and introducing holy names, was able to fill his cellar with coal 'that appeared from nowhere'. Another told of how, when the back wheel of his carriage came off while going along Whitechapel Road, he ordered the coachman to drive on, and the wheel followed the carriage for the rest of the journey. More dramatic was the tale of how when fire broke out in the Great Synagogue on Duke's Place, threatening to destroy the building, and all efforts at dousing the flames failed, Falk was summoned and, offering himself as a *deus ex machina*, inscribed on the jamb of the entrance the four Hebrew letters of God's most-used name (*Yahweh* in English), causing the wind to change direction and the blaze to cease.

Unsurprisingly Falk soon attracted the attention of the feature writers of the day. A feature in the *Gentleman's Magazine* of September 1762 lampooned him as a 'Christened Jew and the biggest rogue and villain in all the world, who has been imprisoned everywhere and banished out of all countries in Germany'. The anonymous writer explained that when he asked the Kabbalist to reveal one of his 'mysteries' Falk had told him to avoid all churches and places of worship, steal a Hebrew Bible and obtain 'one pound of blood out of the veins of an honest Protestant'.

As Falk's reputation grew, so did the invitations to impart advice. In London he was visited by the lothario Giacomo Casanova, who wanted insights into Kabbalistic sexual techniques. He met the great occultist Cagliostro, who over dinner at Versailles with Louis XVI in 1772 had discussed the idea of founding a new Freemasonry that would restore the religion of Adam, Noah, Seth and Abraham. In Paris he met the French Revolutionist Louis Philippe Joseph, Duc d'Orléans, revealing to him the exact date on which Louis XVI would die, and giving him a ring of lapis lazuli, which he claimed would secure succession to the throne of France for the Duc's son, Louis-Philippe. The latter duly reigned from 1830 to 1848 as the 'Citizen King', the last king of France. Falk also met Charles Pierre Paul Savalette de Langes, an adviser to the French government, who had founded the Masonic Rite of Philalethes, or 'Searchers after Truth', and whose aim was 'the perfection of man and his union with divinity'. In his correspondence De Langes noted that the *Ba'al Shem* was 'a very extraordinary man from every point of view . . . the Chief of all the Jews; in all the sects of savants in secret societies a superior man'.

Falk's most persistent client was the German aristocrat and adventurer Theodor von Neuhoff. The German had been elected king of the Mediterranean island of Corsica in 1736, after promising the islanders he could free them of Genoese rule, and had promptly left on a fund-raising tour of Europe. Von Neuhoff brought Falk lavish gifts of a gold tobacco-box and a gold snuffbox, and commissioned him to undertake alchemical experiments which he hoped would transmute base metals into gold that would fund his Corsican campaign. He also invited Falk to his country retreat at Upton, Essex, a mile east of Stratford, on the edge of Epping Forest, where Falk stored for safe-keeping a trove of gifts and contributions granted by grateful clients. There they discussed the origins of Freemasonry, how it had existed since the earliest times (official Masonic history has been rewritten as if its origins date back no further than the founding of the world's first Grand Lodge at the

Goose and Gridiron Ale House near St Paul's Cathedral in 1717), but not under that name, its real purpose never explained, its protectors unable to reveal those secrets even if they so wished.

Falk died on 17 April 1782. His gravestone was carved with the epitaph: 'Here is interred an aged and honourable man, a great personage who came from the East, an accomplished Sage, an adept in Kabbalah. His name was known to the ends of the earth and distant isles.' In his will, Falk granted two exquisite miniature scrolls of the law set in silver cases and an annuity of ten guineas to the Great Synagogue. He also left a commonplace book of fifty-nine octavo pages written in German and Hebrew script. It contains accounts of dreams, lists of charitable gifts, catalogues of books, references to biblical texts, Kabbalistic puzzles, cake recipes and clues about the location of his treasure.

London gossip was rife with theories about the nature of the treasure. Some said it would yield the authentic Great Seal of England, which James II had thrown into the Thames while fleeing the kingdom in 1688, and that the supposedly recovered Seal, stolen soon after from the Bloomsbury home of Lord Thurlow, the Lord Chancellor of England, and never found again, had been a fake. Others claimed the treasure contained the *one* signed first edition of Robert Fludd's early seventeenth-century *History of the Macrocosm and Microcosm*, in which the author attempted to list all the knowledge humanity had acquired by that time. Rumours swept London that Falk's hoard included the carefully wrapped Titian painting *Portrait of Isabella d'Este in Red*, which had once belonged to Charles I but had been lost after the king's execution in 1649, also never to be seen again. Golddiggers spent many fruitless hours digging up chunks of the forest to find Falk's hoard, but none was successful.

Once a few years had passed since Falk's death, and it looked unlikely that there would be a resurrection, the *Ba'al Shem*'s detractors began to blacken his name. They blamed him for the death of Elias Levy, a prominent member of the Great Synagogue congregation and the previous owner of Falk's Wellclose Square villa. After banning members of the Great Synagogue from attending Falk's private place of worship Levy had sent a spy to discover if anyone was disobeying the order. When he found out that one member of the congregation was still visiting Falk's synagogue Levy had the man punished, forcing him to stand up throughout the afternoon service in the Great Synagogue and to repeat line for line an admission that he had sinned by attending the private temple. Falk's opponents claimed that when the *Ba'al Shem* heard of the campaign against him and of the punishment meted out to the 'transgressor', he was so angry he put a Kabbalistic curse on Levy, who died a few months after the row, despite having no history of illness and being only in his early fifties.

They also related the story of Aaron Goldsmid, a friend of Falk who had stumbled across sealed papers among Falk's effects which the *Ba'al Shem* had instructed should be 'securely treasured up, but never opened, nor looked into'. Any attempt to discover their contents would bring about fatal consequences, but anyone obeying the instruction would enjoy lasting happiness. Not possessing the necessary willpower, Goldsmid opened them after months of psychological torment, removed a piece of paper covered with Kabbalistic figures and hieroglyphs, and died 'mysteriously' later that day, before he could discover what that lasting happiness was.

Twelve years after Falk's death Rabbi Shaul Berliner, another Falk acolyte, was found dead in Epping Forest, near the site where Falk had supposedly buried his treasure, following a scandal which left him publicly humiliated. A search of Berliner's clothes uncovered a letter. It revealed that he had decided to starve himself to death, and urged that whoever found the body should bury him not in a cemetery, but in the forest where he had died. Falk's opponents took this opportunity to malign further the *Ba'al Shem*'s name. They claimed that Berliner, in his desperate state, had sought a Kabbalistic solution to his problems, had opened up Falk's treasure trove, of which he was perhaps the only person to know the whereabouts, and on examining the contents had chanced upon revelations so awful he felt his only means of salvation was to undergo a fast to the death and be buried where he dropped, in the same clothes, rather than contaminate a holy cemetery.

# EMANUEL SWEDENBORG MOVES TO WELLCLOSE SQUARE

Wellclose Square was home in the late eighteenth century to another of the era's great mystics, Emanuel Swedenborg, the Swedish visionary, scientist, philosopher and Christian theologian whose work had a profound impact on William Blake. Swedenborg, born Emanuel Svedberg in Stockholm in 1688, left Sweden for Holland and England after graduating from Uppsala University to continue his studies in physics, astronomy, metallurgy, mineralogy and mathematics, as well as the less cerebral disciplines of bookbinding and lens-grinding.

In 1716 the King of Sweden appointed him Extraordinary Assessor in the Royal College of Mines. Three years later, when his father was ennobled, Svedberg changed his name to Emanuel Swedenborg. During his spell as a royal adviser Svedberg planned and designed a submarine, aeroplane, steam engine, air gun and slow-combustion stove. He became the first individual to explain the importance of the pituitary gland and the cerebral cortex, the first to identify electrical phenomena (two decades before Benjamin Franklin) and pioneered the notion that atoms can be broken up into smaller particles, a theory which remained unproved for 200 years.

In 1745 Swedenborg experienced an epiphany. He described his vision to Thomas Hartley, rector of Winwick, as 'the opening of his spiritual sight, the manifestation of the Lord to him in person', and to his friend Robsahm as a vision of the Lord appearing before him announcing: 'I am God the Lord, the Creator and Redeemer of the world. I have chosen thee to unfold the spiritual sense of the Holy Scripture. I will Myself dictate to thee what thou shalt write.'

From then on Swedenborg devoted himself to God. He wrote voluminous works interpreting the Scriptures, and announced that 'no flesh could be saved', according to Christ's words in Matthew 24, unless a New Church was founded. He later moved to London and, when he came to Wellclose Square in 1766 at the age of seventy-eight, he found a once exclusive estate that had been unable to resist commercial development and contained two public houses. Erik Bergström, a Swede, ran one of these, the King's Arms, and there Swedenborg stayed. Bergström kept a record of Swedenborg's typical day: the polymath dressed in velvet, breakfasted on coffee, took a daily morning walk, lunched moderately with one or two glasses of wine, never ate supper, retired early and described him as 'kind, generous and always agreeable, but somewhat reserved'.

The diary made no mention of whether Swedenborg called on his neighbour, Chaim Jacob Samuel Falk, but it is known that the two men met to discuss the origins and history of knowledge – the earliest knowledge, the knowledge saved by Noah before the Flood which, according to ancient myth, was recorded on two indestructible pillars, one of marble that could not be destroyed by fire, the other of brick that could not be dissolved by water. They also discussed Kabbalist sexual techniques that could produce a prolonged erection and state of orgasmic trance through meditation on the male and female Hebrew letters, and how in the spirit world the soul hallucinates a spiritual body to enjoy more wonderful sensations than it experiences on earth.

While living in London Swedenborg also indulged his passion for solving one of the major technological questions of the day: the making of a clock for accurately calculating time at sea. In 1714 the English Board of Longitude had offered a £20,000 prize to the first person to succeed. Over fifty years later the prize had still not been won, the favourite and eventual winner, John Harrison, having been initially derided by the Admiralty because of his lowly birth. Swedenborg visited the board to submit in person a paper, *Method of Finding the Longitude by means of the Moon*, which he had completed in his youth, three years before the Board of Longitude had offered its prize. When it too failed to win he returned to Sweden and presented a copy of the paper to the Swedish Academy of Sciences. He was rejected again, and this time mocked by the academy's secretary, who wrote a letter to a professor in Uppsala, Swedenborg's home town, which came to light only at the end of the twentieth century and reads:

Dear Sir,

Yesterday old man Swedenborg came up to the Academy . . . Although he knows nothing whatsoever of what has been done on the subject during the last thirty years he nevertheless thinks that his own method is the best and only possible one. Still, one ought to try to convince him of his delusion [but] it is difficult to argue with a person who does not even understand the principles. One could expect something better from one who can ask the spirits about everything.

The professor did Swedenborg a disservice. In the 1940s Dr Charles P. Olivier, director of the Flower Observatory in Virginia, re-read the treatise and discovered that 'the principle of Swedenborg's method of longitude determination seems to be entirely correct'. Others have since verified the findings.

Swedenborg died in London on 29 March 1772, a date he had accurately predicted several years previously. Sixteen years later a congregation met at Great Eastcheap in the City of London to mark the centenary of Swedenborg's birth and founded the New Church, according to their mentor's wishes. Now an international movement, it bases its doctrines on Swedenborg's claims about witnessing the Last Judgement, or the second advent of the Lord, with the following list of tenets:

There is one God, in whom there is a Divine Trinity.
That He is the Lord Jesus Christ.
That a saving faith is to believe in Him.
That evils are to be shunned, because they are of the devil and from the devil.
That good actions are to be done because they are of God and from God.
That these are to be done by a man as from himself, but that it ought to be believed that they are done from the Lord with Him and by Him.

Swedenborg was buried in the Swedish church on Princes Square, near Wellclose Square, and when the church was demolished in 1908 his remains were taken to Sweden so that they could be placed in a marble sarcophagus in Uppsala Cathedral. Unfortunately, by that time the corpse was missing its skull, which had been removed by a Swedish sailor who hoped to sell it as a relic. Although the skull was later recovered and returned to London, it was lost while being exhibited with other skulls in a phrenological collection. In a bizarre mix-up the wrong skull was returned to Swedenborg's body while the genuine one went on sale in an antique shop. In 1978 it was auctioned at Sotheby's in London for £2,500.

## THE MISSIONS AND THE HOLY CROSS

Wren and the other post-Fire rebuilders of London made a wise choice in creating Wellclose Square as a haven for like-minded freethinkers. After Falk and Swedenborg came Dr Mayo, the dissenting minister and friend of Dr Johnson, who argued with the dictionary compiler about martyrdom and liberty of conscience in religion, and Dr William Dodd, royal chaplain-in-ordinary and a well-known figure at racecourses, particularly in France, where he was known as the 'Macaroni Parson' due to his extravagant dress sense.

Once, when short of money, Dodd forged a cheque for £4,000 in the name of Lord Chesterfield. Dodd intended to pay it back later – well, that's what he said – but was convicted of forgery and executed at Tyburn in June 1777, despite considerable public outcry. Later came Nathaniel Ward, the celebrated botanist. Ward made great advances in finding methods for storing flowers after saving the pupa of a moth in a sealed jar, finding ferns and grass developing in the soil at the base. In 1833 he sent two custom-built cases filled with native British ferns and grasses to Australia, and despite being at sea for six months they thrived. His experiments encouraged the Victorian craze for orchids, and enabled exotic tropical plants to be sent around the world, particularly from the Pacific region to Kew Gardens.

Wellclose Square's special municipal privileges, which had been gained when James II passed ownership of the land to the Tower Liberty in 1688, meant that residents were exempt from paying various troublesome taxes. But if locals did fall foul of the area's unusual legal system there was a court house and attached prison on the south side of the square, linked by tunnel to the Tower of London, half a mile away, and by passageway to the adjacent Cock and Neptune public house, whose landlord acted as gaoler to the court when the judges were sitting. The prison closed in the early nineteenth century and in 1911, around a hundred years later, the pub's landlord, taking a group of curious visitors round, reopened some of the sealed up passageways, leading the party down a narrow, dark stairway, through a brick kitchen, across a paved yard and through several stout doors where they found plank beds nailed to the wall and a carving that read: 'The cupboard is empty/To our sorrow/Let's hope it will Be full to-morrow.'

The square's special status also allowed the actor John Palmer to open a theatre, the Royalty, here in June 1787, a time when licences to show drama were considerably restricted. The patentees of Drury Lane and Covent Garden immediately issued proceedings against Palmer, and magistrates summoned him to appear before them at a local tavern. When he was asked for the relevant documentation he begged permission to be allowed home to fetch the papers, left the building, turned the key on the magistrates and locked them in, lying low for several weeks. Unsurprisingly, the authorities closed down the theatre.

The incorrigible Palmer later obtained a new licence under an Act of Parliament which stipulated that 'interludes, pantomimes and per-formances of a miscellaneous character' were included on the bill. The magistrates went to tortuous lengths to ensure that the rulings were upheld, but they didn't always meet their target. On 22 May 1789 'two of the Tower Magistrates were fined a hundred pounds each for dis-charging Bannister and Palmer, who had been committed as vagrants for acting plays without a licence at the Royalty'. That year Palmer died on stage in Liverpool during a performance of *The Stranger* after uttering the words 'There is another and a better world.'

The Royalty then changed names a number of times and on 11 April 1826 burned down. A new building, the Brunswick Theatre, opened in its place in 1828 but fared little better. It collapsed a few days later during a rehearsal for *Guy Mannering*, due to the excessive weight of the iron roof, killing a dozen people.

The building of St Katharine's Dock in 1828 turned Wellclose Square from a fashionable enclave to a practical one. The merchants and men of letters who had lived there took advantage of improved methods of travel to move to the suburbs, and sailors and labourers took over the smart houses. Cheap lodging-houses and gin shops soon opened nearby. There was even a music hall on the square – Wilton's – which still stands, the only surviving Victorian music hall in London.

All around were dusty, dismal shops. The most notorious of these was the British and Foreign Medicine Institution at the corner of Wellclose Square and Ship Alley. Its windows displayed wax models with terrible diseases 'rarely to be met with', according to the attached card, and a gruesome collection which included 'bottled babies, children with two heads, a serpent taken from the body of a sailor and the skeleton of a small sailor taken from the body of a serpent'.

The church Caius Cibber and Nicholas Hawksmoor built at the end of the seventeenth century became the mariners' church in 1825. Its new owner and leader was the Revd George Charles Smith – Bosun Smith – who as a young man had been press-ganged into the British Navy to serve under Nelson. When he discovered that the press gang was still active and had seized more than 2,000 local men in only a few months he announced he wanted another press gang in the Ratcliff Highway

for a far nobler service, whose headquarters would be the great rendezvous of the lost and guilty, where the officers of the Captain of Salvation may invite, persuade and impress those poor wretched wanderers who pass by, and graciously compel them to enter the receiving ship of his church universal to wage a good warfare against the Lord's enemies and theirs.

Smith's idea for a Salvation Army predated William Booth by thirty-five years. Having begun his new mission, Smith impressed colleagues for walking through 'the roughest quarters in all London's maze of docks and never being harmed, not because of his powerful build, but because [of] his personality, which made him popular among all classes'. But over the years his behaviour became increasingly erratic, and in 1845 he was imprisoned for debt.

That year the old Wellclose Square church was let to the Anglo-Catholic movement, a new evangelist sect which wanted to reinvigorate the Church of England by reviving certain Roman Catholic doctrines and rituals, something that would have horrified Wren and his fellow Protestants in the Royal Society. The local Anglo-Catholics were led by the charismatic Revd Charles Lowder. He converted Wellclose Square's church to St Saviour's, a mission hall and chapel of ease to St Peter's church on Old Gravel Lane, Shadwell.

St Saviour's ran a strict, ascetic regime, close in spirit to that of the long-lost monasteries which had dominated the area hundreds of years previously. The first bell was rung at 6.30 a.m., Prime Oratory proclaimed at 7.00, and Matins at 7.30, followed by the celebration of the Holy Eucharist. After breakfast the clergy and teachers left to perform charitable works in schools and hospitals. For the remainder of a day that was similarly regimented they took part in choir practice, ran classes, heard confessions and retired early despite the lure of the nearby music halls.

Lowder also co-founded a secret brotherhood for priests, the Society of the Holy Cross. Its members worshipped the True Cross – the Cross of Golgotha on which Jesus Christ was crucified. They promoted the legend that the True Cross had been discovered by Empress Helena, mother of Constantine I, in a Jerusalem cave in AD 326, along with two similar crosses. She had proved which one was authentic by placing a sick woman on each of the three in turn; when the woman rested on the third she was healed.

The Cross passed through many hands over the centuries, but not all its guardians behaved reverentially. Saladin, twelfth-century master of the Muslim world, rode through the streets of Damascus with the captured Cross tied to his horse's tail, dragging in the dust. Some time later the Cross was broken into fragments, one of which came into the possession of Joseph Redman, a member of Lowder's Wellclose Square mission.

One night in 1862 the mission was woken by a distraught woman. Her daughter had died, and frantically she sought help from the missionaries. Redman and his colleague, Father Ignatius of Llanthony, armed with the fragment of the True Cross, headed to the deceased girl's house and laid the relic on the dead girl's breast. As Father Ignatius proclaimed, 'In the name of Jesus Christ I say unto thee, "arise!",' the girl's right hand moved slowly, tracing a cross in the air. The shocked Redman quietly breathed, 'Father, what have you done?', to which Father Ignatius replied, 'I have done nothing, but our Lord has done a great thing indeed.' The 'miracle' was soon explained away by doctors, who averred that the girl had been unconscious, not dead, and that the clerics' arrival had merely catalysed her revival. Nevertheless the St Saviour's clergy insisted that their piece of the True Cross had worked a miracle.

Father Ignatius later made a name for himself locally when he burst into Wilton's music hall one night and, oblivious to the intoxicating atmosphere of mild ale and shag tobacco, let alone the lewd dancing, gingerly made his way to the centre of the dance floor. Once he had everyone's attention and the music had subsided he announced, 'We must all appear before the Judgement Seat of Christ' – to the amazement of the audience.

As the Victorian era proceeded Wellclose Square continued to decline socially. By 1869 even Lowder's people had gone. That year Cibber's old church was demolished and replaced with a school. But the square continued to attract strange religious happenings. In 1884 three Methodists enticed inside Wilton's music hall by the noise and atmosphere were so disgusted with the lasciviousness of the entertainment they witnessed that they fell on their knees in the centre of the hall and in view of the patrons began praying to God that he might 'break the power of the devil in the place and bring the premises into the use of Christian people'. Within a few months the licence was revoked and the venue was converted into a Methodist mission hall.

One day Solomon Ginsburg, a young Jewish refugee from eastern Europe, passing the new mission hall, was enticed by a member of the congregation. Ginsburg heard the preacher discourse on Isaiah 53, the passage that Christians believe predicted the birth of Jesus and His suffering on the Cross, and after desperately pacing the floor of his room until midnight decided to forsake Judaism. He declared his love for Christ, to the consternation of his uncle, who threw him out, and joined Harley House, a training centre for missionaries in Bow.

Ginsburg began addressing open-air meetings in east London. On one occasion he was attacked and kicked unconscious. On another he spoke at a shoe factory to Jewish workmen. They charged at him with hammers and knives. He left for Brazil, where he dedicated himself to converting Catholics on the ground that 'the Roman Church [is] the great hindrance to the evangelization of both Jew and Gentile'. In South America he met with a worse reception than he had been afforded in Bow: stonings, beatings, assassination attempts.

He was ordered out of Brazil by the chief of police, who told him, 'You are prohibited to preach your damnable doctrines in this whole country.' Ginsburg replied that he was a Baptist, and as such would not 'accept orders in matters of religion from any civil authority, neither from you, nor the governor of the state nor even from the president of the republic, but from one superior to all of you'. When the police chief asked Ginsburg who it was that was superior to the president of Brazil Ginsburg quoted Matthew 28:18–19: 'And Jesus came and spake unto them, saying, All power is given unto me in heaven and in earth. Go ye therefore, and teach all nations, baptizing them in the name of the Father, and of the Son, and of the Holy Ghost.' Nevertheless Ginsburg never forgot his roots. He called his autobiography *A Wandering Jew in Brazil*.

## FROM HELL

No East End story is more wrapped up in myth than that of Jack the Ripper, the world's most famous and feared serial killer.

Because he was never apprehended, silently disappearing into the gas-lit, fog-enveloped streets as mysteriously as he had arrived, leaving barely a handful of clues, Jack the Ripper has fuelled an inexhaustible store of books, films, articles, discussions and theories. Although the solution to the mystery continues to evade investigators, the story is well known. An unidentified murderer, or perhaps team of murderers, killed at least five East End prostitutes using similar methods in late 1888. In the early hours of 7 August Martha Tabram, a prostitute, was stabbed to death on Gunthorpe Street, Aldgate. Her body had thirty-nine stab wounds. Nobody was particularly interested, for despite the violence of the slaughter the murder of a prostitute in the East End was not unusual.

On the last day of the month the body of Mary Ann ('Polly') Nichols, her throat cut from ear to ear, was found on Buck's Row, Whitechapel. Crowds of people began gathering at the scene of the murder. Locals canvassed the police for protection. There was fear in the air. On 8 September, two days after Nichols's burial, prostitute Annie Chapman was found in the yard of 29 Hanbury Street, Spitalfields, her throat also cut and her entrails placed around her neck.

Panic gripped the East End. The brutality of the murders, the lack of apparent motive and the inability of the authorities to produce a likely culprit meant that local women, particularly prostitutes, feared they were in danger of imminent unpredictable carnage. The *East London Observer* newspaper summed up people's anxieties. It wrote of a 'painfully deep and unfathomable mystery' that made women 'shrink back to their houses terror-stricken, and made even strong men glance uneasily about, while yet they clenched their brawny hands and muttered vengeance upon the perpetrator of so ghastly a deed'.

On 27 September events took a sinister twist when the Central News Agency received a letter which ran:

Dear Boss

I keep on hearing the police have caught me but they won't fix me just yet. I have laughed when they look so clever and talk about being on the right track. That joke about leather apron gave me real fits. I am down on whores and I shan't quit ripping them till I do get buckled. Grand work the last job was. I gave the lady [Annie Chapman] no time to squeal. How can they catch me now. I love my work and want to start again. You will soon hear of me with my funny little games. I saved some of the proper red stuff in a ginger beer bottle over the last job to write with but it went thick like glue and I can't use it. Red ink is fit enough I hope *ha ha*. The next job I do I shall clip the lady's ears off and send to the police officers just for jolly wouldn't you. Keep this letter back till I do a bit more work, then give it out straight. My knife is nice and sharp. I want to get to work right away if I get a chance. Good luck.

Yours truly

JACK THE RIPPER

This letter, containing the first recorded use of the name 'Jack the Ripper', evidently meant that murder would soon follow, and sure enough in the early hours of 30 September *two* more prostitutes had their throats cut: Elizabeth Stride, who was found on Berner Street, off the Commercial Road, at around 12.50 a.m., and Catherine Eddowes, who was discovered nearly an hour later in Mitre Square, Aldgate. The killer or killers had indeed tried to 'clip the lady's ears off', as 'Jack the Ripper' had warned.

A second note, written on a postcard, was sent to the Central News Agency on 1 October. It read:

I was not codding [joking], dear old Boss, when I gave you the tip. You'll hear about Saucy Jack's work tomorrow. Double event this time. Number one

squealed a bit. Couldn't finish straight off. Had not time to get ears for police.
Thanks for keeping last letter back till I got to work again.

JACK THE RIPPER

Was this a genuine note from the murderer or a hoax letter? There
would just about have been enough time for someone close to the
events other than the perpetrator, such as a journalist, to have written
it so that it reached the agency before the details of the new murders
became widely available.

As the East End tried to make sense of the horror in its midst, a few
weeks later, on 16 October, a gruesome package containing a kidney
was delivered to George Lusk, chairman of the Whitechapel Vigilance
Committee, together with an atrociously spelt note which claimed to
be sent 'From Hell':

Mr Lusk
Sir
I send you half the Kidne I took from one women prasarved it for you tother
piece I fried and ate it was very nise. I may send you the bloody knif that took
it out if you only wate a whil longer.

Signed
    Catch me when
you can
Mishter Lusk.

The kidney could have been Catherine Eddowes's, for one of hers was
missing from the corpse. Interestingly, it is this letter, the one which
does not mention 'Jack the Ripper', that many Ripper experts believe
to be the most genuine.

On 9 November 1888 the worst of the series of murders took place.
Mary Kelly, like the previous victims a prostitute, was found in her
room in Dorset Street, Spitalfields, her throat cut and her body
severely mutilated. The killer had spent considerable time dismem-
bering Kelly, completely disembowelling her as the fire lay burning. By
the time she was found her body was almost empty, the entrails
draped around the room like so many Christmas decorations.

There were more murders of East End prostitutes over the next few years, but none that fitted the pattern of the last five, which now form the 'official' canon of Jack the Ripper victims.

## THE FINAL SOLUTION

So who was Jack the Ripper? Of the many suspects proposed over the years – 176 at the last count! – the most glamorous is Edward VII's wayward firstborn, Prince Albert Victor Christian Edward, the Duke of Clarence (better known as Prince Eddy), who died in 1892, nine years before his father took the throne.

The prince's involvement in the murders was first suggested by the French historian Phillippe Jullien, in the 1962 book *Edouard VII*. The relevant section, translated into English, reads:

Before he died, poor Clarence was a great anxiety to his family. He was quite characterless and would soon have fallen prey to some intriguer or group of roués, of which his regiment was full. They indulged in every form of debauchery, and on one occasion the police discovered the Duke in a *maison de rencontre* [a homosexual brothel on Cleveland Street, near Euston]. The young man's evil reputation soon spread. The rumour gained ground that he was Jack the Ripper.

Jullien's remarkable accusation was taken up in 1970 by a London doctor, Thomas Stowell, who published an article in the magazine *The Criminologist* that made a veiled accusation against the prince. Referring to him as 'S', Stowell explained how Eddy suffered from syphilis, which drove him insane and compelled him to commit the murders. According to Stowell, the royal family knew Eddy was the Ripper, but made no attempt to restrain him until the 'Double Event' (the two murders which took place on 30 September 1888). He was then locked in an asylum, escaping to carry out Mary Kelly's murder.

The prince's alleged involvement in the murders resurfaced during the making of a BBC television series on the Ripper in 1973. The programme's researchers were put in touch with an elderly artist, Joseph Sickert, who claimed to be the son of the better known impressionist artist Walter. He told them an extraordinary story. It was not Eddy, he said, but a team acting on his behalf – Queen Victoria's physician, Sir William Gull, his coach driver, William Netley, and possibly another – who carried out the Ripper murders to prevent a group of East End prostitutes blackmailing the royal family over Eddy's indiscretions.

Sickert provided the BBC researchers with much background. He explained that his grandfather, a Dane, enjoyed connections with the Royal Court of Denmark, from which Edward, Prince of Wales, took a bride, Princess Alexandra. He described how when Eddy, Edward and Alexandra's firstborn, became a disappointment to his parents the princess decided to send him into the real world to gain experience of life. Walter Sickert was asked to take him on as an apprentice in his Cleveland Street studio, but the apprenticeship was not a success. Eddy began courting one of the artist's models, Annie Elizabeth Crook, a Catholic, and secretly married her in 1884 in front of only a few witnesses, including her friend, Mary Kelly (the Ripper's last victim), at the church of St Saviour.

When Annie gave birth to a girl, Alice, the royal family, fearing anti-Popery riots in the ever-volatile East End, and a scandal whose political implications could bring about their downfall at a time of revolutionary ferment in Europe, sought help from the prime minister, Lord Salisbury, to hush up the affair.

Salisbury duly ordered a raid on Cleveland Street. Annie was seized, and she was taken to Guy's Hospital, where Gull gave her drugs to induce memory loss, forcing her to spend the rest of her life in lunatic asylums. Mary Kelly, meanwhile, whisked the child to the 'safety' of the East End. A few years later she and several female friends, including Mary Anne Nichols, Annie Chapman and Elizabeth Stride – all eventual Ripper victims – decided to take the tale to the newspapers unless Prince Eddy paid them sufficient hush money.

Their blackmail attempt spectacularly backfired. Edward, Prince of Wales (Eddy's father), sought help from the Freemasons, of which he was the leading member in the land. Gull, a fellow Mason, hunted down the blackmailers, murdering them according to Masonic ritual and enlisting police officers who were also high-ranking Masons to cover up the crimes.

Before this extraordinary tale was aired Joseph Sickert pleaded with the TV programme's researchers not to use the information. He regretted telling them the story. 'If only I had kept quiet . . . the story would have died with me and the sins of the fathers would not have been visited on the sons', he melodramatically told them. Nevertheless on 17 August 1973 the bizarre story was broadcast, in a format which mixed fact and fiction and had little impact.

The Prince Eddy–Gull–Netley tale was later rescued by Stephen Knight, an East End journalist, who fleshed it out in an enthralling book, *Jack the Ripper: The Final Solution* (1976), by far the most entertaining of the innumerable tracts spawned by the ever-active Ripper industry. Knight visited Joseph Sickert, who repeated to him the entire story. The author, with an extraordinary flourish but with due suspicion, added the rider that Sickert's father, Walter, the great artist, must have also been involved in the murders, probably having been coerced into them by Gull and Netley, and that he left clues in the violence of his paintings to assuage his guilt.

Joseph Sickert, understandably, was mortified to discover that Knight was intending to denounce his father in this manner. 'When the author told me his conclusions about my father's involvement in the case I was disturbed. There is no point in denying that I was also angry. I felt that he had let me down and betrayed my trust. But later I had to admit that my father must have known more than he told me.'

Knight's book, published in 1976, further outraged the Ripper industry. Experts, commentators and sleuths rushed forward to denounce its findings. How dare a Ripper book challenge the prevalent myth of the frock-coated caricature murderer lurking in the shadows? How dare it introduce themes – particularly Masonic lore – beyond the experience and remit of Ripperologists?

Donald Rumbelow, regarded by many as the world's leading Ripper expert, rubbished Knight's theories in his *Jack the Ripper: The Complete Casebook*. He explained how Gull had suffered a stroke in 1887 and therefore could not have committed so violent a series of murders. He showed that there are no marriage or birth records listing Prince Eddy as Annie's husband or as Alice's father, that there is no hard evidence linking Eddy to Cleveland Street, Annie Crook or even Walter Sickert, and that Annie Crook lived longer than Knight claimed.

In turn, Knight's supporters listed their counter-accusations. Gull suffered only a slight stroke, which would have barely incapacitated him. The lack of records or evidence hardly counts as proof that the story is a fabrication, and an elderly source getting dates wrong does not mean the story is a hoax. The anti-Knight side latched on to Joseph Sickert's claim that the tale was a fabrication, but the pro-Knight brigade noted how Sickert had turned on Knight only after the author coaxed out of him an admission that Walter Sickert, Joseph's father, might have been involved in the murders. It seemed that those who decried Knight's findings believed Joseph Sickert only when he said his story was a hoax. When he claimed that his mother was Alice Crook, daughter of Prince Eddy and the shop girl, he was denounced as a fabulist, but when he alleged he had made up the entire thing he was readily believed.

Allegations that Walter Sickert was involved in the Ripper murders culminated with the 2002 release of Patricia Cornwell's *Portrait of a Killer: Jack the Ripper – Case Closed*, in which the thriller writer alleges that Sickert was himself the Ripper. Cornwell spent much of her own money trying to prove Sickert's culpability. Her forensics team performed DNA testing on the backs of envelopes and stamps used in the Ripper letters, as well as Sickert's own correspondence, a rare instance of DNA testing being used on material over a hundred years old, to prove their case. They also attempted mitochondrial DNA (mtDNA) testing, which revealed similarities between the Ripper letters and Sickert's letters.

Did this 'prove' that Sickert was the Ripper? Not quite. It merely proved that the individual who left DNA on Sickert's correspondence cannot be eliminated from the percentage of the population who could have provided an mtDNA match. It also suggested that Sickert wrote some of the Jack the Ripper letters – that he was a serial letter writer rather than a serial killer.

It was a busy year for the Ripper industry, as 2002 also saw the release of the Hughes brothers' sinister Ripper film *From Hell*, starring Johnny Depp, Ian Holm and Robbie Coltrane. Suffused in Masonic imagery, riotous behaviour and substance abuse, *From Hell* was filmed in Prague, whose menacing shadows recreated the East End's dark Victorian alleyways and enveloping courtyards. The film concentrates firmly on the Gull–Netley/Masonic line, and shows the murders being committed in the royal coach, and the bodies then being placed at the locations where they were found. It offers no theory as to why the corpses should have been left at *those* particular places.

## THE THREE JUWES

The Ripper murders spin a web of myth that cannot be explained only by empirical and forensic evidence, as the Jack the Ripper experts insist. Each of the murders bears too many signs of Masonic ritual for it to be a mere coincidence. The ritual in question relates to the murder of Hiram Abiff, architect of Solomon's Temple, one of Masonry's great legends.

Abiff was supposedly killed in the year 959 BC by his three assistants, Jubela, Jubelo and Jubelum, after he refused to reveal to them the secrets of the Temple, that is the secret names of God. When Jubela, Jubelo and Jubelum were found they were in turn put to death, their throats cut from ear to ear, 'their breasts torn open', and their entrails thrown over their shoulder.

The legend of Jubela, Jubelo and Jubelum regularly features in Masonic ritual. To this day many initiates undertake a bizarre ceremony during which they pledge secrecy to the brotherhood, 'binding myself under no less a penalty than having my throat cut across, my tongue torn out from its roots and buried in the rough sands of the sea'.

Those who rise through the ranks of the organization take an oath in the second degree, 'binding myself under no less a penalty than that of having my left breast torn open, my heart plucked out and given as prey to the wild beasts of the field and the foul of the air'.

Those who progress higher face having their body 'severed in twain, my bowels taken from thence and burned into ashes', again, should they reveal certain secrets.

Mary Ann Nichols, the first Ripper victim, had her throat cut from ear to ear, an echo of the threat voiced at the Masonic initiation ceremony, which itself accords with the violent demise of Jubela, Jubelo and Jubelum. Nichols was found on Buck's Row (now Durward Street), just north of Whitechapel station. Was she murdered there or, as depicted in *From Hell*, placed there after being killed elsewhere, perhaps in the royal coach?

Intriguingly, little blood was found at Buck's Row or on Nichols's clothes, and potential witnesses, such as a Mrs Green, a light sleeper who lived in the room above the murder site, and a couple who lived in the cottage opposite, woke at various times in the night but heard and saw nothing.

The next victim, Annie Chapman, was found in the back yard of 29 Hanbury Street, Spitalfields. The possibility that Chapman was murdered elsewhere and placed in the yard is strong; think of the lack of time any murderer would have had to commit the deed in between the comings and goings of the locals. Alongside Chapman's corpse, it was reported, lay an unusual group of objects: some coins, two brass rings and a leather apron. The strange collection has intrigued countless Ripperologists. It defies explanation until one turns to Masonic lore. Perhaps the coins were referring to the money a Masonic recruit is made to remove from his pockets, along with all metallic objects, at an initiation ceremony? The brass presumably was alluding to Hiram Abiff, the master mason of Solomon's Temple, a specialist in brass-welding, who sculpted two hollow brass pillars, Boaz and Jachin, to adorn the entrance to the Temple of Solomon, pillars that are reproduced in all Masonic halls. The leather apron is, of course, well-known Masonic garb, an emblem of innocence, 'more ancient than the Golden Fleece or Roman Eagle, more honourable than the Star and Garter', according to the fraternity.

On the night of 30 September there were two more murders. Elizabeth Stride was killed on Berner Street, off Commercial Road. Whether she was lured there or just happened to be there is impossible to say. A short while later Catherine Eddowes was found dead. According to Stephen Knight she was killed in error, the perpetrator(s) believing with some justification that she was Mary Kelly, as she lived with a John Kelly and often used his surname. Interestingly, Eddowes's body was found on Mitre Square, Aldgate, on the site where in 1530 a woman praying at the high altar of the Priory of the Holy Trinity, which then stood there, was stabbed to death by one of the brothers, much in the same way as Hiram Abiff was killed by three apprentice masons.

The names 'Mitre' and 'Square' further emphasize the Masonic symbolism. The mitre, as worn by the High Priest in the Temple, is used in Masonic ritual, while the square is one of the most important Masonic shapes. It is the trying square of a stonemason which tests that the sides of the stone are right angles, and is used in Freemasonry as a symbol of morality. Mitre Square was also home to one of London's first Masonic lodges – the appropriately named Hiram's Lodge.

Shortly after Eddowes's murder a fragment of her apron was found by the wall of an apartment block on nearby Goulston Street alongside graffiti which read: 'The Juwes [*sic*] are not the men that will be blamed for nothing.' To prevent possible reprisals against Whitechapel's large Jewish community, the local police chief, Sir Charles Warren, himself head of the Quatuor Coronati Masonic Lodge, No. 2076, ordered the words to be wiped from the wall of the block, which at that time was inhabited by many Jews.

When the news of the bizarre message became public knowledge there was considerable speculation on its meaning. The Ripper was a Jew, obviously one who could not spell. Sharper commentators claimed that the slightly indistinct word wasn't 'Juwes' but 'Juives', the French for Jews; obviously the Ripper was a Frenchman. There were claims that the word 'Juwes' was Masonic. Masons came forward to explain that they did not spell Jews 'Juwes'. But their denials were disingenuous. Although it is true that Masons do not write the word 'Juwes' when meaning Jews, they do refer to Jubela, Jubelo and Jubelum as the 'three Juwes'.

Then came the last murder. According to Knight, when the murderers learned that their previous victim was not Mary Kelly, the victims' ringleader, they sought out their real target, finding her in a lodging-house on Dorset Street, Spitalfields, and killed her there. Again the violence of the attack fitted in with the ritualistic killings of the legend.

Similar violence and similar Masonic patterns had governed the style of the Ripper murders' sinister antecedents – the Ratcliff Highway murders of 1811 (see previous chapter). Those murders, also motiveless, purposeless and committed by perpetrators unknown, in this case slitting rather than disembowelling, were enacted using instruments – maul, chisel – that feature heavily in Masonic ritual:

At the end of the ceremony and at the Master's command, the new member is taken by the Junior Warden to perform his allotted tasks on the Rough Ashlar, a huge rough hewn stone placed near to the Junior Warden in the south west corner of the Temple. He has to learn and give the knocks of the First Degree on the Rough Ashlar using in turn the Maul, the Chisel and the Measuring Rule . . .

With the Ripper murders these rituals were taken several stages further, suggesting that the murderer (or murderers) was engaged in some sinister, twisted scheme whose status and purpose may well be more nefarious than Sickert or Knight envisaged. Further bizarre links emerge. Knight and the BBC researchers struggled over the location of St Saviour, the private chapel where the prince supposedly married the shopgirl. They wondered whether it was Southwark Cathedral, which was previously St Saviour, or the long-demolished St Saviour's Infirmary in Euston, near Sickert's studio. They searched the records of both establishments but discovered nothing. As if the marriage of the prince and the shopgirl would be recorded! They expected so controversial a union to be cemented well away from the gaze of London society, probably somewhere in the environs of Whitechapel, but made no more progress.

Perhaps the BBC researchers and Knight, unaware of the biblical/Masonic pattern behind the rebirth of London after the Fire, did not know how to look, let alone where to look. For they never thought of the chapel in the school on Wellclose Square, built on the site of the mission hall of St Saviour and the Cross. At the time of the alleged secret wedding chapels in schools were being used for marriage services, and locals were still calling the Wellclose Square building St Saviour, in the way that people are initially loathe to rename familiar landmarks even after they are demolished and rebuilt.

Consider Wellclose Square's history. Until 1869 it was home to Caius Cibber's Danish church, as Prince Eddy, given his Danish background, would have known. The choice of a chapel on Wellclose Square, the place created according to biblical instruction and Masonic lore, would have also won approval from the high-ranking Masons associated with the prince. Indeed an inspection of the key murder sites and associated locations show that 'Jack the Ripper' must have been acquainted with the esoteric code that lay behind the creation of post-Fire east London.

The Buck's Row/Durward Street location of the first murder stands 2,000 cubits, the distance of biblical instruction enshrined in Masonic legend, from Wellclose Square, which was itself planned by Freemasons and built according to biblical measurements, 2,000 cubits from the edge of London. The Dorset Street location of the last murder, that of Mary Kelly, and indeed the addresses of each of the victims – all of whom lived in that neighbourhood – stand 2,000 cubits from both the first site and Wellclose Square, forming an equilateral triangle of invisible miasma over the East End.

The other three murder sites – that of Mary Anne Chapman on Hanbury Street, Liz Stride on Berner Street and Catherine Eddowes on Mitre Square – stand the same distance from each other. The distance is 1,600 cubits, another length enshrined in Masonic and biblical lore, corresponding to the size of the outer court of the Masons' idealized Temple. The three sites form a smaller equilateral triangle that can be drawn over the area. Placed together the two shapes overlap to burn on to the map a twisted image of the key Masonic shape – the Seal of Solomon or Star of David. It is probably a coincidence.

# 7

# The Mysteries of the Orient

Spice, indigo, saltpetre, tea and other exotic loads arriving in London at the East End quays in the eighteenth century were accompanied by increasing numbers of equally exotic handlers: Chinese sailors and Lascars working the East India Company's vessels. At first the Orientals were brought in to replace English sailors who had fallen ill or deserted ship in the Orient; later they were taken on in their own right. Once the ships had docked in east London the crew were usually left to fend for themselves, and they often absconded, choosing to starve on the streets of Ratcliff, Poplar and Limehouse rather than return to the hell aboard ship.

The Chinese visitors and settlers were barely noticed initially, but in July 1782 a journalist from the *Morning Chronicle*, going through Stepney one Sunday evening, was shocked to see 'a genteelly dressed person' outside a public house annoying a Chinese man who was sitting on a bench and minding his own business. The genteelly dressed person provoked the Chinese man first with a volley of insulting language, then by making remarks on his dress and finally by taking hold of his hair and pulling it. The latter then ran inside to fetch his friends 'who in an instant armed themselves with short bludgeons and rushed out in a body'. And in 1813 Stepney was the setting for the first incident of serious violence involving only the Chinese when two sects, the Chenies and the Chin-Choo, fought with knives at the East India Company's Shadwell barracks in a fracas that left three dead and seventeen wounded.

By the 1820s there were so many destitute Chinese on the streets of London that the government passed a law compelling the East India Company to provide lodgings and basic essentials for Chinese and

'Asiatic' sailors waiting in the capital to sign on with a vessel. But for those Chinese vagrants left to fend for themselves on the streets of east London life was precarious. Crimps would wait outside cafés for suitable-looking potential sailors to coerce on to ships. When they woke up, victims found themselves *en route* for Shanghai. And if they proved not so formidable as marines they could always be found a new use in the galley as a dish of 'long pork'.

In 1857 the government stepped in and, with donations from oriental merchants and shipowners, opened the Strangers' Home for Asiatics, Africans and South Sea Islanders on West India Dock Road, Limehouse. There were 220 beds, but the prices were beyond the means of most who wanted to stay there. By this time there were more than a hundred Chinese and east Asians living in Limehouse. The firemen, boatswains and seamen were from Canton, the cooks from Hainan Island and the stewards from the treaty port of Ningpo. They were nearly all men who, having left their partners at home, soon found themselves new wives from the indigenous population.

## 'A VISION IN A DREAM; A FRAGMENT'

The Chinese who settled in the East End soon opened grocery stores. Inside they sold goods never before seen in east London: areca nuts, betel leaf, lychees, dried seaweed and sam-shu, an alcoholic drink distilled from the juice of boiled rice. They set up gambling houses for playing fan-tan, in which bets are placed on numbers of beans, and pak-a-pu, played on a sheet covered with symbols marked at random by an official known as the Chinese Priest. They also ran laundries and lodging-houses. But, most intriguingly, they opened premises where guests could smoke opium.

A highly addictive drug, opium is made from the sap drawn from the white poppy (*papaver somniferum*) when the plant's petals fall off and mature. It was first manufactured for medicinal purposes in China at the end of the fifteenth century. Three hundred years later it was being used by Londoners to treat diarrhoea and cholera; many a home medicine chest would contain liquid opium in the guise of Collis Browne's Mixture, penny a bottle. With opium came its close relations

– codeine, laudanum (a tincture of opium named after the Latin *lau-dandum*, 'to be praised'), morphine (a vegetable alkaloid of opium) and heroin (morphine laced with acetic acid). But these drugs had greater recreational than medicinal purpose and became popular among eccentrics and dilettantes, especially after the publication in 1821 of the intoxicating *Confessions of an English Opium Eater* by Thomas De Quincey, a Manchester-born writer with an unquenchable appetite for 'just, subtle and mighty opium'.

Blame for the arrival of opium in east London rested with the East India Company, which until the mid nineteenth century was one of the most powerful corporations in the world and was based in Leadenhall Street, on the East End–City border. For 350 years the company enjoyed a royally sanctioned monopoly on trade between London and the Far East. In 1772 Warren Hastings, the company's chief executive, realizing the potential profitability of the drug, began exporting huge quantities of the Indian-grown opium plant into China in exchange for local goods and tea. Opium addiction soon spread throughout China. The emperor banned imports of the plant in 1800, but the policy failed. Traders simply smuggled it into the country instead, while the British bribed Chinese officials to keep the opium traffic flowing and their profits intact.

By the late 1830s more than 20,000 chests of the drug, each yielding around 150lb of extract, were arriving in China every year, and at the end of the decade the Chinese authorities took drastic action. Lin Tse-hsü, the new Imperial Commissioner in Canton, destroyed all existing stores of opium and wrote to Queen Victoria urging Britain to cease its illegal opium trading. Britain refused to back down, and when Lin threatened to expel the British from China war broke out. The British, with their superior weaponry, easily outfought the Chinese, and further humiliated them in the 1842 by forcing the Chinese to cede Hong Kong to Britain.

In 1856 there was a second opium war, in which the British and French defeated China. After that foreigners gained greater freedom to travel into the interior of the country and Christians were allowed to proselytize. All the while the opium trade thrived and consumption increased, as did tax revenue to India, where the opium was grown, to the benefit of the ruling British government.

As the opium wars raged in the Far East, biting ever deeper into Chinese self-respect and dignity, so larger quantities of the drug found their way into London, wrapping parts of Limehouse and Poplar in a barely penetrable haze of yellow, acrid smoke. Many of the shambolic blackened-brick terraced houses set in Limehouse's maze of courts and alleyways were converted into makeshift opium dens. Decoration within followed a similar pattern: rooms gaily decorated with peacock feathers, Chinese characters signifying righteousness and harmony, strips of tinsel and silk, and a stove in the corner; a mantelpiece filled with egg cups, incense-sticks, vases and lamps; a narrow counter piled with blankets, shirts, soap and biscuits; and divans where languid Asians in cotton tunics, fur caps and cloth shoes could satisfy their cravings.

In east London the opium was smoked. This method required considerable preparation, a complex set of operations and a quantity of tools. The opium smoker would need a long steel toasting pin known as a *yen hok* for holding the drug, a pipe or *yen siang*, made of bamboo or ebony (for a favoured visitor it might be an ivory pipe studded with diamonds), opium bowls to fit on to the pipes, scissors to trim the wick in the lamps, a sponge to cool it and a small glass lamp filled with coconut oil hooded to obstruct draughts that might fan the flame. During preparation the smoker would place a lamp on a Japanned tray while holding the toasting pin in the flame until it was suitably hot. He would then dip it into the opium, and when the thick black mass bubbled into a rich brown insert it into the small hole of the earthenware bowl. With the opium ready, the smoker could inhale the drug through the pipe, his mind engaged in celestial luxury, dropping through several psychological stages – 'Caverns measureless to man/Down to a sunless sea' – as Samuel Taylor Coleridge described it in 'Xanadu'.

For many Chinese men opium-smoking was simply a daily routine, as unremarkable as lunch or breakfast. Up at seven, two pipes and off to work. Some disengaged themselves from the drug before the brain was entirely engorged – the best antidote was a small measure of mustard in a glass of warm water followed by further measures of warm water – but most succumbed. And the more opium the user took the more he required, for opium was more than a recreation, it was a religion with its own Ten Commandments – the Ten Chinese Opium Cannots:

He cannot give it up.
He cannot enjoy sleep.
He cannot wait his turn while sharing his pipe with his friends.
He cannot rise early.
He cannot be cured when he becomes ill.
He cannot help relatives who are in need.
He cannot enjoy wealth.
He cannot plan anything.
He cannot get credit even when he has been an old customer.
He cannot walk any distance.

Opium addiction was doubly troubling for the Chinese, for apart from the psychological problems the drug caused, the words of the priests – 'If you eat opium your sons will die out in the second generation' – haunted relatives who feared that the addict would leave no descendants to continue the essential Chinese custom of ancestor worship.

## DESTROYED BY THE MADNESS OF SINS

Opium smoking in Victorian London was legal, and smart society marvelled at the romance on its eastern doorstep. In 1868 Edward, Prince of Wales (the future Edward VII), visited a Limehouse den run by one Chi Ki, and some months later Charles Dickens visited a den in Shadwell, half a mile west of Limehouse, while researching what became his last novel, *The Mystery of Edwin Drood* (1870). There, according to J. T. Fields, the American who accompanied him, they found on a 'large unseemly bed' a Chinaman, a Lascar and a haggard woman 'blowing at a kind of pipe made of an old penny ink-bottle. The two first are in a sleep or stupor; the last is blowing at a kind of pipe, to kindle it. And as she blows, and shading it with her lean hand, concentrates its red spark of light, it serves in the dim morning as a lamp to show him what he sees of her.'

Dickens's den was off Victoria Street, near the junction of Cable

Street and Cannon Street Road. The author's son, Charles Dickens Jnr, even gave directions on how to find it in his 1879 *Dictionary of London*, the most useful London guidebook of the period:

The best known [opium den] is that of one Johnstone who lives in a garret off Ratcliff-highway, and for a consideration allows visitors to smoke a pipe which has been used by many crowned heads in common with poor Chinese sailors who seek their native pleasure in Johnstone's garret. This is the place referred to in the *Mystery of Edwin Drood*.

Johnstone, a corpse-complexioned, sapless-looking man, had been born Ah Sing in Amoy, China, in 1826, and on emigrating to London had married an English woman called Johnstone, inspiring him to adopt the name John Johnstone. When asked by one journalist why he smoked opium he answered that he could not 'go to sillip' (sleep) if he did not smoke it, and that he smoked a barely credible 'five hundred dozen' pipes a day, if he could get them.

Ten years later Oscar Wilde made a similar journey east before writing his only novel, *The Picture of Dorian Gray*, published in 1890. In the story Gray's party arrive at a 'small shabby house', and enter a 'long low room which looked as if it had once been a third-rate dancing-saloon, [where] some Malays, crouching by a little charcoal stove, playing with bone counters and grotesque things, lay in fantastic postures on the ragged mattresses'. Here 'one could buy oblivion, the memory of old sins could be destroyed by the madness of sins that were new, [one could] cure the soul by means of the senses, and the senses by means of the soul'.

This vision inspired Arthur Conan Doyle, creator of Sherlock Holmes, who was present at the Langham Hotel lunch at which Wilde was commissioned to write *The Picture of Dorian Gray*, to begin his 1891 short story 'The Man with the Twisted Lip' inside such a den. Doyle's addict, with a 'yellow, pasty face, drooping lids, and pin-point pupils, is huddled in a chair, the wreck and ruin of a noble man in a long, low room, thick and heavy with brown opium smoke [amid] bodies lying in strange fantastic poses'. Lounging nearby, but resistant to the charms of the drug is, of course, Sherlock Holmes 'in the midst of a very remarkable inquiry'.

Thus were Londoners, who would never dream of making the long trip east, beyond the Hawksmoor church of St George's in Stepney, acquainted with the mysteries of the Orient.

Once the authorities became aware of the particularly hideous conditions of the opium-soaked properties, they intervened. In 1889 the police raided a Limehouse address and found a Chinaman sleeping in a cupboard filled with cobwebs, covered with a few rags 'apparently in a dying state and since expired'. Eight Chinese were huddled together on the kitchen floor covered with slime, dirt and 'all kinds of odious substances'. In another room men had been hung up with weights tied to their feet and flogged with a rope, and a Lascar had been forced to eat pork – anathema to the Muslim – by someone who had rammed the tail of a pig into his mouth and then twisted the entrails around his neck.

One or two opium dens around Limehouse Causeway doubled as venues for the secret Chinese society the Hung League, now better known as the Triads. Members of the Hung League, named after the Chinese character *hung*, which was encased in a triangle to represent the union of heaven, earth, and man, would communicate with each other by pointing first to the sky, then down to the ground, and last to their own hearts.

Their venues featured a shrine containing the tablets of the Five Ancestors, a table with an incense burner, an altar and a red lamp, walls decorated with squares, triangles and dragons' scales, and an adjacent room that contained the temple on whose four 'gates' would be written in turn:

[east] 'To the East where the element of wood stands it is difficult to go/Sun, Moon, mountains, and streams all come from the Eastern seas.'

[south] 'The fiery road to the element of fire is hot/But in the distance Chang, Ts'uen, P'ing and Nankin it is cold.'

[west] 'On the narrow road of the element of metal you must be careful/Of the two paths it is clear that there is no impediment on the one which leads to the West.'

[north] 'At the sign of Yin-kui the water is deep and difficult to cross/But in Yun-nan and Sze-Chuen there is a road by which you can travel.'

Local non-Orientals were desperate to know what happened in these properties, what nefarious purpose their existence obscured. Fanciful legends circulated about a twilight subterranean world which burned with sinister and strange rites; about tunnels connecting the temples with the opium dens where the Chinese were clasping quartz crystals and copper conductors, and indulging in spiritual alchemy.

## AT THE EDGE OF THE ORIENT: LIMEHOUSE AND POPLAR

The East End Chinese, with their opium, pictogrammed grocery tins, exotic compounds in glass bottles, shells, seaweed and dried fish, occupied only a small part of Limehouse and Poplar. Elsewhere the neighbourhood's dusty streets were filled with sooty warehouses. Smells of soap, paint, kippers and allspice wafted in the air.

Limehouse took its name from the local lime-kilns, built in the fourteenth century and used until 1935, where chalk dug in Kent and Essex was turned into quick-lime for making mortar. In the sixteenth century, when the area was still cut off from London by marshland, Limehouse was studded with small boatyards. Here explorers such as William Adams lived when not at sea. It was Adams who made the first English voyage to Japan, staying alive by eating raw penguin, sucking the bones to extract all the marrow, and when that was finished munching the leather around the mast ropes.

The streets that sprang up as industry intensified sported romantic names that contrasted with the hard work oiling the local economy. There was Salmon Lane, the self-evident London Street and Three Colt Street, on which stands the Nicholas Hawksmoor church of St Anne, its spire acting as a beacon for centuries, guiding sailors into the Pool of London. But the most exciting place to live was Narrow Street, the winding lane that still proudly fronts the Thames west of Limehouse Causeway. Here, where the river can be heard but barely seen and only occasionally reached, where the smell of tar and rope has only recently evaporated, stood pretty cottages studded with wooden balconies where their fortunate owners could soak in the richness of river life.

Yet behind the picturesque frontage evil lurked. Rogue watermen patrolled the Thames looking for floating corpses so that they could claim the reward and rob the pockets, as Dickens recounted in *Our Mutual Friend*. The feared press gang (see Chapter 3) made its headquarters at No. 76, the Bunch of Grapes public house, renamed the Six Jolly Fellowship Porters in the novel.

To the east of Limehouse was Poplar. The area probably took its name from the number of poplar trees growing locally; or maybe from one single poplar tree which stood here at the northern end of the Isle of Dogs. Poplar's most famous medieval resident was Edward, the Black Prince, the son of Edward III, who died in 1376, a year before his father, but little of interest happened locally until the docks were built in the first decade of the nineteenth century.

Poplar then grew quickly. The fields were covered with badly built brick houses and noisome factories. In 1866, however, an economic slump saw local unemployment reach 30,000. This disaster was compounded in the same year by a cholera epidemic caused by contaminated water drawn from reservoirs at Old Ford. The water was tainted in all sorts of strange ways. At the height of the epidemic one man who checked his water tank following the death of his two children found a decomposing 14-inch-long eel creating a blockage in the pipe and an unusual-tasting drink. In all more than 8,000 people died from the disease.

Irish and Scottish immigrants filled Poplar during the nineteenth century. The Irish lived around Fern Street and Rook Street, in an area known as the Fenian Barracks, while the Scots settled in the Mcintosh estate, which was begun in the 1860s on what had been Mcintosh's farm, its roster of street names forming a near-complete alphabet from Ailsa to Zetland. Some of these streets were worse than others. For instance, those who lived in Blair Street, to the north of East India Dock, were constantly reminded of the wretchedness of their lot by the stench from a local yard where bones were left to rot. From a cat meat shop in St Leonard's Street came the smell of boiling horseflesh, while a particular brand of nausea arose on Broomfield Street, home of the Fish Guano Company. Up the Lea, the river which separates Poplar from Canning Town, the air was heavy with the even more noxious fumes of blood- and bone-boiling, glue-manufacturing and soap-making.

More fun could be had in Blackwall, at the south-eastern tip of Poplar, by East India Dock. By the mid nineteenth century this isolated spot had been joined to London by a railway line which ran through what the Revd Harry Jones described as 'some of the dirtiest and shabbiest stations and carriages to be found anywhere'. The railway made Blackwall an unlikely but popular summer haunt, affectionately nicknamed 'East End-by-the-Sea'. Day-trippers disembarking at the station would head for the Brunswick Tavern, which stood on the Meridian line and provided superb views of the forest of masts and sails on the Thames, to enjoy the tavern's renowned whitebait suppers. The locale's popularity lasted until the 1870s when the tavern became an emigrants' depot, an overnight stop for those leaving Britain for New Zealand (some 17,000 a year by the middle of the decade). The building was demolished in the 1930s despite plans to convert in into a 'marine residence' for Edward, Prince of Wales.

There was a sizeable German community in Poplar. Hagmaier's, the German pork butcher at 318 Poplar High Street, was renowned for its faggots and saveloys, and locals would bring basins at seven in the evening to take away what the shopkeeper was about to throw out. Within a few hours of Britain's declaring war on Germany on 4 August 1914 Hagmaier's had its windows stove in by a mob who wrenched from the awning the boar's head that had watched over customers for the previous few decades. The mob also made for the Steamship, a pub at the east end of Poplar High Street run by the German-born Weige brothers. But the brothers had been tipped off that they would be targeted, and they had time to prepare their defence – friendly toughs who dissuaded those spoiling for a fight with some persuasive arguments.

When the Germans' limited air warfare came to England in 1917 it concentrated on Poplar. The first daylight air raid occurred on Wednesday 13 June. A bomb fell on a railway station, hitting an incoming train. Warehouses, factories and shops were also damaged, more than a hundred people were killed and 423 injured, 154 of them seriously. Among the dead were eighteen children who had been working in their classrooms at Upper North Road primary school when a bomb dropped through the roof, exploding on the ground floor.

## THE LOTUS LIFE

In the wake of the 1906 Aliens Act, which restricted immigration into Britain, the National Sailors' and Firemen's Union began a campaign to limit the number of Chinese workers on British ships. Yet most sections of society benignly tolerated the Chinese. They were seen as gullible skivvies – one of the pack-ponies on Shackleton's 1908–9 expedition to the South Pole was nicknamed 'Chinaman' – and outright hostility was rare. However, when Orientals had tried to open a laundry on North Street, Poplar, in 1901 a mob laid siege to the premises and hurled stones against the shutters and doors. The occupants had to wait till dark so that it was safe to escape.

Seven years later native dockers tried to prevent Chinese crews from signing on as crewmen at the Board of Trade offices on East India Dock Road. More than sixty police were needed to help the Chinese gain access to the office. However, the police failed to protect them as they came out, and the first group who left were chased down the street, eventually finding refuge in a hostel on Pennyfields.

When Chinese men and white women indulged in sexual liaisons – not a criminal offence, to many people's surprise – there was uproar. A commission of enquiry, which looked into the problem in 1910–11, found it 'undesirable from an English point of view'. An *Evening News* editorial explained how 'to the ordinary decent Briton there is something repulsive about inter-marriage or its equivalent between white and coloured races . . . the time has come to draw a cordon round this area of London and forbid any white woman from frequenting it'. In *Empire News* the Revd W. H. Lax added:

There is something inherently revolting about this union of European girls with black men or Asiatics, and by entering into such unions and marriages girls are fomenting a danger which, I am convinced, will give rise to a great conflagration in the future. The Chinaman is a gregarious creature. He will not live alone. When an English girl takes on the responsibilities of a Chinaman's household she finds he will bring in ten or twenty men to the house.

Not everyone was outraged, though. A detective sent to investigate a complaint in Limehouse concluded that the Chinaman, if he becomes intimate with an English girl, does not lead her to prostitution but prefers to marry her and treat her well. Whatever may be his faults, the Chinaman has the power of fascinating a woman and of holding her in the way the white man cannot do. There is a subtle chance, a romance and a poetry about his lovemaking that makes the efforts of the average westerner seem ridiculous.

Ironically, it was the lotus-eating life that was the problem; Chinatown was too soporific and relaxed, thanks to opium and the love potions made from hashish, geraniums, rose petals, lemon leaves, water, sugar and honey. Even the gambling dens were relatively civilized. But when the drugs laws were tightened through the Pharmacy Act of 1908, allowing only qualified chemists to sell opium, violence increased and drug-taking continued unabashed. New laws introduced in 1909 allowed the authorities to withdraw the licence of any lodging-house keeper who permitted opium-smoking on his premises, but still the practice thrived locally. The government's response was to tighten the law further at the start of the Great War in 1914, passing the Defence of the Realm Act which made it illegal to smoke opium, possess opium without authority, or even possess opium-smoking utensils.

Setting a pattern which still characterizes the drug world, the Draconian laws led not to mass rejection of the narcotic but to the rise of a new crime wave. A powerful syndicate based in Peking took over not just the drugs trade but gambling and vice in London's Chinatown. This syndicate was linked with similar firms running similar pastimes in San Francisco. Because of its cross-national membership the police were largely powerless. An order could come from New York, forcing a Limehouse man to commit some atrocity in London over drug profits or the ownership of a particular woman, and the authorities wouldn't know where to begin their investigations.

To ensure that only the correct personnel gained admittance to the opium dens the Chinese introduced an elaborate ancient ritual. A guard on the door would ask: 'Where do you come from?'

'From the East.' (That was the correct response.)

The ritual then continued: 'For what do you come here?'

'We come to meet our Brethren.'

'If the Brethren eat rice mixed with sand, will you also eat of it?'

'Yes, we will.'

(The guard would then open up and show a sword. More questions would follow.) 'Do you know what this is?'

'A knife.'

'What can this knife do?'

'With it we can fight our enemies or rivals.'

'Is this knife stronger than your neck?'

'My neck is stronger.'

Scotland Yard took little action while the problem was confined to the East End. But when Billie Carleton, a stage actress who had been performing at the Haymarket Theatre near Piccadilly Circus, was found dead from an overdose of cocaine in 1918, the clash of white society and the 'yellow peril' stirred the police and the papers into action. Stories of a dangerous Limehouse where sinister Orientals lived by a code unknown to Londoners, their laws the knife blade, their punishment block the dark and deep waters of the dock, filled the columns. *The Times* ran excited descriptions of orgies which had supposedly taken place at Miss Carleton's flat, where 'the men divested themselves of their clothing and got into pyjamas, and the women into chiffon nightdresses', presumably to have sex, rather than ingest opium or play fan-tan, although the paper didn't elaborate.

The police launched raids. Often they found nothing, for the owners would clear up all signs of disreputable activity, stashing away the pipes and opium, in the time it took for the officers to leave their constabulary cottages on Limehouse's Garford Street and arrive at the targeted address on the Causeway or Pennyfields. Occasionally the police were more successful. When officers raided 17 Limehouse Causeway, home of Ada Low Ping You, where the drug and the utensils used to prepare the actress Billie Carleton's fatal dose came from, they found an electric bell under the lino installed to act as a warning system, and their progress through the house obstructed by several stout oak panels, bells, levers, ropes and pulleys, and a trapdoor at the top of the stairs. They were able to gain access to the opium-smoking room only after clambering out on to a sloping roof and climbing back in to the property. Arrests were made, but those questioned had little to say – none of it in English – and were unbowed by the threat of deportation.

In 1922 a young West End nightclub dancer, Freda Kempton, died from an overdose of cocaine, and this time the blame fell on Brilliant Chang, a stocky, gap-toothed Regent Street restaurateur. Despite being described in the *Daily Express* as an 'unemotional yellow man', Chang was a smooth and accomplished seducer who always wore patent leather shoes and a fur-collared coat. Brilliant Chang was probably his pseudonym. It wasn't so much the cynosural first name, but the use of the word 'Chang' – 'Charlie Chang' is slang for cocaine. Sent to England in 1913 to study medicine, he decided instead to open a restaurant near Piccadilly Circus and deal a little on the side: drugs and white women. Whenever he spotted an attractive white woman at one of his tables he would send over a note that read: 'Dear Unknown, please don't regard this as a liberty that I write to you. I should extremely like to know you better and should be glad if you would do me the honour of meeting me one evening when we could have a little dinner . . .'

When Chang appeared in court on the Kempton charge he was mobbed by women. Even though he was convicted over the dancer's death, he served only a year in jail, and on release moved his business to Limehouse. There he was arrested in 1924 after one of his couriers, Violet Payne, going back and forth between the Commercial Tavern pub in Pennyfields and a Chinese restaurant at 15 Limehouse Causeway, was found to be in possession of heroin. She named Chang as her supplier and he was deported. But Chang was not the mastermind, merely his agent. He was not the first, nor would he be the last. As the newspapers mused, the mastermind would soon send a new 'Brilliant Chang' to continue the nefarious trade with impunity, 'for the Chinese physiognomy is practically a blank page to the average Englishman. They all seem alike.'


## THE CURSE OF FU MANCHU

East London's Chinatown was vividly portrayed by two writers of the early twentieth century: Thomas Burke and Sax Rohmer. Burke, a thoughtful travel and short-story writer, made few moral judgements and avoided much of the hackneyed imagery that limited Rohmer's potency. Even if his plots and twists were too predictable, he had a flair for romantic imagery. His main Chinatown collection, *Limehouse Nights* (1917), opens with the most captivating of descriptions:

It is a tale of love and lovers that they tell in the low-lit Causeway that slinks from West India Dock Road to the dark waste of waters beyond . . . It is a tale for tears, and should you hear it in the lilied tongue of the yellow men, it would awaken in you all your pity.

The book was rapturously received. 'In these Christ-forgotten purlieus of fog and filth and booze [Limehouse], in the lowest sediments of brutality and vice, Burke has found stories that set the soul quivering,' wrote the *Boston Transcript*. The *Brooklyn Eagle* added that 'You have not read a paragraph of Thomas Burke's *Limehouse Nights* before you realize that you are in the presence of a master tale teller. For here is a man whose qualities of greatness are so apparent that it takes not the least discernment to discover them.'

Burke wrote much more than just Chinatown stories; Sax Rohmer, who was obsessed with a clichéd vision of the East, wrote little else. Rohmer (real name Arthur Stansfield Ward) was a dilettante and sensationalist. He was a member of several occult societies, including the Hermetic Order of the Golden Dawn and the Rosicrucians, the secret society so secret no one can be sure whether it exists or not.

In his Herne Hill flat he and his wife, Rose Knox, a psychic, manipulated an ouija board, and their fingers traced out the word C-H-I-N-A-M-A-N, which henceforth would be the source of their literary prosperity. In 1911 Ward was commissioned to write a thriller about the Chinese underworld in Limehouse. Looking for a racy pseudonym, he consulted an Anglo-Saxon dictionary and found the words 'sax', meaning sharp, and 'rohmer' (roamer). Renaming himself Sax Rohmer, he left Rose at home to venture to Chinatown, much as Isa Whitney had done to the faithful Kate in the Sherlock Holmes story 'The Man with the Twisted Lip'. And just as Kate traced Whitney, so Rose, thinking her husband was having an affair, pursued Rohmer to Limehouse.

With a friend she sought help in the Railway Tavern pub. She was shocked to see a Negro playing the piano, but summoned up the courage to ask a barman who had a complexion 'like a dried lemon, an aquiline nose, thick lips and leering blue eyes' if he had seen her husband. Indeed the barman *had* spotted Rohmer (it was not difficult to notice an intellectual in Limehouse). He had spoken with him and noticed that he had ringed the name Fung Wah, that of a local shop-keeper, in a magazine. Mrs Rohmer, her companion and the publican found Fung Wah's shop, which smelled of joss sticks, stale fish and cinnamon. They were ushered upstairs by an assistant and there found an excited Sax Rohmer, who turned to his pursuers and announced breathlessly, 'Thanks to Fung Wah I've found him! I've found Fu Manchu!'

Fu Manchu was Rohmer's *outré* villain, an elderly Chinese physi-cian and scholar, an heir to the Manchu throne, waging a clandestine war against the West as head of the Si Fan, a secret international body of murderers based on the notorious White Lily Society. The figure on whom Rohmer had based Fu Manchu was 'Mr King', Brilliant Chang's predecessor in charge of local crime. One foggy night in Limehouse Causeway Rohmer had ducked back into the shelter of an alley as a car pulled up.

A uniformed chauffeur jumped out smartly and opened the car door for his passengers. A light appeared in a lower window of a house. The street door was thrown open. A tall dignified Chinese, wearing a fur-collared overcoat and a fur cap, alighted and walked in. He was followed by an Arab girl wrapped in a grey fur cloak. I had a glimpse of her features. She was like something from an Edmund Dulac illustration. I knew that I had seen Dr Fu Manchu. His face was the living embodiment of Satan.

Rohmer went on to paint Fu Manchu in glorious detail:

Imagine a person, tall, lean and feline, high-shouldered, [with] a close-shaven skull and long, magnetic eyes of the true cat-green. Invest him with all the cruel cunning of an entire Eastern race, accumulated in one giant intellect, with all the resources of science past and present, with all the resources, if you will, of a wealthy government – which, however, already has denied all knowledge of his existence. Imagine that awful being, his eyes green as the eyes of a leopard, fingernails long, like those of some buried vampire of the

Black Ages, and you have a mental picture of Dr Fu-Manchu, the yellow peril incarnate in one man.

In the first Fu Manchu story, *The Mystery of Dr Fu-Manchu*, published in 1913, Rohmer drew Fu Manchu as a cross between Sherlock Holmes and his notorious foe, Dr Moriarty. There were thirteen sequels, each predictably and eponymously titled – *The Drums of Fu Manchu*, *The Shadow of Fu Manchu*, *Emperor Fu Manchu* – each more preposterous than the last. The stories were translated into a host of languages, dramatized in innumerable radio plays and cast in a succession of Hollywood films. These films were filled with hunched-shouldered Orientals – inscrutable advocates of torture and mercilessness – each armed with 'menace in every twitch of their fingers, threat in every twitch of their eyebrows and terror in each split-second of their slanted eyes'. Naturally they wore their hair in pigtails, a dangerous weapon that could be used to strangle foes.

Rohmer was remorseless and disingenuous in defence of his creation.

Fu-Manchu is Fu-Manchu. He can't help that; no more than I can. When I close my eyes he communicates with me. 'You have sought for and you have found me,' he says. 'I am here. You have followed me through the forests of Burma. You have tracked me to my palace in Kiang Su. Because you have made me, you think that you *know* me. Do you dream that you can conquer me? That my mastery of the secret sects of the East can be met by the simple efficiency of the West? I shall prove a monster which neither you nor those you have created to assist you can hope to conquer.'

But by the time the Fu Manchu craze was at its peak, the Chinatown of Limehouse and Poplar had already begun to be dismantled by the local council who ordered slum clearance to sanitize the area and bring it under English, rather than Asiatic, law. New regulations that made it illegal to sign on a Chinese crew in any British port also led to a severe drop in the number of oriental sailors.

When Eric Blair, an aspiring writer keen to expunge the bourgeois guilt he had accumulated while serving in Burma as a military policeman, came to Limehouse Causeway in 1928, to stay in the most loathsome lodging-house he could find while researching what became his first book, *Down and Out in Paris and London* (published under the pseudonym George Orwell), the mysteries of the Orient were already receding into a myth-wrapped past. In 1934 the authorities announced that Limehouse Causeway was to be demolished 'in the interests of a better London'. Second World War bombing exacerbated the decline and further mass demolition continued into the 1960s, leaving only the street names – Ming Street, Amoy Place, Pennyfields, West India Dock Road – as a reminder of a vanished exotic oriental London.

# 8

## The Jewish Ghetto

There are no records of the first Jews to arrive in east London, but Jews have been coming to Britain since King Solomon sent over tin traders *c.* 960 BC to negotiate with the miners of Cornwall. The tin traders included a number of Phoenicians – inhabitants of what is now the Gaza Strip – whose word for this island was 'Berat-Anach' ('country of tin'), which is phonetically similar to 'Britain'.

Some time around AD 20, according to a once popular legend, Joseph of Arimathea, a merchant from the Holy Land, journeyed across the Mediterranean, past the Straits of Gibraltar, and landed in Cornwall to trade tin. His party allegedly included his great-nephew, Jesus Christ. Better known is the legend of how Joseph of Arimathea returned to Britain after Jesus' crucifixion with the Holy Grail, the vessel used by Jesus and the Apostles at the Last Supper, and preached the first Christian teachings heard in England at Glastonbury.

Yet if Joseph did visit Britain on an evangelical mission – with or without the Holy Grail – it is more likely that after crossing the Channel from France at the closest point (Calais to Dover) he would have explored the nearest estuary (the Thames), rather than heading a long distance west by sea and journeying forty miles through woodland to get to a remote spot such as Glastonbury. If so, he may well have disembarked only once the marshland on the riverbank gave way to the settlements dotted around the huge lake known to locals as Llyndin, which was later drained to form Wapping.

## THE INVISIBLE COMMUNITY

After the Norman Conquest significant numbers of Jews came from Rouen in France to London to aid William I's commercial activities, settling mostly in the City, rather than the East End. Hostility to the Jews grew steadily over the next two centuries and in 1290 Edward I expelled them from England. In the ensuing 400 years there were no Jews in England – officially. They were the invisible community.

Occasionally Jewish refugees landed in London. For instance, following the Spanish Inquisition of 1492 a number of Jews settled around Aldgate. They were disparagingly known as Marranos ('pig' in Spanish), the name given to those who had publicly eaten pork to prove their gentile credentials, and they worshipped in secret behind a cloak of Catholicism.

When Oliver Cromwell became Lord Protector of England following the execution of Charles I he cast envious eyes at cities like Hamburg, Amsterdam and Leghorn in Italy where Jews had been instrumental in creating a new prosperity. Cromwell began to allow Jewish bankers and merchants to settle in London, hoping they could improve the city's naïve and primitive banking methods.

They settled in Aldgate and found, to their astonishment, a fascination among educated Londoners for all things Judaic. For example, Cromwell's Little Parliament had replaced the English constitution with the Old Testament. The Protector told the MPs that God's message to Israel in the 68th Psalm was addressed to them for they were chosen by God to preside over the establishment of His rule on earth. Cromwell had also set the total of privy councillors at seventy-one in honour of the seventy-one elders who had comprised the ancient Jewish kingdom's Sanhedrin council. Banners paraded by his New Model Army were inscribed 'The Lion of Judah'. This was an England dominated by religious leaders, mostly Puritans. Their ideology had been shaped by the reading of the Bible, which had only recently been translated into English for the first time, and they were fascinated by the notion that not only must God have created the world in Hebrew, but that Adam, the first man, must have spoken Hebrew.

Hoping that the Jews' pan-European links might do more than

merely boost English commerce, but might improve his fledgling secret service as well, Cromwell invited the Dutch rabbi Menasseh ben Israel to England to discuss the official return of the Jews. The discussions, held in December 1655, were dramatically interrupted by a Flemish Jew, who approached England's ruler and carefully and deliberately began to touch his body. A minion rushed up to stop the man and seek an apology or explanation for this outrageous behaviour. The Jew explained that he meant no harm, and that he had journeyed from Antwerp to London solely to ascertain whether his Highness, the Lord Protector, 'was of flesh and blood, as his superhuman deeds indicated that he was more than a man and must have emanated directly from heaven'.

The outbreak of war with Spain in 1656 complicated matters. An edict was passed allowing the state to seize the goods of all Spaniards in England, putting the Marranos' status in jeopardy. However, when they revealed themselves to be Jewish refugees from hostile Spain, Cromwell allowed them to stay, and a synagogue was opened in a house on Creechurch Lane, near the border of the City and East End, that December.

The demise of Cromwell's Commonwealth and the restoration of the throne in 1660 left the thirty-five Jewish families in London with no legal protection. But fears that the advances made under the Protector would be lost proved groundless when Charles II showed himself to be amicably inclined to the community on account of the help the Jews of Amsterdam had afforded him in exile.

Within a few years east London's Jews were involved in a new controversy. Shabbatai Zevi, a Turkish Jew known for indulging in religious ecstasies and mystical speculations, declared he would appear as the Messiah in September 1666. When the year arrived Jews in an East End ravaged by the Plague prepared for His coming, while a number of gentiles nervously noted that 1666 was a juxtaposition of 1,000 (Christ's millennium) and 666, the Number of the Beast.

A rumour swept the capital that a barque decked with silken sails and rigging and manned by a Hebrew crew, was waiting at Ratcliff to take believers to the Promised Land. Hebrew prayer books fronted by pictures of Zevi sitting on a royal throne were circulated within the Jewish community. Members of the Exchange wagered large sums on whether Zevi would take control of the Ottoman Empire, and Samuel Pepys noted in his diary for 19 February 1666 that speculators were offering 10–1 if a 'certain person now at Smyrna [Turkey] be within these two years owned by all the Princes of the East, and particularly the grand Signor as the King of the world, in the same manner we do the King of England here, and that this man is the true Messiah.'

In April 1666 Zevi landed in Constantinople, Turkey, and was captured by the sultan's troops. The sultan gave Zevi the chance to prove himself. Troops would fire arrows at him, which he would ward off using his divine powers. Rather than risk humiliation, or even martyrdom, Zevi immediately renounced his views and converted to Islam. This shocking news led many, understandably, to denounce Zevi as a false Messiah, and meant that London had to wait a little longer for the Second, or perhaps the First, Coming.

William of Orange, the Dutch Protestant who took the English throne from his father-in-law, the Catholic sympathizer James II, in 1688 in a bloodless coup known as the Glorious Revolution, formed even closer links between the Jewish communities of London and Amsterdam. Greater numbers of Jewish Dutch merchants moved to the City and East End. They were in turn followed by poorer Jews – hawkers, peddlers and second-hand traders – from Germany and Russia, and it was this image of the impoverished Jewish street trader, rather than the wealthy Jewish merchant, that formed the anti-Semitic stereotype of the next few hundred years.

By the mid eighteenth century east London had four German Jews (Ashkenazim) to every Mediterranean Jew (Sephardi). The main Ashkenazi centre was the Great Synagogue on Duke's Place, built on the site of Holy Trinity Priory Aldgate, which became the seat of worship of the Chief Rabbi and was destroyed by the Germans, ironically, during the Second World War. The main Sephardic place of worship was the still surviving Bevis Marks synagogue, also in Aldgate, which opened in 1701.

By 1800 there were about 10,000 Jews in London, mostly in the East End. They relied on precarious jobs, mostly street-selling of second-hand clothes, birds, shells, oranges and lemons, sponges, pencils, knives, combs, pocket-books and razors. They had little other choice, for although London's Jews enjoyed more rights than those of any other European community, even those of Holland, in the first half of the nineteenth century, they were not allowed to own a shop, teach, hold government office or practise at the Bar. In 1845 the offices of alderman and Lord Mayor were opened to them, but when Alderman Salomons won the seat of Greenwich at the 1851 general election, and refused to use the words 'in the true faith of a Christian' on taking the oath, he was expelled from the House. It took another seven years before the requirement was dropped.

The public ridiculed the Jews as misers, usurers, extortioners, cheats, coin-clippers and pimps. In *Our Mutual Friend*, Charles Dickens highlighted this problem through a character, Mr Riah, who muses:

For it is not, in Christian countries, with the Jews as with other peoples. Men say, 'This is a bad Greek, but there are good Greeks. This is a bad Turk, but there are good Turks.' Not so with the Jews. Men find the bad among us easily enough – among what peoples are the bad not easily found? – but they take the worst of us as samples of the best; they take the lowest of us as presentations of the highest; and they say 'All Jews are alike.'

In *Oliver Twist*, Dickens cast Fagin, the shifty hook-nosed leader of a gang of pickpockets, as a Jew. The author based him on a real-life Jewish fence, Ikey Solomons, who lived on Bell Lane, Spitalfields. The novel's readers knew nothing of Dickens's source. Eliza Davis, who bought Dickens's Bloomsbury house from him, wrote to the author, damning his portrayal of Fagin as 'a great wrong' to her people. 'If Jews thought him unjust to them,' he replied, they were 'a far less sensible, a far less just, and a far less good-tempered people than I have always supposed them to be'. He pointed out that all the other villains were Christians and that he had made Fagin Jewish because at that time 'that class of criminal almost invariably was a Jew'.

There was no let-up in this typecasting for a generation or two. Researching *The Wild Tribes of London* in 1855, Watts Phillips visited a fence's house near Petticoat Lane, where the resident Fagin motioned with a sweep of his hand to the inhabitants of the room and explained, 'These are what we call Petticoat-lane fencers; they're Jews, every one of them. You know the old saying, that there was never roguery yet but a Jew or a woman was at the bottom of it. The

Jews are downy customers, I confess, and plaguey hard to catch.'
Pointing to a little old man warming his shrivelled hands by the fire,
the fence told Phillips: 'that's Solomon Hart, a regular Californy. His
father was the rummest old codger I ever knew. He'd read somewhere in the Scriptures that David was laid on a bed of gold. Now,
that's my ambition.'

Jews were always on the defensive. When early in the nineteenth
century the Jewish community opened a hospital in Mile End, a
Christian evangelical body, the London Society for Promoting
Christianity Among the Jews, opened a rival school in Bethnal Green.
Instead of setting fees for those who wished to attend, the governors
offered to pay any Jew who wished to join them and be Christianized.
A Jewish solution to such predicaments came about in 1817 in the
shape of the Jews' Free School, which had become the largest school
in the British Empire by the end of the century.

## ARRIVAL OF THE ALIENS

In 1871 the *Jewish Chronicle* celebrated the 'decrease in the number
of poor foreign Jewish immigrants arriving in London'. At the time
this was a major theme within the city's Jewish community whose aim
was to win greater acceptance in British society. If there were too
many foreign-looking Jewish immigrants in London assimilation
would be harmed. The number of arrivals continued to decline over
the next ten years. When Alexander II, Tsar of Russia, was assassi-
nated on 1 March 1881 by a terrorist group that included a Jewish
seamstress, this gave the Russian authorities a convenient excuse to
exact reprisals against the Jewish community living in the Pale of
Settlement ghetto on the Polish–Russian border. As the pogroms raged
more than 200,000 Jewish families fled, most of them making the tortuous journey overland to Hamburg, Germany. For the chance of
landing in what many thought was America, but turned out to be
Britain, they boarded cattle boats and endured intolerable conditions,
herded together in the hold in near darkness, eating salt herrings out
of a barrel, sleeping on bare planks or a filthy rug, finding a toilet
where they could.

There was no legislation preventing the Jewish immigrants entering the country. No passport was required; the only stipulation was that the master of the ship entering British waters declared to the chief officer of customs the number of aliens on board. From 1881 to 1906 some 100,000 east European Jews came to the East End, mostly landing at Irongate Stairs by the Tower of London. The arrival of a boat produced one of the most bizarre sights in London: hordes of exotic, gabbling, theatrical, hirsute characters, the men with pointy beards and Homburg hats, the women with dark wigs and darker curls, landing in a country where they probably knew nobody and spoke no more than a few words of the native language.

Most of the boats were met by chancers looking to ingratiate themselves with the new arrivals. They would help them with their luggage but also offer them bogus tickets to America, or send them to 'free' lodgings where they were charged punitive sums to be escorted around London looking for work. If the immigrants were lucky they would be met by welfare workers from the Hebrew Ladies' Protective Society or the Poor Jews' Temporary Shelter who would escort the refugees past gangs of stone-throwing youths to an office on Church Lane at the north-west end of Commercial Road. There they would be interrogated by a tall bespectacled man sporting a short blond beard and a satin skull cap who would ask them, 'What is your name? Where have you come from? Do you have any relatives in England? Do you have any money?' Those who naïvely answered 'Yes' were abandoned to their own fate. Those who sensibly answered 'No' were whisked off to Schewzik's Russian Vapour Baths on Brick Lane – 'Best Massage in London: Invaluable relief for Rheumatism, Gout, Sciatica, Neuritis, Lumbago and Allied Complaints' – before being sent back to the shelter for afternoon prayers, dinner, evening prayers and bed at 9 p.m. This pattern continued for fourteen days, after which they were thrown out.

The immigrants met hostility not just from the gentiles but from Jewish groups. For instance, the Jewish Board of Guardians wrote to their counterparts in eastern Europe pleading with 'all right-thinking persons among our brethren in Germany, Russia and Austria to place a barrier to the flow of foreigners, to persuade these voyagers not to venture to come to a land they know nothing about. It is better that they live a life of sorrow in their native place than bear the shame of famine and perish in a strange land'.

Their inhospitability did not have the desired effect. By the end of the 1880s there were about 30,000 Jews in the East End, living in an unofficial Jewish ghetto which stretched from Spitalfields beyond Gardiner's Corner (the junction of Commercial Street and Commercial Road, and the traditional gateway to the East End) into Whitechapel. Predictably, Jews new to London wanted to live near other Jews already settled, so they moved here.

Jobs for the immigrant Jews were severely limited. In eastern Europe, banned from working on the railways, in factories and state-sponsored industries, they had become artisans – bootmakers, tailors, hatmakers – insecure trades on the margins of the economy. Now in their new homeland they faced hostile trade unions constrained by arcane regulations about the enrolment of new members, major East End employers such as the breweries refusing to take on Jews, and jobs at the docks at the mercy of a small number of patriarchal Irish families in Poplar and Shadwell. The immigrants' inability to speak English, their strange clothes and their religious strictures, which forbade them to work on a Saturday, put them at further disadvantage, so they continued to embrace the same insecure tailoring and associated trades.

Work took place on the top floors of the damp crowded cottages in what became known as 'sweatshops', named after their most conspicuous product. These sweatshops needed little space or capital, and could be serviced by a huge pool of local cheap labour. The immigrant Jews worked thirteen-hour days, starting at six in the morning, fuelled by starvation wages, and were therefore an ideal investment for owners desperate to compete with provincial factory owners by minimizing costs and manufacturing cheap goods.

Each task in the sweatshop – fixing, filling, button-holing and pressing – was clearly delineated and performed as if on an assembly line to the constant jackhammer crashing of the newly invented Singer sewing machine. The air was foul, the atmosphere thick with woollen particles, and the heat of the gas appliances used for warming the pressing irons was an excellent breeding ground for diphtheria and bronchitis. Sustenance was near non-existent. When one Pole appeared before the authorities he explained that a cup of tea and a herring did him for most of a day. Sure he worked harder in London than in Warsaw, but at least London was a city overladen with riches. Sure the riches weren't coming his way, but one day . . .

Overcrowding in the ghetto was rife. The medical journal the *Lancet* found a Jewish potato dealer living with his wife, five children and some sacks of potatoes in a room measuring six yards by six yards, furnished with nothing other than a bed. A Whitechapel sanitary inspector conducting a spot check found twenty people living in a house let to an immigrant named Cohen in Goulston Street, just off Whitechapel High Street, and twelve fowls feeding under the bed in a back room.

But despite the poverty, unrelenting grime, confusion and congestion the area soon attained a vibrancy that its gentile members could not understand or match. On Friday nights the streets from Bell Lane to Stepney Green would come to life in a blaze of light as the women lit candles in the windows to welcome the Sabbath. On Saturday evenings, after the Sabbath, the ghetto's youth, dressed up in their finery, turned Whitechapel Road into a preening ground. On Sunday mornings lengthy queues would form in the dark side streets alongside enormous women sitting astride barrels of olives and gherkins soaked in salt water.

These queues were nothing compared to the barely moving juggernaut of clamour and haggle that was the main East End market – Petticoat Lane – then one of London's most colourful sights. Officially Middlesex Street, the traditional boundary between the City and the East End, Petticoat Lane opened as a second-hand clothes market in what was then a Spanish enclave in 1608, and soon began a trade in local clothes made by the Spitalfields Huguenots. By the late nineteenth century the market was mostly Jewish. Here the undiscerning *flâneur*, dodging the thimble riggers, card sharps and assorted swindlers, could buy a thousand useless goods: headkerchiefs, fur boas, peacock feathers, oilcloths, damaged lamps and chipped china shepherdesses et al.

The Lane's stallholders began their apprenticeship at the age of ten, usually by selling thinly cut cakes known as boolers made of egg, flour and candied orange or lemon peel, with a slight colouring of saffron.

They would spend much of the day 'getting around' – becoming known in the neighbourhood – and at sunset head off to the West End to wait for a servant who might have old shoes or suits for sale. He would then take the clothes back to the Lane and try to interest one of the established stallholders in buying them. Later on in the evening he would toss up ha'pennys in the alleys with his pals, cleverly secreting about his person a coin known as a gray, which had a head or a tail on both sides. At the age of fifteen he would be as sharp as a man of fifty and twice as nimble, maintaining his agility longer than the gentile by avoiding the excessive use of alcohol.

By the end of the century Petticoat Lane was also known for a selection of food that more than anything else identified the Jewish community. It was not so much the locally crafted brown sweet butter cakes, or the puddings made of eggs and ground almonds, but the Spanish olives and Dutch cucumbers, the Norwegian herrings steeped in brine, the German sausages, the Scotch smoked salmon, the fish stewed with lemons and eggs in the Dutch manner and the Polish chollas – long plaited loaves that were still edible long after the gentile loaf had turned blue.

The Jewish ghetto divided itself into an elaborate and implicitly accepted social hierarchy. At the top were the German Jews (the bakers), followed by the Lithuanians (tailors), Poles and Russians (also tailors, but not quite as skilful), Rumanians (woodworkers), Spanish and Portuguese, and lastly the Dutch (the cigar makers), whose lowly status reflected the political and commercial demise of Amsterdam, by then usurped as the centre of the financial world by London.

The Judaism of the 'ruling' German Jews was a religion open to reform and anglicization. Prayer books were printed with Hebrew on one side and English on the other. Those from further east, such as Lithuania, Poland and Russia, tended to maintain the most conservative aspects of their culture. They took refuge in the Sabbath, the annual festivals and the most minor anniversaries and holy days as a safeguard against a hostile world. Oblivious to the role of the Chief Rabbi, whose status they dismissed as negligible (it has no basis in Jewish law) and whose Hebrew they found mostly unintelligible, they worshipped in *stiebels*, tiny home-based synagogues.

Inside them long-bearded men and ringleted boys discussed the finer points of Jewish law: how many white hairs may a red cow have before it becomes a white cow? Why can a louse but not a flea be killed on the Sabbath? (The first is allowed; the second is a deadly sin.) The *stiebels* acted as unofficial social centres, occasionally even as lodging-houses, being always open, like a twenty-first-century East End mosque, rather than closed and intimidating like the more established synagogues, which the east European Jews damned as being more like cathedrals than Jewish places of worship.

Each *stiebel* housed a different sect. The most unusual of these were the Machzikei Hadas V'Shomrei Shabbas – 'strengtheners of the law and guardians of the Sabbath' – whose members complied with the strictest Sabbath laws, refusing to carry out all manual tasks on the day of rest; even going as far as tying their handkerchiefs around their waists. For the execution of vital but menial tasks they hired a flunkey known by the semi-insulting term 'Shobbos Goy', who could not be directly ordered – 'It's rather dark in here', rather than 'Could you find some light, please?', 'It's getting cold', rather than 'Could you place another log on the fire?' – but had to guess what was required.

The Machzikei took over a Georgian building on the corner of Fournier Street and Brick Lane that had been a Huguenot chapel, the Neuve Eglise. It was one of a number of local places where John Wesley hosted the earliest Methodist services, and in 1809 it had become the headquarters of the London Society for Promoting Christianity Among the Jews. (It is now the Jamme Masjid mosque, the only building outside the Holy Land to have housed the world's three major monotheistic faiths: Christianity, Judaism and Islam). Ironically the Machzikei received most harassment not from gentiles, but from non-religious Jews. On the Day of Atonement 1904 Jewish anarchists pelted worshippers taking a break from the service on this day of fasting with bacon sandwiches.

The lingua franca of the Jewish ghetto was Yiddish, a Babylonian mix of German, Hebrew and Aramaic, sprinkled with Slavic and Romish words, which was particularly suited to the cut-throat atmosphere of the tailoring sweatshop. It was also rich enough in dramatic-sounding, heavily guttural cusses to be particularly effective in warding off hostile gentiles and contained its own in-built levels of irony, part self-deprecating, part insulting, part antagonistic, best summed up in the following typical late nineteenth-century East End Yiddish joke:

Edward I, having expelled the Jews from England in 1290, receives a telegram from the distinguished European rabbi Yossel Ben Akiva. To the king's amazement the telegram supports his stance in ordering the Jews from England. So in front of his admiring court the king reads the telegram out loud:

'Your most distinguished Majesty, Edward, King of England, Conqueror of the Welsh, Hammer of the Scots, Slayer of the Infidel Saracen, *kain ain' hora*. You were right to expel the Jews from England. The Jews have perverted the ancient teachings. We killed Christ. You are the heir to Solomon and David. The gentiles are the chosen people. We should apologise. Yours, Rabbi Yossel Ben Akiva.'

Edward revels in this unexpected admission from the spiritual leader of his latest victims and turns to his courtiers for approval. He basks in their applause until the court jester approaches: 'Your Majesty, may I be so bold as to read the telegram again, but this time in the intended Yiddish style. Please allow me.' The jester picks up the telegram and reads it, this time with the appropriate inflection:

'Your most distinguished Majesty Edward, King of England, Conqueror of the Welsh, Hammer of the Scots, Slayer of the Infidel Saracen, *kain ain' hora*. You were *right* to expel the Jews from England? The *Jews* have perverted the ancient teachings? *We* killed Christ? *You* are the heir to Solomon and David? The *gentiles* are the chosen people? *We* should apologise? Yours, Rabbi Yossel Ben Akiva.'

Unlike other foreign nationals who had made their home in the East End, the immigrant Jews had no affinity with the natives. Huguenot immigrants may have spoken a different language, but at least they shared a religion with the majority of the population. The Irish may have followed a different religion, but at least they spoke the same language. The Chinese, with no common language or religion, were at least working on British ships and involved in British trade. But the Jews spoke incomprehensible languages (Yiddish, Lettish, Russian, Polish) written largely in indecipherable characters, followed a different religion, and had no connection with any outpost of the British Empire.

Nevertheless they prospered. The Jewish pauper living alongside a chicken that he might have to eat became the exception rather than the rule. Amid the impoverishment of Stepney and Whitechapel the Jew tended to live in more comfort than the gentile. The proletarian Jew was taught that manual work was not to be worshipped as an end in itself, but was simply a stepping stone to a greater calling – making or managing money – which would require greater social skills and subtleties than could usually be found in a roomful of Hoffman presses.

From birth great store was made of education. The Jewish system trained the child to think, analyse, question and investigate, to marvel at the syntactical beauty of the psalms and prayers, to indulge in the lexical dexterity of the ancient language, to be aware of a deeper meaning, a greater presence, whereas the Irish Catholic child was enwrapped in a barely understood ritualistic experience involving incense, wafers, transubstantiation, wine and threats of eternal damnation, and the Protestant child often simply wasn't taught.

But this analytical approach had its own drawbacks. The Jew constantly queried the nature of Judaism. What did it mean to be Jewish? Was the nub of the religion the pursuit of a life devoted to scripture, the unravelling of Talmudic esoterica in pursuit of some ethereal goal, or was it a quest for moral purity through works of self-lessness, charity and kindness? How far should the Jew go in complying with a series of seemingly inexplicable rituals – the proscription of linen and wool combined together in one's clothes; the Sabbath laws which prohibit all work, even writing and cooking; the strict dietary requirements that render as edible only fish with fins *and* scales? And what appearance should the chosen people display? Could a Jew be a good Jew if he dressed like a Victorian English gentleman rather than an eighteenth-century Pole? Was it sacrilegious to speak English instead of Yiddish?

To the Jewish philanthropist Lord Rothschild, who founded the East End-based Poor Jews' Temporary Shelter, the role of the established Jewish community was unequivocal: 'Our business is to humanize our Jewish immigrants and then to anglicize them.' Anglicization took place most emphatically at the Jews' Free School on Bell Lane, Spitalfields, which stood next to a chicken slaughterhouse amid the most densely populated part of the capital, the population 600 people per acre compared with a London average of fifty-four.

The school's aim was to turn the children of the Jewish immigrants into English gentlemen; to replace their heavily guttural Slavonic growl with an affable Cockney inflection that would be acceptable in Dollis Hill and Dalston, to churn out young Jews who would unstintingly support their country at its time of need, Jews who, while remaining kosher, would develop a taste for London products and culture – porter, Gilbert and Sullivan, Lord's.

As a new generation of anglicized Jews appeared they created their own quasi-secular community, with the Chief Rabbi the *heimische* Archbishop of Canterbury and the United Synagogue as the Church of England. Their synagogues, resplendent with stained glass, Classical pillars and rows of pews, resembled the Baroque English churches of Nicholas Hawksmoor and Thomas Archer. They called their clergy 'reverend' rather than 'rabbi'. In turn, Edward, Prince of Wales, called Dr Hermann Adler 'my Chief Rabbi'; Adler with his gaiters and dog-collar was more of a chief rabbi to the Protestant king than he ever was to the east European pauper immigrants with their *stiebels* and vapour baths.

Those who emerged most successfully from this background – writers, artists, entertainers, moguls – managed to appear conspicuously Jewish, but in a British way. Isaac Rosenberg, born in Bristol in 1890 but brought up in Stepney, had worked out by the age of fourteen that 'wealth, with its soul-crushing scourges placed into hands by fate/Hath made the cement of its towers, grim-girdled by our despair'.

He left school to train as an apprentice engraver, like his hero, William Blake, took art classes in the evening, and when he was twenty-one joined the Slade School of Art, helped by some wealthy Jewish ladies who clubbed together to raise the funds. Rosenberg had escaped the Jewish ghetto for the Bloomsbury Group and the Fitzrovians. When he needed money in 1915 he signed up for war duty. Being opposed to killing, he enlisted for the medical services. Now, instead of analysing the direction of modern art and literature with Wyndham Lewis at Omega studios, he found himself in the trenches: 'Down – a shell – O! Christ,/I am choked . . . safe . . . dust blind, I/See trench floor poppies/Strewn. Smashed you lie.' Many were impressed with his evocations of the war, and he even managed to be patronized by the American poet Ezra Pound: 'He has something in him horribly rough, but then "Stepney, East . . . we ought to have a real . . . burglar, *ma che* !!!"' Rosenberg suffered considerable pain from his ill-fitting boots, which should have been soaked in cod liver oil, but rubbed the skin off his feet, making marching agony. When his unit was caught by the Germans on 28 March 1918, he was killed in close combat.

Reuben Weintrop, born at 12 Hanbury Street, Spitalfields, eight years after Jack the Ripper murdered Annie Chapman at nearby No. 29, was so humiliated by his sergeant-major while serving in the army in the First World War that he vowed to exact revenge by turning the man into a laughing stock. Weintrop took the sergeant major's name – 'Bud Flanagan' – and with Chesney Allen formed the double act Flanagan and Allen, part of the popular Crazy Gang team. The Jewish authorities' determination to see the children of the ghetto talking the same language as the natives worked perfectly in this case, for his most reassuringly English of voices continues to haunt the nation's consciousness as the singer of the sublimely executed 1940s pastiche 'Who Do You Think You Are Kidding, Mr Hitler?', the theme tune of the television programme *Dad's Army*.

Barney Barnato, born Barnett Isaacs near Petticoat Lane, first became a stand-up comedian and then went into diamond mining – in South Africa, not the East End. He bought worked-out mines in Kimberley and increased his fortune through speculation, before merging his business with Cecil Rhodes's De Beers company. Barnato was often caught up in embarrassing misunderstandings. At a party in a luxurious Cape Town villa lined with expensive works of art a duchess invited him to come upstairs and examine her Watteau. Barnato followed enthusiastically, expecting something more visceral than an eighteenth-century French painting.

On returning to London to trade in gold shares he began brandishing a visiting card inscribed: 'I'll stand you a drink, but I won't lend you a fiver'. When he tried to buy land on Park Lane in 1897 the landlord, the Duke of Westminster, rejected his offer on the grounds that Barnato did not 'stand in a high position in South Africa and that he is a land speculator' – a euphemism for saying he was Jewish.

Overladen with money, Barnato bought Spencer House, the grand mansion by Green Park now owned by the Rothschilds. When he was obliged to appear in court in London and gave his address as 'Spencer House, St James's', the judge enquired, 'Are you the owner's major-domo?' To which Barnato replied, 'No, I'm my own bleedin' major-domo.' Barnato committed suicide in 1897 in mysterious circumstances while aboard a ship in the Atlantic, much in the same way as the late twentieth-century roguish Jewish financier Robert Maxwell met his end.

Louis and Boris Winogradsky, brothers born in the early years of the twentieth century in the village of Tokmak in the Ukraine, fled the pogroms in 1912 and arrived in Brick Lane speaking mostly Russian, a little Yiddish and even less English. Louis entered the rag trade, but developed a passion for dancing, becoming the Charleston Champion of London as Louis Grad, which he changed to Lew Grade after a Paris newspaper spelt it that way during a review of his act at the Moulin Rouge.

Grade began working as a talent spotter, and in the 1950s founded the Incorporated Television Company. He and brother Boris (by then known as Bernard Delfont) became the dominant figures in television programme making in the medium's early days, broadcasting shows as diverse as *Sunday Night at the London Palladium*, *The Avengers* and *Thunderbirds*, thereby demonstrating once again that what is thought of as quintessentially British culture has often been introduced by immigrants. Now both deceased, their legacy is carried on by their nephew, Michael Grade, who was appointed chairman of the BBC in 2004.


## PIMPS, FENCES AND GANGSTERS

A myth has persisted of the immigrant Jew in late-Victorian England as righteous victimized martyr, upholder of the law, protector of a fractured morality in a near-godless land. But the Jewish immigrant community harboured as many villains as any other group. Pimps targeted attractive unaccompanied females as soon as they had stepped off the boat at Irongate Stairs. Claiming to be representing organizations that were little more than fronts for the white slave trade, they would lure girls to a shabby boarding-house on Heneage Street, off Brick Lane (the kosher catwalk) and there, amid much schmooze, prepare her for a bordello in the West End or the most desirable brothels in South Africa. During this period 151 aliens in Great Britain, most of them Jewish, were convicted for keeping brothels, and 521 for soliciting, figures which horrified the Rabbinate and led to accusations that any acknowledging of these problems by the Jewish community could only lead to increased anti-Semitism.

Of the many Jewish pimps, the best known was Ikey Bogard, who liked dressing as a cowboy, openly carried a gun (at that time it was still legal to do so) and had so swarthy a complexion he was given the nickname 'Darky the Coon'. His gang, who supplied muscle for street traders, were known predictably as 'The Coons', and their headquarters was Clark's café at 119–121 Brick Lane, a rough caff in a rougher area. It was there that they came up against the nastiest local non-Jewish 'firm', led by Arthur Harding. In his memoirs Harding explained that the streets off Brick Lane were 'a hotbed of villainy, where women sold themselves for a few pence. Thieves hung about the corner of the street; in the back alleys there was garrotting.'

The two gangs arranged a showdown at the nearby Blue Coat Boy pub on Norton Folgate in December 1911. Once they had met Bogard offered Harding a drink, but Harding threw it and the glass back at Bogard, leaving the latter's face 'looking like a map of England', according to one witness. This was the cue for a mass brawl that left the room littered with smashed glass, broken chairs and tables, and scores of villains too injured to resist the charms of those police officers who arrived to sort things out.

A bigger menace than Bogard's Coons was the Stop At Nothing mob, who were based at the Rumanian café at the corner of Settles Street and Commercial Road. Also known as the Bessarabians as they mostly originated from the Bessarabia region of Rumania, they were the 'greatest menace ever known to London', according to the East End detective Benjamin Leeson.

The Bessarabians were easily spotted on the streets of Whitechapel and Stepney. They wore wide-brimmed Panama hats cocked at an angle, huge peacock feathers, pointed shoes, mustard-coloured shirts, silk socks held up by garters, trousers sporting a low-hanging crotch, which tapered to a tight clutch around the ankles, and oversized pinstripe jackets with shoulders so wide and padded that from a distance members of the gang looked like upside down triangles.

Their leader was the enigmatic 'Perkoff', and their number included one Max Moses, better known as the light heavyweight boxing champ Charlie 'Kid' McCoy. He had a wonderfully quick left hand, the best ever seen according to many commentators, fast feet and shifty, slippery, crafty, clever moves. When roused McCoy would rip his opponent's face open with a series of slicing punches, which may explain why he lost only six of some 200 fights.

In 1891 Moses became Norman Shelby as Irish boxers were popular at this time. He was rebranded Kid McCoy – 'the Real McCoy' (the first individual to be referred to in this way) after being heckled in a bar by a man who said he did not believe that he was speaking to the real McCoy, the prize fighter, until the Kid smashed him in the face, which made the man rub his jaw and exclaim: 'Geez, you are the real McCoy, all right.'

The Bessarabians specialized in blackmailing prospective brides. A few days before a wedding, they would approach the bride's parents and threaten to expose all manner of embarrassing indiscretions unless they were paid. They were not, in fact, experts in the family's background, but in human psychology, for the victims, terrified of a scandal, *would* often pay, to hide whatever skeletons were lurking in their closet.

Occasionally the Bessarabians targeted those who had been married for some years. Finding a Jewish couple who had reputedly saved considerable amounts of money, they burgled the property but came away empty-handed. They then sent one of the gang to knock on the door a few days later, urging the couple to pay protection lest they be burgled again. The terrified couple handed over a small sum and were warned in turn not to leave anything valuable in the house, just to be on the safe side. When the couple went to synagogue on the Day of Atonement they sewed their savings into the wife's dress. Unfortunately, during the service a smoke bomb was thrown into the congregation, and amid the confusion the woman was attacked. Once the chaos had died down, she found that her money had been taken.

The Bessarabians' next victims were Jewish shopkeepers. They ordered the proprietors to pay protection money. If the owner protested the gang would descend on the premises armed with coshes, clubs and knives to exact punishment. The victims rarely went to the police. Being east European immigrants – first generation and second generation – they had a psychopathic, and justified, fear of the authorities. The police in their homelands were agents of the state, ordered to make life as difficult as possible for all Jews, so the immigrants, knowing nothing of the relatively civilized behaviour of the Metropolitan Police, thought it best to take no chances. Or perhaps their reticence to elicit help from the authorities was correct? The police's unwillingness to confront the Bessarabians suggests they were in the villains' pay, and it was left to another gang to rid the East End of this nefarious menace.

This other gang were the Odessans, patrons of the Odessa restaurant in Stepney. The owner, one Kikal, not only refused to pay the Bessarabians protection money, but attacked five of them with an iron bar when they came to 'persuade' him, which led to a swift adjournment of hostilities and a spell of treatment in the London Hospital. From then on the inhabitants of the East End felt safer, knowing that their tormentors were now spending their time attacking each other rather than them. Predictably, the two gangs decided to settle the question of who was to run the streets of Stepney and Whitechapel through a showdown, which took place some fifty years before the Krays and the Watney Streeters arranged a similar summit on the same patch.

The Odessans' plan was simple and violent: they would cut off the ears of the Bessarabians' leader, Perkoff, and nail them to the door of the Bessarabian café on Settles Street. One night a woman attached to the Odessan gang lured Perkoff into a side street and indeed slashed off one of his ears with a razor. Surgeons at the London Hospital sewed it back on, and when the police asked Perkoff who had committed this foul deed he feigned ignorance (or perhaps he couldn't hear them!). Nevertheless, he and his gang plotted revenge. In 1902 the two gangs fought their final battle at the York Minster public house on Philpot Street on a night when the pub's clientele were being entertained by a group of Russian 'dancers'. The ensuing mass brawl resulted in the death of a gang member, Henry Brodovich, who stumbled out of the premises one hand on his own knife, the other on his stab wound, and collapsed in the street. Those who sustained less threatening injuries had only a few yards to stagger to reach the London Hospital.

That was the end of the Bessarabian–Odessan menace in east London, and some of their number soon left for Chicago, where they drifted into the various gangs that controlled the city's alcohol supply during Prohibition. One of them even became a cop. McCoy served in the US army during the First World War, acted in a few Hollywood films, and went through eight wives (halfway towards the marriage service's optimum of sixteen – 'four richer, four poorer, four better, four worse . . .' When his mistress refused to marry him after he had divorced wife number seven, he shot her, escaping a murder charge by pleading insanity due to his boxing injuries. On his release after serving seven years, and with a promise of a job from Henry Ford himself ringing in his ears, McCoy married wife number eight. He committed suicide in Detroit in April 1940.

## JACOB THE RIPPER

By 1888 the *East London Observer* newspaper had become openly contemptuous of the Jews and was demanding their exclusion from the neighbourhood. 'We are justified on the ground that they depreciate our home products and depress our markets. Their low state of civilization tends to demoralize whole populations of native workers,' ran an editorial.

When the body of Mary Ann Nichols, a prostitute, was found disembowelled, her throat cut from ear to ear, in a Whitechapel back street in August 1888 – the second local woman to have been found violently murdered in that area within a month – public suspicion centred on these mysterious, inarticulate, dishevelled, east European East End Jews.

No gentile could have perpetrated such a crime, the *East London Observer* reasoned, ignoring the fact that only two Jews had been hanged for murder since the return of the Jews to England in the

1650s. A Jewish culprit for the murders had to be found, and Jews were randomly abused and attacked. Before long the police revealed that they were looking for a local Jew known popularly by the exotic nickname 'Leather Apron', on account of his customary garb, who was known for mistreating prostitutes, and who had been spotted in the area at the time of the murders acting suspiciously and holding a knife.

On 8 September another prostitute, Annie Chapman, was found murdered and mutilated in the East End, this time on Hanbury Street, Spitalfields. Near the body was a leather apron. The East End buzzed with anticipation about the probable involvement of the mysterious 'Leather Apron'. Two days later the police identified him as John Pizer, a cobbler who had been arraigned before Thames magistrates a month previously charged with indecent assault, but had been cleared. Pizer was swiftly rearrested at his home, 22 Mulberry Street, Whitechapel. Conveniently, he turned out to have the typical East European Jewish appearance: swarthy face topped with strips of grizzly black hair and an expression which the *Manchester Guardian* described as 'sinister . . . full of terror for the women who describe it . . . eyes small and glittering, lips parted in a grin, but excessively repellent'.

The case against Pizer looked strong. Timothy Donovan, Annie Chapman's lodging-house keeper, recalled ejecting him from the property a few months previously for threatening a woman. In an identity parade set up at Leman Street police station Pizer was picked out by a Spanish/Bulgarian immigrant, Emmanuel Violenia, who identified him as the man he had seen threatening to stab Annie Chapman early on Saturday 8 September. Pizer pleaded innocence vehemently. He was saved only because Violenia failed to identify Chapman in the mortuary. Further inconsistencies then emerged: it turned out that the leather apron found near Chapman's body belonged to a neighbour; Pizer's alibi was confirmed; Violenia was unmasked as a crank whose main interest was in seeing the victim's corpse. Pizer was released, but only after a twenty-four-hour delay for fear that he would be dismembered by the mob.

This did not bring an end to the Ripper murders, nor to the allegations of involvement of Jews. At the end of the month, during the early hours of 30 September, Elizabeth Stride, a 45-year-old Swedish woman, was found with her throat cut, the blood still pouring out, on land adjoining the Berner Street International Workmen's Educational Club, a haunt of Jewish anarchists and socialists.

This time there was a witness, of sorts: Israel Schwartz, a Hungarian immigrant. Schwartz told police that, on turning into Berner Street from Commercial Road, he had seen two men speaking to a woman at the gateway where the body was found and had watched as they tried to pull her into the street and throw her on the ground. The woman screamed three times, and as Schwartz crossed the road one of the men hissed at him, 'Lipski.' Schwartz walked away, but to his horror found himself being followed briefly by the other man. The 'Lipski' incident, chillingly recreated in the 2001 Johnny Depp film *From Hell*, was an allusion to the 1887 murder and sexual assault of a young Jewish girl, Miriam Angel, who had been found dead in her bed at nearby 16 Batty Street with a curious yellow staining around her mouth. Under the bed lay the prostrate, semi-conscious figure of fellow tenant Israel Lipski, a 22-year-old Polish-Jewish umbrella maker. He had the same yellow staining around his mouth.

On being revived, Lipski claimed that two Jewish hawkers he had invited home to discuss some work had attacked him when he asked them why they were entering Angel's bedroom, and had made him drink nitric acid. One crucial piece of evidence weighed against Lipski: the bedroom door where he and Angel were found was locked from the *inside*. However, the door was in such poor condition, with a hole by the catch that the key could have been turned from the *outside*.

Lipski's case was taken up by the crusading journalist W. T. Stead, and public opinion began to turn in favour of him. But before the home secretary was able to recommend commuting the death sentence, Lipski confessed. This sudden, unexpected twist of events predictably stymied the growing support Lipski had been receiving and he was hanged at Newgate on 22 August 1887, the day after his surprise confession. Still some defended him. They claimed a rabbi had pressured him into pleading guilty to quell growing anti-Semitism in London. Or perhaps, like Robert Hubert, who, 200 years previously, falsely claimed to have started the Fire of London, Lipski had admitted to a crime he had not committed? Instead of dousing anti-Semitism in the East End the confession seemed only to exacerbate it, and for a while the name 'Lipski' was used as a slur for all Jews.

Stride wasn't the Ripper's only victim that night of 30 September 1888. An hour later another prostitute, Catherine Eddowes, was killed on Mitre Square, near Aldgate station, about half a mile from where Stride had been slain. Eddowes's white apron was torn during the attack, and part of the garment dropped on nearby Goulston Street. There it was found by a policeman who, looking up at the wall, saw graffiti proclaiming: 'The Juwes are not the men That will be Blamed for nothing', a message which has strong Masonic connotations (see Chapter 6) but could also be taken anti-Semitically.

Fearful of a pogrom in Whitechapel, the police wiped the message without photographing it, before it could be spotted by the early-morning market traders. Sir Robert Anderson, the assistant commissioner of police at the time of the Ripper murders, later explained how the police had been 'certain that the murderer was a low-class foreign Jew. It is a remarkable fact that people of that class in the East End will not give up one of their number to Gentile Justice.' Or as the Jewish commentator Chaim Bermant later explained, 'If Jack the Ripper was a Jew then one can be fairly certain that his fellows would have kept quiet about it, for the simple reason that the whole community could have been held culpable for his deeds.'

By October Jewry itself was in the frame. The Vienna correspondent of *The Times* recalled how four years previously a Polish Jew, Ritter, had been arrested near Cracow for murdering and mutilating a non-Jewish woman in a ritualistic killing that was an obligatory part of the atonement a religious Jew needed to undertake for having sexual relations with a gentile. The Chief Rabbi quickly stepped in to explain that such practices had no place in Judaism. Then another theory circulated. The murderer must be a Jewish animal slaughterer; such a man would have the knives and the anatomical knowledge. Two slaughterers were duly arrested, but both had plausible alibis, and once again Jewish leaders were obliged to clarify religious minutiae, in this case that the *khalef*, the implement used to kill an animal according to the kosher method, is single-edged and not pointed, as the one used in the murders. Nevertheless there were many who *wanted* the culprit to be Jewish, and the *Jewish Chronicle* warned East End Jews that it might not be safe for them to venture out at night while the murders were in the news.

One possible lead, which surprisingly has not been explored by the omnipresent Ripper industry, came from the local newspaper, the *East London Observer*. Its 15 September 1888 edition, published soon after Chapman's murder, contained a bizarre letter on the atrocities sprinkled with biblical references to 'Pharisees', 'the marriage feast of the Lord' and 'the Kingdom of Heaven'. The letter suggested setting up a national fund to find 'honourable employment for some of the daughters of Eve [prostitutes], which would greatly lessen immorality'. It was signed 'Josephus'.

Given the level of theological allusions, it is most likely the writer named himself after the first-century Jewish historian and scholar Josephus, who during the war against the Romans hid in a cave near the fortress of Jotapata with forty others. Deciding their only escape was death, they drew lots to determine the order of their demise. Whoever drew the first lot was to be killed by the drawer of the second, who in turn was to be killed by the drawer of the third, and so on. Josephus was lucky enough to draw the last lot. However, he and the penultimate participant chose not to complete their pact but surrender to the Romans. Many suspected that Josephus had 'fixed' the lots, sending scores to their deaths, a view reinforced when he swiftly moved from the Jewish priesthood to the role of adviser to the Roman emperors Vespasian, Titus and Domitian.

Surprisingly, commentators have paid little attention to the significance of the *Jewish* dates of the murders, something which caused much consternation within the community at the time. Martha Tabram, the first of the prostitutes to be violently murdered in Whitechapel in 1888, was found on 7 August. This was a few hours before the start of the month of *Elul*, a time of contrition and repentance in the Jewish calendar, heralded in synagogue by a blast of the ram's horn warning that the Day of Judgement (the Hebrew New Year) is at hand.

Mary Ann Nichols was killed on 31 August, the 24th of *Elul* in the Jewish calendar, just before the commencement of the special prayers for forgiveness known as *selichos* that lead up to the New Year.

Remarkably 7 September, the date when the body of Annie Chapman was found mutilated and disembowelled on Hanbury Street, Spitalfields, was the second day of the Jewish New Year – the last hours of the 'Day of Judgement'.

So were the slayings the work of a deranged Jew enacting some arcane chronological Biblical ritual to rid the East End of sin, or that of a disturbed gentile steeped in Judaistic knowledge intent on humiliating East End Jewry? Jewish leaders braced themselves for fresh murder on 15 September. For this day was not only the Jewish Sabbath, but the Day of Atonement, the holiest day of the Jewish year, the day when the worshipper begs forgiveness for all sins. In Biblical times the high priest conducted a special Temple ceremony on the Day of Atonement to clean the shrine, slaying a bull and two goats as a special offering. Perhaps there would be a human slaying this time?

Well, no murders occurred that day, dashing the theory that the killings were linked to significant dates in the Jewish calendar. Or maybe the murderer was interrupted while about to commit a fresh atrocity. *The Times* reported how on the evening of 14 September, as the Day of Atonement was being ushered in at synagogue with the mournful, heart-thumping prayer *Kol Nidre*, Aldgate police arrested a slightly built shabbily dressed man, Edward McKenna, of 15 Brick Lane, who was wearing a cloth skull cap in the religious Jewish manner and had been seen acting suspiciously in the neighbourhood. He may have been the man who, on coming out of Tower subway, asked the attendant, 'Have you caught any of the Whitechapel murderers yet?', and then produced a foot-long knife with a curved blade, remarking, 'This will do for them', before running away. A search of McKenna's pockets at Commercial Street police station yielded what the newspaper described as an 'extraordinary accumulation of articles': a heap of rags, dress fabrics, old and dirty linen, two women's purses, two or three pocket handkerchiefs, two small tin boxes, a small cardboard box, a small leather strap and one spring onion. Although McKenna was unable to produce an explanation for his behaviour he was released. Subsequent Ripper murders took place on dates insignificant to the Jewish calendar.

# THE ALIENS ACT

Allegations that Jews were involved in the Ripper murders exacerbated xenophobic feelings in the East End. Although some community leaders held sympathetic views – the Revd D. Ross told a meeting of the St George's Vestry that 'the Jews cherished thrift, sobriety and industry . . . I wish they were all Jews in the parish [and that] New Road could be called Jew Road' – they were a rarity.

Increasingly common was what the First World War poet Isaac Rosenberg later described as 'the thoughts that are prompted by hate'. For example, Captain Colomb, MP for the East End seat of Bow and Bromley, announced that he objected to England 'with its overcrowded population, being made a human ashpit for the refuse population of the world', while the writer Arnold White railed against 'foreign paupers replacing English workers and driving to despair men, women and children of our blood'.

In 1894 Lord Salisbury introduced a Bill in the House of Lords to block the immigration of 'dangerous aliens', what would now be called terrorists, but it was rejected by the Liberal government. However the arrival of nearly 3,000 Rumanian refugees in the East End in 1899 terrified not only most conservative gentiles but many embourgeoised Jews. An 'anti-alien' candidate, Major William Evans-Gordon, overturned the Liberals' majority at the subsequent general election. He was helped by the Jewish financier Lord Rothschild, the wealthiest and most powerful anglicized Jew, who felt that he, his family's and his friends' hard-won status in various company boardrooms, if not the golf clubhouse, was being jeopardized by the presence of these ill-mannered Transylvanians who spoke Yiddish and dressed like peasants.

In 1901 a businessman called Stanley Shaw founded the anti-immigration British Brothers' League, warning that 'thousands of alien paupers were pouring into London, driving English people out of their native parishes and literally taking the bread out their mouths'. The league's first meeting took place at the People's Palace, Mile End, in January 1902, in front of a crowd of 4,000; many more were turned away at the door. Stirring songs such as 'Soldiers of the Queen', 'God Bless the Prince of Wales', 'There's No Place Like Home' and 'Britons Never Shall Be Slaves' were sung in between speeches from those who railed against not just the east European Jews, but international Jewry.

A councillor called Williams asked the audience, 'Who is corrupting our morals?', and then went on to answer himself with the reply, 'The Jews.' A call-and-response session continued: 'Who is destroying our Sundays? – The Jews.' 'Who is debasing our national life? – The Jews. Shame on them. Wipe them out', which must have been embarrassing for spectators such as the Jewish Harry Samuel, MP for Limehouse, but presumably not for Henry Norman, MP for Wolverhampton South and also a Jew, who told the gathering, 'This is England. It is not the backyard of Europe, it is not the dustbin of Russia.'

The growing campaign against an excessive Jewish presence in Britain led the Tory prime minister, Arthur Balfour, to set up a royal commission in 1902 to investigate alien immigration. Despite opposing the arrival of Jews in the country, Balfour supported Zionism, and therefore began to assume heroic status in the Jewish community. The headquarters of the Zionist Federation in Britain was later named after him. But if the Tory Balfour had problems reconciling one personal view of the Jews with another, consider the psychological problem the newly formed Zionist Federation faced. At the 1900 general election the organization declared its support for the anti-Semitic Tory candidate for Whitechapel, David Hope-Kyd, simply because he supported the infant Zionist movement. They did not care that his support was governed by a desire to rid the East End of Jews and send them anywhere else – the Holy Land if they so wished – and that he had described Jewish immigrants as 'the scum of the unhealthiest continental nations'. Supported by Lord Rothschild, Hope-Kyd lost to the Liberal by only seventy-one votes.

Balfour's royal commission received contributions from members of the police, local government officials, doctors, lawyers, factory inspectors and trade unionists. Evans-Gordon, the anti-alien MP, told them that 'the aliens will not conform to our ideas and have no sort of neighbourly feeling. A foreign Jew will take a house and move in on a Sunday morning, which upsets all the British people there. He will use his yard for storing rags, mountains of smelly rags, or perhaps he will start a little factory in the yard and carry on a hammering noise all night.'

The commission reached a compromise. It refuted the vitriolic accusations made against those already settled, and recommended that, while it was not necessary to block all immigration, new arrivals should be allowed to settle only in particular areas. It also recommended that a department be set up to examine the character of those wishing to enter the country, so that political and religious extremists, religious zealots, prostitutes and 'idiots' were weeded out, and certain 'undesirables' deported.

A bill was rushed through for parliamentary discussion in 1904. Hastily drawn up, its proposals were barely workable and it fell. A new bill was drafted, defining more carefully which aliens were to be excluded from Britain, and allowing the right of appeal to an immigration board. It received considerably more backing, and even the Chief Rabbi, from his East End headquarters, was reluctant to condemn it. When the Liberal opposition mostly abstained, the bill was easily carried. The Liberals took over the government in 1906, but instead of repealing the legislation simply instructed the authorities to adopt a casual approach to it. Nevertheless Jewish immigration decreased by 40 per cent as east European Jews learned that Britain was no longer so welcoming.

The outbreak of the First World War on 4 August 1914 changed the debate over Anglo-Jewish identity. The *Jewish Chronicle* threw its weight behind the war effort from the start. Ignoring the recent hostility Britain had shown to incoming Jews, the paper declared: 'England has been all she could be to the Jews; Jews will be all they can be to England.' And in case readers had not taken in the message, the same words were included on a banner hung up outside the paper's Fleet Street offices.

As most British males of suitable age were keen to fight, the armed forces found themselves augmented by more than 40,000 British Jews. Services in many East End synagogues were turned into patriotic rallies, choirs adapting the liturgy to incorporate the melody of 'Rule Britannia'. Meanwhile, public suspicion fell on the 3,000-odd Jews of Austrian and German origin in the East End. Those who chose not to volunteer for the armed forces were condemned as shirkers or accused of stealing Englishmen's jobs; those who did join were denounced as fifth columnists.

Abraham Beverstein of Whitechapel, worried that his family would be humiliated if their son became a soldier, joined the army in September 1914 under the false name of Abraham Harris. He also gave a false age, claiming to be eighteen when he was only fifteen. The following spring Beverstein was sent to fight in France, but he was in hospital by the end of the year suffering from shell shock. When he was sent back to the trenches he walked out. 'I felt nervous and lost my head. I thought I'd stay at a farm for a few days and go back to the company when they came out of the trenches,' he wrote in a letter to his parents. Those words condemned him. He was court-martialled and shot for desertion.

The authorities exempted from the forces some naturalized Jewish foreigners, in particular Russians. The Jewish home secretary, Herbert Samuel, understood that Russian Jews would be unable to find much enthusiasm for fighting on the same side as Tsarist Russia, which had been so harsh and unfeeling an oppressor. When the Tsar's regime fell in 1917, the policy changed, and the British authorities presented the 'alien eligibles' with a choice: fight for Britain or return to Russia. Hundreds were taken to Euston, from where they were deported by train, forbidden from taking out of the country 'English gold or intoxicating liquor'.

The Russian Revolution attracted many East End Jews. They saw the new Soviet Union as their saviour, believing that now that they had a political solution to anti-Semitism they no longer needed their religion or nationality. They flocked to the Communist Party, joining trade unions such as the Jewish Furniture Workers' Union, which conducted its business in Yiddish and had its own banner inscribed with Hebrew letters, and the Jewish Bakers' Union, each of whose loaves of rye bread and chollas displayed a little label proudly inscribed: 'Baked by Union Labour'. An end to the sweatshops, casual labour, bad conditions, and low pay was close at hand, it seemed. The Communists would make sure of it . . .

Those who were leading the campaigns against Jewish immigration were the first to condemn Communism as a Jewish plot. A number of the main protagonists *were* Jews, therefore the overthrow of the Tsarist regime became a Jewish plot in the minds of those who wanted it to be. The Revd B. S. Lombard, chaplain to the British forces, told the Foreign Office that when all Russian businesses 'became paralysed and shops closed Jews became possessors of most of the business houses and horrible scenes of starvation became common'. Leo Maxse, the editor of the *National Review*, who back in 1898 had supported Alfred Dreyfuss, the French-Jewish army captain falsely accused of providing military secrets to the Germans, had performed a 180-degree turn by 1919. He was convinced that international Jewry was pulling the strings not only for the revolution, but for the British government: 'Whoever is in power in Downing Street, whether Conservatives, Liberals, Radicals, Coalitionists or pseudo-Bolsheviks, the International Jew rules the roost.'

That year Henry Hamilton Beamish founded the Britons, a London-based society that claimed Jews were engaged in a worldwide conspiracy and were responsible for all wars and revolutions. Membership of the Britons was originally limited to those who could prove their parents or grandparents were 'of British blood', although this was soon changed to allow admittance to 'other branches of the Aryan family'.

The Britons advocated an ingenious solution to the 'Jewish problem': expel the British Jews to a suitable and distant location – if not Palestine then Australia or Madagascar. In August 1922 they set up a publishing company to release vehemently anti-Semitic tracts, in particular *The Protocols of the Meetings of the Learned Elders of Zion*, a supposedly ancient text explaining how throughout history Jews had instigated political movements to hasten a takeover of the world. Jews had, for instance, promoted the French Revolution to usher in liberal democracy, a form of government ideal for Jewish manipulation.

That some Jews, such as Chaim Jacob Samuel Falk, the eighteenth-century *Ba'al Shem* of London and one-time East End resident (see Chapter 6), *had* been involved in the move towards revolution, meant, according to the Protocolers, that *all* Jews were involved. *The Protocols of Zion* was eventually exposed as a fraud dating no further back than 1903, and written in St Petersburg by a Russian mystic, Sergei Nilus. Nevertheless many anti-Semites refused to accept the evidence. They wanted the work to have existed from antiquity. It made more sense.

Meanwhile, a new generation was being born to London's east European immigrant Jews. They knew nothing of Transylvania or the Pale of Settlement, and were keen to put some distance between themselves and their forefathers' backgrounds. Their first move was to leave the East End for the nearby gentile petit-bourgeois suburbs of Dalston, Stamford Hill and Clapton. But those who remained in the East End would discover that no amount of appeasement, anglicization and legislation could protect them if the enemy were intent on destruction.

# 9

# In Darkest London and the
# Way Out

As the metalled roads and iron railways began to obliterate what had been mostly rural land to the east of the City in the early nineteenth century, as huge deep-water docks were cut into the mud banks, and factories and sweatshops were built where there had been fields of grazing sheep and cattle, the East End became darkest London.

Nowhere escaped the gloom. In Bethnal Green, according to John Hollingshead, writing in 1861, the men were 'the lowest kind of thieves, the most ill-disguised class of swell-mobsmen; the women mainly hawkers, sempstresses, the coarsest order of prostitutes'. Mile End, to the east, as Charles Dickens noted in *Uncommercial Traveller*, was 'a poor, busy, and thronged neighbourhood [where] old iron and fried fish, cough drops and artificial flowers, boiled pigs'-feet and household furniture that looked as if it were polished up with lip-salve, umbrellas full of vocal literature and saucers full of shell-fish in a green juice which I hope is natural to them when their health is good, garnish the paved sideways'.

St George's was over-built. Where there should have been a back garden there was often another house or rather a chaos of brick, usually just one storey – little more than a glorified cowshed. Spitalfields was riddled with overcrowding. Beds were let on the three-relay system: one occupant would sleep in it from, say, midnight to eight a.m. Then his or her place would be taken by another, who would lie there from eight to four in the afternoon. When that occupant left the bed would be seized by its third inhabitant for the four to midnight shift. How wonderful to get into a warm bed! And such economy was not the only piece of ingenuity used in allocating residency, for the space underneath the bed would be taken up according to the same system. Notices advertising 'part of a room to let' were commonplace.

By Stepney and the Thames lay Tiger Bay, where the violence, like the name of the locale, was exotic to the point of theatrical. A new magistrate taking over the local bench in the 1850s was shocked to be presented with an ear wrapped in a cabbage leaf which had been bitten off by a man in a fight. 'God bless my soul!' he exclaimed, to incredulous looks from the court. 'It must be a very shocking neighbourhood.'

The worst East End neighbourhood was, by common agreement, Whitechapel. According to Hollingshead, 'The houses present every conceivable aspect of filth and wretchedness; the broken windows are plastered with paper, the faces that peer out of the narrow windows are yellow and repulsive. It should be renamed "Blackchapel", for it overflows with dirt, and misery and rags.'

To Arthur Morrison, writing at the end of the century, Whitechapel was peopled by 'dark, silent, uneasy shadows passing and crossing; human vermin like goblin exhalations from all that is noxious around. Women with sunken, black-rimmed eyes, whose pallid faces appear and vanish by the light of an occasional gas lamp, and look so like ill-covered skulls that we start at their stare.'

An 1888 survey found that Whitechapel contained 233 common lodging-houses, accommodating 8,530 people, and sixty-two brothels. Its streets were patrolled by 1,200 prostitutes, although the true number was probably higher, for many local women resorted to casual prostitution from time to time. By the end of the year the number of local prostitutes had decreased by at least five, the victims of Jack the Ripper, all Whitechapel prostitutes.

With the Industrial Revolution, which brought dirt, squalor and poverty to the East End, came the factory system and a vast new hierarchy of manual workers. Most revered was the skilled craftsman, typically the Huguenot descendant fine-tuning an intricate timepiece in a Spitalfields attic. Next came the skilled artisan: the east European sweatshop machinist or the brewer of Brick Lane. Under them was a host of jobs – prostitution was the most popular – whose skills diminished until they vanished. The less skilled the labourer, the more rigid the demarcation between his job and that of a rival. For example, the casual who worked irregular hours and days in the docks and markets, reliant on the tally of ships pulling into the Port of London or, in the case of the market trader, on the weather, knew he was socially superior to a full-time employee such as the pure-picker who made a living collecting dog turds dropped in the streets. The pure-picker would in turn pour scorn on the bone-picker, who rose at two in the morning – sometimes earlier (was it worth their going to bed?) – leaving the house with a bag on his back and a stick in his hand to turn over the heaps of rubbish thrown out of houses in search of goods worth seizing and selling. And both looked down on the midden men, who ran from house to house collecting buckets of human shit to empty into the sewers.

At least the midden men only did the emptying. The toshers had to wade through the mud at the points where the sewers emptied their contents, on the look out for anything 'interesting' discharged along with the lavatorial waste. They were truly the lowest of the low, barely a social rung above the discharge they were examining. Yet they had their pride. They insisted on dressing in velveteen coats that sported huge pockets, and always went to work suitably equipped, carrying a seven-foot pole with an iron hoe at the end. They travelled in threes or fours, not for moral support, but for the physical strength to withstand attack from the sewer rats that seemed to grow in size every year. Their findings were often lucrative, but the occasional sovereign or necklace could not be counted as guaranteed income, and such riches as appeared were soon converted into pints of porter at the nearest tavern.

## CRIME PAID

There was no such thing as an everyday common criminal in the Victorian East End, and those involved in the various types of scams had their own idiosyncratic names: beak hunters stole chickens; bit fakers made their own coins; bouncers stole from shops, while pretending to make an honest purchase; bug hunters waited outside pubs to rob drunks; buttoners enticed people to play in crooked card games. And those were just the Bs. There were scores of others: nobblers, palmers, smashers, abbesses (women who ran brothels), abbots (the madames' misters), dragsmen (who stole from carriages), shofulmen (who spent bent money) and those who flew the blue pigeon (stole lead from roofs).

At the beginning of the nineteenth century the authorities launched a campaign to wipe out another group of rogues – sharpers, who had obtained pawn-broking licences but were really trading in stolen goods, and their drivers, who would wait in a neighbourhood until a robbery had been completed, and then draw up to spirit away the burglar and his hoard. They also railed against rogue auctioneers holding mock auctions at which attractive-looking rubbish was sold as precious goods with the help of stooges in the audience (puffers), who would raise the stakes by making excessive bids to spur on the gullible, much as still occurs in Oxford Street today.

By 1837 a different kind of menace was terrorizing London. A businessman returning home from work late at night saw what he described as a tall, thin figure with red glowing eyes, large pointy ears and nose spit white and blue flames, and jump some twenty feet into the air to vault the railings of a cemetery. The strange figure was given the nickname 'Spring-heeled Jack'. He was soon being spotted regularly, but in more worrying circumstances. He attacked three women, tearing the top off Polly Adams's blouse, grabbing her breasts and clawing at her stomach. A month later he struck again, this time in Clapham.

In January 1838 the Lord Mayor of London declared him a 'public menace', but Jack was not put off by the mayor's antipathy, and on 20 February he jumped out in front of eighteen-year-old Lucy Scales and her sister Margaret, as they walked through Limehouse, spitting blue fire and blinding Lucy, before jumping from the ground to the roof of a house to escape.

Two days later, on 22 February, another eighteen-year-old East End girl, Jane Alsop, answered the door at her home on Bearhind Lane, Bow, to a black-cloaked man. 'I'm a policeman. For God's sake, bring me a light, for we have caught Spring-heeled Jack.' The girl didn't suspect anything was amiss, as a black cloak was what most policemen wore, but when she gave the caped figure the torch he shone it at her and spat blue and white gas into her face. It was Spring-heeled Jack himself!

As Jane tried to run back into the house, Jack held her tightly by her hair. She was eventually rescued by one of her sisters, and gave police a statement which explained how 'Spring-heeled Jack's hands were as cold as ice and like powerful claws', but that the most frightening thing about him was his eyes, which shone 'like balls of fire'.

The next day Jack was again spotted in the East End, when, 'with glowing orange eyes and clawed hands', he waved his fist at a servant who answered the door of a property on Turner Street, off Commercial Road. The description led police to suspect that Spring-heeled Jack was Henry, Marquis of Waterford, an Irish nobleman known for his cruel sense of humour, and that his leaping feats were accomplished with the aid of springs hidden in his shoes. But as there was no evidence to implicate the Marquis the accusation faded, and the case against him collapsed when the attacks continued after his death following a fall from a horse in 1859. Spring-heeled Jack was last seen in London in 1877, hurdling over several houses. Perturbed locals fired their shotguns at him to no avail; the shots sounded as though they were hitting a metal object.

Criminals and villains could always find sanctuary in a church – except in 1859. That year the Hawksmoor church St George's-in-the-East, where the funerals of the Marrs, victims of the first Ratcliff Highway murders, had taken place in 1811, became the setting for 'No Popery' riots. These broke out after parishioners discovered that the vicar, Bryan King, had co-founded a secret brotherhood for priests, the Society of the Holy Cross. So angry were they at King for indulging in supposed 'Romish practices' that they pelted the altar with bread and butter and orange peel. They also brought in barking dogs to disrupt services, seized the choir stalls, tore down the altar cross and spat on and kicked the clergy. They even urinated on the pews. The mob would have thrown King into the docks had his friends not made a cordon across the dock bridge, enabling him to get to the Mission House safely. The church was forced to close and was allowed to reopen only when King promised to abandon the wearing of vestments, ceremonial robes worn by a priest during mass. Even when services recommenced there were often as many as fifty police officers in the background, ready for trouble.

Some things which should have been criminal were not – at the time. The nefarious activities of the brewers and pub landlords, obsessed with experimenting with the beer, were particularly cynical. A typical East End pint at the time might contain a pinch of foxglove, a plant with large purple flowers and a bitter taste, which taken in quantity induces nausea and giddiness. Or it might include a trace of green copperas, an iron-based compound which gives porter a frothy head and was therefore a must for the enterprising landlord. Other unusual ingredients included hartshorn shavings – the shavings from the horns of the male deer, boiled in the worts of ale – which prevented the beer from going sour (as well as giving off ammonia) and nut galls, the excreta of an insect which attacks trees in Syria and is used to colour the liquor. All sorts of unpalatable substances were added to increase the beer's powers of intoxication: henbane, a mildly poisonous plant that induces delirium, nausea and vomiting; multum, an opium-based mixture; and nux vomica, smell-less seeds of a violent acrid nature. Yet none of these unusual additives ever seemed to dis suade the workers from indulging.

## PLAGUE AND PESTILENCE

Dangerous diseases often arrived in London via the East End. In 1348 locals found themselves covered with black swellings 'about the bigness of a common apple' which oozed blood and pus. They did not realize it at the time, but they had caught the Black Death. Sufferers prayed, wept, gnashed their teeth and pulled their hair. They were treated with blood-letting, boil-lancing and a soak in a bath of vinegar or rose water. They were told to avoid excitement. But they suffered extreme pain none the less and were usually dead within a few days of developing the swellings.

During the Black Death's most virulent period, between Candlemas (2 February) and Easter (12 April), some 200 Londoners died of the disease each day. Their bodies were stacked five deep in visible mass graves, which upset the king, Edward III, who remonstrated with the town council about the sight of so many dead bodies. The council explained that it could do nothing, as all the street cleaners had died of the epidemic. The church was even more mortified by the carnage, as many sinners died without being administered the last rites because priests, fearing contamination, failed to appear to hear confessions, just as lawyers refused to witness wills and parents deserted their children.

There were many theories about why the Black Death had struck. Some cited an Italian earthquake, which had supposedly 'corrupted the air with foul odours'. Others spoke of an unholy alignment of the planets Saturn, Jupiter and Mars in the fortieth degree of Aquarius on 20 March 1345. Whatever the reason – geological, astrological or perhaps purely bacteriological – around a third of Britain's 6 million population died of the Black Death in 1349.

A pestilence more savage even than the Black Death – Bubonic Plague – attacked the East End in the 1660s. It reached London in December 1664, when a group of Flemish weavers in Holborn opened a parcel of clothes imported from Holland. The parcel contained fleas that live off black rats, which had survived in the wrapped warmth, and the fleas contained the bacteria that causes Bubonic Plague. Soon after a doctor was called out to treat a young man who had 'two Risings about the bigness of a nutmeg on each thigh'. Before long the man and his neighbours were covered in small black growths – bubos – in the armpits and groin. Once the bacteria had taken root they travelled to the liver, spleen, kidneys, lungs and brain. This induced in the victims shivers, terrible headaches and vomiting, produced a white coating on the tongue and led to broken blood vessels which turned the skin black.

Although physicians did not know what caused the plague, they realized it was contagious and protected themselves by wearing a suit that sported a large and grotesque beaked headpiece containing sweet oils to nullify the stench of the dying victims. People believed they could ward off the plague by inserting a clove of garlic or a piece of rue, the herb of grace, in their mouth. They thought it could be cured by washing the head in vinegar or by sitting next to a blazing fire, as the Pope had demonstrated successfully in 1348. They tried remedies such as holding mercury in a walnut shell, dangling a toad on a leather string, or taking up the advice of the fourteenth-century surgeon Guy de Chauliac, who explained how the swellings could be softened by figs and cooked onions mixed with yeast and butter.

Alas, these weren't cures, and barely worked as placebos, so it was just as well that the affliction did not last long and death was swift, though agonizing.

By the nineteenth century the Black Death and the Bubonic Plague were ancient history. Now there was a new deadly disease – cholera. It came from India in 1817, spread to Russia six years later, and arrived in east London in 1832. In a land marked by dunghills, cesspits and an open sewer called the Black Ditch that ran from Spitalfields in the west to Limehouse in the east, cholera was able to spread easily. It thrived in the local water – not that people realized this – a problem which was exacerbated by the fact that the water companies took their supply either directly from the infected rivers or from standing pipes in the street, the water from which tasted fresher but was equally infected.

Those who drank water containing the cholera bacterium, vibrio, contracted a mild fever, which usually cleared within a week. But the poison produced by the bacterium caused diarrhoea, and that could prove fatal if the sick person did not guard against dehydration by drinking vast quantities of water. Physicians, unaware of this, tried to *restrict* fluid intake in their treatment, thereby aggravating the condition. One doctor explained:

Cholera was something outlandish, unknown, monstrous. Its tremendous ravages long foreseen and feared, its insidious march over whole continents, its apparent defiance of all the known and conventional precautions against the spread of epidemic disease invested it with a mystery and a terror which thoroughly took hold of the public mind and seemed to recall the memory of the great epidemics of the Middle Ages.

Some blamed the outbreak of the disease on a political faction opposed to parliamentary reform. Others claimed the epidemic had been spread by drug shops profiting from sales of Anti-Cholera Peruvian Tonic Drops and Asiatic Anti-Pestilential Essence, medicines based mostly on brandy. The first East End cholera victim was a sailor who had arrived from Sunderland on a collier. He was taken ill with vomiting and cramps and sent to the Shadwell workhouse where instead of recovering he died. After the post-mortem a twenty-inch length of his intestines was extracted and given to the parish beadle to take to the Central Board of Health at Whitehall. But the beadle's journey was in vain. The inquest, held at the George and Dragon public house on Ratcliff Highway, had already found that 'the deceased had died by the visitation of God, from natural causes, and not from Cholera'.

Those who were not convinced that political, pharmaceutical or divine intervention was responsible formed boards of health to deal with the epidemic. Poplar's was the busiest. It kept a free supply of brushes, buckets and unslaked lime at the Town Hall for people to borrow if they wished to clean up the overflowing cesspits and stagnant pools, and remove the pig faeces that could be found in most backyards.

Typical of Poplar's victims was 53-year-old Elizabeth Connolly, who first felt unwell on 17 February 1832, a day after eating a dinner of ox's cheek. Connolly blamed her malady on having eaten meat for the first time in a week, and at lunchtime went to a shop to buy some herring. As she returned home she had an attack of diarrhoea, which forced her to beg the use of a stranger's house. She never made it back home, continued vomiting until 5 p.m., when the doctor was called, and was taken to the workhouse where a hot-air bath, emetic, enema and brandy failed to prevent her dying.

It was often hard to tell what was a dose of influenza, cholera in its early stages or chronic food poisoning, as food adulteration was common, particularly the practice of adding alum to brown bread to make it look white, which was banned. When it *was* cholera the authorities weren't particularly helpful. The London Hospital refused to admit anyone who was infected. But this unchristian act, rather than causing resentment, was welcomed by many locals, for there was a fear among East Enders that admission into hospital would not lead to a place in a bed but to a spot on a slab under the dissectors' knife, such was the demand for corpses. The Central Board of Health demanded that the bodies of cholera victims be wrapped in a tar-soaked blanket and their coffins filled with lime to make the bodies unsuitable for dissection. An East End mob even attacked a hospital, threatening to destroy the building and murder the surgeon for 'Burking' the patients – killing them for their body parts in the fashion of the bodysnatchers Burke and Hare.

At the height of the epidemic the government announced that 21 March 1832 would be a National Day of Fasting and Prayer, as 'the disease was proof of the judgement of God among us'. Some pointed out that a fast was unnecessary in an area where people were already starving, and so the National Union of Working Classes asked for the day to be changed from one of fasting to one of *feasting*.

Debate continued to rage over the cause of the disease. Many, including Florence Nightingale, believed it was induced by a 'miasma' in the atmosphere, until a Soho surgeon, John Snow, convinced the authorities that contaminated water was responsible. But Parliament took action only when the Thames outside the Palace of Westminster began to reek so pungently during the hot dry summer of 1858 that MPs were able to carry on their business only after hanging disinfectant-soaked cloths over the windows.

Desperate to eradicate the problem, the government commissioned Joseph Bazalgette, chief engineer to the Metropolitan Board of Works, to build sewers and drains. Bazalgette constructed an eighty-two-mile network of sewers for London, lined with special bricks, Staffordshire Blues, baked to extremely high temperatures to make them more durable.

The sewers took waste and rainwater to treatment plants at Plumstead, south-east London, and Beckton, in the Essex wastelands, beyond the East End, in pipes which in central London were buried out of sight below the pavement, emerging in Wick Lane, Bow, at the edge of the East End. From there to Beckton the pipe runs at ground level, in what is now a landscaped walk, and has been used by countless hikers, most famously the Indian leader Mahatma Gandhi, who took lengthy strolls along it in 1931 while he was staying in Bow during the talks about India's independence.

The sewers worked. Cholera soon vanished from those parts of London that were connected to Bazalgette's system, and when the disease returned in 1866 only to Whitechapel, which was not connected, the public were convinced that sophisticated drainage obstructed its spread. Indeed it was the last cholera epidemic London suffered.

## THE BLACKEST HELL – THE OLD NICHOL

The English social system allowed anyone – Huguenot, Jew, German, Irish Catholic, Highlander, Chinese, Negro, Indian – to live anywhere, earn anything, be anyone. Successive swathes of immigrants knew this and swarmed to London, in most cases arriving in the East End to seek political protection, economic betterment or simply the chance to feed off the scraps of the world's most dynamic empire.

No matter what privations they endured to survive, immigrants knew that in the East End, despite the everyday indiscriminate violence and the all-pervading destitution, there were no secret police, no pogroms, no restrictive laws on liberty and little religious persecution. They also knew that future generations would be able to reap the benefits of their labour, most obviously by living in a more pleasant part of the capital.

But what of those who were indigenous to the locale? Those who knew no other home? For them, the English, no end appeared to be in sight to the overcrowding, the dark stairways, the broken windows, the filth, vermin and crime. And nowhere in the East End of the nineteenth century was overrun with these problems to a greater extent than the Old Nichol.

A parish of 8,000 people and seventeen pubs but no church, set around Old Nichol Street to the immediate east of Shoreditch, the area suffered from a death rate four times the national average. It had once provided the workforce that kept the Spitalfields silk industry going. 'Here they are born, live and labour, and die. They neither migrate nor change their occupation; they can do nothing else,' wrote the diarist Charles Greville. But by the early nineteenth century silk was dying and more than a thousand locals had been confined to the poorhouse, five or six in a bed.

To the East End novelist Arthur Morrison the Old Nichol was 'the blackest pit in London'. The *Daily Graphic* claimed it had a 'worse reputation than any other neighbourhood in London'. The *Illustrated London News* went further, damning the place as

a neighbourhood as foul as can be discovered in the civilized world, [its] population, huddled in dark cellars, ruined garrets, bare and blackened rooms, teeming with disease and death, and without the most ordinary observations of decency or cleanliness, depressed almost to the last stage of human endurance.

The locals ate mostly offal – cow-heels, bullocks' hearts, kidneys, livers, tripe and sheep's heads – enlivened by the occasional black pudding or faggot. Indeed, it was as close to being a totally non-vegetarian diet as any creature outside the cat family could endure, consisting of meat, meat and more meat. Sure there were vegetables in the shops, but who wanted to bother with potatoes or peas if there was a saveloy to munch?

Housing conditions were intolerable. Hector Gavin conducted an investigation into East End life in 1848, published as *Sanitary Ramblings*, and found dwellings 'constructed in defiance of every law and principle on which the health and lives of the occupants depend'. The decaying cottages, often built below pavement level and oblivious to the sun, had been stuck on the ground with scarcely any foundations. They were liable to flooding and were prolific sources of disease. There were no sinks or toilets, and outside were rubbish tips made of dung, decomposing cabbage leaves and animal remains, which congealed with the wet soil to form a foetid mass of putrescence.

A survey conducted by *The Builder* magazine in 1863 found that the party wall between Nos. 20 and 21 Old Nichol Street bulged to such an extent, its brickwork so fractured, that it looked as if it might fall down at any moment. In each of half a dozen rooms at No. 20 lived a married couple with six or seven children, and in the basement there was a mound of dust that had not been removed for fourteen years. Water came from a small tub without a lid, and because there was no efficient drainage to take away the waste, the basements were soaked with pools of stagnant water, which also collected in the yards.

Worse was an underground room at No. 59 Old Nichol Street, where the reporter from *The Builder*, peering through the narrow space of the window eventually managed to make out through the gloom and polluted atmosphere two figures on a broken truckle, naked except for some black rags – and this at noon. Inside he found plaster fallen from the walls and ceilings, a narrow staircase which had become rotten and shaky, and damp refuse piled up against the wall.

The Old Nichol had long suffered from the worst crime rate in London. In 1826 the authorities petitioned the home secretary, Robert Peel, founder of the Metropolitan Police, to suppress the 'dreadful riots' being perpetrated by a lawless local gang of some 500 thieves, whose exploits were causing much alarm. On market days the gang would lie in wait for the cow-boys marshalling cattle from the Home Counties' farms to the meat markets, capture a beast or two, and hide them in the marshes. They would then slaughter the animals and cook the meat with a few boiled potatoes, mostly plundered from local shops, in the open air, so fearless were they of the authorities.

Their confidence unassailable, the gang eventually turned to more serious robbery, attacking a couple in a chaise on Bethnal Green Road, robbing and beating them, and cutting the reins of their carriage to prevent pursuit. Only when a squad of forty officers was sent to the area did the trouble abate. But it was no surprise that things had gone that far. For decades the leading local JP was the notoriously corrupt Joseph Merceron, who filled the various parish offices with members of his family, and was jailed for fraud in 1818.

In 1831 the Old Nichol was in the news again when two local men, John Bishop and his brother-in-law, Thomas Head, abducted Carlo Ferrari, a fourteen-year-old Italian boy who made his living exhibiting performing mice. They forced him to drink rum laced with laudanum, which swiftly brought on unconsciousness, and then drowned him in a nearby well. When Bishop and Head tried to sell the body to surgeons at King's College, the police were called. They arrested the pair, who were convicted and hanged at Newgate in front of a crowd of 30,000 people.

Bishop and Head were just two Old Nichol hoodlums. Scores more were involved with the Old Nichol gang, who specialized in forcing protection money out of prostitutes. They used as bait local girls who would charm the targeted victims and convince them to hand over a percentage of their earnings by following their example, which involved little more than one Old Nichol girl handing some money to her brother.

The Old Nichol gang was blamed for the violent murder of

prostitute Emma Smith on Easter Monday 1888, the first such incident in the year of Jack the Ripper. Later, when the Old Nichol was razed, the surrounding area, Bethnal Green, took up its underworld status, specializing in 'villains' – those who rely on intimidation or run protection rackets. Skills in villainy and wrongdoing were handed down zealously from father to son, from mother to daughter, from brother to brother – a state of affairs which reached its peak in the 1960s with the locally based Krays.

In the 1880s a saviour came to the Old Nichol in the shape of the Revd Osborn Jay, whose dynamism and selflessness tore into the status quo. Jay opened a working men's club in a cheese and bacon warehouse, where locals could sing, box and play cards or dominoes. Despite the Old Nicholians' initial scepticism there were soon 500 members.

Finding that the district had no church, Revd Jay took over a row of stables as a place of worship, and raised the money to build Holy Trinity. He wanted to civilize the locals by providing a moral foundation to their lives through the church. Services were crowded every Sunday, as were the Sunday Schools. Mothers' meetings held on Tuesday and Thursday afternoons attracted 600 members. A mission house was built, with two large halls, committee rooms and a bathroom where mothers could wash their children. And next to it was a lodging-house, where a man could get a clean bed and his own cubicle.

In the mid 1890s Jay received help from an unlikely quarter, the writer Arthur Morrison, whose *Tales of the Mean Streets* (1894), a collection of short stories about life for the ordinary East Ender, had impressed him. The reverend wrote to Morrison, praising the accuracy of his East End descriptions, and adding that in the Old Nichol life was rougher than he had portrayed it in the *Tales*. He invited Morrison to the area, who, as a result, began writing a novel-cum-dramatized documentary that would bring the plight of the Nichol to a wider audience.

Morrison called his new work *A Child of the Jago* in honour of Jay, sympathetically recast in the book as Father Sturt. By the time it appeared, the county council had begun to clear the area. They demolished the tenements of crime and despair, and built model flats on wide new streets radiating from the open space of Arnold Circus, with its bandstand and elevated setting above the slurry of Shoreditch. Ironically, redevelopment created fresh problems, for little care was taken to rehouse the displaced tenants while it was being rebuilt, and when the new Nichol was ready few who had suffered in the Old Nichol could afford the rents. But at least one problem had been solved; some light now poured into darkest London.

## THE ABYSS – FLOWER AND DEAN STREET

Once the Old Nichol had been razed, the search was on for London's new hell hole. The obvious choice was the territory around Flower and Dean Street, a claustrophobic and overpopulated estate on the Spitalfields/Whitechapel boundary, known as the 'evil quarter-mile'. It was a favourite haunt of prostitutes, of whom there were over a thousand in Whitechapel, working in more than sixty brothels, and was where the Pre-Raphaelite artist Ford Madox Ford placed the home of his ragged wretch in *Work*, his epic canvas of 1863.

To Arthur Morrison, debunker of the Old Nichol, Flower and Dean was 'black and noisome, the road sticky with slime, dark, silent, uneasy shadows passing and crossing, [peopled] by human vermin and women with sunken, black-rimmed eyes'. J. Ewing Ritchie, researching *Days and Nights in London* (1880), found every Flower and Dean property to be a lodging-house, holding as many as 400 beds (those with a bed were the lucky ones; some had to sleep leaning over a rope). The men, 'unshaven and unwashed', played pitch and toss. The women, 'who have sunk exhausted in the battle of life, and who come here to hide their wretchedness and shame, were covered with filth, innocent of all social virtues, and robbery, drunkenness, fighting and midnight brawls were the regular and normal state of affairs'.

Being a resident of the Flower and Dean Street neighbourhood could be a precarious business. All five 'official' victims of Jack the Ripper, murdered in 1888, lived in or had connections with this collection of streets. Yet if that year marked the nadir in the area's fortunes, it was also the year in which major improvements to the neighbourhood were made. The increasing number of immigrant Jews moving into the locale led the Board of Guardians for the Relief of the Jewish Poor to take action. Lord Rothschild, the unofficial leader of Anglo-Jewry, formed a company to build cheap tenement dwellings that would provide its shareholders with a reasonable dividend – 4 per cent – from the rent. What became the Four Per Cent Industrial Dwellings Company built Rothschild Dwellings to replace the mid-Victorian slums. The new block opened in April 1887 and was a considerable improvement on the previous housing. The company bought further chunks of Flower and Dean Street in 1891, demolished more of the slums, and built new blocks of flats aimed at newly married couples, most – but not all – of whom were Jewish.

By the time the American writer Jack London arrived in Flower and Dean Street in 1902, on a fact-finding mission that resulted in the book *The People of the Abyss*, the area had improved so much it was by then a respectable slum. When London, who wrote in the social realist style later perfected by George Orwell, told friends who lived in more respectable parts of the capital that he was coming here their response was swift and dismissive: 'You can't do it, you know. You had better see the police for a guide.'

Undeterred, he headed for the intrepid travel firm Thomas Cook, 'path-finders and trail-clearers, living sign-posts to all the world and bestowers of first aid to bewildered travellers'. He entered Cook's Cheapside branch in the City of London but found they were keener on darkest Africa and innermost Tibet than the Stygian wastes of Stepney. A clerk begged the American not to attempt the journey. 'We are not accustomed to taking travellers to the East End; we receive no call to take them there, and we know nothing whatsoever about the place at all. It is so – hem – so unusual. Consult the police.'

London explained to the man that he wanted to make him aware of his plans in case of trouble. 'Ah, I see,' responded the assistant, 'should you be murdered, we would be in position to identify the corpse.'

Nonplussed, London ventured outside and hailed a cab, instructing the driver to drive him down to the East End.

'Where, sir?' he demanded with frank surprise.

'To the East End, anywhere. Go on.'

The hansom pursued an aimless way for several minutes, then came to a puzzled stop. The cabman peered down perplexedly at me.

'I say,' he said, 'wot plyce yer wanter go?'

'East End,' I repeated. 'Nowhere in particular. Just drive me around anywhere.'

'But wot's the haddress, sir?'

'See here!' I thundered. 'Drive me down to the East End, and at once!'

Eventually the cabbie complied, possibly following Arthur Morrison's injunction that the East End is 'down through Cornhill and out beyond Leadenhall Street and Aldgate Pump'. Once inside the impenetrable eastern underworld, Jack London found streets filled with a new and different race of people, 'short of stature, and of wretched or beer-sodden appearance, [and] the air obscene with sounds of jangling and squabbling'. Alighting at Stepney station, he found an old clothes shop where he exchanged his American attire for something less conspicuous – 'a pair of stout though well-worn trousers, a frayed jacket with one remaining button, a pair of brogans which had plainly seen service where coal was shovelled, a thin leather belt and a very dirty cloth cap'.

London returned to civilization (friends in respectable, suburban Highbury Vale), had dinner, and there transformed himself into a typical East Ender, sewing into the armpit of his stoker's singlet a gold sovereign for emergencies. He then went back to the netherworld. All servility had vanished from the demeanour of the common people; inconspicuous in his new mufti, he had become one of them. Foreshadowing George Orwell twenty-five years later, London was able for the first time 'to meet the English lower classes face to face, and know them for what they were'. Like Margaret Harkness, author of *In Darkest London*, he was shocked to find people starving. 'It is only in the civilized world that men starved. Among the tribes who lived on the banks of the Yukon River everyone shared out what little they had; no one starved alone, either everyone was fed or everyone starved.'

He went to the workhouse, the only means of survival for the poorest, where he was given a loaf of bread which felt more like a brick (you were meant to dip it into water and then rub it in the salt spread over the tables before eating), searched for knives, matches and tobacco (all forbidden) and given a canteen of Indian corn and hot water, which his stomach could not take. At bath time men entered the water in pairs. When they got out another pair jumped in, the water remaining unchanged, even though, as the writer pointed out, one man's back was a 'mass of blood from attacks of vermin and retaliatory scratching'.

London fell asleep at around midnight but soon woke to find a rat on his chest. After a fitful night reveille at 6 a.m. was a relief. Breakfast was skilly (a thin porridge flavoured with meat), followed by the first labours of the day: pounding stone into dust. He came upon great numbers of unemployed men marching in procession through the streets crying for bread, besieging the Salvation Army's headquarters. Unable to take any more of this horror he fled, only to find outside Hawksmoor's Christ Church Spitalfields 'a mass of miserable and distorted humanity, the sight of which would have impelled Doré to more diabolical flights of fancy than he ever succeeded in achieving. It was a welter of rags and filth, of all manner of loathsome skin diseases, open sores, bruises, grossness, indecency, leering monstrosities, and bestial faces' – mostly women, who would sell themselves for a few pennies or a loaf of stale bread.

London later returned to his investigations. This time he was escorted around the streets of the East End by a carter and a carpenter who kept their eyes down as they walked and talked, stopping now and then to pick something up from the pavement. He thought they must have found a cigar or cigarette butt, but later noticed that they were picking up bits of orange peel, apple skin, grape stems, stray bits of bread the size of peas and apple cores 'so black and dirty one would not take them to be apple cores, and swallowed them – and this, between six and seven o'clock in the evening of August 20, year of our Lord 1902, in the heart of the greatest, wealthiest, and most powerful empire the world has ever seen'.

## SAUCY WINKS AND BLUE CHEESE

What passed for entertainment in this den of depravity? There was a fascination in the East End for the macabre, the bizarre, the ridiculous.

In 1884 John Merrick, the so-called Elephant Man, who suffered from neurofibromatosis, a disorder of the lymphatic system that severely disfigured him, was kept in a cage in the window of a shop at 159 Whitechapel Road and made to act like a dog to entice people inside to see a freak show, until he was rescued from his plight by Dr Treves of the London Hospital.

More sophisticated were the penny gaffes where for a 1d entrance fee entertainment was provided by hairy men, hairless dogs, gorillas, Aztecs and giants. But most typical of the character of the East End was the music hall, the repository for anything that did not fit into the established categories: song and dance, tragedy and comedy, low culture and base crassness.

The music hall arose from the tavern and coffee house of the eighteenth century, where performers sang while customers ate, drank or joined in. By the 1830s many taverns had rooms devoted to musical entertainment. Here acts performed amid incessant audience chatter and were subjected to missiles ranging from bottles to dead cats. Soon, the theatre taverns were supplanted by purpose-built halls. London's first was the Canterbury, which opened in Lambeth, south of the Thames, not the East End, in 1852. But it wasn't long before the high streets of east London filled with similar venues – the Paragon Theatre of Varieties in Mile End Road, the Cambridge on Commercial Street, the Queen's in Poplar and the Eastern Empire in Bow.

The grandest was Wilton's on Wellclose Square, built into what had been the Prince of Denmark tavern in 1858 by John and Ellen Wilton. It is now the only surviving music hall in London and film set *extraordinaire*, where Tom Cruise and Brad Pitt filmed *Interview with the Vampire*. The Wiltons wanted to compete with the West End theatres, and so they fitted the hall with private boxes, mahogany furnishings and plush carpets. The walls were covered with mirrors, and from the ceiling hung a chandelier made from 27,000 cut crystals. There was a dedication to 'Great Apollo, God of early morn/Who wakes the song of birds from Eastern sky' and a roster of acts that had played 'proper' theatres, rather than just music halls. But Wellclose Square was not St James's Square. Wilton's attracted few respectable folk and its audience, as described by James Greenwood in *Music Hall*

*Luminaries*, was mostly women, 'wild-eyed, boisterous, with cheeks red with rouge and flabby with intemperance, all alike equally coarse, and insolent, and unlovely in manners and appearance', and sailors so saturated with drink they could not remember whether they were still on board ship, were sailing on an ocean of mild and bitter, or had already drowned in a sea of porter.

The bill differed little from venue to venue. Most nights the first act, advertised without any trace of irony or calumny, would be a 'nigger minstrel'. He would be followed by a comic singer – perhaps 'the Inimitable Brown' or 'the Irresistible Smith' – singing about how 'She shoved me right bang into a dish of fried Dutch plaice/Took hold of a bowl of butter, and threw it in my face'. There would then be a clog-dancer, sword-swallower and some flying children. By this time the rough types in the pit would be drowning out the repertory with piercing whistles. But they would hush momentarily for the farce, specially if billed with the grand rider: 'licensed by the Lord Chamberlain expressly for this theatre'.

During the course of the evening twenty to thirty songs would be sung, mostly patriotic numbers proclaiming the virtues of John Bull, 'gentle and kind/a better friend you'll never find', or love songs in which 'the girls, oh! the girls, and the boys, yes, the boys!/You'll find them together in all sorts of weather/They go kiss, kiss – yes! they go kiss, kiss!/And they squeeze, and they spoon, and they say, "Oh, what joys!"'

Occasionally a comic masterpiece would appear from this mawkish nonsense. It warmed the public, even those who would never be seen within a curtain call of a music hall, to know that somewhere in London someone had sat down to compose a song as ingenious as 'Waiting at the Church' or 'A Nice Quiet Day'.

In 'Waiting at the Church' Vesta Victoria sings of her expected betrothal to Obadiah Binks (how could she have trusted a man with such a name?) which is dashed when the cad fails to turn up at the service: 'There was I, waiting at the church, waiting at the church, waiting at the church/When I found he'd left me in the lurch/Lor, how it did upset me!' Binks had kindly sent a note ('Here's the very note/This is what he wrote') in which the rotter explains: 'Can't get away to marry you today/My wife won't let me!'

Gus Elen's 'A Nice Quiet Day' tells a story that all hard-working folk with a skeleton in the family closet could relate to: 'There was me and the missus and me half a dozen kids/With nothing in the bottle but the bung/But I gave the kids a treat/When we got to me old street/ 'Cause I showed them where their uncle, he was hung.'

The main East End music-hall stars were Charles Coborn, Dan Leno and Marie Lloyd. Coborn's success rested on just two songs; but what songs! 'Two Lovely Black Eyes', which was a hit in 1886, achieved the impossible – it captured Bethnal Green in lyrical form – and even impressed the notoriously unmusical George Orwell, who noted how 'there are music-hall songs [such as 'Two Lovely Black Eyes'] which are better poems than three-quarters of the stuff that gets into the anthologies'.

Five years later Coborn chanced upon an even smarter song, one of great drama, wit and movement. It revolved around the story of Charles Deville Wells, an English gambler who had arrived in Monte Carlo in July 1891 and after eleven hours gambling at roulette turned his stake of 100,000 francs into 250,000. Despite a few losses, Wells recovered and went on to break the bank a dozen times, winning half a million francs.

The songwriter Fred Gilbert turned the tale of the man who broke the bank at Monte Carlo into song and offered it to Coborn, who turned him down. Coborn later had second thoughts, and, after spending a day mulling over the chorus ('As I walk along the Bois Boulogne/With an independent air/You can hear the girls declare/He must be a millionaire!'), he realized the song's worth and desperately sought out Gilbert, handing him £10 for it. In his recording Coborn cleverly conveyed with each verse and chorus the slurring speech of somebody becoming increasingly drunk on the proceeds of his newly found wealth, creating a comic masterpiece. Unfortunately, he sold the copyright for £600, a fraction of what he and his estate, let alone Gilbert and his estate, could have earned.

Dan Leno, born George Galvin, 'a mere child', as he later claimed, was performing a routine with his uncle at the age of nine which ran: 'I once had an I.O.U.'/'So had I, but now I've only got U left.'/'Yes! Poor I. O. died.'/'What did I. O. die of?'/'Don't you know? Iodide of potassium.' Later on stage, recalling how his St Pancras birthplace, Eve

Court, was bulldozed to build the Midland Railway station, he would ask philosophically: 'Ah! What is man? Wherefore does he why? Whence did he whence? Whither is he withering? Then the guard yelled out: "Leicester, Derby, Nottingham, Manchester, Liverpool."'

Dan Leno was more than just a comic. He was champion clog-dancer of the world, a title he won at the Princess Music Hall, Leeds. Formidable at the most complex steps, shuffles, twizzles and taps, he boasted of being able to put 'more beats into sixteen bars of music than a drummer can with his drumsticks'. But when Leno made his adult London debut at Forester's Music Hall, Mile End, the clog-dancing bombed – it was, after all, 200 miles south of the clog-dancing border near Rochdale – and he had to rely on his songs to win over the London crowds.

Leno could not handle success, and used to drink himself into a stupor. In 1902 he began to go insane, writing contracts for the bits and pieces members of the company on scraps of paper and handing wads of notes to the paperboys in Haymarket. He died of a brain tumour on 31 October 1904. Max Beerbohm described him as a man 'unlike anyone else we had ever seen. That face so tragic, with all the tragedy that is writ on the face of a baby monkey, yet ever liable to relax its mouth into a sudden wide grin and to screw up its eyes to vanishing point over some little triumph wrested from fate.'

The brightest music-hall star was Marie Lloyd, whose songs captured the bittersweet frailties of east London life, its presumed violence and malevolence, its fidelity and honesty – an existence that teetered between outright poverty and muddling through. Born in 1870 as Matilda Victoria Wood in Hoxton, just outside the East End, she achieved her first triumph in her mid teens with 'The Boy I Love Is up in the Gallery', sung in a schoolgirl outfit she used throughout her career. By the 1890s she was playing pantomime at Drury Lane.

Lloyd captivated audiences with her saucy winks and asides (if her parasol failed to open she would quip, 'I haven't had it up for ages'), but not Mrs Ormiston Chant of the Purity Party, who forced her to appear in 1896 before the Vigilance Committee and was more shocked when she charmed them with a performance of unimaginable innocence. Her act twisted and turned on innuendo. A typical Marie

Lloyd number, 'She Sits among Her Cabbages and Peas' appears innocent to the point of blandness until the title is spoken out loud.
Because of her support for the performers during the music-hall strike
she was overlooked for the first Royal Command Performance in
1912 and defaced the show's posters with: 'Every Performance by
Marie Lloyd is a Command Performance' and 'By Order of the British
Public'. While appearing at Edmonton in 1922 she staggered about on
the stage to the delight of the audience who thought it was part of the
act. Three days later, on 7 October, she died.

## THE PHILANTHROPISTS

The Victorian century that threw up the nightmare that was the East
End also provided its would-be saviours: Samuel and Henrietta
Barnett, Thomas Barnardo, William Booth, Angela Burdett Coutts
and Frederick Charrington.

When the Revd Samuel Barnett took up a post at St Jude's,
Whitechapel, in 1873 the Bishop of London warned him and his wife,
Henrietta, that Whitechapel was the 'worst district in London, containing a large population of Jews and thieves'. The Barnetts were
pleased. Its dismal, dark alleyways, crowded tenements, filthy ver-
minous lodging-houses and population of prostitutes, beggars and
hawkers seemed to be just the sort of thing they were looking for.
They could not make people richer, but they felt they could ease
suffering by stimulating the intellect. They organized mind-improving
lectures, adult education and art exhibitions, opened clubs for girls to
keep them away from prostitution and held summer evening dances
that occasionally descended into what Henrietta described as
'Bacchanalian scenes'.

The Barnetts believed indiscriminate charity to be among the curses
of London as it meant the poor never learned to work or save. Instead
they wanted the wealthy to come and live among the poor, 'to learn
as much as to teach; to receive as much as to give'. With this in mind
they opened a settlement – Toynbee Hall – in 1884. It had sixteen full-
time live-in settlers working among the East End poor to improve
adult education, housing and health.

Toynbee Hall was built to look like an Oxford college. The lecture hall was full nearly every evening for talks on history, physiology, astronomy and English literature. There was also a room used by mind-improving societies such as the Adam Smith Club, the East London Antiquarian Society and the Toynbee Shakespeare Club. Well-spoken, well-educated young men, burning with plans for social reform, flocked there. Among them were Richard Tawney, who arrived in 1903 and helped found the Workers' Education Association; William Beveridge, who arrived at the hall the same year and played a central role in the creation of the Welfare State in the 1940s; and Clement Attlee, post-war Labour prime minister, who implemented the Beveridge-inspired National Health Service. Toynbee Hall became the model for a world-wide movement, inspiring an American woman, Jane Addams, who had been a visitor, to open the similar Hull House in Chicago in 1887. In 1931 she became the first American woman to win the Nobel Peace Prize.

Thomas Barnardo came to the East End in 1866 during a cholera epidemic to study medicine at the London Hospital. He harboured hopes of becoming a missionary in China, but first opened a school at Hope Place, Limehouse. As he was locking up one night, he spotted a dishevelled shoeless boy in the street. Barnardo told him to go home but the lad replied, 'Home? I don't live nowhere, sir.' Barnardo enquired about the wretch's father and mother – he had neither – and, when he asked if there were any more boys like him, was told, 'Yes, sir, loads of 'em, more than I can count.' He took Barnardo to the back of some offices by the City where they found eleven more unfortunates sleeping on a tin roof.

The would-be missionary abandoned the Far East for the immediate east. He sought the help of the philanthropist Lord Shaftesbury, who was sceptical about the level of deprivation Barnardo claimed to have encountered, but went with him to see for himself. In an alleyway near Billingsgate fish market they saw a naked foot peeping out from under some tarpaulin covering a pile of crates. Soon, the entire tarpaulin began to move; no fewer than seventy-three children were found to be sleeping there in abominable conditions. Shaftesbury was mortified and announced, 'All London shall know about this.'

In 1872 Barnardo opened a home for destitute children at 18 Stepney Causeway. He drew up a balance sheet for each charge: 'Bread, water, shame, flogging; cost per young criminal in prison, £80 per annum for all the term of a lost life. Meat, bread, honour, the Bible, Christian teaching; cost in a Christian workshop and training home, and then emigration, £19 once and for all.' Barnardo selected the 'flowers of the flock' and sent them to the empty plains of Manitoba. 'They have no family responsibilities to handicap them. They are decent, honest and industrious.'

Not everyone was impressed. Detractors spread dark rumours about his homes: that his charges were underfed and mistreated; that the photographs of starved children, which Barnardo released to elicit support, were faked; that he was embezzling funds. Barnardo set up an independent board of enquiry. It absolved him of misplacing money or mistreating children, but found him guilty of doctoring photographs and keeping the boys in solitary cells. To avoid further criticism he enlisted trustees to help him oversee the homes. Public support returned, and by the end of the 1880s Barnardo was running twenty-five homes, as well as a hospital in Stepney, and had raised over 3 million pounds.

More thunderous in his Christianity than the Barnetts, more evangelical than Barnardo, was William Booth, a tall, white-faced, dark-eyed, fierce-looking revivalist preacher who sported a long black beard over his chest. In 1849 Booth moved to London and drew up a personal code of conduct which read:

I do promise – my God helping – that I will rise every morning sufficiently early (say twenty minutes before seven o'clock) to wash, dress, and have a few minutes, not less than five, in private prayer. That I will as much as possible avoid all that babbling and idle talking in which I have lately so sinfully indulged. That I will endeavour in my conduct and deportment before the world and my fellow servants especially to conduct myself as a humble, meek, and zealous follower of the bleeding Lamb.

Despite, or perhaps because of, these strictures, Booth became prone to black moods of despair and was tempted to give up preaching altogether. One evening in June 1865 he heard two missionaries holding an open-air meeting outside the Blind Beggar public house in

Whitechapel invite any Christian bystander to join them. Booth did so and told them that 'there is heaven in East London for everyone who will stop to think and look to Christ as a personal saviour'. He told them of the love of God in offering salvation through Jesus Christ in terms so clear they invited him to take charge of a special mission tent they were holding nearby. A year later Booth's mission had over sixty converts. His wife Catherine said that he was stumbling home 'night after night haggard with fatigue', 'his clothes torn and bloody, bandages swathing his head where a stone had struck'.

Booth relied more on 'visions' – images of fire and brimstone – than on theology. He preached passionately across the East End, surrounded by what a supporter called 'blaspheming infidels and boisterous drunkards', condemning the usual vices – drinking, gambling, watching cricket and football – anything that people enjoyed which could lead to unchristian behaviour.

In 1878 he reorganized the mission along quasi-military lines as the Salvation Army, with preachers fighting for Jesus given ranks such as major and captain, and Booth himself cast as the General. The Salvation Army's banner in red, blue and gold sported a sun symbol and the motto 'Blood and Fire', the blood being the blood of Christ and the fire that of the Holy Spirit.

The marching bands of the Salvation Army began marching into town 'to do Battle with the Devil and his Hosts and make a Special Attack on his territory'. Their services provided the model for what became known disparagingly in the following century as 'happy clappy' – joyous singing, Hallelujahs, beseeching for repentance, the clapping of hands. Evil-doers and lost souls flocked to repent, even when the organization's enemies, the so-called 'Skeleton Army', marching under a skull and crossbones banner, attempted to drive them off the streets. Occasionally Booth's Salvation Army met naked evil. In Whitechapel a group of Army women were captured by the heathen, roped together and pelted with burning coals.

Within ten years Booth commanded 3,000 corps and 10,000 full-time officers, and had opened branches in Iceland, Argentina and Germany. By the time he died the Salvation Army had spread to fifty-eight countries worldwide. His findings were detailed in his famous 1890 publication, *In Darkest England and the Way Out*, which began with the words: 'The lot of the Negroes in the Equatorial Forest is not, perhaps, a very happy one, but is it so very much worse than that of many a pretty orphan girl in our Christian capital?'

In 1837, the year that Victoria took the throne, the richest woman in England was not the new Queen but Angela Burdett-Coutts, the banking heiress. After Charles Dickens had introduced her to East End poverty, she began giving away much of her money – to the Ragged Schools Union, the Temperance Society, soup kitchens and new churches. Burdett-Coutts went to Ireland during the famine, feeding and clothing whole towns and donating money to fishermen in County Cork to restore their fishing industry. She had model dwellings built in Bethnal Green with £9,000 of her own money.

Horrified at the dishonesty and criminal behaviour of the East End costermongers, Burdett-Coutts financed Columbia Market, a Gothic monstrosity of soaring turrets, Tudor arches, cloisters and crypts which resembled the new flamboyant town halls of the northern industrial cities. Columbia Market was meant to set new standards in trading, but it was a flop. The traders preferred the street markets. They despaired of rules preventing them opening on Sunday on religious grounds and mocked signs displayed on the walls urging them to 'Be Sober, Be Vigilant, Be Pitiful, Be Courteous'. One poster warning them against swearing and spitting simply led to more cussing as they expectorated on the floor.

In 1881 the 67-year-old Burdett-Coutts, after spending a lifetime fending off men she thought wanted her only for her money, married William Ashmead Bartlett, an American forty years her junior. By Royal Assent he became 'Mr Burdett-Coutts'. Two years later she set up the National Society for the Prevention of Cruelty to Children. By the time she died, in 1906, she had given away nearly 3 million pounds.

Charrington's Anchor Brewery in Mile End opened in 1766 and was soon one of the biggest local employers. Successive master brewers became the most respectable of citizens, often MPs. Frederick Charrington, born in 1850, looked set to follow the same path of dispensing liquor and formulating laws, but when he was twenty he experienced an epiphany that led him to give away his inheritance.

Outside a public house he saw a woman with a young daughter plead with the father not to enter the bar but to give them some money instead. As the man turned round, knocking the girl down, the brewery heir looked up and saw his own name: 'Charrington', emblazoned in gold on the bar-room door.

'I can't stay with liquor!' he told friends and family. 'It suddenly flashed into my mind that that was only one case of dreadful misery and fiendish brutality in one of the several hundred public houses our firm possessed . . . It was a crushing realization . . . What a frightful responsibility for evil rested upon us.' Charrington moved out of the family mansion and found cheap rooms in Stepney. He became temperate, ascetic and celibate, and spent his time raising money for charity and spreading the word of God to make the East End a 'purer' place in which to live.

In 1886 Charrington opened the Great Assembly Hall on Mile End Road as the largest prayer hall in Europe. Five thousand people turned up Sunday after Sunday for meetings which began with the command, 'Stand up, stand up for Jesus' and were enlivened by Charrington, gripped by religious fervour, crying out, 'Down on your knees.' People marvelled that a man who bore a name so indelibly associated with drink should campaign for temperance, but Charrington had become obsessed. He strode the streets with a notebook and a companion looking for 'the foulest sinks of iniquity'. He found one in Nelson Street, Mile End, where, he claimed, 'scenes of unqualified bestiality' were taking place. Touring local brothels he would remonstrate with the owners. If the brothel keeper was amenable he would invite them to breakfast, not a meal they usually took formally, and they would feast on ham, beef and coffee to the strains of 'Auld Lang Syne'.

Charrington began to receive letters from beyond the East End, written by fathers pleading for the closing of brothels that had ruined their sons, and by wives pleading for the closure of brothels that had broken up their families. By spring 1888 he had set in motion a national campaign against sexual immorality. During one raid on a brothel he was mortified to find a portrait of himself hanging in one room, until it was explained to him that every brothel had a picture of him on the wall so that the occupants would know the identity of their nemesis. One East End madam, a Mrs Rose, when told that Charrington was coming, fled inside her house, collapsed and died. Divine retribution, he claimed. In all, Charrington was responsible for closing down some 200 back-street brothels. Cynics said he did so in order to buy up the properties cheaply. Indeed he carried out his mission so zealously many suspected *he* was Jack.

# 10

# Riot and Revolution

The East End has a long history of rebellion. When John of Gaunt imposed the poll tax on the public in 1381 some 20,000 protesters marched into east London demanding its abolition and an end to serfdom. They camped at Mile End, and on 12 June called on King Richard to meet them. The king travelled east by royal barge but took fright when he saw the size of the crowd and hid in the Tower of London. The peasants, angry at being snubbed, marched from Mile End through Whitechapel into London, where sympathizers had opened the gates for them, and burned down the Savoy, John of Gaunt's Strand palace.

In 1450 a group of rebels led by Jack Cade, a Kent landowner furious at heavy taxation and government corruption, also camped at Mile End to prepare an attack on London. The men stormed the Tower, where they decapitated the Archbishop of Canterbury and the king's treasurer, Sir James Fiennes. They then skewered their heads on to poles, held them together to make it look as if they were kissing, and attached them to London Bridge. The rebels successfully stormed the city, but their aggressive behaviour exasperated Londoners and the revolt was quelled. In defeat Cade suffered the same ignominy as his victims: his head was severed and displayed on a pole on London Bridge.

In the nineteenth century the sudden and savage industrialization of the East End encouraged significant numbers of east European agitators to settle and organize locally. These immigrant radicals introduced to London an unprecedented range of new ideas. As the Nobel Prize-winning writer Isaac Bashevis Singer explained in *The Manor* in 1967: 'All the spiritual and intellectual ideas that triumphed in the modern era had their roots in the world of that time – socialism, nationalism, Zionism, nihilism, anarchism, suffragettism, atheism, the weakening of the family bond, free love; even the beginnings of Fascism.'

## ANARCHISTS

The first significant group of such agitators to move to the East End were the anarchists. Kicked out of Russia and Germany, they arrived in London in the 1870s. At least here, in England's capital, they would be able to congregate freely. They would also find the poverty, squalor, low wages and shifting population that were fertile breeding ground for their ideology.

Although anarchism disapproved of leaders, a figurehead for the London anarchists emerged in the shape of Aaron Lieberman, a clerk in an insurance company. Lieberman, a Lithuanian, was well versed in several European languages, though not, initially, English. He also had a thorough knowledge of the Bible and Jewish lore, was a powerful orator and a talented propagandist.

Lieberman's first involvement with revolutionary politics had been at a rabbinical seminary in Russia. When in July 1875 the Tsarist police had attempted to break up his clique, he and his anarchist colleagues fled first to Germany and then to Britain, declaring that 'London, or England, is the only place where we can operate openly'. They moved into a squat already filled with sympathizers at 3 Tollington Park, Stroud Green. But this uneventful tract of suburbia at the edge of London's northern heights was no place for revolutionary anarchist agitators, and so Lieberman was sent out to find headquarters closer to the pulse of capitalism.

He went to the East End, naturally, and chose 40 Gun Street, a house a few yards east of Spitalfields market. There, on 20 May 1876, Lieberman and his group founded the Hebrew Socialist Union (*Agudah Hasozialistim Chaverim*). The *Jewish Chronicle*, the community's main newspaper, claimed otherwise. On 23 June it published an article warning against a document being sent round the East End immigrant community that 'purports to contain the rules of the

Hebrew Socialist Union – a body which possesses no existence what-soever, except in the imagination of the insane originator'.

There were many who believed the Hebrew Socialist Union *did* exist. They railed against it in the *Chronicle*'s letters pages, in the boardrooms, from the pulpits and on the shop floor. They thundered against its advocacy of free love, its support for the class struggle and its desire to overthrow the 'system' which, the anarchists claimed, had 'usurped all men's rights for its own profit'. They railed against its triumphant claim that God was dead and that there was no worthy human source of authority – 'not the church, nor the state, nor the family'.

The anarchists were unfazed and announced their first programme. They would unite the East End Jew, living in the 'narrow, crooked streets of Whitechapel, in the smelly and dirty holes and corners of the workshops, working twelve to fourteen hours a day for paltry starvation wages', with the East End Irishman. Jew and Irishman would rise up against Mammon together. The programme failed. The Irish proletarian had no interest in uniting with the Jewish proletarian on *any* matter.

Unbowed, the anarchists held a public meeting at the Zetland Hall, 51 Mansell Street, just south of Aldgate, on 26 August 1876. A succession of speakers outlined the struggles of the Jewish immigrants and the miserable conditions they endured in the factory. The revolutionaries raged against the machine, which was squeezing out the poorer worker, and declared that the 'emancipation of the working class from the oppression of capitalism as a stage on the ultimate road to full anarchy' was the only way forward.

The meeting was a success until Lieberman spoke. He tore into the Jewish financiers and the local rabbinate with rhetoric that would be echoed by Oswald Mosley's British Union of Fascists on nearby Cable Street sixty years later, until one member of the audience could take no more and leapt on to the platform to challenge Lieberman for insulting the Chief Rabbi. Anarchy of a more brutal and decisive kind than Lieberman and his supporters had envisaged was swiftly enacted as fists were slammed into faces and chairs were smashed over opponents' heads. The meeting ended in anarchy.

That December Lieberman was sacked from the journal where he was working and he left London, travelling to Berlin, Leipzig and St Petersburg, where he disseminated propaganda and helped move political refugees out of Russia. He was arrested in 1878 by the Austrian police and charged with assuming a false identity, using a fake passport and belonging to a secret society (evidently not so secret). After completing his sentence Lieberman returned to London, taking rooms at 21 Elder Street, Spitalfields. Posing as one Arthur Freeman, he sought work in a variety of jobs – shoeshiner, photographer, teacher – but by this time, late 1880, few of his former associates remained. His one-time chief comrade, Lieb Wainer, had so gentrified himself that he refused to speak the old language.

It was not long before Lieberman met his nemesis in Rachel, a comely daughter of Zion. When she rejected his advances, he fled to Syracuse, Sicily, a city well acquainted with *amour fou*, where he shot himself. He was thirty-one.

With Lieberman gone there was a vacuum in the East End. It was filled by Rachel's brother-in-law, Morris Winchevsky. Also a Lithuanian Jew, he too had attended a rabbinical seminary, and on arriving in London in 1884 secured himself a job in a Jewish banking firm. That July, Winchevsky began publishing a left-wing Yiddish newspaper, *Der Polisher Yidl* (the Little Polish Jew), from 137 Commercial Street. Its aim was to politicize East End Jewish tailors, cure them of their mania for gambling, teach them English and encourage them to form trade unions.

But when the paper's business manager accepted an advertisement from the Liberal MP Samuel Montague, Winchevsky quit in disgust and founded a rival publication, *Arbeter Fraint* (Workers' Friend), 'to spread true socialism among Jewish workers'. The back page of the new publication carried an appeal in heavy type: 'Workers, do your duty. Spread the *Arbeter Fraint*!' The Jewish establishment responded by bribing the typesetter, and Issue Number 26 appeared with the wording of the ad changed to: 'Workers, do your duty. *Destroy* the *Arbeter Fraint*!' The typesetter promptly disappeared, fleeing the wrath of the editors. The anarchists then bribed the printer to change the message back.

At the time of the Jack the Ripper murders in 1888, while the Jewish community prayed through the Day of Atonement, the most important religious date in the calendar, apostate anarchist Jews at the Berner Street International Working Men's Club held a banquet as their personal snub to the day of fasting. In their speeches the anarchists explained that the miseries and degradation of the people should not be blamed on divine power but on capitalism, which monopolized the means of production and paid starvation wages. They anticipated trouble from orthodox Jews, and were not disappointed. Religious zealots who had gathered outside the building began to smash the club's windows. When three of the audience went outside to intervene more troubled flared, and a mêlée of around a hundred Jews fought until dispersed by the police.

A year later the anarchists again commemorated the Day of Atonement in their own special way. This time it was with a social event at Hanbury Hall, Spitalfields, held to compete with local synagogue services. Benjamin Feigenbaum, the main speaker, discoursing on the topic 'Is There a God?', thundered, 'What is God? It is an abstract word coined to designate the hidden forces of nature, while the belief in God is but a mechanical habit of childhood, a prejudice handed down from father to children. If there is a God, and if he is as Almighty as the clergy claims he is, I give him just two minutes to kill me on the spot so that he may prove his existence!' Two minutes elapsed during which God, being sought for forgiveness at the Spitalfields Great Synagogue on the corner of Brick Lane and Fournier Street, and innumerable other Jewish establishments, failed to respond. Feigenbaum turned to the room and exclaimed: 'See! There is no God!', to considerable applause and strains of the 'Marseillaise'.

The years 1888 and 1889 were marked by significant strikes: the matchgirls' (1888) and the dockers' (1889), which abutted the tailors' strike, also of 1889. The latter was London's first industrial dispute to affect mostly immigrant workers. It started with spontaneous walkouts, the tailors switching off their Hoffman presses and heading out of the sweatshops. The strike leaders demanded that the sweatshop workers' hours be reduced to twelve and their pay aligned according to trade-union rates. They received support not only from those dockers who had also downed tools, but from established Anglo-Jewry. But not all the donations sent to the strike headquarters on Old Montague Street were kosher. When a cheque for £1,000 sent by

'Lord Rothschild' arrived, eight men went to the bank to cash it (one man might be tempted to run off with the money), only to find it was a forgery. Remarkably the strikers won their demands, but glory was claimed not by the anarchists, who had led the action, but by the Liberal MP, Samuel Montague, whose intervention had led to arbitration.

What Lieberman and Winchevsky sowed, Rudolf Rocker reaped. A German, Rocker fled the Fatherland to escape imprisonment for his political activities and settled in the East End. Disturbed by the sight of the poor, who 'went about in foul rags through which their skin showed, dirty and lousy, never free from hunger, starving, scavenging their food out of dustbins and the refuse heaps that were left behind after the market closed', Rocker joined the Jewish anarchist movement, announcing, 'I am an anarchist not because I believe anarchism is the final goal, but because there is no such thing as a final goal.' In 1898 he relaunched the Yiddish left-wing paper *Arbeter Fraint* – not bad for a Roman Catholic who could neither read nor speak Yiddish – which he published intermittently from Dunstan Houses, a gloomy apartment block by Stepney Green which still survives.

In 1904 the East End anarchists found their meetings being broken up by heavily tooled-up Jewish gangsters – the Bessarabians. When they discovered that the Bessarabians were being paid by the Federation of Synagogues to cause disruption, they decided to exact revenge, and hired the Bessarabians themselves to break up the Federation's religious services. That year, on the Day of Atonement, a mob made its way to the Spitalfields Great Synagogue and, despite Rocker's opposition, pelted worshippers coming out of the building at the end of the service with bacon sandwiches. The worshippers fought back and Brick Lane soon became a battleground, with fists and lumps of bacon sandwich flying amid the cashmere coats, *shtreimel* hats and ringlets.

Rocker, the gentile anarchist editor, was horrified. Jew against Jew. A bad business. Those who had organized this *treife* post-fast party were so annoyed with Rocker's lack of support that they spread rumours that he was a spy in the pay of the German government (what gratitude for years of selfless service to anarchism!). He was called to answer the charge at a meeting held at the Archers public house on Osborn Street, Whitechapel, and after much fiery debate was cleared.

In 1906 the anarchists helped organize another tailors' strike. The working day was reduced to ten and a half hours as a result. But other clothing unions, such as the Jewish Trunk and Pursemakers' Union, who staged similar strikes, won more advances and better pay. Many tailors left their unions in disgust and two leading writers on *Arbeter Fraint* emigrated to New York.

Meanwhile, the anarchists opened a new East End club in a former Salvation Army depot at 165 Jubilee Street, Stepney. It had a meeting hall, library and reading room. Classes were held in Hebrew and English. Lecturers discussed the merits of anarchist doyens such as Michael Bakunin, Pierre Proudhon and Adam Weishaupt. Unfortunately, it had no bar, but the premises sold typical anarchist food of the time – gefilte fish, pickled herring and chopped liver.

One of the club's most enthusiastic visitors was Charles Lahr, a German-born baker who came to anarchism from Buddhism. After arriving in England in October 1905 Lahr was soon being watched twenty-four hours a day by the Metropolitan Police. While eating one day at the German restaurant on Leman Street, Lahr overheard a conversation in which the Kaiser was being lavishly praised. He stood up and shouted, 'The bastard should be shot,' only to be promptly thrown out. The next day, noticing he was being followed, he confronted his pursuers, who doubtless wished to be spotted, and was told he was being watched because he was considered to be a threat to the Kaiser, who was due to visit England. Seven years later, at the start of the First World War, Lahr was interned at Alexandra Palace as a potentially hostile alien. There he was recognized by one of his former shadows from the Metropolitan Police, who greeted him amicably and remarked, 'Pity you didn't shoot the Kaiser then, Charles.'

## THE HOUNDSDITCH MURDERS

The anarchists were keen on what they called 'expropriation' – removing the goods of the bourgeoisie for redistribution among the oppressed classes (themselves); what non-anarchists called stealing.

Always keen to put their policies into practice, a group of Latvian anarchists targeted for expropriation jewels supposedly belonging to the Tsar himself which were on sale in a shop at 119 Houndsditch in December 1910.

The gang included William Sokolow, a jeweller; Peter Piatkow, a sallow-looking handyman who went by the nickname 'Peter the Painter' (Peter Wyngarde played him in the 1961 film of the events); and Jacob Peters, a short, snub-nosed man with bristling brown hair. Their leader was Poolka Mourrewitz, a smartly dressed revolutionary who would walk only in the middle of the road, lest he be seized by Tsarist agents lurking in a doorway, and who in England went by a wonderfully anglicized false name – George Gardstein.

The team rented premises at 11 Exchange Buildings, Cutler Street, only a few yards from the jeweller's they were planning to rob, and began digging a tunnel that would connect their lair with the shop. They made such a racket digging that they were overheard by a jeweller working nearby. Concerned at the intense banging he could hear in the vicinity, the jeweller contacted the police.

A constable knocked on the door of Exchange Buildings and, after being answered by a 'suspicious-looking' foreigner, left for reinforcements. When he knocked again the door was opened by Gardstein. 'Is anyone working out the back?' the officer asked him. 'May we have a look?' The police entered and were greeted by Peters, who fired a pistol at them. A shot went through the rim of one policeman's helmet and pierced the shutter behind. Another bullet hit one of the officers in the neck, killing him instantly. When another officer, a Constable Choat, caught hold of Mourrewitz/Gardstein and tried to wrest the gun from him, he was shot eight times by the other anarchists. He did, however, manage to partly shield himself with Gardstein, who was fatally wounded by a bullet meant for Choat.

The gang had no scruples about shooting the officers. The Tsarist police had pulled out Jacob Peters's fingernails after arresting him at a demonstration in Latvia. It was they who had led the pogroms against the anarchists' Jewish brethren. How were the anarchists to know that the Metropolitan Police were a gentlemanly body of men who played by a civilized rule book?

After debating whether to abandon the dying Mourrewitz in the street, the gang took him to a hideaway at 59 Grove Street, St George's. There they felt they had no option but to call out a doctor, who in turn felt he had no option but to call the police. By the time they arrived Mourrewitz was dead and the gang had fled. The officers searched the room and found a loaded pistol, ammunition and incriminating documents. A manhunt was now on. Posters were displayed throughout the neighbourhood, advertising a £500 reward for the capture of Fritz Svaars, who had occupied the room where Mourrewitz had died, and gang members Joseph Marx and Peter the Painter.

Even if the Houndsditch murders weren't the precursor to revolution they were a dramatic enough landmark event after thirty-five years of local anarchist activity. The story had everything: robbery, riches, murder, revenge, escape. There was even a woman involved.

## THE SIEGE OF SIDNEY STREET

Events moved on. Some of the gang fled further east to 100 Sidney Street, a few yards south of Whitechapel station, home of Sokolow's mistress, Betsy Gershon. There they were spotted by a Russian immigrant who had become a regular police informer. In early January 1911 officers swarmed to the street and one by one began to remove from the property all the occupants unconnected to the gang. The landlady, half-dressed at the time, was not at all happy about coming out. 'And let these *yokishe* policemen see me in my underwear,' she wailed in Yiddish.

Nevertheless she complied and managed to lure Betsy Gershon downstairs by pretending that her husband had been taken ill. The police told Betsy Gershon curtly that if she didn't tell them which gang members were hiding on the upper floors, or it any officers were shot dead, she would be hanged as an accessory. Gershon cooperated, and the police waited overnight in the snow.

At first light an officer banged loudly at the door. There was no response. A group of policemen threw pebbles at the windows of the room where the men were believed to be sheltering. The stones were met with a volley of shots, one of which hit Detective Sergeant Leeson, who fell to the ground, spluttering to his superior, Detective Inspector

Wensley, 'Mr Wensley, I am dying. They have shot me through the heart. Goodbye. Give my love to the children. Bury me at Putney.' He survived to write an engaging set of memoirs.

In need of reinforcements, the police contacted the home secretary, Winston Churchill, who sent in the Scots Guards. Churchill soon appeared at the siege, wearing a top hat and a fur-collared overcoat. Locals greeted him with taunts of 'Oo let 'em in?', a visceral critique of the Liberal government's liberal immigration policies. When more shots rang out from 100 Sidney Street the heckling abated, and a couple of hours of stalemate ensued. Eventually fire broke out and No. 100 collapsed, just as the postman came by on his round. The fire brigade arrived to quell the blaze, but the chief police officer told them they would be shot if they attempted to intervene, which led to a public row between officers from the two bodies.

When the blaze abated police entered the burnt-out property and found the bodies of two men, Fritz Svaars and Joseph Marx. There was no sign of Peter the Painter, who was never officially seen again. His success at escaping capture enshrined him in legend. Churchill later described him as 'one of those wild beasts who, in later years, amid the convulsions of the Great War, were to devour and ravage the Russian State and people'. Some claimed that Peter the Painter was an alias of the Latvian artist Gederts Eliass, who smuggled arms for Lenin, was involved in the 1917 Russian Revolution and later became People's Artist for the Republic of Latvia. Others said that he was a double agent who became a member of the Soviet secret police. Some even believed he was Comrade Stalin himself.

Churchill's secretary, Charles Masterman, was horrified that his master had personally attended the siege, and when Churchill returned to the Home Office, Masterman accosted him with a cry of, 'What have you been doing, Winston?', to which Churchill responded, in full lisp, 'Now, Charleth, don't be croth; it wath such fun!' At the inquest Churchill was accused of muttering at the time of the fire 'Let the bashtards burn', and his political response was the 1911 Criminal Bill, which set penalties for carrying unlicensed pistols, clamped down on illegal immigration and proposed sureties for aliens with criminal records coming into the country.

The Houndsditch murders and the siege of Sidney Street brought anarchism out into the open. It was now public property, a philosophy threatening the fabric of London life. The newspapers, especially the *Daily Mail*, seized on the events with relish. 'The time has come to stop the abuse of this country's hospitality by foreign malefactors,' it thundered. Rudolf Rocker was worried: 'The way the newspapers linked the Houndsditch murderers with the foreign revolutionaries made us fear the affair would be used to work up agitation for withdrawing the right of asylum in Britain, which was the only country where political refugees did not live with the constant dread of expulsion hanging over their heads as in France, Belgium or Switzerland.'

Rocker's fears were mostly unfounded. He went on to mastermind the 1912 tailors' strike which, for a brief period, ran alongside the dockers' strike. Mutual support between the two groups fostered the warmest race relations and the tailors' strike ended after three weeks with the men winning many of their demands – shorter hours, improved sanitary conditions and union recognition. It was not an end to exploited sweated labour but it helped.

Anarchism boomed. The *Arbeter Fraint* expanded to twelve pages. The Jubilee Street club became popular once again and held dances, lectures and social events. Rocker was mobbed in the streets of the East End. Walking through Whitechapel one day, he was stopped by an old Jew with a long white beard who greeted him, 'May God bless you! You helped my children in their need. You are not a Jew, but you are a *mensch*.'

There could be no trial of the Sidney Street siegers, but a trial of the Houndsditch raiders took place at the Old Bailey. Conveniently and convincingly, they blamed the shootings on the late Poolka Mourrewitz (aka Gardstein) and were freed. The *Daily Mail* was horrified: 'The police can hardly be congratulated upon their success in dealing with this formidable conspiracy; but, in excuse, it must be remembered that in the vast alien population of East London it is a matter of peculiar difficulty to obtain evidence or run down the offender.'

Churchill was mortified at the acquittal of Jacob Peters, who then made the unusual reverse journey of the alien fleeing persecution – Russia to England – by leaving England for Russia, where he became a leading agitator during the October 1917 Revolution. When the ruling Bolshevik communists established a secret police, the Cheka,

Peters was appointed its deputy chairman. The Cheka had powers to shoot anyone it considered undesirable; no charges or trial were needed. Peters had come a long way from Houndsditch, or indeed from the Holloway Road tailors' where he had once worked. Now there were no running-dog lackey capitalist policemen to obstruct the path to true socialism. Assassination was carried out impassively in garages and cellars. A single shot was all that was needed. Sadly Peters later fell out of favour, and in 1939 was shot, under Stalin's orders. Perhaps when Churchill met Stalin at Potsdam in July 1945 the British premier took time to congratulate his Soviet counterpart on implementing suitable if belated punishment to the one-time expropriator of the East End.

## COMMUNISTS

During the Great War of 1914–18 East End radicalism came to be dominated by a different strain of left-wing ideology: communism. Unlike the anarchists, the communists saw politics not in terms of an ideology that railed against the very nature of leadership but in terms of an ideology which pitted an entire class – the working class – in a historic struggle against the leisured classes.

Like anarchism, communism was an international phenomenon, a monster whose heart was in Paris, whose head veered from Moscow to St Petersburg, and whose hands could often be found in London. And it was on the streets of London, the most class-ridden metropolis in the industrialized world, rather than on those of Moscow or St Petersburg, that the Russian Revolution was bred.

The absence of immigration laws in Britain meant that the communist leaders – Lenin, Stalin, Trotsky – and their many minions were able to enter the country at will. They could melt into the population and enjoy a level of political freedom unavailable elsewhere in Europe, and which they themselves never tolerated in the Soviet Union when they came to power.

Of these communist cynosures it was Lenin who spent most time in London. He and his wife, Krupskaya, first arrived in the capital in 1902, when Tsarist censorship and police persecution rendered it difficult for them to publish their revolutionary newspaper *Iskra* (the Spark) in Russia. They settled in King's Cross as Mr and Mrs Jacob Richter, eating food that they could not stomach – 'ox-tails, skates fried in fat and indigestible cakes not made for Russian stomachs' – and journeyed regularly into the most proletarian quarters of the East End.

Lenin remembered the area as being full of 'mean little streets tenanted by London's work people, with clothes lines stretched across the road and anaemic children playing on the doorsteps'. Observing the startling contrasts between wealth and poverty, he would mutter in his Irish-inflected English accent through gritted teeth, 'Two nations!' (the title of Benjamin Disraeli's novel about the contrasting wealth and poverty in England). Lenin frequented a bookshop at 106 Commercial Road kept by Petrov, a seven-foot Siberian with a huge black beard. He also visited the Stepney anarchist club on Jubilee Street, as recalled in 1970 by an 89-year-old woman, who described the budding revolutionary to the East End chronicler Bill Fishman as 'a small balding taciturn man brooding alone at a table in the corner'.

In 1907 the communists came to London *en masse* for a congress. Their number included a galaxy of stars the brightness of which has never since been matched in the East End. Among them was the writer Maxim Gorky, who, at the age of twenty-one, had attempted suicide by shooting himself in the lung. He survived, but the injury caused by the bullet rendered him tubercular. Then there were the revolutionary agitators Rosa Luxemburg, Lev Bronstein (Leon Trotsky), who had recently led the St Petersburg Soviet to a General Strike, and Joseph Dzhugashvili, the future Joseph Stalin, who claimed to represent the Bolshevik workers from the Borchalo district, even though no party branch existed there at that time.

The communists arrived by train, disembarking at Liverpool Street station, at the edge of the East End, where they were met by curious journalists, local socialist dignitaries such as Lansbury and Comrade Lenin himself, who greeted Gorky with the words, 'So glad you've come. I believe you're fond of a scrap. There's going to be a fine old scuffle here.'

Lenin had found them rooms. He arranged it so that opponents such as Stalin stayed in some discomfort in the fearsome-looking

Gothic lodging-house on Fieldgate Street, the one that Jack London had decried as 'the Monster Doss House' in *The People of the Abyss*. In the cubicle alongside the future Soviet leader slept Maxim Litvinoff, who became the Bolsheviks' representative in London at the time of the Russian Revolution, and was later Soviet ambassador to Washington. Nearby were Lev Kamenev and Grigori Zinoviev, who, together with Stalin, emerged as the three most powerful figures in Russia on the death of Lenin in 1924, and whose executions Stalin ordered during the show trials of the 1930s.

After unpacking, the Russians headed to Whitechapel, where the English Friends of the 1905 Russian Revolution had laid on a dinner for them. The Russians were pleased with the attention their English comrades showed them but were shocked to be told that they were to attend in evening dress. None of them owned such bourgeois attire, nor had any of them thought of hiring such outfits before packing.

It was at this dinner that Stalin first met Trotsky. Two mad mavericks whose contrasting ideologies, the former bureaucratic and authoritarian, the latter evolutionary and organic, continue to rend asunder left-wing philosophy wherever it is practical. To cap the unique evening the last toast was proposed by James Ramsay MacDonald, who went on to become Labour's first prime minister some twenty years later, by which time socialism, let alone communism, was a distant memory for him.

With the communists desperately short of money – the party was bankrupt financially, as well as morally – Lenin went to Chelsea, to the luxurious home of the artist Felix Moscheles, and after a stirring speech asked those assembled there to give generously. He received an ovation but no cash. The communists were saved by George Lansbury, the leading East End socialist, who arranged a loan with an English soap manufacturer, which allowed the congress to go ahead in the now-demolished Brotherhood Church in Dalston.

The Dalston congress was watched over by twelve Tsarist spies, who infiltrated the meeting to check up on their exiled political adversaries, and a number of Scotland Yard officers, disguised as Russians, who were attending to check on the Tsarist spies. Historians now believe the congress contained more policemen and secret service infiltrators than communists.

Lenin felt that Russia was too backward to stage a revolution; London was a more likely choice. But after visiting a 'socialist' church on the Seven Sisters Road with Trotsky he wrung his hands in despair. 'Among the English proletariat there are many revolutionary and socialist elements, but it is all so intertwined with conservatism, religion, and prejudices, that it cannot reach the surface and become the property of all,' he wailed.

When in 1917 a revolution took place in Russia, despite Lenin's predictions, there were plenty of British sympathizers in the East End. Understandably they wanted to help, and so a People's Russian Information Bureau opened at 400 Old Ford Road, the former headquarters of the East London Federation of Suffragettes. This one East End cell soon became part of an enormous network of communist cells whose deliberations moved more slowly than a Moscow bread queue. All local decisions had to be sanctioned by those on the next rung of the hierarchy. They in turn needed guidance from their superiors, who themselves required the nod from those above them, and so on through each successive layer of bureaucracy. A chain of command stretched upwards from the card-carrying proletarian engaged in dirty work at Le Bas Tubes on the Isle of Dogs to the East London Representative Committee, to the British Communist Party's imposing headquarters in Covent Garden, and from there through the various strata of Soviet communism . . . all the way up to Comrade Lenin himself. It was not easy to get a quick answer to a simple question. It was not easy forming a political manifesto. By the time word had travelled from Stepney to Moscow and back again the central Politburo had probably changed its policy.

## THE GENERAL STRIKE

Perhaps there would be revolution in Britain, starting in London, after all? In the summer of 1925 all the talk was about the imminent General Strike following the coal-owners' wage cuts and lengthening of working hours. On the day the strike was meant to start, Friday 31 July 1925, the government granted a nine-month subsidy to the coal industry and set up a royal commission to review the industry.

The unions and their supporters hailed the announcement and pro-claimed 31 July 'Red Friday', but the government was simply playing for time, rather than conceding.

When the findings of the royal commission were delivered in 1926 the wage reductions were approved. The unions rallied behind the miners with a new slogan: 'Not a penny off the pay, not a second on the day.' Talks between the TUC and the coal-owners failed to find an agreement, and on 20 April George V proclaimed a State of Emergency. The Special Constabulary was mobilized. Hyde Park became a military camp, and troops in war kit patrolled the streets of Manchester, Birmingham and London's East End, where the miners' most vociferous supporters were the dockers. Communist Party leaders were arrested and sent to prison. Street meetings boomed. Debate intensified.

On 1 May 1926 the TUC met and announced that a General Strike 'in defence of miners' wages and hours' would begin on the 3rd. Communist leaders in the East End wrung their hands at the hastiness of it all; the Party rank and file were exhilarated at the prospect of a real revolution! The Tory government had prepared well for the strike. They had arranged it so that there were enough supplies to last for a month. In the East End food wagons protected by armed guards, foot soldiers marching four by four, tanks and armoured cars, left East India Docks . . . slowly, bound for the supply depots.

George Lansbury, the East End MP, issued his own strike news-paper, *Lansbury's Bulletin*. It had a peculiarly Christian slant. 'Tomorrow is Sunday. You will come to our meetings at night, but I would like you to attend the Church services nearest your home. It is Christ's gospel of passive resistance which you are practising today.' The docks were besieged by pickets and guarded by soldiers toting machine guns who had been told by the home secretary, 'Make your own plans. Use whatever force you require. I give you carte blanche, but my orders are that the London Docks must be opened at all costs.' On the Wednesday evening of the strike a group of dockers meeting outside Poplar Town Hall was scattered by a lorryload of police, who drove through the crowd scattering people to each side as the Revd Groser – the so-called 'red cleric of Poplar' – held up a crucifix. Officers stormed the headquarters of the Poplar branch of the

National Union of Railwaymen, beating with truncheons everyone they found.

With the strike less than a week old the TUC took fright and sought a truce. The meeting that brokered a settlement was held at Toynbee Hall in Spitalfields. On 11 May the TUC General Council visited 10 Downing Street, offering to call off the strike as long as the government guaranteed there would be no victimization of the strikers. When the government refused to do so, the TUC capitulated. Lord Birkenhead, a member of the Tory Cabinet, later confided that the TUC's surrender was so humiliating 'that some instinctive breeding made one unwilling even to look at them'. Although the General Strike was over, the miners held out till November, and when they returned to the pits they discovered that they were working longer hours for less pay for less tolerant bosses. It was a shattering blow for the communists, who had put so much effort into the strike and were so expectant of seizing the state.

By the mid-1930s a new dynamic political creed, fascism – intensely opposed to communism – was gaining support throughout Europe. By this time it was also clear that Stalin's Soviet Union was not the workers' paradise Marx had envisaged – or rather that a workers' 'paradise' would inevitably be like this. Somehow the Revolution had been betrayed. The proof for local communists came via the story of East Ender Rose Cohen. It was a tale laced with duplicity, disloyalty, betrayal, lost love, vanquished dreams and tragedy.

Born in 1894 to an immigrant Polish-Jewish family, Cohen, through self-improvement – the Workers' Educational Association, long sessions at Whitechapel public library – secured a job with the London County Council. She also became a founder member of the British Communist Party. In the early 1920s Cohen left for Russia with Max Petrovsky, Comintern representative in Britain, to live a life of thrilling cloak-and-dagger adventures as a spy and foreign envoy. She later became foreign editor of an English-language Russian paper, the *Moscow Daily News*.

When Stalin's show trials began in August 1936 some of those who once bestrode the streets of the East End, proudly confident of their future role righting world-wide injustice, found themselves in the dock. Kamenev and Zinoviev, Stalin's fellow lodgers in Stepney's

Tower House, and once the second and third most powerful figures in the Soviet Union, were accused of betraying the Revolution, of being 'mean degenerates' and 'abominable traitors', in league with Trotsky and Hitler. They were shot, as was Petrovsky, Rose Cohen's husband, who, East End communists were told, had been arrested for being a 'wrecker'.

On 13 August 1937 Rose was arrested. It was the same day that Harry Pollitt, leader of the British Community Party and once her most devoted suitor, arrived in Moscow to meet her. He was told she was 'unavailable'. A few months later East End communists were told of Rose's arrest. The British press demanded that the Soviets charge her publicly; the *Daily Worker* told them they had no right to meddle in Russian affairs. There was no official complaint from the East End Communist Party. After all there had been no directive from Moscow advising them to make one. Rose was shot on 28 November 1937, two months after her husband's execution. Enemy of the state.

In the East End support for communism dipped. The communists found it increasingly hard to offer a programme dynamic and exciting enough to attract the masses. Fascism, particularly in Stepney and Whitechapel, was able to stir the blood with tales of an heroic struggle against a swarthy enemy. It was able to attract those who thrilled to the feel of a black, perhaps a leather, uniform and tingled with excitement at the prospect of a passionate public meeting ending in a fist-fight and a stirring song, preferably sung in a shouty language.

But what could the communists offer in comparison? They could not, after all, disclose their real agenda: one of violent bloody revolution, regicide, the overthrow of the British state and its traditional institutions; the abandonment of free elections, open debate, tolerance, compromise and enterprise; the removal of choice over even the most basic of human needs and wants; the installation of a rigid bureaucracy and authoritarian centralized government bolstered by an endless pyramid of workers' councils; the establishment of a rarefied elite, afforded privileges unavailable and unknown to the masses; the creation of a secret police to ensure that individuals desisted from the evils of capitalism; the opening of labour camps to punish those who indulged in the old habits none the less – it is unlikely that the inclusion of such items on a manifesto would have attracted many supporters.

At least the communists, for all their faults, could be relied upon to lead the confrontation against Nazi Germany, so people assumed. The public watched and waited for a lead. In the summer of 1939 Stalin, under pressure from the Nazis, replaced the Jewish foreign minister, Maxim Litvinoff, whom he had lodged alongside in Stepney back in 1907, with the non-Jew, Vyacheslav Molotov.

On 23 August Soviet Russia and Nazi Germany announced a non-aggression treaty, part of a secret pact to divide eastern Europe between the two countries. It was the political shock to dwarf all others. The communists had been the most vociferous opponents of fascism, yet here was Molotov excusing fascism as a 'matter of taste'. Here were the communists allied with the British Union of Fascists, their deadly enemies. In June 1941 Hitler reneged on the pact and attacked Russia. The Soviet Union then joined forces with the Allies to fight fascism.

At the end of the war the East End communists achieved their greatest coup – the election of a communist candidate, Phil Piratin, as MP for Stepney. A photograph of the victor standing alongside the re-elected Labour MP for the neighbouring seat of Limehouse was flashed around the world. The Americans were horrified: the Limehouse MP was Clement Attlee, the new British prime minister. How could these limeys be trusted if their premier was associating with commies?

About that loan, the one that financed the communists' 1907 congress in Whitechapel. Although it should have been repaid by 1 January 1908 the lender wasn't in the least surprised when nothing arrived by that date. However, the debt was not forgotten. After the 1917 Russian Revolution, Krassin, the Soviet ambassador to London, returned the money, to the astonishment of the lender's heirs, with a letter signed by all the participants in the congress, including Trotsky and Stalin.

# SOCIALISTS

By the end of the nineteenth century English-flavoured – as opposed to continental-inspired – socialism was dominated by the 'muscular'

Christianity of Revd F. D. Maurice and the poet Matthew Arnold alongside the florid medievalism of William Morris, the great designer.

At that time there was no Labour Party, and the major left-wing movement was the Social Democratic Federation. Founded in 1881, the SDF was run by Henry Hyndman, an aristocratic socialist and barrister, who had converted to socialism while on a business trip to Utah in 1880. When William Morris became their treasurer the group gained the most beautiful membership cards ever possessed by a socialist society: a banner proclaiming 'Liberty, Equality, Fraternity' surrounded by a typical Morrisian arboreal pattern framing another banner announcing: 'Educate, Agitate, Organize'.

At the end of 1884 William Morris and Eleanor Marx, Karl's daughter, quit the foundation to form the Socialist League. The split led to farcical events in Dod Street, Poplar, on 20 September 1885. At one end of the street stood a speaker from Morris's and Marx's Socialist League. At the other end a member of Hyndman's Social Democratic Federation. Thousands filled the street, torn between the two orators, and when proceedings finished the police swooped, arresting two banner-bearers and six onlookers. In court there was another mêlée, during which Morris himself was arrested, for supposedly hitting a policeman. The following Sunday a huge crowd again assembled in Dod Street. This time they were more united. They decided to march south to the docks, and seize control of this bastion of capitalist trade. When the mob arrived they found police guarding the premises zealously. The would-be revolutionaries thought better of it and dispersed.

## THE MATCHGIRLS' STRIKE

Few East Enders joined either the Social Democratic Federation or the Socialist League. Both groups seemed too concerned with sophisticated views and fine living. But there was an alternative route to socialism, and it came from the trade unions.

By the late 1880s only 5 per cent of the British labour force were members of unions, and they tended to be skilled workers in the textile and mining industries. Then came the 1880 matchgirls' strike. Annie Besant, a member of the Social Democratic Federation, was shocked to hear about the horrific conditions in which the Bryant & May matchmakers of Bow, mostly young women, worked. The yellow phosphorus the Bryant & May matchgirls used caused a yellowing of the skin and hair loss. It withered away the jaw, resulting in what was dubbed 'phossy jaw', an often fatal form of bone cancer in which the face discharged foul pus.

Many firms had banned yellow phosphorus, but not Bryant & May. When Besant visited the factory she discovered that the women were working a fourteen-hour day for low wages, from which fines were levied for talking or dropping matches. She also found out that six years earlier, when the factory owner, Theodore Bryant, erected a statue to his political hero, William Gladstone, the former Liberal prime minister, he had forced his workers to contribute to the cost by taking a shilling from their wages. He had also deprived them of half a day's work by closing the factory to 'celebrate' the unveiling, a ceremony at which a number of the women had cut their arms and let the blood trickle on to the marble, as they considered they had paid for it, metaphorically, with their blood.

When Besant complained, Bryant & May tried to force staff to state their enthusiasm for their working conditions. A group of women who refused to do so were sacked, and so on 5 July 1888 the rest of the women went on strike.

Besant was used to controversy. Ten years previously *The Times* had condemned her book, *The Laws of Population*, in which she had advocated birth-control, as 'indecent, lewd, filthy, bawdy and obscene'. Now, with the strike on she successfully lobbied her well-connected friends to boycott Bryant & May's matches. She also organized the workers into a union. After three weeks the company announced it would rehire the sacked workers and end the fines system. It was an unexpected victory for the strikers.

Three years later the Salvation Army opened its own match-factory nearby, using relatively harmless red phosphorus instead of yellow, and paying employees twice the Bryant & May rate. William Booth, the Salvation Army's founder, invited MPs and journalists to his works and then took them to the homes of the Bryant & May employees. More unfavourable publicity. Ten years later Bryant & May stopped using yellow phosphorus.

## VOTES FOR WOMEN

At the 1892 general election Keir Hardie won the seat of West Ham, just outside the East End, as an Independent Labour candidate. The Labour Party did not then exist. His clothes were odd for a Member of Parliament. Rather than wearing the typical garb of top hat and long black coat, he chose a cloth cap and tweed suit. His politics were equally unusual, for he supported votes for women.

At that time the campaign to win women the vote was led by the National Union of Women's Suffrage Societies. Members favoured using constitutional methods to achieve their aim, but Emmeline Pankhurst, a leading Manchester-based supporter, wanted a more militant approach. In 1903 she helped found a breakaway organization, the Women's Social and Political Union. It moved its headquarters from Manchester to London, and took up direct action, which included throwing stones at the windows of 10 Downing Street and demonstrating outside the House of Commons.

The East End began to figure prominently in suffragette affairs in October 1912 when Sylvia Pankhurst, Emmeline's daughter, who saw the 'rousing of the East End as of the utmost importance', opened a women's suffrage campaign headquarters in a disused bakery at 198 Bow Road. It was a central spot on the busiest road in the area, and the huge 'Votes for Women' sign painted in large gold letters shocked the staid Bow public. A month later George Lansbury, the local MP, resigned his seat to show his support for women's suffrage. Sylvia Pankhurst wanted to co-opt him on to the campaign, but when Emmeline and Christabel, another daughter, ruled that the WSPU would not work alongside men, Sylvia broke away to form the East London Federation of Suffragettes.

The new group was soon staging passionate meetings in the East End. On 27 July 1913 police broke up a Federation of Suffragettes meeting at Bromley Hall on Bow Road (now the Tower Hamlets Registry Office). Sylvia Pankhurst and two colleagues fled and hid in a nearby stable, from which supporters rescued them at four in the morning. Concealed in sacking, the three women were driven off in a cart to Woodford. Sylvia was eventually arrested and sent to Holloway prison. Supporters marched there from Bow in torchlight, besieging the prison.

Sylvia was released only on condition that she did not campaign for votes for women in public. Nevertheless, three months later she appeared at a meeting at Bow Baths in disguise. No sooner had she begun speaking than police rushed to arrest her. As cries of 'Jump, Sylvia, jump!' went up from the audience, she leapt into the seating area and ran off, pursued by officers, who in the mêlée knocked one woman unconscious. A month later she was back at Bow Baths to speak, again evading police, who arrested Daisy Lansbury, daughter of George, believing that, as she was wearing Sylvia Pankhurst's hat, she must be Sylvia Pankhurst.

The suffragette movement was thrown into disarray by the outbreak of the First World War on 4 August 1914. Sylvia Pankhurst declared the hostilities to be a 'capitalists' war', and took her supporters weapons training in Victoria Park. In contrast Emmeline Pankhurst's WPSU threw its weight behind the war effort, asking, 'Could any woman face the possibility of the affairs of the country being settled by conscientious objectors, passive resisters and shirkers?'

Local women, though denied the vote, were encouraged to take on any difficult jobs vacated by the men who had gone to the trenches. They drove lorries, stoked the burners at Beckton Gas Works and helped manufacture munitions such as TNT at Silvertown's Brunner Monds Works, which exploded on 19 January 1917, killing seventy-three and injuring hundreds.

Sylvia refuted the argument that women needed to prove themselves by carrying out war work, and maintained her radical East London Federation of Suffragettes. Her organization moved its headquarters to another Bow address, 400 Old Ford Road. A large, angry crowd gathered outside in June 1914 when Sylvia, weakened by hunger strike and tied in a bath chair, was arrested.

On 11 January 1918 the Representation of the People Act gave the vote to all women who were over thirty, householders, wives of householders, occupiers of land over a certain value and university graduates. In 1928 all women over twenty-one were granted the vote. The East End had played a significant role in this success.

## POPLARISM

The most popular political philosophy in the East End in the early years of the twentieth century was a form of socialism that was moralist rather than Marxist, methodical rather than militant. It could be heard in union branches, town halls and churches. It could be heard in the intensely urban communities around the River Lea. By 1900 it had organized itself into a new party – the Labour Party – which was particularly active in East End districts such as Poplar, where thirty-seven different unions formed the Poplar Labour Party to challenge the Liberals as the main local political force.

Poplar was one of the poorest areas in Britain. Its population was almost entirely blue collar, low paid and economically fragile. Almost a third of Poplar men were labourers, and more than half of these were dockers, working casual shifts, employed day by day with no guarantee of work. At the beginning of the century the area veered from Liberal to Conservative. Alfred Yeo, a local shopkeeper, won the seat for the Liberals at the 1911 general election, beating the conservative Emery, with the help of a song sung enthusiastically by local children, which went: 'Vote, vote, vote for Mr Yeee-o/Punch old Emery in the eye/If it wasn't for the lore, we would break his bloomin' jore/An' 'e wouldn't come a-votin' no more.'

By the end of the decade Poplar council had become Labour. Its leader was George Lansbury, the Christian pacifist who had earlier resigned his parliamentary seat over women's suffrage. Lansbury's vision was of a well-organized, municipally dynamic borough. Poplar became one of the first London councils to provide public services such as baths, wash-houses and free libraries. At a time of growing unemployment and disenchantment with the First World War Lansbury wanted the council to be a model employer. Accordingly, Poplar introduced a minimum wage and paid men and women equal salaries. Local sanitation was better than in most similar areas and death rates were surprisingly low. Even the Poor Law Guardians, who administered the workhouse, had a more humanitarian reputation than their rivals in neighbouring districts.

In 1921 Poplar councillors voted to pay more poor relief to the local unemployed rather than hand their levy to the London County

Council. The government took Poplar to court over the issue and on 29 July the council leader, George Lansbury, and 2,000 supporters, accompanied by a mace-bearer and brass band, marched from the town hall to the High Court to demonstrate the authority's resolve. Thirty councillors were arrested and sent to prison – the men to Brixton, where they continued to hold council meetings in Lansbury's cell, the women to Holloway. When other councils expressed support for Poplar the jailed councillors were asked to negotiate. The government then relented, agreeing to apportion the precept according to each borough's means. It was a rare example of mass action resulting in a swift change in the law.

Lansbury became a major national figure. He later edited the left-wing daily newspaper the *Daily Herald*, and won re-election to Parliament in 1929, joining the new Labour government as First Commissioner of Works. He protected Hadrian's Wall from quarrying and passed an Ancient Monuments Act which still stands. When the Labour premier Ramsay MacDonald abandoned the party during the economic crisis of 1931 to form a coalition government, Lansbury became Labour leader by default, presiding over a withered rump of a party, whose loudest voices had either joined the national government or lost office.

By 1939 Lansbury was no longer Labour leader but mayor of Poplar. He journeyed to Berlin to meet Hitler and Mussolini in an ambitious but fruitless attempt to seek peace, but never saw world war return for he died on 7 May 1940, four months before the Second World War began. Ironically, his home, 39 Bow Road, was one of the first East End houses to be destroyed by German bombs.


## FASCISTS

Where communism preached world revolution, fascism embraced revolution in one country. It promoted the egalitarianism, but not the internationalist outlook of socialism, and its egalitarianism did not always include all sections of society.

Fascism was founded by an Italian socialist, Benito Mussolini, who, after being expelled from the country's main socialist party for urging Italy's participation in the First World War, gained power on his own idiosyncratic socialist platform. He called his new group *fascia di combattimento*, the *fascia* being the bundle of rods Roman civil servants carried in front of magistrates to symbolize the latter's powers. Needing a creed, Mussolini came up with the idea of the 'corporatist' state: commerce and industry divided into corporations run by representatives of employers, workers and the government. This was a system derived purely for the benefit of Italy; other countries would have to find their own solutions.

By the 1920s a new generation of Europeans, shaped by the horrors of the First World War, was coming of age. It wanted a better world to emerge from the bloodbaths of Flanders. Of these new men with new ideas, the loudest in Britain was Oswald Mosley, an aristocratic war hero, who had been invalided out of the forces with one leg three inches shorter than the other.

Mosley impressed the Harrow Conservative Party with his oratory and enthusiasm, and won the seat in what was known as the 'Khaki General Election' of 1918. His platform was left wing for a Tory: a belief in higher wages, shorter hours, slum clearance, public ownership, and improved services in education and health. In the House of Commons Mosley proved to be one of the few MPs willing to stand up to the bullying Liberal minister Winston Churchill, and he was earmarked as a future premier by many commentators.

When the Liberal–Conservative coalition broke up in 1922 Mosley chose to re-stand as an Independent. He won. A national figure already and he was only twenty-six. Here was the man who would surely become Britain's great leader. When two years later Labour formed a government for the first time, Mosley saw an opening and joined its left-wing adjunct, the Independent Labour Party, applying for the parliamentary Labour whip. Given Mosley's left-wing views, it was no surprise that he soon drifted to the Labour Party, for whom he advocated a 'third way' (a phrase recently purloined by Tony Blair) between Bolshevism and reaction.

When Labour won the 1929 general election Mosley was appointed Chancellor of the Duchy of Lancaster. By the end of the year he was advocating his own programme for tackling the growing problem of unemployment with the Mosley Memorandum, a twenty-five-page dossier produced with the help of the great East End radical George Lansbury, and the country's leading economist, J. M. Keynes. The House gave him passionate support, but the government rejected his proposals. The Chancellor of the Duchy of Lancaster solving the nation's problems; really. Or as Richard Crossman, who later became a Labour minister, wrote in 1961: 'Mosley was spurned by Whitehall, Fleet Street and every party leader at Westminster simply and solely because he was right.'

When Mosley failed to carry the Labour Party conference he formed a new political party, the prosaically titled New Party. But at the 1931 general election New Party candidates were humiliated. Even in Whitechapel the East End folk hero Kid Lewis, who drilled Mosley's force of tough young security guards, denigrated in the press as the 'Biff Boys', polled only 154 votes.

Realizing there was no future in his lightweight New Party, Mosley visited Italy to find out how he could remould his party in the continental style. The New Party became the British Union of Fascists. Because of his opposition to communism and the Soviet Union, Mosley enjoyed support from businessmen – Jewish businessmen such as Israel Sieff of Marks and Spencer and the publisher Paul Hamlyn. And why not? Mosley himself had no record of acting anti-Semitically in public or private. Nor was it unusual that Jews would be fascists. After all, the chief rabbi of Italy was a member of the Italian Fascist Party.

By the end of 1932 hostile references to Jewish capitalists had crept into BUF speeches. Jews were untrustworthy, the British fascists claimed, for they played key roles in the two anti-fascist camps: communism and capitalism. Fascists who were already anti-Semitic (there were plenty in all parties) became bolder and louder. The fascist programme was designed to protect national interests, but the Jews were an international body which respected no national boundaries and therefore had to be opposed. The richest Jews, the Rothschilds, had founded their banks at the time of the Napoleonic wars with a conscious policy not to serve any national government exclusively, the fascists pointed out. The Rothschilds were able to tell the British prime minister Lord Liverpool, the result of the Battle of Waterloo one-and-a-half days before Wellington's official dispatch. Even

Catholics could not match that network. One minute the Jew would swear allegiance to the Tsar and a few weeks later, after emigrating to London, to the British king. The Jew was too powerful. 'All States, all things, all sovereigns they control, And waft a loan from Indies to the Pole,' as Lord Byron had explained in 'The Age of Bronze'. Jews were soon ousted from BUF membership.

The fascists concentrated on the East End, where economic hardship and poverty abutted the City, with its financial institutions and bold traditions. Beyond, in the West End, were bright lights and glamour. Here was the East End, where no light shone. Here was the East Ender, Britain's forgotten man, who would be rescued by Oswald Mosley, cast as a millennial religious substitute. Mosley began to prey on the simmering resentment the impoverished white working-class East Ender felt towards others, particularly non-Christians. With an ideology that was apocalyptic and centred around the idea of imminent catastrophe, he identified a scapegoat in the heart of the East End in the shape of the Jew.

In 1933 the British Union of Fascists opened an East End office in an empty cowshed at 64 Squirries Street, off Bethnal Green Road. They decorated the premises with their new symbol – a bolt of lightning inside a circle – ridiculed by opponents as the flash in the pan. The Squirries Street office saw much heel-clicking and arm-swishing. Members would salute even when just answering the phone. They were duty bound to wear a uniform: black polo neck shirt and black trousers; fascists on more than three days' service a week were obliged to wear black riding breeches with jackboots. HQ was soon full of men carefully placing razor blades in potatoes and apples, secreting piping in their jackets and hiding tiny knives in their hob-nailed boots.

Through a nostalgic haze the British Union of Fascists venerated a vanished harmonious community of workers and feudal lords united in duty and custom. It claimed that Jewish landlords had priced out white residents, forcing them to move to the new overspill estates of Becontree and Harold Hill. It explained how Jews had corrupted society by introducing alien culture – jazz, surrealism and the cinema – to British arts. From Squirries Street poured forth anti-Jewish propaganda explaining how Jews worked not for social advancement, but for personal pride. How rich Jews purposely remained in the East

End to look down on the gentiles. Here was the Jewish businessman, cigar in mouth, sleeked-back hair, cuff-links, arm-bands, braces and snazzy shoes urging hard work and long hours, with few prospects of advancement for his workers. One batch of bad orders and he would close down the firm, sending the workforce on to the dole queue while he reopened elsewhere. There was his brother, the communist agitator with wild demonic eyes and the keys to the local printing press, a batch of *Daily Workers* under his arm, urging strikes and revolutionary activity that would jeopardize the livelihood of the working man who simply wanted to earn an honest crust and had no time for alien political ideology.

The fascists took advantage of the incompetence of the main political parties in the East End. The Labour Party was relatively powerless in an area where the lack of heavy industry meant weak trade unions. They preyed on the fears of local small businesses – furniture workshops, tailors – of which there were many (many Jewish!) in the area, and activated the East End as a launch-pad for a national assault. Their open-air meetings in Victoria Park were driven by intimidation and aggression amid a terrific clamour of boos and cat-calls. Objects were thrown at the speakers, not by opponents, but by the fascists themselves, trained and primed to create havoc by contriving the existence of a violent enemy who needed to be vanquished. (Later there was a real enemy, but the trick had worked by then.) Snatch squads rushed from party headquarters to whisk imperilled speakers away in black vans, the windows covered by wire mesh and armour plating.

At public meetings held in East End pubs – the Salmon and Ball by Bethnal Green tube station was a favourite venue – fascist guards lined up below the stage across the width of the room eyeing the crowd. The speaker would begin his discourse by warning that he would tolerate no heckling. A shiver of excitement would run through the audience. Surely such a warning could only increase the likelihood of violence. No sooner had the speaker begun his discourse than he would be shouted down. Was this a genuine interruption or had it been stage-managed? Either way the same pattern would follow. Fascist stewards would sweep through the crowd and noisily remove the heckler. If the heckler were a fascist stooge, planted to create a commotion, he would be bundled out painlessly. If the interrupter were a genuine opponent, he would be silenced with a fist, taken outside and kicked repeatedly. There would soon be another fracas, and within seconds such pandemonium would have broken out that no more debate could take place. On cue the police would arrive to close down the meeting. Back at party HQ punishment would be meted out to fascists who had disobeyed the leadership, or who had genuinely brought the organization into greater disrepute than anticipated. Calculated pain was inflicted on the guilty: a needle driven into the testicles; messy operations involving castor oil.

With the havoc planned by the British Union of Fascists having taken hold of the East End by the mid-1930s, Oswald Mosley arrived in the area, striding through the streets of Stepney at the head of a growing band of followers, arms raised in salute to shouts of 'Hail Mosley'. Now that the Jew had been suitably demonized, battle could commence. The East End became a war zone. By day groups of black-shirted young men would 'urge' people to buy their newspaper. At night they would be replaced by rabble-rousers running open-air meetings where the crowds would chant, 'The Yids, the Yids, we got to get rid of the Yids' and sing 'Roll on the Pogroms' to the tune of 'Roll Out the Barrel'. Graffiti gangs roamed the streets scrawling 'PJ' (Perish Judah) on the walls of synagogues and 'This is the home of a Jew' at Jewish addresses. On 30 August 1936 fascists boarded buses in Whitechapel, throwing off those they suspected of being Jewish. Letters were sent to Jewish MPs and councillors which read: 'Each of you has a lamppost ready and waiting'. Anti-Semitic attacks escalated after BUF members toured the East End sticking cards bearing the word 'Jew' on suspected Jewish shops. BUF members would walk into Jewish-run shops and announce: 'This won't be your shop for long. It will soon be ours.' The roar of the fascist amplifiers meant that Jewish children went to sleep to a soundtrack of hate, and scrapped in school playground games of 'Jew' and 'Blackshirt'.

By autumn 1936 a new map had been drawn across the East End, dividing it into Jewish and gentile. Unaccompanied Blackshirts kept away from Mile End, Brick Lane and the streets off Commercial Road. On the other hand, no Jew would willingly cross Burdett Road eastwards, Ratcliff Highway southwards, or venture into the hinterland of

Bethnal Green around Old Bethnal Green Road and Quilter Street (featured unchanged sixty years later in the Mike Leigh film *Secrets and Lies*); streets where there had been little Jewish immigration and there had long been a siege mentality, the police loath to enter; streets run by their own local guv'nors which obeyed no law other than that of fist smashed into face.

## THE BATTLE OF CABLE STREET

The climax to 1936, the fascists' *annus mirabilis*, was to be a march on Sunday 4 October. The BUF would stride proudly through the heart of the Jewish ghetto, stopping at four designated points to rally support and create a spectacle. There they would be joined by tens of thousands of locals, mostly youths, stirred by Mosley's breathless devil-may-care oratory. These young foot-soldiers had already been engaged by constant appeal to their baser sentiments. After all, what more enjoyable way to spend a Sunday afternoon could there be than a pint or two in the Lord Rodney's Head on Whitechapel Road, some banter with the lads, a bit of shouting and singing, a bundle with the commies and the Old Bill, a left hook, a chase? Back home, exhilarated, euphorically weary before Monday morning work.

The Jews were worried that the march would be followed by a pogrom. The communists, with one eye on the Spanish Civil War, which had recently broken out, wanted to prevent the fascists organizing support for the Spanish fascist leader, Franco. All sides prepared for battle. East End Labour politicians such as Clement Atlee warned that the march would lead to much bloodshed, and urged a ban.

Instead, Sir Philip Game, the Metropolitan Police Commissioner, sent 6,000 police officers – a third of the Met's force – into the area on the morning of the 4th as fascists, communists, Jews and the masochistically curious gravitated to Stepney and St George's. A group of communists infiltrated the enemy camp. One of them, Hugh Faulkner, was a doctor at the East End's London Hospital. He approached the thick line of policemen guarding a large contingent of fascists near the Tower, shouted 'doctor, let me through', and was allowed past. Among the fascists he found a colleague from the hospital. 'I've made up my mind. I want to join you,' Faulkner told the man. He was shown the route of the fascists' intended march. 'I better go and move my car,' Faulkner added. He left, crossed the police lines again and phoned through the details to his communist friends. Unfortunately, they didn't believe him.

At noon a large group of Independent Labour Party members demonstrating against the march collided with some fascists coming out of Mark Lane station. A car bearing the slogan 'Mosley shall not pass' swept into Royal Mint Street, which links Tower Hill and Cable Street, where some 2,500 Blackshirts were parading in front of a thick line of policemen. By 1.30 p.m. the Blackshirts were congregated around Tower Hill and Royal Mint Street, while some 500 anti-fascists and Jews were assembled at Gardiner's Corner, the junction of Whitechapel High Street and Commercial Road, a few hundred yards to the north, chanting, 'They shall not pass.'

It was around a quarter past two when the cry went up: 'Everyone to Cable Street!', where opponents including, Trotskyite legend has it, Ted Grant, leader of the Militant Tendency in the 1980s, had overturned a lorry and thrown alongside it barrels, corrugated iron, timber, paving stones and piles of bricks. The crowd surged along Leman Street, throwing marbles at the police horses' hooves, tearing down a barricade and arming themselves with the jagged wooden pieces. The police kept the two sides apart as the crowd waited for the arrival of Mosley. Just before 3.30 p.m. the fascist leader's bodyguards arrived in vans with barred windows. As they jumped out the crowd surged forward, but were obstructed by mounted police with batons drawn, who drove them into side streets.

A few minutes later Mosley arrived at the junction of Dock Street and Cable Street in an open-top car, driven at walking pace and flanked by police motorcycle outriders. He was wearing a black military jacket, grey riding breeches, jackboots, black peaked military cap and a red arm-band. An autogiro (an early type of helicopter) flew overhead. Opponents, held back by a huge cordon of police officers, showered a volley of stones and bricks on the motorcade. One smashed the window of Mosley's car; another struck him in the face. As Mosley's Bentley tried to turn into Cable Street, the fascists began singing 'M-O-S-L-E-Y, We want Mosley.' The communists retorted with the 'Internationale'. Mosley, surrounded by his wrestler body-guards, gave a Hitler salute as his car was attacked by a band of men whose leader attempted to hit Mosley's bodyguard, Roughneck, with a chair-leg. The man doing the attacking was Jack Spot, who became one of London's leading post-war gangsters.

While Mosley got out of the car to review his troops, Fenner Brockway, secretary of the Independent Labour Party, smarting from being trampled on by police horses, phoned the home secretary, John Simon, urging him to call off the march. Simon phoned Mosley and told him that in view of the large crowds and the risk of further clashes, the procession would have to be diverted to central London. Fascism had lost the day.

Instead of marching through the East End, Mosley's British Union of Fascists were diverted to the empty City, where to strains of the 'Horst Wessel Lied' ('Raise high the flag/The ranks are closed and tight/Storm Troopers march/With firm and steady step/Souls of the comrades shot by Reds') the fascist leader thundered; 'The government has surrendered to red violence and Jewish corruption. We never surrender. We shall triumph over the parties of corruption because our faith is greater than their faith, our will is stronger than their will and within us is the flame that shall light this country and light this world.' Meanwhile, at Limehouse more fascists waited several hours for Mosley, unaware that his car had not been able to pass through Cable Street.

Over the course of the afternoon eighty-four people were arrested and taken to Leman Street police station. Among them was the sixteen-year-old Charlie Goodman, picked up for climbing a lamppost and shouting at the top of his voice, 'Don't be yellow bellies, forward, we are winning.' Also brought in was the teenage Jack Shaw, who later recounted the incident: 'I was chased into Royal Mint Street and I could not get over the barricades. An old lady, a Christian lady, smashed the policeman in the face and said "Leave that boy alone". I was grabbed. Four policemen dragged me to Leman Street police station. My head went through the door and the shout was "Another Jew bastard". One of the old-time coppers was so shocked he dragged me away and said "Keep quiet, sonny. These bastards'll kill you."'

Shaw saw the floor and walls covered with the blood of those who had been beaten by the police. He remembered seeing one officer drag in a non-Jewish woman, rip off her blouse, and hold his truncheon as if to strike her in the face until she yelled at him, 'I am not afraid of you', at which point he called her a 'Jewish bitch' and threw her into a cell.

Shaw was charged with throwing a brick at a police inspector, and a Jewish doctor gave evidence against him. When Shaw asked the doctor why there was no scar on the police inspector's face the witness disingenuously replied: 'It's all according to how the brick landed on his face', which led the magistrate, the feared Basil Henriques, to intervene quickly. 'Quite right, doctor,' he said, sentencing Shaw to three months' hard labour for grievous bodily harm. Henriques, despite being Jewish, then made Shaw suffer a little more. 'You're a hooligan,' he told him. 'You should have let Mosley march,' and transferred him from Wormwood Scrubs to Bristol so that his parents would not be able to visit him easily. Shaw didn't even get a call from a Jewish chaplain. He found out why on his release when a Jewish member of the prison governors told him, 'This sort of thing doesn't happen in England. You should be ashamed of yourself.'

A week later, on 11 October, the communists staged a counter-demonstration between Tower Hill and Victoria Park. One banner proclaimed: 'Fascism burnt the Reichstag, don't let it set Europe in flames'. When the crowd dispersed, violence began. Over a hundred police broke up the fights between communists and fascists near Whitechapel station and forced the fascists into Shoreditch and Hoxton, their heartlands, where the trouble abated.

Meanwhile, a gang of about 150 Mosley youth stormed Mile End Road, smashing the windows of every Jewish shop. They pulled Samuel Jelen, a hairdresser, off his feet and threw him through a shop window. Glass smashed all around him. A few moments later they threw a four-year-old girl after him. On White Horse Lane, Stepney, the fascists captured a Jewish girl and hoisted her to an advertising hoarding so that it looked as if she had been crucified. Another gang of older fascists, led by Mosley, marched from Victoria Park to Limehouse, along the eastern boundary of the Jewish ghetto, to cries of 'Good old Mosley'. Hundreds tried to shake the leader's hand.

Within a few weeks of the events in Cable Street Jewish shopkeepers in the East End were being plagued by a new menace – protection racketeers capitalizing on their misery, insisting that they pay a premium to a 'window- and property-protection society' that would safeguard them against further trouble. The society's representatives were suave and smartly dressed, and they were Jewish. The shopkeepers refused the offer, and within a week the newly glazed windows of their shops were smashed again. Behind the scam was Jack Spot, the aspiring Jewish gangster who had attacked Mosley in his car as it had tried to turn into Cable Street.

Despite the fascists' failure to 'take' the East End, they maintained their campaigning zealously. The East End became one vast political parade ground. Open-air meetings continued almost nightly, with small groups of Blackshirts, communists and Jews dotted around the streets, particularly those near Victoria Park, looking for action. Surprisingly the fascists' progress was stymied by the government. Realizing it could outflank the BUF by playing on the party's deference to the law, Parliament introduced restrictive legislation – the Public Order Act – a clever law which banned the wearing of political uniforms and meant that the fascists, to their horror, would no longer be able to identify each other easily in public (or be recognized by the public).

Of course this was not the end of the BUF, merely the end of the paramilitary BUF. At the March 1937 London County Council elections the party averaged 18 per cent of the East End vote, some achievement given the negative publicity it had endured. When Mosley heard the results he smashed his fist into his hand and shouted, 'Better than Hitler!', referring to the German dictator's poor results four years before gaining power. But Mosley got no further. The advance of fascism and national socialism in Europe thwarted the BUF for, when Germany became a serious threat to Britain, Mosley replaced his lust for thunderous rhetoric and political violence with a programme of peace; peace with Nazi Germany. Few Londoners wanted a reflective, considerate fascist party.

When German troops crossed the border into Poland on 1 September 1939 fascist activity in the East End ceased. Fascist bookshops were emptied of stock; fascist offices were boarded up overnight. Britain declared war on Germany two days later. But during the quiet early months of the Second World War (the Phoney War) fascist activity recommenced. The padlocked British Union of Fascists headquarters, by now on Roman Road – the main route connecting Bethnal Green and Bow – reopened as a 'Peace Centre'. At night fascists crept round London committing small acts of sabotage such as cutting telephone cables. They placed stickers proclaiming 'This is a Jews' war' on anything that didn't move (lampposts were particularly popular). They sprayed anti-Semitic graffiti on walls asking: 'Why should you die for Poland's 3,500,000 Jews?', even daubing 'PJ' on a property once occupied by the gentile Lenin. They urged East Enders to 'Support Christianity. Oppose atheism', and proclaimed: 'No alliance with the Jew atheist Bolsheviks against our fellow Christians.' At street meetings the chants would be heard:

MOSLEY: What is international power?
CROWD:  The Jews!
MOSLEY: You know, my friends . . .
CROWD:  The Jews!
MOSLEY: Yes! International finance!

In May 1940 Oswald Mosley was arrested at his Pimlico flat and detained under emergency Defence of the Realm laws. It was an ignominious end for the man who had expected to be by then striding the world stage arm in arm with Francisco Bahamonde, Benito Mussolini and Adolf Hitler.

# 11

# The Unlucky Isle of Dogs

A flat, low-lying, U-shaped peninsula, a mile and a half long, three-quarters of a mile wide. Around it snakes the Thames. Within it lie marshes and meadows cut by ditches. The land is forlorn, windswept and devoid of life save seagulls, sheep and cows. The nearest settlements are more than a mile to the north. By the water's edge are rushes that can be used for weaving mats or making wicker cages for catching fish. At the foot of the land are wooden gibbets where the swaying corpses of recently hanged pirates warn seamen arriving in London on the Thames that they are entering a tough place.

This was medieval Stebunhethe Marsh, a mostly empty and terrible stretch of land. Nothing much happened here until 1800. Then, within a few decades, it became the hub of London industry: Planet Vulcan, a burning smithy of iron and steel powering shipbuilding and engineering. In the twenty-first century it houses Britain's tallest skyscrapers at Canary Wharf, a commercial empire of granite and glass, the shining city of the dream – home to Mammon and the media.

From Saxon times until the sixteenth-century Reformation the land was owned by the Bishop of London, who sent Cistercian monks from Eastminster Abbey, near Tower Hill, to maintain the river wall and drain the marsh. In the fourteenth century the island acquired its first building, a chapel for pilgrims journeying between Canterbury and Waltham Abbey, which stood near the modern-day Chapel House Street. The building was abandoned when the river overflowed in 1448.

By the late sixteenth century Stebunhethe Marsh had been given a nickname – the Isle of Dogs – though nobody knows how this strange name came about. It may have been a corruption of 'Isle of Ducks' or

'Isle of Dykes'. It may have referred to real dogs – Henry VIII's royal hounds – which were kept here. Locals tell a fanciful story about a dog which swam around the body of his dead master, who had been thrown into the sea, and later growled at a waterman who turned out to be the murderer. Perhaps the island is named after this dog.

The land was prone to constant flooding until the sixteenth century when Vanderdelf, a Dutchman, drained the marsh, built an embankment, and made it suitable for cattle, whose meat was salted and barrelled for the army. But the island remained a lonely place. Samuel Pepys, journeying to a wedding dressed 'in a new coloured silk suit and coat trimmed with gold buttons and gold broad lace round my hands, very rich and fine', was forced to stay here for a few hours on 31 July 1665 when his horse-drawn ferry became stuck in the ebb tide. He captured the predicament in his diary: 'So we were fain to stay there, in the unlucky Isle of Doggs, in a chill place, the night cold and wind fresh . . . to our great discontent.'

Pepys never explained why he felt the Isle of Dogs to be 'unlucky', but the physical difficulty in leaving the area meant that he had to send the licence and wedding ring ahead by horse while his party waited for a coach and six to take them across, thereby missing the service, though luckily not the celebration party.

A scurrilous play written by Thomas Nashe and Ben Jonson in 1597, now lost, was called *The Isle of Dogs*. The play so irked the monarchy that the authors and the leading actors were jailed for a few months, and all London's theatres were closed. To William Blake, writing his epic poem 'Jerusalem' in the first decade of the nineteenth century, the Isle of Dogs was one of many London haunts of Los, embodiment of imagination, inspiration and wisdom, 'the eternal prophet'. It was also home to the dogs of Leutha, who lapped 'the water of the trembling Thames' and whose only purpose was to destroy their masters.

For much of the seventeenth century the island had only two 'official' inhabitants: the man who drove the cattle off the marshes and the man who operated the ferry to Greenwich on the opposite bank. Then, between 1679 and 1740, twelve mills containing granaries and bakehouses went up along the western bank. Cottages were built, and a new community formed: Millwall.

There was now life on the island, even though it was mostly limited to traders stopping to unload grain and load flour. A row of smart houses was built at the north-eastern corner of the island on a street called Coldharbour, the name taken from the most impressive of the new houses, built for Sir John Poultenay of Coldharbour in the City, who was Lord of the Manor of Poplar in the fourteenth century. At the northern end of Coldharbour was another magnificent brick mansion, Isle House, built in 1824 for the Blackwall Dockmaster. Alongside was No. 3, where Admiral Nelson reputedly stayed in 1799 before leaving to fight in the Battle of Aboukir. Coldharbour still stands; the oldest development on the island.

The building of West India Dock at the northern end of the peninsula at the end of the eighteenth century tore apart many of the remaining rural features of the island. An army of navvies, bricklayers, carpenters, surveyors, engineers and architects descended on the area, wiping out the hedgerows and lanes to excavate huge basins for the docks. Bricks were made from the extracted earth and were built into a forbiddingly high wall around the site to protect it – implying a mystery within which tantalized visitors and locals for the next 150 years. Around the same time a new waterway, the City Canal, was cut across the north of the island to allow vessels – mostly whaling ships laden with spermaceti oil – to reach the more westerly docks near Tower Bridge without having to negotiate the lengthy trip around the peninsula. The Isle of Dogs was now an island.

## CITY OF BURNING NIGHT

Steadily the population grew: from 200 in 1800 to 1,400 in 1830. They came from all over Britain to power London's industrial revolution. A new wide road running alongside the perimeter of the island was built, financed by businessmen remembered in the names of nearby streets: Price, Byng, Tooke, Batson. A bus service began, 'the smallest of all metropolitan omnibuses', according to Charles Dickens, who caught it in 1853. Then came trains; William Cubitt engineered a railway line that linked Blackwall Dock with Tower Hill, the trains being hauled into the London terminus at Fenchurch Street by cable.

Cubitt also created a new estate at the south-east corner of the island – Cubitt Town – built in the 1850s on land leased from the Countess of Glengall. Cubitt Town solved the housing shortage created by the rapid increase in the local population, mostly made up of immigrant Scots and Irish brought in to man the docks, iron foundries, flour mills and paintworks. Unfortunately, the builders completed the project too swiftly and did not take sufficient care in the construction of the houses. Nor was the fabric of the properties maintained properly, and when floods came in 1879 pools of sewage poured into the basements. More care was taken in the construction of the smart villas on Saunders Ness Road which offered a view across the Thames to the Renaissance glories of Greenwich. But there were never enough wealthy merchants willing to live this far away from civilization to maintain the gentility of the locale.

Millwall, the older community on the western side of the island, became intensely industrialized. Here were shipyards, workshops, warehouses, factories, ironworks, brass foundries, cement works, potteries, shipbuilding yards and engineering firms. By 1817 Johnstone's London Commercial Directory was listing thirty-two firms built on the site of the Millwall windmills, which between them made cement, chains, masts, ropes, barrels, boilers and rivets; especially rivets ('Rivets, by heaven! Rivets. To get on with the work – to stop the hole').

As for which firm was the dirtiest, noisiest, loudest, biggest stain on the environment, it was a close call between Cassell's Pitch, Tar, Oil, Paint, Naptha and Varnish yard, Burnett's works for the manufacture of disinfecting fluid, Jukes, Coulson and Co., working scrap iron into anchors and chains, Sir Charles Price and Co., where rapeseed and linseed were crushed and turpentine distilled, and Brown and Lenox, making chain cables to lay across the ocean floor.

It was noisy, noxious, nasty work which began at five in the morning, as official wakers strode the streets to rouse the bleary-eyed an hour before the workshop bell rang and three hours before their breakfast of herring, watercress and shrimp. It was a thriving working-class community. Tiny houses of four rooms: two-up, two-down, no inside toilet; houses notorious for their lack of privacy, houses which refused to remain clean.

Still the island's population kept growing. The 1,400 of 1830 became 5,000 by 1850, and 14,000 within ten years. But there was room for only a small proportion of those who needed to be here. Most of the workers manning the factories had a three-mile journey to their jobs. In 1868 the Millwall Dock and Canal Company opened a new dock that turned much of Millwall into water. The City Canal was converted into another dock, which meant that the Isle of Dogs was no longer an island. To the sides of the dock were bridges linking the area with the rest of London. Horse-drawn cabs, horses and carts, herds of cows and sheep, pedestrians, and even caged circus animals being brought in from the docks, had to wait for a ship to make its way through before being able to cross the bridge – 'catch a bridger', as it became known. But islanders felt themselves cut off from the rest of the world. They developed a siege mentality. They knew more of the far-off countries whose goods passed through the local import docks than they did of the rest of London.

Shipbuilding began to dominate local industry in the mid-nineteenth century. Under a sulphurous sky filled with shoots of hissing steam cranes shifted their loads through the smoke and oily grime, and hunchbacked men with blackened faces turned vast cog-wheels, bashed their hammers on sheets of steel and trained vats of molten metal into containers. Steam power and metal fired the ancient industry.

Britain's wealth depended on the quality of its merchant ships and fighting vessels, so yard after yard was geared into producing iron-clad ships for the navy and sea-borne cities plying the British Empire for the great entrepreneurs. This was a boom period for London shipping, when coal cargoes coming into London rose from just under 10,000 tons in 1852 to a million tons ten years later.

As east London had become the world's fastest growing shipbuilding location it was only right that it was here, at Russell's yard in Millwall, that the world's largest ship was built. *Leviathan*, designed by Isambard Kingdom Brunel, at least four times bigger than any other ship in the world, was able to take 6,000 passengers on the 22,500-mile route to Australia and back, and weighed 22,500 tons, one ton for each mile.

To locals watching *Leviathan* being built it looked as if a metallic Tower of Babel was rising out of the dock. The world waited in wonder. Finally, in November 1857, the great day arrived. *Leviathan* was ready to be launched. Ten thousand people gathered at Burrell's Wharf (now Blasker Walk) in Millwall. Brunel asked for perfect silence before giving the go-ahead to let the 12,000-ton hull edge into the water sideways on iron rails. Then calamity struck. The chains snapped and the ship remained stuck on its rollers. *Leviathan* would not move! So many people had gathered that, as the drama unfolded, one man died in the severe crush. The press ridiculed Brunel, who desperately organized another launch. And another. It was only after three more aborted attempts that the vessel was water-borne. By then the owners had gone bankrupt.

*Leviathan*'s maiden voyage was another disaster. Everything was running smoothly until about half past five in the afternoon, when there was a tremendous explosion as the vessel passed Folkestone, scattering broken glass, fragments of wood and slithers of iron through the skylight. The centre of the ship was a confusion of fire and vapour. The funnel had been blown apart and had smashed through the ornate dining room – empty, fortunately – destroying the gilt mirrors and chandeliers. Somehow the ship managed to struggle on to Portland. It was repaired but found to be too costly to run and too cumbersome on rough seas. The shock was too much for Brunel, who was seriously ill, having suffered a severe stroke. He soon had a relapse, and died shortly after.

*Leviathan* was renamed *The Great Eastern* and finally made the open sea, plying the trade routes between India and Australia. It also carried the first telegraphic cables to be laid down on the Atlantic seabed, although the first cable snapped halfway across the ocean. In 1886 the vessel was converted into a showboat for the Lewis's store of Liverpool. Two years later it was broken up. During the demolition two skeletons were found entombed between the double hull: a shipwright and his apprentice had been trapped during construction and had starved to death.

The boom in heavy industry in Millwall could not last. By 1866 the prohibitive costs of importing huge quantities of iron, coal and steel hundreds of miles from the North to east London had led to bankruptcies and closures in the shipyards. It did not take long for the ship-building crash to affect the smaller supporting industries, local shops and the service sector. Thousands were thrown out of work; there were 6,000 unemployed in the borough where a few years previously there had only been 600. Destitution took hold. Many of those who had emigrated from distant parts of Britain to work the yards returned home with their families.

Yet bust soon returned to boom, for this was Britain's most economically expansive century. New industries involved in packaging and distribution for the enlarged docks were established. The railway was extended through the island in 1871. Saw mills, pump manufacturers and cask makers sprang up; here an antimony ore works, there a coal and coke company. The new local firms were bigger and bolder than anything that had gone before. Typical of these was Yarrow's of Cubitt Town, which won a contract in 1875 to build a steamer for use on Lake Nyasa in southern Africa, and was soon making iron bridges for export around the world. But none was more powerful than Thames Ironworks. The company occupied locations on both banks of the Lea's confluence with the Thames, and took some 200 workers on ferries between the two shores. Like Russell's, Thames Ironworks suffered one major disaster: the launch of the *Albion* in 1898.

The *Albion* was a 130-yard-long cruiser, commissioned by the Admiralty. On the launch day, 21 June 1898, 30,000 spectators turned up, 200 of whom lined the slipway bridge. Surely the bridge could never hold this many? It was signposted as dangerous, after all. There were three attempts to smash a bottle of champagne against the hull. They all failed. When the vessel hit the water the momentum created a huge wave which poured over the bridge, smashing it to pieces and throwing those on it into the river. Thirty-seven spectators lost their lives, their cries drowned out by the cheers of those who were applauding the launch. Those celebrating included the Duke and Duchess of Windsor, who didn't realize there was any problem and left the scene in their own boat.

Thames Ironworks was run by Arnold Hills, who, unusually for the time, was a teetotaller, campaigning anti-smoker and vegetarian. He was the first president of both the London Vegetarian Society (Mahatma Gandhi was another committee member) and the Vegetarian Cycling and Athletic Club. Hills was a benign patriarch who disliked trade unions and employed non-union labour, to his workforce's disgust. During a strike in 1891 his own workmen hissed at him as he entered the yard, but he held no grudges and the following year he implemented a 'Good Fellowship' scheme of bonuses, as well as reducing the working day from nine hours to eight. That extra hour of leisure could now be devoted to recreational activities, for Hills was obsessed with sport. Thames Ironworks had a cycling club, a cricket club and a works football team. Not any old works football team either, but one that went on to become one of England's greatest clubs – West Ham United – cup-winners of Europe in 1965. By that time Thames Ironworks was long defunct. The company collapsed just before the First World War, unable to compete with yards on the Tyne and Clyde.

## 'CITY OF DESOLATION'

The island has never been a pretty place. Thomas Wright, in *Some Habits and Customs of the Working Classes* (1867), railed against the 'slushy, ill-formed roads, tumble-down buildings, stagnant ditches and tracts of marshy, rubbish-filled waste ground', and concluded his survey with the most damning epithet he could find by describing the Isle of Dogs as the 'Manchester of London'. George R. Sims, author of 1911's *In Limehouse and the Isle of Dogs*, described it as 'Desolation-Land – a vast expanse of dismal waste ground and grey rubbish heaps . . . a black fringe of grim wharves and towering chimneys, belching volumes of smoke into a lowering sky that seems to have absorbed a good deal of the industrial atmosphere.' The Revd Richard Free was also keen on the word 'desolation'. In a parish magazine he described the island as 'City of desolation, badly lighted, astonishingly foul, inconceivably smelly and miserably bare and lifeless'.

The wind, fog, smoking chimneys and unrelenting noise of metal on metal meant that anyone who could afford to live elsewhere did so. Thus the island's population was almost entirely working class, tempered by those few professionals obliged by their station in, say, the church or medicine, to stay. For the latter there were no Beethoven recitals, dramatic performances or poetry readings to while away the long nights. The concert halls of Mayfair and St James's may have been only five miles away, but in terms of ease of access it might as well have been five light years. For those of refined manners and tastes there was next to no social alternative to the back-slapping bonhomie, porter-fuelled games of bowls and jingly piano of the local public house, where the conversation veered from sailors' talk of cyclones and typhoons, of the dark places of the sea, of Borneo, Sarawak and Celebes, to intense debates about pigeon-racing and greyhounds.

At least there was no shortage of pubs to fill the small patches of land between docks: the Gun on Coldharbour, looking over the water to the ghostly wastes of Bugsby's Marsh (now home to the Millennium Dome); the Newcastle Arms, taken over by the TV presenter Daniel Farson in the 1960s and visited by Clint Eastwood; and best of all Charlie Brown's.

Officially the Railway Tavern, and standing in the shadow of the railway bridge at the corner of Garford Street and West India Dock Road, it was run by Brown, a former boxer who liked to ride, and be seen riding, on horseback along the West and East India Dock Roads. He stuffed every corner of the tavern with a collection of eccentric curiosities gathered from around the world: a half-fish half-baby mummy, a two-headed calf, poisoned arrows, opium pipes, busts, statues, totems, trinkets and musical instruments. Brown ran the pub from 1893 till his death in June 1932, and his funeral procession was east London's best attended until that of Ronnie Kray in 1995. After arguments about who should be Brown's rightful heir, Charlie Junior took over the Blue Posts establishment opposite and renamed that Charlie Brown's. The two Charlie Brown's pubs stood for a few years as rivals, displaying parts of the original collection of curios. Both pubs are long gone.

There were almost as many pubs on the island as there were children, who would stand on the bridges over the inlet to the docks watching ships of the Blue Star, Cunard and Furness lines just in from Rangoon, Manila or Amoy make their way through the docks, their Lascar crews dressed in white robes, carrying drums of ashes on a pole, ready to dispense their cargoes of jade, onyx, malachite, betel-nut and bhang.

To the isle's children the place was one huge magical adventure playground of bowsprits, rotting barges and broken-down cranes. In its numerous dark corners the enterprising youngster could effortlessly obtain all the bits needed for a go-kart or a custom-made bike. And when that paled, there was the river, tantalizingly close, mostly unreachable, blocked off by docks and depots, but secretly accessible at Blackwall Stairs, where from a patch of sand below the London, Midland & Scottish Railway's Goods Depot wharf youth could brave the vessel-filled river to swim to the opposite bank.

The most unusual local playground was the huge mound of earth excavated in building the docks that was piled high near Cubitt Town and cordoned off by the land owners, the Port of London Authority. It became known as Mudchute, and the uncovered ditch which ran through it, often filled with dead animals and rotting vegetable matter, turned it into a cesspit that wobbled like a jelly and did wonders for the number of local outbreaks of typhoid. Anti-aircraft guns were sited at Mudchute during the Blitz, and it was later cordoned off by the dock police. In 1977 it reopened as an urban farm – Mudchute Farm – safe, sanitized and sober.

For adults leisure was almost entirely male orientated and made up of demanding pastimes to complement the demanding manual labour. Men fought each other with bare fists and raced each other in the Thames. They pitted cock against cock, pigeon against pigeon, dog against dog. On one occasion Custom House stadium staged a race between a pigeon and a whippet over 100 yards. The contest attracted more bets than anything else that took place at the venue. Many were convinced that the pigeon would simply soar over the dog to the winning line. Others thought that the bird, being of limited intelligence compared with the intellectual muscle of the dog, would fail to keep to the prescribed route and flap into a panic. The pigeon was carried to the starting line, while the dog confidently preened itself. The starting pistol cracked, the whippet took off, and the pigeon careered from lane to lane uncertainly. But just past the halfway mark the bird took to the air and zoomed past the amazed dog to fill the pockets of its backers.

Food on the isle was a barely nutritious cartoon diet, but this was hardly surprising given that so many local women worked for firms such as Morton's, specialists in potted fish and jam, and Maconochies, purveyors of Pan Yan Pickles, whose slogan was 'My, you're in a fine pickle'. Schoolchildren would come home at noon for a lunch of herring decorated with generous helpings of vinegar. After school it was time for tea – bread and marge with a spoonful of sugar sprinkled on top – washed down with sarsaparilla wine. Later they might be sent out to buy a ha'porth of jam – another nutrition-less feast – with their own container, which would be weighed before and weighed after to make sure the difference coincided with the weight a ha'porth could buy. Sunday mornings meant salt fish soaked overnight to remove the brine.

A significant part of the Isle of Dogs diet was medicine, taken perfunctorily rather than practically: syrup of figs, castor oil, gripe water. Two ounces of citrate of magnesia for clearing the bowels. A course of sulphur tablets, followed by brimstone and treacle, in the spring to clear the blood. In winter a daily dose of cod-liver oil and malt with a dollop of Scotts' Emulsion from an engaging-looking bottle whose label featured a man carrying a fish almost as big as himself. A particular treat for all occasions was locust beans – the seed of the carob tree, the favourite food of John the Baptist. Sacks of them by the thousand, which had somehow lost their place on cargo ships, were always rife.

In 1885 the Scottish jam manufacturers at Morton's formed a football club and named it after the locale. They went on to become the most loathed club in English football history, the very name – Millwall – enough to send a frisson of fear along the spine of opposition fans, their supporters traditionally meting out casual violence and flaunting their defiance to the chilling refrain: 'No one likes us, no one likes us, no one likes us, we don't care.'

Originally the team was called Millwall Rovers. Most of the players were Scottish, and they played in the incomers' native colours of Protestant blue and white. Their first pitch was on Glengall Road (now Tiler Road) and they used the Islanders' Public House as changing rooms. In 1910 Millwall left the Isle of Dogs for a ground on the other side of the Thames, where they have remained, albeit with the solecistic name unchanged. In a history spanning over 120 years Millwall have never won a major trophy.

New football clubs sprang up to meet interest in this newly

professionalized sport. Another works team, who in 1886 played their first match on the island, was Dial Square, formed by ammunition workers from the Woolwich Arsenal. They beat Eastern Wanderers 6–0 on a field at the south-eastern end of Glengall Road, but soon found a more permanent ground near the Woolwich works on the opposite bank of the river. The club turned professional in 1891 and twenty years later moved to north London as Arsenal. They, too, are now feared, but for their trophy-winning success, rather than their anti-social behaviour.

Into the twentieth century the island found it hard to keep its industry contemporary. Whereas west London embraced cars, recording, broadcasting and other exciting new technologies, the Isle of Dogs relied too much on the heavy stuff: lumps of metal, iron and steel. Employers knew the island had a stagnant, poorly educated population and few capable white-collar workers. Transport links were poor. The station at the southern tip of the peninsula was incongruously called North Greenwich, as if the authorities were embarrassed at giving it a name that smacked of the Isle of Dogs. It closed after the 1926 general strike, and didn't reopen until it was subsumed into the Docklands Light Railway in the 1980s. Firms left. Yarrow's, bridge-makers to the world, found the cost of operating by the Thames too high and headed for the Clyde in 1906. The mighty Thames Ironworks closed a few years later. Duckham's Oil left Millwall in the 1920s and was later absorbed into BP.

The economic crisis of the late 1920s and early 1930s hit the island hard. When unemployment was at its worst, the island's able-bodied men became so desperate for work that they took to making a living 'toshing' – collecting driftwood from the shore at low tide. To compound the economic grief the Thames had its worst ever flood in 1928. As the waters rose hundreds abandoned their homes to whatever watery fate the river had in store. Furniture floated down the streets. But at least the employers made sure that the barrels of merchandise recently unloaded from the docks were secured.

Yet it was not all doom. The expansion of the docks in the 1930s brought similar improvement in related commerce. The island resounded to the clash of iron hammers on steel joists. At Matthew T. Shaw's rolled steel, which had arrived by ship from Sheffield, was cut, drilled, beaten, bolted, riveted and welded into dredgers sent to the Malay marshes, and then abandoned in the jungle. Westwood's made iron and steel for the new extensions on the London underground. Snowdon's, which had nearly gone bust in 1917 when the Russian Revolution cost them their main client, recovered to develop a new type of oil that contained detergent.

In the 1930s the council demolished many of the most decrepit island cottages and built blocks of flats for which they, rather than private investors, were the landlords. The new blocks, icons of streamlined functionalism, dressed in sturdy muscularity with their decks of banded brick, strangely echoed the shape of the ocean liners berthed at the royal docks two miles east. The tenants were impressed. They had a kitchenette, rather than a parlour, an inside toilet, electricity and hot water. They had, however, lost their gardens and sense of privacy. One woman complained to the *East London Advertiser* that there was no drying ground and 'nowhere for the menfolk to have a hobby'.

In 1938, with another mass war expected, islanders prepared to defend their land, digging trenches in football grounds and making clubhouses over to anti-aircraft units. Once war was declared, on 3 September 1939, local children, each with a label bearing their name and school, left on coaches to rural safety. By the time it was safe for them all to return much of the island had been obliterated by German bombs.

# 12

# Blitz and Bombs

Britain declared war on Germany at 11.15 a.m. on Sunday 3 September 1939. Seven minutes later air-raid sirens sounded over east London. Policemen on bicycles rode up and down the East End streets brandishing placards bearing the message: 'Take Cover'. People blacked out their windows, for the bombs were surely about to fall. Barrage balloons were positioned over the river and anti-aircraft 'emplacements' erected in Victoria Park, east London. Sandbags were placed outside public buildings.

The East End public displayed none of the jingoistic flag-waving and cheering behaviour that had marked the beginning of the 1914–18 conflagration. The countdown to war had been long and tortuous. A sequence of failed utopian solutions to unemployment, poverty and inequality – various strains of communism and fascism – had brought the threat of conflict. No one knew when war would arrive, but it was inevitable, and, when it came, the East End, with its docks and heavy industries, would be in the front line.

There was a tacit agreement among locals that life was getting worse: it was harder getting a job; wages weren't rising in keeping with the higher cost of living; houses weren't being modernized fast enough; some, but not all, had electricity, kitchens, inside toilets.

When war was declared East Enders looked for the gas masks the government had issued. These masks sported pig-like snouts which made them look as grotesque as the beaked headpieces used as protection during the Bubonic Plague, some 300 years earlier. Alice Beanse of Wapping recalled how 'we had to go to a nearby hall to be fitted for these, and to me this was quite frightening. I felt as though I could not breathe. Nevertheless we all had them and always took them with us, especially during the early years of the war.' Less useful were the leaflets which explained that, if people suspected poison gas was in the air, they should look for one of the pillar boxes that had been painted with a special liquid which would change colour in the presence of poison.

Food rationing was soon introduced, and people had to live on unusual fare. Whale meat was popular because whales were not bound by the same regulations as cows. One Poplar man commented that it tasted 'strongly of fish, unless you soaked it for twenty-four hours in vinegar, after which it tasted of vinegar. But there was so much of it, great big bloody steaks as big as your plate, that we didn't care what it tasted like.'

Tens of thousands of local women and children were told to prepare for evacuation to the countryside. Some took the initiative themselves. The Gleeson family on the Isle of Dogs decided to move away and proceeded to the foot tunnel that connects the island with Greenwich, but found it shut. Watermen were taking people across the Thames in small rowing boats, and so they crossed the water by this, the ancient method. After walking in confusion *towards* London, they stopped at New Cross station, where they found a train leaving for Sevenoaks, then a mostly rural village separated from the London sprawl by a sliver of Kent countryside.

The Gleesons had no plan; they just wanted to get away. Alighting in Kent they stood in the road 'bewildered' as the regular commuters shuffled off home. A man stopped and offered to help. 'I shall go and phone my wife. I will do my best to get you settled for the night.' He found them board in a public house in the countryside. The Gleesons were safe from the bombs but they were stranded in an alien land, though less than twenty miles from home. And they had to pay rent.

Many evacuees found their rural hosts inhospitable, flinching from their coarse manners and tongues. In turn the East Enders wondered why they had uprooted themselves, leaving their homes undefended to be patronized and ridiculed by strangers. Those who were sent to the then sleepy villages around Epping Forest, barely ten miles from the East End, found no arrangements had been made for them, and that they were expected to sleep in the forest itself or in a cinema, upright in the seats. Some of the Epping contingent were taken to a school, marshalled into the assembly hall and told, 'The first thing we do with you East Enders is scrub yer.' They insisted on being driven immediately back to east London.

Britain might have been at war, but in the capital there was little concern until 19 September, when Adolf Hitler gave a speech in Danzig, referring to a weapon that could be used against Britain and France if they persisted with the war. What could this be, the public wondered? In East End pubs the talk was of long-range artillery which could bombard London from across the sea, of a death ray, nerve gas, germ warfare using a 'malignant pustule'. When no such weapons materialized, the press dismissed Hitler's talk as bluster.

The authorities decided to take no chances. They closed down cinemas and theatres, and imposed a 6 p.m. curfew on all shops except newsagents. Yet the war still did not appear to be a real threat for those left in London, only a minor inconvenience, such as when a barrage balloon in Bow broke free on 3 October, damaging a gas holder and causing a small fire.

There was considerable debate about what kind of shelters were needed to protect the public against the inevitable bombs. Mayor Lewey of Stepney argued for deep shelters but was told they were too costly. Many proposed the tube stations as an obvious and instant solution, but the government feared that the public would crowd the stations and refuse to leave, that children would fall on the tracks and that the streets would be choked with potential victims scurrying to get underground. And what if the public thought the shelters were too safe or too comforting? They would go down during the air raids and refuse to come out. The tube stations would flood in the rain. There would never be enough toilets or washing facilities. They would be a breeding ground for every possible infectious illness. More people might be killed by the germs of the shelters than by the bombs of the Germans.

The government unveiled its own domestic refuge, the Anderson Shelter – small corrugated steel huts with curved roofs, named after the home secretary, Sir John Anderson. The shelters arrived in parts and had to be assembled in the garden, where they were sunk three feet into the ground. They had no lighting, heating or toilet facilities, and would not be much use in heavy rain. Nevertheless hundreds of thousands of them were erected and many lives were saved, even though when the Blitz began many people did not want to leave their houses, either for an Anderson shelter or a tube station, preferring a cupboard under the stairs.

Once 1940 arrived with little outward sign of battle the war became ridiculed as the Phoney War or the Bore War. Evacuees returned. Theatres and cinemas reopened. Life appeared to be returning to normal. But the mood changed that spring with the German bombing of the Dutch port of Rotterdam and the invasion of surrounding countries by airborne troops.

The first German bombs did not fall on the London area until June 1940, hitting the countryside near Croydon. Then there was a break until August, when Croydon airport, at that time larger than Heathrow, was hit. Nazi invasion – what Hitler called *Unternehmen Seelöwe* (Operation Sealion) – seemed imminent. On 13 August the Germans launched an air battle over Kent and Sussex – the Battle of Britain. Although the German Luftwaffe outnumbered the RAF by four to one, the British had the advantage of being close to their airfields, while the German fighters could stay over England only for about half an hour before they needed to fly back and refuel. The RAF also had better radar than the Germans and more intelligence on the enemy than the enemy had on them. Nevertheless the British suffered heavy losses, and it looked as if the Germans would win the air battle.

The East End was not attacked until late at night on 24 August. An air raid warning which sounded in Mile End caused panic. People ran around wildly in all directions. However, at the People's Palace on Mile End Road, where a production of *La Traviata* was taking place in front of the mayor of Stepney, the audience was told that bombs were dropping outside only when there was a convenient break in the libretto. Management helpfully announced that anyone who wished to leave the theatre was welcome to do so, but no one moved. When the German bombers arrived they found it difficult to navigate the area, and damage was lighter than expected – only nine people were killed and fifty-eight injured, all in Bethnal Green.

## THE EAST END ALIGHT

Saturday 7 September 1940 was a wonderful late summer's day. In the East End people were going about their weekend business, shopping, visiting friends and relations, walking the dog, lazing in the park. Just outside the East End at Upton Park more than 10,000 people were watching West Ham United play Tottenham Hotspur; 'unofficial' war-time football. At Cap Gris Nez, in France, senior Luftwaffe officers, including *Reichsmarschall* Hermann Goering, who had overall command of the German war machine, were watching growing numbers of German bombers leave the continent to cross the coast bound for the area they called *Zielraum* – the loop of the Thames around the Isle of Dogs. Twenty-one British squadrons went to meet them, resulting in the biggest air battle ever seen.

At half-time at Upton Park, with West Ham leading 4–1, the crowd looked up as the sky blackened with German planes. A stick of bombs fell about 100 yards from the stadium. Thousands fled through a rain of debris as shrapnel danced off the cobbles. In the compression that followed the clothes were ripped off fleeing victims, who later described their ordeal as the feeling of having your eyeballs sucked out.

Some 300 German planes dropped bombs on the Ford motor works at Dagenham, on Beckton gas works (the largest in Europe) and on West India Docks, where the warehouses gushed flaming spirit that lit up the shore on both sides of the river. Many East End houses collapsed in seconds. A shelter in Poplar lifted up and moved, bashing the occupants against the walls.

In Millwall horrified locals who had left their houses to watch the events somehow managed to make a cup of tea with water from a standpipe in the street, which one man boiled using his welding torch. In Mile End the teenage George Mooney was shopping on the Waste when the air raid sounded. Desperately he sought the whereabouts of his mother. While talking to his uncle at the George pub he saw his house destroyed. Was his mother inside? A neighbour told him he had only just seen her, standing at the window with her arms outstretched. They began digging, finding a cousin whose legs had been blown off and his grandmother, who had been decapitated. When the rescue team arrived it forced them to leave so they went on a trip around all the local hospitals, where Mooney found seven members of his extended family in various mortuaries. There was still no sign of his mother.

Her absence from the mortuaries was peculiarly reassuring. Her continued absence was not. And if she were still alive, somehow, where would they find her, given the destruction of the house? When Mrs Mooney had spotted the bombers she had fled, and continued running until she reached Victoria Park; the planes would not bomb a park. So she stayed there till the fuss died down.

When the bombers returned after dusk, they were guided back by the fires that blazed along the Thames. This time the planes dropped another 300 tons of explosives and thousands of small incendiary bombs on the East End. Only the Thames, which provided the firemen with vast amounts of water, prevented the flames spreading.

Rescuers uncovered bodies and body parts from damaged houses as those spared looked out for falling masonry. Tens of thousands were made homeless. Sixteen hundred people were injured, 430 dead. Many of the victims later were found lying in their gardens or in the street. A German Messerschmitt plane crashed between Ranelagh Road and Meath Road in West Ham, but news of this unexpected and unwanted arrival was suppressed by the authorities for fifty years, and was admitted only after curious journalists asked the current house-holder for permission to dig up his back garden, where they found pieces of wreckage.

That September bombing raid was the start of the Blitz, a new phase of the Battle of Britain, and it continued relentlessly. The following day 171 planes attacked the East End, killing 400. Two local clerics, the Revd W. W. Paton and Father John Groser, took it on themselves to clear up the mess. The Revd Paton, 'The Guv'nor' as he was known locally, who had launched the National Old Age Pensions Association in the 1930s, stayed out all night comforting those who had lost their homes and relatives looking for survivors.

Father Groser broke open government stores of food he had located and distributed the contents. He also lit bonfires in his Stepney churchyard and visited Whitehall ministries to demand evacuation and shelter. But the civil servants were too busy to listen. They were organizing the production of millions of cardboard coffins and arranging for teams of psychiatrists to treat the expected outbreak of mass neurosis.

At Agate Street school in Canning Town hundreds were sheltering, mothers nursing their children in the passages and classrooms while waiting for coaches to take them away from the bombed East End to countryside towns. They had seen the bombers destroy the area, the planes dropping four bombs, then pausing, banking in a tight turn before dropping the final remorseless fifth bomb. When the coaches failed to arrive there was growing panic. The children became impatient. They begged to be allowed to play in the crater a bomb had formed in the playground. Ritchie Calder, surveying the scene for the *New Statesman*, went to Whitehall and urged the authorities to clear the school before another raid occurred. They took little notice. A few people left the school, but there were still over 100 taking refuge there when the bombs dropped on the building at 3.45 a.m. the next morning, killing nearly everyone. The children who had been playing in the crater the day before were now buried in it.

The Ministry of Information at Senate House, Bloomsbury, which had been set up to organize propaganda (George Orwell satirized it mercilessly in *1984* as the Ministry of Truth), decided to suppress information about the extent of the East End bomb damage and the number of deaths. Films and photographs showing people dying in bombing raids were banned, press reports of casualties were censored and the newspapers were told to be cheery and positive, to show that life in London was carrying on as normal.

The press duly complied and ran stories of people going to parties or dining out in the West End. Malleable journalists churned out stirring nonsense epitomized by Hannen Swaffer's 'The Cockney is Bloody but Unbowed', which appeared in the *Daily Herald* of 9 September 1940:

The Cockney can take it! East London paused for a moment yesterday to lick its wounds after what had been planned by Hitler as a night of terror. But it carried on. During a five-hour tour of the bombed area I met only one disgruntled person – a youth who complained that in his district there were not enough shelters. Elsewhere I saw only a quiet calm that amazed me. Even the homeless chatted smilingly in the schoolroom in which they had been housed.

In private Home Office officials wrung their hands. They drew up a (secret) report which noted how 'the population [in the East End] is showing visible signs of its nerve cracking from constant ordeals'. The next day another Home Office report recorded:

There is increased tension everywhere. When the siren goes people run madly for shelter with white faces. The exodus from the East End is growing rapidly. Taxi drivers report taking party after party to Euston and Paddington with their belongings. Thousands of terrified East-Enders trekked out of London. They struggled through cratered streets, pushing babies in prams, the elderly in wheel chairs and their possessions loaded in handcarts.

In the east London of late 1940 daily life assumed a pattern of air raids, blackouts, shelter, exhaustion, sleeplessness . . .

## DEEP-SHELTER MENTALITY

Long before the first bombs dropped the public realized that there was not enough room to shelter everybody, despite the months of expectation and planning, and that what shelter did exist was inadequate.

When the planes appeared in the sky on Sunday 8 September, a crowd surged from Spitalfields towards Liverpool Street tube station, and were shocked to find it shut, with troops protecting the entrance. Panic-stricken, they refused to disperse. After much heated argument the authorities let them in the station. Once inside, the shelterers decided they were staying; that this subterranean sanctuary was now their home. More people came to Liverpool Street, bringing with them bedding, flasks of tea, sandwiches, packs of cards, books and wirelesses. The police, ordered to move on anyone who looked as if they were about to bed down for the night in the station, were powerless.

The government soon changed its mind about not using tube stations – it had little choice, after all – and began supplying bunk beds and toilets. Rules were set. Before 7.30 in the evening shelterers had to keep behind a line drawn eight feet from the edge of the platform. From 8 to 10.30 they could encroach as far as a second line, four feet from the edge, and when the trains stopped running, the lights dimmed and the current in the rail was cut, they could make use of the entire platform.

By the end of September nearly 200,000 people were using the stations. They had created another London, a city obscured from light, an underground world with its own capricious social order and unrelenting angst. Many became trapped psychologically. They went down but were afraid to leave; they had acquired deep-shelter mentality.

Few saw the tube stations as the last word in shelter. They wanted proper protection. Frustration with the inadequacies of the tube shelters reached a climax on the evening of 15 September when a group of about forty members of the East End Communist Party raided the Savoy, the luxurious hotel off the Strand, where the management unsuccessfully tried to stop them and called the police. 'What was good enough for the Savoy Hotel parasites was reasonably good enough for Stepney workers and their families,' their leader, Phil Piratin, later explained. The all-clear sounded before the officers arrived, and the situation was defused, but the point was made: there was a need for specially designed, comfortable and safe shelters.

Piratin had chosen the Savoy rather than any other major West End building with a large shelter because the American newspaper correspondents were staying there. The communists knew that censorship would prevent the British press reporting the story but calculated that the journalists would cover it in the US papers. Unfortunately, the German press picked up the story as well and, with predictable embellishing, turned it into a tale of mouth-foaming mobs rampaging this bastion of English gentility before being *shot down* by the police.

Meanwhile, people found shelter in all sorts of unusual places; empty coffins in Christ Church Spitalfields were popular. The massive vaults below the Fruit and Wool exchange on Brushfield Street, Spitalfields, were opened to house some 10,000 people pressed into a space that would have been suitable for about half that number. Those who braved the inhuman conditions dubbed the Spitalfields vault the 'black hole of London'. They slept on piles of rubbish or in passages grimed with filth, the lights non-existent, the floor awash with urine. Eventually, conditions improved due to the selfless work of 'Mickey', a three-foot-tall hunchback optician; what became known as Mickey's Shelter was soon the best equipped in east London.

The biggest and worst East End shelter was the Tilbury goods depot on Gower's Walk, off Commercial Road. The building was a ten-storey monster of strictly utilitarian industrial architecture with a roof of metal girders. The floor space was broken up by a network of archways, and platforms four feet from the ground ran along the length of the basement. Queues to enter the Tilbury began forming at lunchtime, and when the doors opened at about 4.30 p.m. the shelterers would rush to grab space among the crates of marge and bales of newspapers. Soon every bit of floor was taken with deckchairs, blankets and pillows.

By night time crowds of around 12,000 had gathered to sleep head to toe. It wasn't long before the floor was wet with pools of urine, for there were only two toilets, both of which were nominally for women only; to defecate shelterers had to walk down the tunnels and use the tracks. Eventually, more sophisticated toilets, made out of cardboard cartons, were installed.

At first there was chaos in the Tilbury. 'The place recalled the horrors of London before the Great Plague,' claimed Ted Bramley, a local Communist Party activist. Wardens were accused, with considerable irony, of behaving like 'Little Hitlers'. Then the Tilbury's owners, the Port of London Authority, established a number of important rules. No sex was allowed . . . 'officially'. Another rule banned the communists from selling their newspaper, the *Daily Worker*, for their attitude to the war had been addled by Stalin's pact with Hitler, and they were spreading defeatist propaganda, persuading the public that the war was not worth fighting. There might have been a war going on, but inside the Tilbury there was to be no fighting, the Port of London Authority decreed. However on 10 October a drunken Dunkirk veteran stabbed a market porter over some stolen bedding, and two months later one Eleanor Harding fought with wardens who refused to allow her to bring her pet monkey inside. Disease flourished in the Tilbury, in particular various strains of influenza and cerebro-spinal meningitis, the so-called 'spotted fever'. As people remained in the same wet clothes day after day the Tilbury reeked of a fusty atmosphere which incubated lice and fleas.

Cynicism and hatred festered in the Tilbury shelter. Shelterers could be heard muttering about Jews; how this was a Jews' war, how the bombs were chasing the Jews, whose abundance in the East End was making the area a popular target. Every action in the shelter by a Jew was magnified and singled out for complaint. The prams which Jewish mothers were bringing in were not protecting a baby but valuables, many claimed. The prams of all Jewish women were searched. There was a baby in all but one, which yielded a stash of rings and jewels under a blanket. Should any Jews be discovered committing a selfless act – driving an ambulance, helping carry a stretcher – the newspapers would describe them as 'plucky East Enders' rather than as Jews.

## THE MYTH OF THE BLITZ

The war created another East End myth: the myth of the Blitz. An idealized vision of a burning, bombed-out Stepney gallantly defended by the plucky East Ender endures in British society. Less publicized are the stories of how East End criminals worked largely undisturbed while the Blitz raged. One gang obtained an ambulance, painted on the appropriate civil defence logos, put stretchers inside and journeyed round London lifting not injured bodies, but broken material – anything that was worth a bob or two. Looting was rife. Some was the seemingly innocent work of carefree children rummaging excitedly through the rubble; some was more concerted and veered over the blurred edge between helping oneself and stealing. Food shops whose windows had been blown in were prime targets. Rings and jewellery were torn from dead bodies.

In the East End people had long lived by their own social rules, outside the law. Authority was usually decided by *ad hoc* soi-disant local government – a fist in the face, a boot on the knee-cap, a 'quiet' word. Here the charm and sophistication usually associated with London was in short supply. There was huge resentment against the City next door, for little of the enormous wealth it generated permeated through to the East End. Here the army, police and church were barely recognized. Not like us. Not to be trusted.

Although the East End population was almost entirely working class, there was little local unifying industry or regular employment. Many had to rely on casual work, living on their wits, in the docks or

on the markets. East Enders still resented the way that during the First
World War the previous generation had joined the fighting on a wave
of spurious patriotism, only to be massacred in the trenches, and that
those who survived were thrown out of work to starve a few years
later. Many were unconvinced by the arguments for the new war. A
prevalent attitude was 'It's *their* war, not *our* war.'

Forced to fight this time, many deserted. They used a variety of
ingenious ruses. Men would register and fail to attend the medical,
thereby clogging up the bureaucracy. Or they would feign epilepsy.
They would register and then send along to pose as them someone
who had already failed the medical. There was a healthy trade in
stolen or forged medical exemption certificates, and on Brick Lane
one doctor received a hefty jail sentence for obstructing conscription.

Some would simply ignore the summons. Many men spent the
1940s dodging the military, and the area where the railway bridge
crosses Vallance Road was known as 'Deserters' Corner', so great was
the proportion of able-bodied men who lived there but shirked war
duty. One of these was Charles Kray Snr, the twins' father. Working-
class deserters such as Kray became heroes in some parts of the East
End, but not so the genteel, middle-class draft dodger, the so-called
Tube Cuthbert, who fled into the underground system and refused to
come out, dodging from shelter to shelter to evade the authorities, his
only daylight the open stations east of Whitechapel.

On 14 November 1940 there was no bombing of London for the
first time since early September. The break gave the East End an
opportunity to tot up the extent of the damage, to plan rebuilding and
repairing. Much of the district had been destroyed. Churches, schools,
hospitals, factories, shops and whole streets had been reduced to
rubble. Forty per cent of houses in Stepney had been wiped out.

The councils were obliged to rehouse those who had been bombed
out of their homes, but Stepney borough was run so badly that it had
no rehousing or billeting department. In another London borough, its
name expunged from the official records, the chief billeting officer was
also an estate agent, who devoted his energies to finding buyers for
available houses, rather than takers for empty properties. By the end
of October not one homeless family had been placed in an empty
house in his borough.

In 1941 a new spirit of optimism, fostered by the arrival of the Soviet Union as allies against the Nazis, was matched by increased production to support the war effort in the East End and surrounding suburbs. Bryant & May, the match manufacturers of Bow, setting of the infamous 1888 strike, began making demolition charges and safety fuses. Albright & Wilson of Canning Town stepped up its production of shell-fillings. Ford at Dagenham produced more army trucks. An aircraft components factory was opened in the tunnels of the unfinished Central Line tunnel heading out of the East End into the Essex countryside. By the end of 1942 the Allies had made half a million sub-machine guns – a factor instrumental in the British Eighth Army's victory over Rommel at El Alamein in November 1942.

The following year brought one of the most tragic East End incidents of the war – the Bethnal Green tube disaster. The station had been turned into one of east London's main shelters, with room for 5,000 bunk beds, but it was accessible through only one narrow entrance, which led to a staircase lit by just one 25-watt bulb. When an air-raid warning sounded at 8 p.m. on 3 March hundreds made for the station.

A little while later a thunderous sound came from the park. It couldn't be bombs; they didn't make that sound. Word went round that it was land mines. In fact it was anti-aircraft fire, but the crowd panicked, which led to a stampede at the top of the station. At the bottom of the steps a girl stumbled. Someone fell on top of her, and someone else on top of them. The people still outside feared they wouldn't get to the shelter and felt in danger while in the open air. They pushed, increasing the crush at the bottom. Soon the entire stairway was a heaving mass of gasping, breathless, dying bodies. Within minutes 178 people had died, mostly from suffocation, and a further sixty-two were seriously injured. The government insisted that news of the disaster mentioned neither the place nor the number of casualties.

## ROCKET ATTACK

By the end of 1943 Londoners were getting used to the war. Some even believed it would end one day without Hitler marching down

Cable Street alongside Oswald Mosley. Air attacks were still occurring, but less frequently. Sirens were still wailing, but they seemed less threatening.

From January to April 1944 heavy bombing returned to London in what became known as the 'Little Blitz'. Then came early summer, which was relatively peaceful for a war-torn city. But it did not last. At around 4.25 a.m. on 13 June 1944 an unusual noise, which sounded like a huge mechanical toy or, some said, a fleet of old motorbikes, was heard over east London. A few seconds later the source of this odd noise was explained when a flying bomb landed on Grove Road, Bow, killing six people.

Kathleen Williams was lying in bed in her sister's house on the same road when the sirens went off. She heard a plane above and the noise of the engine suddenly cut out. The next second 'I could see the house falling in on me'. She was under the rubble for three hours, as was her sister's one-year-old daughter, who was thrown to one side and was rescued by the local vicar, who gave her a sip of brandy. 'She used to cry a lot after that and her mum used to sing "Any Old Iron" to comfort her.' The couple who lived upstairs were not so lucky: 'They got killed outright, they had their heads blown off.' Kathleen kept getting recurring nightmares: 'I thought the man from the plane would come and get me. The hospital had to give me sleeping tablets as I was too frightened to go to bed any more. I lost weight and went down to under six stone.'

The flying bomb was a fearsome new weapon, more deadly than anything that had previously been dropped on the East End. What was so shocking was that this time the aeroplane had no pilot; *it* was the bomb. The pilotless plane was the *Vergeltungswaffe*, or reprisal weapon, better known as the V1 rocket. Like much Second World War paraphernalia, the V1s soon acquired a matey nickname: doodlebugs. As they flew over houses there would be a throbbing drone, the whistle growing louder. Then, when the engine stopped, people froze in fear, because they knew it was about to fall. You prayed it did not cut out directly above you. In fact, if you could hear it you were relieved – it was about to cut out over some other poor bugger. Finally the machine would explode with a terrific noise. Ten V1s were launched in that first wave, of which five crashed at once, one fell in the Channel and three in Kent, causing little damage. Only one got through – the one that landed on Grove Road.

News of the V1 rocket was suppressed, but two days later seventy-three more flying bombs attacked London, and the government was forced to concede that the Germans had a new more advanced, more frightening weapon. Hitler had examined maps of London in detail and worked out which areas would yield the most casualties; he wanted to kill as many Londoners as possible. People again took to the tube shelters, and stayed there. Thousands more evacuees left London, and hundreds of V1s dropped on east London, causing considerable damage and loss of life, although when one landed on the London Hospital on 3 August 1944 only one person died.

How could the military combat the V1? It would be futile trying to bring it down over London, and so the anti-aircraft guns were moved out of the city into the countryside. Allied success in dealing with the V1s came after D-Day, 6 June 1944, when troops landed in northern France to liberate that occupied country. In August British troops, led by General Montgomery, destroyed the V1 launching sites in the Pas de Calais. A week later London was gripped by euphoria – victory fever – following the announcement from the minister Duncan Sandys that the V1 rocket problem was almost solved. Surely the end of the war was imminent? Not quite. The victory celebrations were premature.

On the evening of 8 September unexplained explosions were heard in Chiswick, west London, and in Epping to the north-east of the capital. More of these strange explosions occurred over the following few days, but nobody knew what they were, for the government had once again suppressed the news. In fact it was a new and even more dangerous weapon of unparalleled ferocity – the V2 rocket – produced by slave labour drawn from the concentration camps and like the V1 fired from western Europe. The V2, considerably more powerful than anything that had previously been used in airborne combat, was 45 feet long, weighed 14 tons, and could reach a speed of 3,600 m.p.h. at a height of 60 miles, which meant that it briefly left the earth's atmosphere during flight, re-entering at a speed that made defence against it impossible.

This time there was no drone, no noise, no warning that anything was about to happen until it exploded. And then the noise, like a thunderclap, was more earth-shattering than anything that had gone before. With it came a blinding blue flash and a tumultuous roar – the after-noise produced by the V2's supersonic speed. It led to people complaining about what George Orwell called the 'sudden unexpected wallop with which these things go off. They complained that there was no warning, and there was even a tendency to talk nostalgically of the days of the V1.'

Between 8 September 1944 and 27 March 1945 more than 1,000 V2s fell on Britain, about half of which dropped on the London area. Many hit the East End; a V2 which fell on Spitalfields on 10 November almost destroyed Petticoat Lane. But it was the suburbs east of the East End, such as Ilford, Walthamstow and Dagenham, that suffered most. Residents, incensed at the carnage, lambasted the government, claiming that it would have provided more protection had it been central London being attacked. And once again the government suppressed news of the bombardment so as not to affect morale, or let the Germans know where they had landed. It was not until 10 November, two months after the first V2 was dropped, that Churchill announced that London was under attack.

The V2s continued to fall until March 1945, the last one on Hughes Mansions, Vallance Road, near the home of the ten-year-old Kray twins. But Hughes Mansions was not hit by accident; the Germans had intended to hit Jewish parts of the East End. William Joyce, the one-time British Union of Fascists propaganda chief, who had left for Germany at the start of the war to broadcast for German radio, had continually told his many listeners that the Luftwaffe would 'smash' Stepney and that 'those dirty Jews and Cockneys will run like rabbits into their holes'. The V2 that landed on Hughes Mansions killed 130 families, 120 of whom were Jewish. By the end of the war the East End had lost half its 100,000 Jewish population.

The winter of 1944–5 was one of the coldest ever recorded in London. George Orwell wrote about being obliged to burn his son's wooden toys to keep warm. There were few vegetables available and even the ink froze in school ink wells. But Britain was making rapid progress on the battlefield, reaping the rewards of D-Day. The threat from the air was over. There were fears that the enemy had one last surprise left, and Allied planes soared to Germany, prompting complaints from Londoners about the noise the planes made passing over the capital – and when they stopped more complaints about the silence.

The Germans did have another trump card – the V3 – a fifty-barrelled long-range gun, which they nicknamed the 'London Gun', and whose launch site was buried in a fortified emplacement in the Pas de Calais. Each V3 rocket was over 400 feet long and could fire some 300 lbs of explosive 100 miles every six seconds. But when they were launched the shells from the weapon toppled in the air and turned end over end, losing speed and range, and failing to reach London.

Gradually the blackout was relaxed. The underground reverted to being a transport service, rather than an alternative home, the barrage balloons were taken down, evacuees returned, food rationing eased and the theatres reopened. Prisoners-of-war were removed from the Oval, while at Lord's 100,000 people knew that life was getting back to normal as they watched Australia beat England. The Nazis surrendered and 8 May 1945 was VE Day, celebrating Victory in Europe. Triumphant rockets fired from ships on the Thames lit up the sky. Singing crowds danced in the streets. Euphoric people hugged strangers. The war was over.

# 13

# Dark Ages

A wrecked, burnt-out East End. The people shattered and exhausted after six years of war. The streets devastated. Forty per cent of houses in the borough of Stepney destroyed by German bombs, 85 per cent of properties near the docks wiped out. Tens of thousands homeless.

The horror of life in the East End in the late 1940s was evoked by George Orwell in *1984*: 'A decaying, dingy city where underfed people shuffled to and fro in leaky shoes, in patched-up nineteenth-century houses that smelt always of cabbage and bad lavatories . . . London, vast and ruinous, city of a million dustbins . . .' And of all the problems the East End faced the most acute was housing. It had been sub-standard since the area's population had shot up during the Industrial Revolution, socially unacceptable in London terms. Now its inadequacies were critical. Town hall housing departments struggled to find accommodation for the homeless. There were so many more people without homes than they or the government, despite meticulous and zealous planning, had estimated. After telling desperate bombed-out locals to move in with friends and relatives, the councils also found a short-term fix to East End homelessness – prefabs (pre-fabricated homes).

These glorified single-storey huts in charmingly utilitarian metallic white contained one or two bedrooms, a living room, kitchenette, bathroom (with hot water!), the latest electrical fittings and a small garden for growing vegetables. At first they were made from reconstituted bits of damaged aircraft and assembled by German prisoners-of-war interned in Britain, but they were soon being mass produced in factories, arriving at designated East End bomb sites on the back of lorries, ready to be used by dinner time.

By the mid-1950s there were 150,000 prefabs in the UK, several thousand in the East End. They were supposed to be temporary but many lasted thirty years. Their popularity foxed the town halls, but the reason for it was obvious: there could be no greater contrast with the damp, dismal East End terrace preyed over by the snarling landlord. Nevertheless councils were horrified that many of those obliged to live in prefabs liked them, and they gradually abolished the structures . . . for people's own good.

Prefabs were only a partial solution. It would have been absurd to fill the East End bomb sites with temporary homes, no matter how cute. There was a major housing problem, and debate raged in town hall committee rooms about how it should be resolved. What should a council do with a bomb site if there were undamaged houses of reasonable quality nearby? Should the entire street go, including the unscathed properties, or should the rebuilding take place only where there was damage? And how should the rebuilding be carried out? Should the new properties look like the old properties, only better built and with modernized amenities, or should the buildings be something different, structures that owed nothing to the traditions of the East End?

The problem was solved by the lack of public debate. Decisions were made quickly in the town halls. The planners put to one side notions that many East End communities, though slums, were successful socially, that people enjoyed where they lived, that they simply wanted better houses, not a new community. They decreed that since the old communities were slums they had to be wiped out. Clean it up! Remove the mess! Rid the East End of this chaos! Good-quality houses in the way? There was, they claimed, no such thing as the good-quality East End house. Everything would have to go: Spitalfields merchants' homes, cutesy Mile End cottages, houses with chimneys, picture-rails, coal cellars and Butler sinks.

Even the smartly built late nineteenth-century apartment blocks aimed at the poorest residents, which had been constructed to much acclaim and had served locals admirably and popularly for six decades, were needlessly demolished, rather than modernized. Redevelopment instead of rehabilitation. Such was the case at Brady Street Dwellings, Whitechapel. Tenants urged Tower Hamlets council to update the estate rather than destroy it, but the council ignored them. They moved out the occupants, left the buildings to rot and then claimed that the properties had deteriorated so badly that they had to be demolished. Six months after the tenants had gone the council announced a plan to build offices and a shopping centre on the site.

That the council was wrong to compound the Nazis' destruction with their own was proved when a generation or two later the streets of traditional houses that had not been demolished, such as those around Christ Church Spitalfields and Tredegar Square in Bow, became the most desirable properties in east London.

Nowhere was the needless destruction more marked than on Wellclose Square, once the grandest address in the east, home of Scandinavian sea captains, scholars and mystics, the crown jewel of London, the New Jerusalem, as chosen by those who rebuilt the capital after the Fire (see Chapter 2). Although Wellclose Square avoided the Blitz, the authorities chose to destroy the square none the less. They condemned its unique weather-boarded houses, with their Venetian windows; the Danish Embassy; the 1700 Court House; and the west terrace of five-storey Georgian houses, where the gardens were decorated with flagpoles and ship's figureheads. This sort of stuff was now passé. People no longer wanted dark cellars and open fireplaces, the council claimed. So it all went, even the last vestiges of the villa where Chaim Jacob Samuel Falk contemplated the deepest mysteries of the Kabbalah – everything apart from Wilton's music hall, saved after John Betjeman lodged an appeal against its demolition, and the school where Prince Eddy may have married the shopgirl Annie Crook, as witnessed by Mary Kelly, the last victim of Jack the Ripper.

Another casualty of the wrecking ball was nearby Cable Street, where the communists and Jews had prevented the fascists from marching in 1936. After the war Cable Street became the main red-light area in east London – the 'coloured man's village', as it was popularly known, due to the abundance of West Indian seamen, their pockets laden with their newly acquired wages, who came to hire 'wives' at one of the street's thirty-four cafés, brothels, gambling dens and doss houses.

Here it was the residents, for once, who urged the authorities to take action. It was they who fought for a clean-up, for the banishment of the Maltese pimps and the lorry drivers looking for underage prostitutes. The owner of a Greek café told the evening paper, 'I've been round the world and this is a wicked street all right,' while the black journalist Roi Otley explained that 'few slums in the US compare with this area's desperate character, unique racial composition and atmosphere of crime, filth and decay'. But the council's response was too extreme: they wiped the street clean between Cannon Street Road and Dock Street, leaving to this day little other than grass verges on the south side and rubble-strewn empty lots on the north.

## A MACHINE FOR LIVING IN

In rebuilding the East End the planners looked to Le Corbusier, Mies van der Rohe and other exponents of the international style of architecture for revolutionary notions of how the community should be rearranged. War-torn London became a battleground again, this time attacked by planners, civil servants and bureaucrats.

In planning a new East End the London County Council took into consideration four 'themes': traffic congestion, the 'confusion of business and residential areas', the 'lack of open space' and housing. Each campaign was a failure. Sixty years later traffic congestion in the East End is so intense that the roads of the mid-1940s would now be considered empty in comparison.

'Confusion of business and residential areas'? There was no 'confusion of business and residential areas'. It was the planners who were confused; their belief that businesses and houses needed to be separated, that the public should not live near their place of work, was misguided. Their rush to destroy the old East End condemned the traditional economic pattern of a low-paid workforce living in close-knit communities within walking distance of the breweries, docks and sweatshops, and encouraged firms to move out of these 'poor' areas, to relocate to greenfield sites and suburban industrial estates. Alas these were too far from home for even those who enjoyed walking to work, and were mostly inaccessible by public transport. The planners foresaw this but did not see it as a problem. Either people would drive to the new sites – and so they encouraged a glut of new roads – or they would move out of the dismal East End into the new suburban housing estates on the windswept Essex flatlands of Dagenham, Grays and Basildon.

In tackling the 'lack of open space' the planners asked themselves several questions. Why stay with the traditional street pattern of buildings set in a line, separated from the road by pavements? Why have neighbourhoods of short parallel streets separated by gardens, crossing other similar roads at right angles? Why not set down the new blocks of flats, large and small, randomly on open space? A new townscape began to appear. Instead of the interesting jumble of roads, alleyways, side streets and junctions that made neighbourhoods such as Spitalfields, Stepney and Whitechapel so visually interesting, the new estates were set in a poor man's version of the late nineteenth-century garden city idyll: 'access' roads that dissolved into endless culs-de-sac, sprinkled with concrete slabs or low-rise rabbit-hutch 'cottages' dumped arbitrarily on bare patches of grass.

The *Architectural Review* of 1944 summed up what the East End needed to do about housing: 'The devastation of war has given us an opportunity that will never come again. If we do not make London worth the spirit of those who fought the Battle of Britain, posterity will rise and curse us for unimaginative fools.' Thus they have been cursed, for in almost every aspect the authorities got it wrong. The London County Council and the four East End councils – Bethnal Green, Poplar, Shoreditch and Stepney – chose to rebuild the area insensitively and inappropriately, with tower blocks and landscaped smaller estates based on a scheme outlined by Ralph Tubbs in his 1942 book *Living in Cities*.

Tubbs advocated communities in the form of terraces 'around open quadrangles of lawns and trees, punctuated with high blocks of flats'. He dreamed of 'how pleasant [it would be] to walk from one quadrangle to another, with a skyline of . . . towering flats'. Cynically taking advantage of the depleted population numbers and the fractured political organization in the East End, the councils used the area as a template to indulge in their high-rise dream, without first calculating whether that style would be suitable for east London. Into the East End came all the modernist trimmings – concrete towers, uniformity, mass production, the 'house as a machine for living in' (Le Corbusier's famous dictum), the occupant as cog in that machine – but little thought of how this might work. The councils vied with each other to build higher, quicker and cheaper. The towers are 'good to live in and look at', claimed Tory minister Keith Joseph to the Tory Party conference, as he promised 400,000 new homes. Except they were not.

The model used for the new estates – high and low – was Le Corbusier's *Unité d'habitation* in Marseilles, which became the single biggest influence on domestic building on post-war East End architecture. *Unité d'habitation*, built from 1946 to 1952, is a vast housing complex of 337 flats with a laundry, school, sports and health facilities, and shops contained inside. Its rigid brown concrete lattice face is broken up with inset windows, each of which features a gaily coloured canvas awning that chimes well with the daytime light-blue sky. The building stands on slender columns – pilotis – which means that no space is wasted by its bulk; people can come and go underneath as if the building were floating in the air. On the roof, which offers views across to the Alpilles mountains, there is an open-air swimming pool surrounded by a shapely concrete funnel and a wall speckled with coloured squares. David Hockney's richly technicoloured *A Bigger Splash* may have been set in California, but it is so *Unité d'habitation* as well.

When similar blocks went up in the East End only the shape – the high-rise slab – was kept. There were no school, sports facilities or medical services. The laundry usually didn't work for long, the shops were of the most utilitarian kind – often a Co-op. There could be no rooftop open-air swimming pool 1,000 miles north of the Mediterranean. Whereas the budget for *Unité d'habitation* allowed for all the extras that made it so attractive, English town-hall budgets were never able to stretch beyond the most basic amenities. Whereas *Unité* was built by one of the most inspired architects of the century, the East End blocks that superficially resembled it came mostly from the town hall architects' department. The moral? *Unité d'habitation* was a superb choice for Marseilles. East London should have found its own answer to its problems; not have someone copy Le Corbusier.

Even using a 'name' architect was not the solution, for the system itself was flawed. For instance, Denys Lasdun, best known for the National Theatre on the South Bank and now considered one of Britain's greatest post-war architects, was responsible for Keeling House, a Bethnal Green tower so severely executed that the tenants were soon pining for the old slums.

Keeling House has a 'butterfly' shape of four towers branching from a central service column containing lifts and stairs. There are only two flats on each floor and they are maisonettes, providing the residents with an upstairs. But any architectural finesse deployed in devising the block was wiped out by the utopian fundamentalism that went into its creation. 'Let's wipe out the old streets and everything that went with them,' thundered Lasdun.

Keeling House did not work as a place to live. Tenants of the old neighbourhoods, who in the past had acted as unofficial local guardians, watching over the street and looking out for their neighbours, were unable to do so on a 'street in the sky'. Bethnal Green council was unwilling to take an interest in the block once the initial publicity had faded, and was abolished soon after during local government reorganization, which complicated matters further. The newly formed Tower Hamlets council had not built the thing, so why should it feel responsible for its problems, officials mused. Keeling House descended into anarchy. Burglary became rife and responsible tenants who moved out were replaced by problem families. By 1990 the flats were covered in fungus, there were cracks in the stairwells, and safety nets had been installed to catch chunks of falling masonry. But when demolition loomed in the 1990s, English Heritage stepped in and, to many people's surprise, listed the building.

They explained that they were concerned with the originality of its architecture, which should be divorced from its social implications. At the end of the century Keeling House was sold to private developers, who carried out the full programme of repairs that the council should have enacted, added penthouses on the roof of each tower, and stationed a concierge in a glass foyer decorated with fountains. Keeling House, now aimed at single people working nearby in the City or in the artists' studios of Shoreditch and Hoxton, was functioning at last, even if not as originally intended.

At Balfron Tower in Poplar Erno Goldfinger, the flamboyant Hungarian *émigré* on whom Ian Fleming partly based Goldfinger in his James Bond books, created an iconic tower block to be compared with his better-known Trellick Tower in North Kensington. Balfron has twenty-six storeys and flats on two levels, each of which features a balcony. A separate side tower connected by walkways contains the services – such as rubbish chutes and lifts. On completion of Balfron, Goldfinger announced to general incredulity that he was going to live in a flat on one of the upper floors for a few weeks 'as a sociological experiment' before returning to his (low-rise) Hampstead terrace. He would pay the going rent. 'I want to experience, at first hand, the size of the rooms, the amenities provided, the time it takes to obtain a lift, the amount of wind whistling around the tower, and any problems which might arise from my designs, so that I can correct them in the future,' Goldfinger explained. At the end of his period of residence Goldfinger announced himself pleased with the result. He even applauded the much derided 'street in the sky' system, maintaining that people could sit on their doorstep and chat to the people next door. 'A community spirit is still possible even in these tall blocks, and any criticism that it isn't is just rubbish.' The architect also praised tower blocks for 'enabling us to bring the countryside into the towns', as they allowed for 'enough room for green spaces, lawns and trees where children can play'.

Despite his unquestionable gifts as an architect, Goldfinger showed an inability to grasp basic psychological concepts. Two factors prevented the 'street in the sky' from working. No one wanted to sit chatting about the Common Market, West Ham's chances in the FA Cup or the price of haddock, out in the open, ten, fifteen or twenty flights above the traffic, even were they able to find anyone else to chat with. To make things worse the council began filling blocks such as Balfron with the social misfits, psychopaths and eccentrics on their housing waiting list. Other residents soon learned it was best to avoid eye contact with such neighbours, rather than take out the deck chairs and socialize with them.

Goldfinger's 'countryside into the towns' concept was soon debunked. Organized communal space did not work. It was taken over by local gangs of vandals and owners of dangerous dogs. It took only one anti-social type to ruin the place for everyone. Estate staff were never going to preserve the communal greens as if they were the royal parks, and they soon became eyesores. People wanted their own individual private gardens, not public spaces.

And that was just the walkways and the communal grass. There were all sorts of other intractable problems with the new blocks. The lifts rarely worked. The towers' height created a wind tunnel that whipped up every scrap of litter in the neighbourhood into a vortex of chip wrappers and used nappies. It was so far to the shops or the pub that people stayed in more than they wanted to; older people and children felt particularly trapped. In 1978 a survey of Balfron's 400 residents found only disgruntled inhabitants. Fifty-nine-year-old Harold Byford told journalists from the *East London Advertiser* that he felt like a 'battery chicken in a box', that the design of the flats contributed to the 'indifference' people showed each other. The same week the county council housing chairman, George Tremlett, told a meeting of the Royal Institute of British Architects, 'Tiptoe through the mess beneath Balfron Tower and see the legacy your profession has left.' Unfortunately, throughout the East End there were scores of similar blocks, unsuitable as homes, and built without the 'benefit' of named architects such as Lasdun or Goldfinger. They were all blighted by similar problems. No matter how snazzy the models of the new towers looked in the town hall housing committee rooms, they quickly became slums, prisons for a fractured lonely community.

Of the legion of modernist slum estates that disfigure the East End the most embarrassing, by common consent, is Peter and Alison Smithson's Robin Hood Gardens at the northern entrance of Blackwall Tunnel in Poplar, built from 1968 to 1972. The Smithsons' brochure for the estate was liberally peppered with gibberish terminology – 'cluster', 'aggregation', 'foci', 'nodes'. They explained breathlessly how 'the moment the man or child steps outside his dwelling, here our responsibility starts, for the individual has not the control over his extended environment that he has over his house'. The Smithsons were obsessed with the notion of 'community', not in the traditional sense of a neighbourhood that grows and comes together under its own dynamic, but as something imposed by them on the locale. They put considerable thought into how communities exist, how they function, without realizing that typical successful London communities of that time – Dalston, Crouch End, Willesden, for instance – had evolved independently, not by imposition.

The estate has been a disaster. Austere and frighteningly utilitarian, it consists of interminable concrete. There are walkways running through two long slabs of pre-cast concrete separated by a no man's land of landscaped open space and surrounded by a concrete segmented wall that makes it look like an East German prison camp built for deviants who have committed the most abominable crimes. The horrors are sadistically emphasized by the proximity of the thunderous motorway approach to the Blackwall Tunnel. Indeed Robin Hood Gardens is so inexcusably, unarguably, unmitigatingly awful that the only solution would be to turn it into student housing. Imagine the irony.

The high-rise honeymoon was officially declared over with the Ronan Point tragedy of 1968, the worst peacetime housing disaster in London's history. Here was a twenty-two-storey tower in Canning Town just outside the East End, populated mostly by East Enders decanted from the bombed neighbourhoods. A fire test, which should have been carried out soon after it was built, was aborted. Tenants went to County Hall to complain and were told by Horace Cutler, the Tory politician and later leader of the Greater London Council, that all the flats were safe. They were told not to put electric storage heaters on the outside wall as that would make flats more likely to collapse. Then the residents began to hear loud creaks. The window frames twisted, rain poured in. At 5.45 in the morning of 16 May 1968 a tenant, Ivy Hodge, struck a match by her cooker and caused an explosion that blew out the panels which formed the side of the building. A section of the tower collapsed like a house of cards, killing five people, although Mrs Hodge survived.

It turned out that in building Ronan Point pre-cast re-enforced concrete blocks had been slotted into place on site and then bolted and cemented together like pieces of a gigantic DIY kit. Only later tests showed that the joints within the structure were filled with newspapers instead of concrete. Ronan Point had been rushed off by a council that wanted to erect housing 'units' as quickly and as cheaply as possible. Interestingly, investigations unearthed a number of dubious connections between local politicians and the developers who had built Ronan Point.

After that no more towers were built. The councils' preoccupation with building 'streets in the sky' was over. So who was to blame for the high-rise failures? Lasdun, Goldfinger and co. were simply fulfilling the terms of their brief: design a block of *this* height, in *this* style, on *this* site; it was not their choice to create a tower. The fault was the councils' for choosing this unsuitable style of housing and the government's for empowering the councils in the first place. But most of all the fault was in the public's acceptance that the state – national and local – could be trusted to run people's lives.

In the 1990s councils gradually began blowing up the worst blocks. At the same time they started peddling a false history about the towers with specious arguments about why they failed. The claim was that the towers failed because they were built without public consultation – as if the public were united by its understanding of quality architecture; as if the public, rather than the professionals, planned the beauty of Hampstead, Barnes and Chelsea. Indeed surveys and consensus can still produce slum areas – as in the new Hulme of twenty-first-century Manchester.

Many claimed that the tower block as a design choice was inherently flawed. So how does one then explain the qualities of Berthold Lubetkin's Highpoint in Highgate, the Post Office Tower in Fitzrovia or Canary Wharf? These are clever, witty and handsome blocks; they are beautifully presented and add to the richness of the cityscape. The problem in the East End was that the tower blocks were cheap, nasty, unsuitable and badly built with paper-thin walls and hideous concrete street furniture. The problem was that the councils aimed them at families rather than single people. The problem was that the councils failed to spend the required money maintaining them. The problem was that there were too many of them. Had Lasdun's Keeling House and Goldfinger's Balfron Tower been the only tower blocks in the East End there wouldn't have been a story. But instead the planners wanted to turn the entire area into high-rise hell; towers of Babel reaching to heaven, higher, bigger, bolder, meaner. More and more and more of them. The tower block to display the might of the municipality; higher than the church spire to symbolize the town hall as the new source of spiritual power.

It was only because the councils ran out of money, allowing dissenters to organize opposition, that they did not cover the entire East End in these slabs. And once the novelty had worn off, and the tenants had been decanted *en masse* from bombed out Bethnal Green or Bow to the new concrete jungles of Canning Town and Poplar, the loneliness, alienation, misery and shabbiness of the towers brought a new hell to the East End, as diabolical and depressing as the Old Nichol and 'Blackchapel' of the early nineteenth century.

## FROM OUR HOUSE TO BAUHAUS

While the new towers of the East End were created with Le Corbusier in mind, the low-rise estates and public buildings – health centres, schools, colleges, libraries – were drawn from a different continental template.

This time the model was the Bauhaus ('building house' in German), the early twentieth-century design school where creativity and craftsmanship combined to produce goods, furniture and industrial fittings with the emphasis on the machine age – clean lines, geometry, science, technology. Bauhaus director Walter Gropius designed the company headquarters in Dessau, a building which did more to usher in the new hi-tech era than any other. The Dessau Bauhaus has no bulk, no heavy masonry. It is a basic cube with a glass frontage covered by a steel mesh, a look that was shocking at that time for its use of industrial ideas and lack of obvious historical influences (Gothic, Baroque, Egyptian . . .) used in other buildings. This was a truly internationalist style.

Architects and planners schooled in the first decades of the twentieth century were so enamoured with all things Bauhausian they decided to cover the East End with scores of mini Bauhauser. But the offspring did not inherit the qualities of its parent. They were banal, uninspiring, worthless copies, instantly loathed and then left to rot.

Typical was Poplar's Lansbury estate of maisonettes, schools, churches and shops (Britain's first shopping precinct, no less), built on a fifty-acre site devastated by wartime bombing as a 'live' architectural exhibition for the 1951 Festival of Britain. It was designed by Frederick Gibberd, best known for Liverpool's Roman Catholic Cathedral, and named after George Lansbury, Poplar's great early twentieth-century political dynamo. At first the residents, helped by the porters, kept the communal areas clean and tidy, but the problems the council had created for itself by introducing modernist architecture and experimental ideas on a whim soon began to appear. The clock tower, triumphed by the estate's creators as a beacon attracting the world to wonder at the marvels therein, was shorter than planned, as the money needed to build it higher ran out. Although the tower had been imaginatively cast as a look-out post, the council cordoned it off no sooner than it had opened, decreeing it a suicide risk. Before long the four clock faces showed different times. The joke going round the estate was that one clock showed the time it was, one showed the time you wanted it to be, one the time it might be and the other the time it would never be.

It soon became clear that the layout of the Lansbury estate precluded the development of a community. Few inhabitants knew, trusted or could depend on their neighbours. As the council began to get bored with the estate, it reduced funding, closed facilities, overlooked repair work and moved problem families in. The Lansbury became a 'no go' estate, riddled with drugs, street crime and random racist violence. George Lansbury, who, as a long-time councillor and MP, did so much to improve life in impoverished Poplar, would be horrified today at the estate that bears his name: horrified by the bleak architecture, the decrepit shops, the blight, litter, rubble, boarded-up buildings, brutality, mindlessness and meanness – not to mention shattered Poplar beyond, bereft of public amenities and care.

The thinking behind the new estates was socialist, but bore little resemblance to the inspired early twentieth-century municipal socialist vision of Poplar's George Lansbury. It was a socialism cobbled together in the planning director's office, rather than evolving from industrial struggle. It preached that all tenants should live in similar buildings featuring identical front doors, identical decor, identical appliances. All should share the same outlook on life. No one need do anything for themselves. From cradle to grave lives would be overseen by the state. Born in NHS hospitals, brought up in council-owned flats, educated in council-run schools, studying in council-owned libraries, working in the public sector, watching television (the BBC) administered by government-appointed governors, going on holiday in nationalized trains, eating government-rationed food and retiring to local authority-run rest homes. The only escapes from the state and public sector, the pub and football.

It was a cold and callous philosophy, wrought with no small measure of cynicism, for it was prescribed only to the poor and powerless; the executive class would not be living in the new council estates or be relying very much on public services. The smart suburbs beyond the East End – Chigwell Row, Buckhurst Hill, Abridge – were not being remodelled by the town hall, nor were the independent schools, City jobs and privately patronized arts under threat.

For a few years the public accepted this new statism without question. Then the money ran out. The government and the town halls lost interest. The gleaming new estates, which looked so attractive on the architects' boards, the state-decreed existence that appeared so perfect on paper, didn't work out in real life. People tired of being told what to do. They saw that there were never enough funds to keep all the houses, schools and libraries in good repair, often because the government, realizing that town halls could not be trusted to act responsibly, slashed their budgets for education, health and social services. Yet, even by 2004, this impasse was still governing life in east London. That year Hackney council, which had lost the right even to run its own schools, such was its incompetence, and had destroyed one of the most successful communities in London, announced plans to build a new town hall for £64 million.

From the end of the Second World War until the 1980s the East End continued to decline economically. Fewer jobs, dying industries, emigration of the middle class to Wanstead, Chigwell and Loughton. No one working in the finance houses of the City wanted to set foot in the East End, let alone live there, despite its proximity. After all, why would anyone who had the choice want their lives run by the council? Even those with the best local blue-collar jobs – the skilled labourers and foremen – were quick to flee Bethnal Green and Stepney for West Ham or Romford, leaving the East End even more at the mercy of the planners, housing experts and those who wanted to destroy everything Hitler's forces had not managed to.

The greatest decay could be found on the Isle of Dogs. To Poplar council the island was an embarrassment: a land of rusting cranes, deep dark docks and dying industries peopled by a strange race that never ventured beyond the peninsula. One Poplar councillor described it as the 'forgotten island' when pleading with the town hall for attention, to no avail, for the island remained at the bottom of the queue.

The baths and the Glengall Road bridge over Millwall dock, near where Arsenal had played their first game in 1886, remained unrepaired, as did the streets of tumbledown housing surrounded by their debris of German bombing for a few decades. Many shops had been destroyed, forcing locals to make lengthy trips – often across the river – for anything beyond the most basic provisions. The one thing the council did achieve was to slap compulsory purchase orders on a number of properties, almost at random. The CPOs did nothing other than blight the area – catalyse more decay during the long wait for enthusiastic developers.

The island declined from a bombed, burnt-out wreck inhabited by close-knit communities at the end of the war to a bombed burnt-out unrepaired wreck, barely populated, inhabited by fractured depressed communities by the end of the 1970s. Heavy industry, which had converted the island from an uninhabited swamp into a dynamic metal world of manufacture, began to collapse in the 1960s.

Typical of the demise was Huish's road haulage firm. The family company was nationalized in 1949 during the Attlee government's peak period of state interference in industry. British Road Services took over the business, and work continued with some success, but in 1963 Poplar council placed a compulsory purchase order on the firm's island premises. It moved to a nearby bomb site at the same time that changes in working patterns saw goods arrive not in packing cases but in twenty-ton containers. The company did not have the vehicles to cope with such heavy loads, thanks to under-investment by the state. Again they struggled on, till 1972, when their main customer closed its shipping business, rendering Huish's obsolete. By that time many other island firms had gone the same way: Burrell's, colourists and paint-makers; Stephens Smith and Co., the medical equipment suppliers; Hawkins and Tipson, ropemakers . . .

Even the docks were closing down. By the early 1980s West India, East India and Millwall docks, once teeming, vibrant waterside cities, worked by tens of thousands of men, worlds within worlds, twenty-four-hour havens of ardour and hard labour, were empty. As the island closed in on itself the newly formed Tower Hamlets council began to break up the last local communities as part of a deliberate policy of smashing the local fiefdoms, with their extended families and independent attitudes. In this era of municipal madness the council wanted total control, even if it was only over empty land. There was one amusing interlude in this depressing story. One night in 1970 Millwall councillor Ted Johns wondered what would happen if the Isle of Dogs declared UDI as Pimlico did in the Ealing comedy *Passport to Pimlico*. Johns proclaimed himself president, and the world's media flocked to his council flat where he poured out to them the privations of living on the 'forgotten island', the lack of transport and shops. The authorities denied anything was wrong while simultaneously making lukewarm improvements. Real change was afoot on the Isle of Dogs, though. It would take another decade, but it would not proceed in a way that island traditionalists such as Johns approved.

## RETURN OF THE FASCISTS

Although Britain fought a six-year war to rid Europe of fascism, fascists flourished openly in Britain once the war had ended. They were able to do so because the government decided it was legally unable to obstruct the fascists' right of assembly.

The new post-war fascism was far removed from the corporate state quasi-socialism of Mussolini. Now the accent was on nationalism and racism. The new fascists' targets were Jews, communists, lefties, bohemians, liberals – anyone who was not prepared to march behind Oswald Mosley holding a rude banner and ready for a fight. A bewildering collection of new nationalist parties formed to champion Britain: the New Order Group, the Britons Patriotic Society, the Union of British Freedom, the British Vigilance Action Committee, the British National Party (a name now back in vogue), the Imperial Defence League, the Order of the Sons of St George, the Gentile-Christian Front, the League of Christian Reformers and the strange folk who appeared at an auction of Von Ribbentrop's effects in London and bought a bust of Hitler for £500 and Nazi flags for £102, then promptly disappeared into the Sussex countryside.

In 1947 Mosley formed a new political party, the Union Movement. 'I have not changed my political ideas one iota. I do not retract anything I have either said or stood for in the past,' he announced. He peppered his speeches with references to 'alien politicians', 'international Jewry' and 'the financiers' war'. He set up book clubs and discussion groups across the country. This time his fascism had not just a pro-British, but a pan-European flavour: Mosley wanted a fascist Europe that would wilfully plunder Africa for resources. Anti-Semitism remained, reinforced by the Zionists' anti-British terrorist activity in the Holy Land in setting up the State of Israel in 1948.

Union Movement speakers referred to Jews as 'filthy lice, underhanded swine, black marketeers corrupting the children of the country' – race hate under the guise of free speech. Like Mosley's BUF, the Union Movement sought popularity in the East End by appealing to the natives' distaste for the Jewish caricatures they lived among – the mean landlords and sweatshop owners – all of whom would, of course, be deported under a Union Movement government. Outside Whitechapel tube station Mosleyites sold their newspaper and denounced the Holocaust as Jewish propaganda, explaining that the German gas-chambers were filled with the corpses of Jews killed not by the Nazis but by British bombs.

Jewish ex-servicemen passing by were horrified. Harry Rose, who had been a sergeant in General Wingate's Chindit force in Burma, and had just been demobilized, told the man alongside him, 'I'm going to shut that bastard up!' Harry's mate remonstrated with him, 'You can't. Cause a disturbance and those police over there will arrest you, and what good would that do?'

Frustration grew. Eventually a number of East End Jews set up their own guerrilla body – the 43 Group. They wanted a war of attrition against the new fascists; they wanted to shatter the stereotype of the weak, cowardly Jew. The 43 Group sent infiltrators into Mosley's reading clubs and Union Movement meetings. It sent large numbers of men who were handy with their fists to the fascists' rallies, which had moved from Victoria Park and the Salmon and Ball public house to new territory, Ridley Road market, Dalston, in east London.

Mosley arrived in Ridley Road on May Day 1948 to launch the Union Movement with some 200 policemen guarding him. The 43 Group made sure the event soon descended into chaos. There was prolonged fighting. Many were arrested. As a policeman grabbed the 43 Group's Morris Beckman and began frogmarching him away, Beckman commented on the officer's war ribbons. 'Convoy duty?' he asked. 'What were you on – Corvettes? Destroyers? Armed merchant cruisers?' 'Corvettes. Why?', replied the policeman. 'I was picked up by the *Dianella* off Iceland. We were hammered on the way back from Halifax, Nova Scotia,' explained Beckman. 'The *Dianella*. That was one of the flower class,' said the officer. 'That's right,' replied Beckman. 'Are you still going to hang on to me?' The policeman let him go with a friendly warning, 'You'd better beat it fast before the Marias get here from Dalston Lane and Stoke Newington stations.'

Street fighting was all very well, but the 43 Group decided it needed one dramatic event, something that would bring big publicity and catapult the debate about fascism into the public arena. The events committee came up with a brainwave: they would kidnap Oswald Mosley, strip him naked and dump him in Piccadilly Circus. The operation would run as follows. A couple of 43 Group members would wait for Mosley outside his flat in Dolphin Square, Pimlico, and, as he tried to drive off, block his car, wrench him out of the vehicle, and bundle him into their Singer saloon. Inside they would remove his clothes and then drop him off at Piccadilly Circus at a time arranged with waiting photographers. Group members even went as far as to stake out Dolphin Square. But when their lawyers explained the likely length of the sentences 43 Group leaders could expect at Wormwood Scrubs as a result of these events, the scheme was dropped.

Instead they turned to sabotage. The target was the headquarters of the British League of Ex-Servicemen, led by Mosley acolyte Jeffrey Hamm. One evening 'Martin' and 'Jack', two Aryan-looking members of the 43 Group, knocked at the League's headquarters, greeted the former SS paratrooper who kept guard with salutes and cries of 'Hail Mosley', and made their way upstairs to Hamm's office. There they dropped their cover, attacked the British League leader, and began shoving files and official-looking papers into a bag. Jack ran downstairs and out first, but when Martin went to leave he found the ex-SS man waiting for him on the stairs with a length of pipe. In a flash of inspiration he yelled at the German, 'You stupid idiot! Why didn't you stop that Jew bastard who ran down the stairs?' It was enough to unsettle the German, who relaxed his grip enough for Martin to overpower him.

Fascism peaked in the early 1950s. There were only a few thousand Londoners interested, and outside the capital fascism had made little headway. Most Mosley sympathizers were nationalists but not fascists. They had no time for Jews, but were tired of the tirades against Jews and tired of mass, manic political movements. Indeed the war had tired them out. It was not until the Mosleyites had a new scapegoat for the empire's ills – the blacks – that nationalism resurfaced, and then it was not in the East End but in west London – Notting Hill.

As the racial shape of London changed, so the Jewish East End declined. Change was not evident in 1945, certainly not when the Jewish Phil Piratin won the main parliamentary East End seat, Stepney, for the communists. It was not evident as you walked through Brick Lane, past shops such as Katz's, which sold only string (kosher string, mind), or along Wentworth Street, where Marks' delicatessen dispensed onion-rich *latkes* cooked to crispy perfection and a peculiarly pungent artichoke and mozzarella salad. It was not evident on Petticoat Lane, where Jewish stallholders sold Teddy boy jackets and wash-leathers, while gently mocking their gentile rivals in barely intelligible Yiddish. But it became clearer that change was afoot when one considered that those who ran these businesses, like many of those who bought their wares, no longer lived in the East End. They had decanted from Whitechapel to Wembley, from St George's to Shacklewell. They had transcended their origins; the dream of every immigrant.

For a generation the Jewish organizations and clubs continued to operate from the East End, as if this were their Holy Land from time immemorial. At Brady youth club on Hanbury Street anglicized young Jews forsook a life of rabbinical study to play football to the point of nausea and trade R&B records. At synagogues on Fieldgate Street and Sandys Row they continued to talk through the prayers and dive into the olives at the post-service *kiddush*. But every year the exodus to the London suburbs continued. Another family left Settles Street; another shop closed on New Road.

The official demise of the Jewish East End came in 1996 when Bloom's, the most famous Jewish restaurant in the world, closed its Aldgate branch. This was not just a tragedy for the East End, but a tragedy for the entire world of fine eating. Rebecca and Morris Bloom had opened their first restaurant at 58 Brick Lane in 1920, and built a reputation through their unique recipe for pickling beef. They later moved to bigger premises at No. 2, which became known as Bloom's Corner, and when that was destroyed in 1943 by a German bomb the restaurant moved round the corner to 90 Whitechapel High Street. Not only was Bloom's renowned for its food, but its waiters were among the most feared individuals in the East End. Their rudeness and conceit was legendary. Diners would find themselves bullied into eating at breakneck speed by their waiter, who at the conclusion of the meal would prowl unattractively, practically extracting a sizeable tip from their wallet uninvited. It was not unknown for patrons who had not tipped generously enough to be chased down the street. The waiters' extraordinary excuse was that they had to buy the meals from the kitchen, and were then paid commission on what they sold – the more customers they served, the more they earned.

The end came in January 1996 when the branch had its food licence removed by the Court of the Chief Rabbi after a breach of the Jewish dietary laws. The family's Michael Bloom then set up his own café off Hatton Garden, serving Jewish-styled, rather than kosher, food, open twenty-four hours a day and patronized emphatically by Jewish taxi drivers, Jewish media folk and curious gentiles. It was a daring attempt and survived gallantly until 2004.

## THE MAKING OF BANGLATOWN

The late 1960s witnessed a new East End phenomenon – immigration from the Indian subcontinent. Although the East End had a long history of Chinese settlement, complemented by the odd Lascar and Bengali, Chinatown was at the far eastern end of the district, a few streets in Limehouse and Poplar, well removed from the hub of the East End. These new Asian immigrants were from Sylhet at the north-eastern corner of the Indian peninsula, which, with its 600 years of Islamic history, had voted to join Pakistan at the time of Partition in 1947. Unlike the Chinese they moved into the heart of the East End – Spitalfields, Stepney and Whitechapel.

The first arrivals were mostly men who had jumped ship or been left stranded at the dockside, with no passage home for a few weeks. There were just two properties – both in Spitalfields – that welcomed them. Soon large numbers of Bengalis were taking advantage of the growth in air travel to flee the harshness of life in humid, rainy, impoverished, overcrowded Bangladesh and move to British cities. They came mostly from rural backgrounds and had no experience of cities, let alone the world's most famous city. They came to make enough money to buy a farm back home, and had little intention of staying.

To help them find their way around the East End they left bricks along the pavements to mark the way. They adopted pictorial codes to remember the bus routes: two eggs for the No. 8 to Oxford Street, two hooks for the No. 22 to Piccadilly Circus. Almost all of them were men, married men – few wives came – and they lived in male-only dormitories. But the 1981 Immigration Act meant that dependants of those already in the UK were allowed to enter the country, and numbers rose. Indeed, during that decade Bangladeshi immigration increased to such an extent that, according to the 1981 census, there were 10,000 people of Asian background in the East End.

The Asian newcomers were usually shunted into the worst local housing, where there was room for little other than a bed, and no inside toilet or hot water. The properties were slums, but at least the desperate tenants could take heart in knowing that their landlords were fellow countrymen. This surely was a step up from the early 1960s when property ads were still allowed to stipulate 'no coloureds'? The wealthier Asian arrivals soon took action. They invested in cheap, semi-derelict properties and rented out rooms to Bangladeshi workers. But they also trapped the new arrivals in a labyrinthine housing scam. Tenants who wanted to leave were told they would have to carry on paying a portion of the rent, which amount they could recoup by selling the rent book on to the new tenants and upping the rent accordingly. Because the next lot of tenants were now paying a higher rent, they would probably need to take in a friend to help meet the cost. And so it went on until the properties were as overcrowded as in the early days of the Jewish ghetto.

In one set of flats in Wentworth Model Buildings, where in 1888 Jack the Ripper had daubed the cryptic graffiti 'The Juwes are not the men That will be Blamed for Nothing', there were twenty Bengali residents in 1971 and 200 at the end of the decade. Unfortunately, demolition was unlikely to be a solution. The first victims in the chain had a vested interest in ensuring that the property, no matter how substandard, was not pulled down, for they would then lose everything.

The Bangladeshis joined the flickering local textile industry. Actually, they did not have that much choice, for the kind of job opportunities that the average white working-class East Ender took for granted were closed to them. They couldn't really work in pubs or the local breweries, for their religion forbade alcohol. They couldn't speak English very well, if at all, so that put paid to many more positions. Jobs at the docks were disappearing fast, and even if it had been boom time in the port the Irish gang leaders around Watney Street wouldn't have allowed them within six fathoms of the Call On. Even jobs at the lower end of the public sector, such as binmen, were not available, for hiring was the strict preserve of racist, beery, trade union barons.

It was easy, however, to start up in the rag trade. Little capital was needed to buy a few machines or rent a small workshop. Making clothing needs a lot of sub-contracting, which meant many opportunities to employ relatives or share out tasks during lulls in what is mostly seasonal work. These lulls meant time off to visit families in Bangladesh. And when the wives arrived they were able to join in the work or mind the children in what were, and still are, highly conservative patriarchies. The new immigrants also fitted neatly into the textile industry's pyramid system, a pyramid that featured the big-name high-street retailer at the top and the Bangladeshi women button-holing, cutting and trimming in poor light with antiquated, hazardous machines in a Spitalfields hovel at the bottom.

Eventually the Bangladeshis created a new mass industry – the curry house. Before the 1970s it was hard to find a curry in London, even though it was as early as 1773 that curry first featured on a menu in the capital – at the Coffee House in Norris Street, near Piccadilly Circus. Dean Mahomet, from Cork, not India, opened London's first curry house, at 34 George Street, Marylebone, in 1809, 'for the Nobility and Gentry, where they might enjoy the Hookha with real Chilm tobacco and Indian dishes of the highest perfection'. The first such eaterie in the East End was set up at 120 Brick Lane in the 1930s.

When Bengali immigrants arrived in the late 1960s London's few curry restaurants were mostly too expensive, staffed by suffocatingly subservient waiters, and mainly in the West End. But opening a curry house in Spitalfields was an ideal venture for Bangladeshis who had served as cooks and chefs on ships using the Port of London. They could work with friends and relatives, and as they lived nearby they were not inconvenienced by the late finishing times, long after the last tube had gone. The only drawback was that they believed that to attract whites they had to provide food that was not authentic: chicken with cream; lamb *off* the bone. But who cared? Not the owners, who started making money, and not the customers who could now eat fiery viscous liquid meat washed down with vats of lager after the pubs shut.

Just as the threatened gentile population of the late nineteenth century had railed against the Jews, so the whites of late twentieth-century Spitalfields snarled and spat at the Bangladeshis. They greeted the first arrivals by pushing dog turds through their letterboxes, waxing up keyholes, and hanging pigs' trotters over the doors. They blockaded the stairs to prevent furniture being delivered. Then came the politically motivated attacks. A new post-Mosley sometime-fascist force arrived – the National Front – claiming it wanted democratic fascism, through the ballot box. Its intelligentsia dreamed of a mythical world in which a cross between Adolf Hitler and Winston Churchill won a world war against a Jewish Stalin to free the British Empire for the white man . . . all of whom looked strangely like Captain Mainwaring. The Front passed over classic Mussolini/Franco corporate state fascism for uncompromising racist propaganda. Its one main policy was repatriation of non-whites – 'by the most humane means possible'.

The first serious assaults on Bangladeshis took place in 1969. On 3 April 1970 came the first public references to 'Paki-bashing' when two Asian workers at the London Chest Hospital in Bethnal Green were attacked. The *Observer* claimed that 'any Asian careless enough to be walking the streets alone at night is a fool'. They might as well have added that any individual who was not between the ages of fifteen and twenty-nine, working class, white and lippy was in danger walking at any time in Bethnal Green, with its battered, dingy streets, blighted bomb sites, slum estates, 'no go' pubs and bereft shops.

Later that month there were mini riots in Brick Lane, Spitalfields' high street. The new street thugs, skinheads – crop-haired Artful Dodgers in laced-up Doc Martens, Sta-prest jeans, button-down check shirts and Harrington jackets – randomly chased Asians, attacked passers-by and threw stones at the police. A group of Bangladeshis marched on Arbour Square police station to demand protection. They soon realized that the police, like their 1930s prede-cessors, were not enthusiastic about responding when Pakistanis were attacked, but would come out in force to protect the fascists if a counter-demonstration was staged. Receiving no help from the police or council, the Asians formed themselves into vigilante groups, which did little to curb the violence, but at least made the fights more equitable.

The Asians received little popular support from the existing popu-lation. While West Indian immigrants were grudgingly tolerated, then accepted, because they spoke English, were interested in football and cricket, visited public houses, placed bets, went to church, took interesting drugs and lived to a backdrop of funky music, the Asians were snubbed because they spoke strange, chattery languages, had no interest in football, played cricket without any rain, wouldn't drink or bet (on religious grounds!), prayed in mosques and listened to unlistenable music.

The West Indian wanted to integrate, the Asian wanted to remain separate. The West Indian was respected because, if challenged, he would answer back, and more beside, but the Asian tended to cower or run. The American writer Rawle Knox put this down to a fatalism drawn from the Bangladeshis' native experiences. They came from an area lashed by typhoons, where entire villages could be wiped out and turned to mud. Faced with a few street thugs they shrugged their shoulders. 'They never give up and they never expect to win.'

If the Asians had anything in common with anyone, it was with their Jewish immigrant predecessors. Both were united by a Semitic religion. Both observed dietary laws based around the preparation of meat. Both threw themselves into the local clothing industry. Both overran Spitalfields. Now Bangladeshis took over Jewish shops, often with Urdu lettering inscribed alongside the Hebrew characters; kosher butchers became halal butchers; children came home from school and went to religious classes, just like Jewish children had done in the East End for decades. Mosaic law to Moslem law. The Spitalfields Great Synagogue on the corner of Fournier Street and Brick Lane, where the anarchist Jews had pelted worshippers with bacon sandwiches on the Day of Atonement in 1904, became the Jamme Masjid mosque.

Meanwhile, the National Front stepped up its onslaught. Its support increased. The party won nearly 10 per cent of the vote in Bethnal Green in October 1974, but lost ground when people began to spot contradictions, apparent at every turn. While the strange-looking chap with the awkward moustache and ill-fitting clothes selling the party's *Spearhead* newspaper outside the Ben Truman brewery on Brick Lane played down hostile references to Jews, and was keener to talk about withdrawal from Europe, the NF meetings at the back of the Seven Stars pub, a few hundred yards down the road, were full of hardcore zealots cracking jokes about the Auschwitz gas chambers.

And what exactly were the Front's policies, other than hate? It did not seem too interested in the corporate state of Spain or the socialism-in-one-country of Nazi Germany, which had enthused millions of Europeans. The party advocated strong charismatic leadership, the veneration of a Franco, Mussolini or Hitler figure, yet its supremo was the seedy, creepy-looking John Tyndall, a man of non-existent charm, lacking in original views and style – accusations that could never be levelled at Oswald Mosley. Tyndall's views were all the predictable Jewish-conspiracy rubbish – that liberal democracy was a Jewish tool of world domination that needed replacing by authoritarianism – but he lacked the chutzpah to localize the battle imaginatively. He probably didn't even realize that the liberalization of Britain could be traced back to the Wellclose Square villa where Chaim Jacob Samuel Falk and his cohorts debated dangerous ideas that helped foment the French Revolution.

When Tyndall stood in Dalston at the 1979 general election his vote topped 4,000, but with his public concern for the 'democratic' route to nationalism and racism he cut a pathetic figure – as if the British public would vote for rudderless fascism in the way that the Germans of the 1930s had voted for the ideologically consistent and smartly led Nazis. Fascists, and those attracted to the movement, wanted a lead. They wanted excitement. The National Front didn't even have the guts to attempt a proper fascist putsch.

Meanwhile, the racist violence continued into the 1980s, especially after the National Party's John Kingsley Read, referring to the murder of a young Southall Asian, announced publicly, 'One down – a million to go.' There was more street fighting; no end in sight to the predictable weekly battles on Brick Lane between Asians and skinheads, between National Front and Socialist Workers' Party newspaper sellers.

On 4 May 1978 twenty years of racial violence in the East End culminated in the murder of Altab Ali, an Asian youth, who was chased along Brick Lane and stabbed to death near Aldgate East station. Even this event did nothing to stem the violence, for vengeance needed to be had, retribution exacted. Seven thousand Bangladeshis marched to Downing Street behind Ali's coffin.

In the 1980s the violence gradually declined. One thing contributed mainly to this. Not the politicization of the white working class during the Winter of Discontent of 1978–9, as Militant Tendency claimed. Not the election of Margaret Thatcher on a supposedly right-wing and racist platform in May 1979, as the papers claimed. Not the visit of President Ziaur of Bangladesh, who came to Brick Lane on 18 June 1980 and took a street sign back to Dacca to rename a street there Brick Lane. Not even the aggressiveness of the new generation of Asian youth, who forsook their parents' passivity and began to fight back.

The violence receded because Spitalfields became almost entirely Asian. The skinheads and their feckless parents left, mostly grudgingly, to the new slummy suburbs of Romford, Barking and Canning Town. It became hard to lead a native charge on infiltrators when the infiltrators outnumbered the natives. The 1980s were much quieter than the 1970s, and the 1990s were quieter still. There was still the odd racist murder, but the weekly battles died away; fights seemed to be of Asian upon Asian now, turf wars involving Asian heroin gangs.

There was still the occasional reminder of Brick Lane's violent past. In April 1999 a bomb left by David Copeland, a lone Nazi sympathizer waging a one-man war against 'deviants' and immigrants, exploded near the police station. Copeland's incompetence showed how low the fascist/nationalist campaign had sunk. He couldn't even get his day right, choosing to plant the device on a Saturday, the quiet day, rather than on Sunday, when the street would have been full of curry eaters and market folk.

## THE PROFESSION OF VIOLENCE

The East End of the 1950s lacked credible leaders; public figures of gravitas. There was no one capable of picking up the mantle once worn by the Barnetts, Thomas Barnardo and George Lansbury. Oswald Mosley had tried but been humiliated. Clement Attlee, one time mayor of Stepney, was now prime minister, but had no leadership qualities. A vacuum was waiting to be filled by an heroic figure; someone of the East End, who understood the people, the land and its history. The East End was fortunate enough to get not one, but two such powerful charismatic leaders: the Kray twins.

Like Jack the Ripper, the Krays' name has become synonymous with East End myth. Except that in their case they were highly visible, without being compromised by their conspicuousness. The Krays ruled an alternative East End in which they set themselves up as overlords, unquestioningly accepted by their subjects, ignored by those of the other, 'real' world. They even retained their thrones when the real world called a halt to their activities. Death has created a setback, but the myth continues to grow, fuelled by endless newspaper articles, documentaries, books, biographies, confessions of former associates, analyses, treatises, dissertations and walking tours created by those in a hurry, anxious to capture the East End of the Krays, the grey days of the 1950s and 1960s, before it vanishes, like the almost extinct world of Jack the Ripper.

The Krays were Reginald and Ronald, identical twins, born in October 1933 in Stean Street, Dalston, near Haggerston station. Their mother, Violet, was a formidable matriarch, strong-willed and fiercely possessive. In another life she might have been Margaret Thatcher or Boadicea. There was an elder brother, Charles Junior, who became a charmingly pleasant big-time crook, rather than a disturbed, evil bastard. Their father, Charles Senior, worked as a 'pesterer', a travelling trader roaming the countryside buying and selling silver, gold and clothing.

In 1939 the family moved a mile south to 178 Vallance Road, Bethnal Green. All around extended what seemed to be a continuous family: uncles, aunts, grandparents, cousins . . . Opposite No. 178 was a café run by Grandad Jimmy 'Cannonball' Lee, which sold food of the kind that has now almost disappeared from the East End – bacon sandwiches, cups of strong tea, liver and onions. Lee, a bare-knuckle boxer in his youth, later made a few bob on the Mile End Waste licking a white-hot poker. It wasn't as dangerous as it sounds. Red-hot pokers are the ones to avoid: they take your tongue off. Violet's sisters, Rose and May, lived either side of No. 178. It was Rose who told Ronnie, upset about being teased in school about his eyebrows being too close together, that it was a sign that he was 'born to be hanged'. Had the Labour Party not brought in the Murder (Abolition of Death Penalty) Act of 1965, which suspended hanging for an experimental period of five years, she would have been right.

When Charles Senior's call-up papers to join the army arrived he went on the run, claiming that having never previously 'worked for a guv'nor he couldn't start taking orders now'. Kray was not a coward – he came from a family of boxers – it was just that the war was not his battle; he had other things to do. One day the military police raided the Kray home, demanding entry with a search warrant while Charles was hiding in the coal cellar. When the officer touched the handle of Kray Senior's hidey-hole the young Ronnie affected what was probably his last angelic appearance and piped up, 'Do you think my old man would be stupid enough to hide in a place as obvious as that?' The officer admitted it was unlikely and turned away.

The twins missed much schooling during the war – evacuation did not work in their case; they came back – and spent their time playing in gangs among the rubble of the bomb sites. In their teenage years they became boxing champions, and gained a reputation as the most fearsome toughs in the neighbourhood. They strode the streets of Bethnal Green and Whitechapel, out for trouble, tooled up. They had to be; the East End was a dangerous place, not least because of the number of local gangs like theirs. Before their seventeenth birthdays the Krays were charged with GBH after attacking a rival gang outside a dance hall in Mare Street, Hackney. They were acquitted due to lack of evidence – their beaten opponents would not 'peach', in accordance with the East End underworld's code.

When the twins turned nineteen they came up against the outside world again in the formidable shape of the army. They were called to Waterloo Barracks at the Tower of London to enlist for national service. After listening to a welcoming speech, and receiving instructions for cleaning boots and laying out their kit, they walked out, telling the astonished corporal, 'We don't care for it here. We're off home to see our mum.' The next day the military police turned up at No. 178, much as they had done for Kray Senior twelve years earlier. This time there was no hiding in the coal cellar. The twins came readily, and were sent to an army prison where they met Charlie Richardson, who in the 1960s became their only rival as London's godfather of crime.

The road from slummy Bethnal Green to glitzy Knightsbridge and Soho began with a snooker club, the Regal, in Eric Street, Mile End. 'Put us in charge of security and there won't be any trouble,' the twenty-year-old Krays told the manager. 'But there isn't any trouble,' they were told in reply. No, but there soon was. The fights, stage-managed by the Krays, were so fierce that the manager fled, leaving the twins in charge. They redesigned the Regal as an American-style pool hall with low-slung lights. A machine blew cigar smoke around the room for two hours before opening time to create a suitable speakeasyish atmosphere.

There is a hierarchy of villainy in the East End. It's a simple hierarchy. At the bottom are street toughs out to make a quick buck at the expense of the hapless passer-by. At the top are the feared gangsters. And top of the top, even though they could barely read, write or count, were the Kray twins. So how did they get from the bottom to the top? Easy. By challenging or intimidating everyone in their way. When there was nobody left to fight, they had won.

Once the Krays had established a reputation they were 'invited' to visit Ziggy's café on Cobb Street, just off Petticoat Lane, to meet the Jewish villain Jack Spot – he who had attacked Oswald Mosley's car during the battle of Cable Street. Spot and his cohorts Sammy Ross and Franny Daniels, with their greased hair, torpedo cigars and back-slapping bonhomie, would sit inside Ziggy's day after day, downing endless cups of tea amid a haze of Senior Service smoke.

In a bid to gain the crown of the London underworld they planned a raid on Heathrow airport, where they would remove a cargo of valuables from a bonded warehouse. The raid was aborted when one of the team began helping police with their inquiries before the police were aware that any inquiries were needed, but the plan was enough to send Spot shooting up the London underworld league table. Spot took the Krays under his wing. When rivals later knifed him in a feud, the Krays assumed his place.

Only the most foolish crossed the paths of the young Krays. Like the Watney Streeters, drawn from the feared Irish families of Shadwell, who organized labour at the docks. In 1956 the Watney Street gang chose to overlook the Krays when organizing a post office van scam, and so the Krays plotted revenge.

Armed with a Young America revolver and a small crew, Ronnie Kray decided to storm the Watney Streeters' public house, the Britannia. When he entered it at 9 p.m. only one member of the Watney gang, Terry Martin, was left; the rest had escaped through the back door. Kray dragged Martin from the pub, attacked him with a bayonet, and then toured the local streets in his car looking for the rest of the gang. Kray was stopped by the police, who found him in possession of a revolver, crowbar and machete. He received three years for GBH and unlawful possession of a revolver.

While Ron was away, Reg opened a club in Bow – the Double 'R'. Reg showed a flair for legitimate impresarial activity among the sharp-suited clientele of socialities, villains, businessmen, actors and sportsmen that patronized the venue. Well, almost legitimate. Opponents were dispatched with a fist holding a lighted cigarette secreted between two fingers, the glowing end slightly protruding and hitting the face first.

Aunt Rose died while Ron was locked up. Her death had so profound an effect on him that he was sent to Long Grove asylum. It was easy to escape from there. When Reggie came to visit one day, Ronnie left as the visiting brother. When warders attempted to lock up Reggie he explained that, as he was not Ronnie, he could not be held against his will. Frustrated officers had no choice but to let him go.

Ronnie went back to Vallance Road in the boot of a car, but once he was free his paranoia raged. He refused to believe that the woman who greeted him was his mother. He claimed Reg was a Russian spy 'got up to look like him'. He began turning up at the Double 'R' when the place was known to be free of police officers, jeopardizing the smooth running of the club by meting out disproportionate violence to those who crossed him. He stayed on the run from the police for five months, drinking two bottles of gin a day. The family realized that the only thing to do was to hand Ron in.

On his release in 1959 Ronnie found it hard to readjust. His time in prison and on the run had twisted his appearance. He was no longer an identical twin. His face and neck were fuller. His speech was slow and he walked stiffly. He spent the first few months huddled by the fire at No. 178, going out only after dark, always carrying a swordstick and .32 Beretta.

Reg had acquired other establishments while Ron was inside, usually only a few days after they had been firebombed. By the 1960s the twins had an empire of about thirty venues. Every Friday members of the firm would go round collecting the premium the owners paid for protection, mostly protection from the Krays; it was known as 'the milk round'. Of these venues Ron's favourite was the Kentucky at 106 Mile End Road. He opened it in 1962 to coincide with the première of the cockney comedy film *Sparrers Can't Sing*, starring Barbara Windsor, at the Empire Cinema opposite. The decor was up-market for the East End – black leather upholstery and red walls – spoiled by Ron's insistence that smokers lit up as often as possible to produce an authentic 'club' atmosphere. Entertainment often came from Ron leading a chorus of 'Knees Up Mother Brown'.

Late in 1959 Reg was jailed for eighteen months for demanding money with menaces. With Ron left in charge business suffered. There was too much violence. He would lend those he wanted to control inordinate sums of money, just to make them subservient, and then turn nasty when they couldn't pay back on time. But once Reg was out, the Krays were invincible. It was said that if anyone made a complaint against the twins they would know about it by the time the person complaining had left the police station. They were involved in hi-jacking lorries, trading National Service exemption certificates, protection rackets and long firms.

Thanks to Jake Arnott's book *The Long Firm* and the well-crafted television adaptation shown in 2004, this type of scam has come to the attention of the wider public. In a long firm gangsters form a trading company, enlist a compliant dignitary as non-executive director (to win credence) and fill up with stock, which could be toasters, stereos, golf clubs or silk stockings. Anything that moves quickly.

The villains settle their bills with frightening speed. They buy more goods, and again settle the bills rapidly. Eventually, they buy huge quantities of stuff, but don't pay up so quickly, which is fine as they have a thirty-day credit period. They then make their final stock purchase, again paying on credit, and sell off all the goods in a cheap 'fire sale'. The firm promptly disappears. Registered company officers turn out to be long dead, having been resurrected with purloined birth certificates and fake signatures. Creditors find empty offices and no trace of the businessmen.

The best long firm was the Richardsons' on Mitre Street, Aldgate, a few yards from where Jack the Ripper killed Catherine Eddowes. Instead of staging a fire *sale* the Richardsons decided to set the warehouse housing the goods on fire and to claim the insurance. Unfortunately, the gang's explosives' expert planted too much dynamite. Not only did the warehouse explode, it took with it a gas mains, which set off fires and explosions in nearby shops and factories, and saw the entire street catching light. Twenty-seven fire engines were called out to quell the flames. Nevertheless, the Richardsons made around a quarter of a million pounds' profit from the enterprise.

The Krays also ran a number of minor scams which netted considerable income. Typical of their brazen resourcefulness was the 'Sting'. One night at the Double 'R' Reg Kray spotted a fence and decided to ensnare him. He called the man over and told him of a forger, Ossie, who had £10,000 in counterfeit £5 notes which he wanted to sell for 30 shillings (£1.50) each. Kray explained that the deal didn't particularly interest him, it wasn't enough money, but the fence's mouth watered at the prospect of making an easy £7,000 profit. Not wishing to appear too keen, the man told Kray he'd go away and think about it.

A few days later the fence rang Kray. 'Is the counterfeit cash still for sale?' Kray repeated it was not his to sell, and reiterated that he was not interested, but the fence persisted. Kray 'reluctantly' agreed to meet him at the Terminus Café in Mile End Road. He was accompanied by Ossie, who had with him samples of his stash, which of course were perfectly clean notes and which he used to pay for his tea. When the café owner took the notes without a murmur the fence was impressed, and asked to see more. Ossie pulled out a roll of valid fivers and the man marvelled at the notes, agreeing that they looked indistinguishable from those issued by the Bank of England. When the fence insisted on buying all the remaining notes Kray asked to be counted in, and so the party drove off to Ossie's flat to retrieve the rest of the cash.

As the three men pulled up outside Ossie's address he explained that he wanted to go up to his flat alone, as his wife was unaware of his shady business. The fence saw nothing amiss and sat with Reg Kray in the car. Ossie went up, phoned the police, and came downstairs with two wrapped bundles which he handed to the two men. Kray sat with the parcels, making small talk. But when they heard the sound of a police car in the distance, they cursed and decided to get away fast. Quickly Reg cried, 'Don't go without the money', handing Ossie £1,500 in exchange for his parcel. The fence did likewise and gave over his £1,500, before rushing off to avoid the police. Reg then gave the fence his parcel of the easy fivers, shouting to him, 'Be careful with my share of the notes.'

The fence returned home with £10,000 worth of fivers that had cost £3,000. He opened the first parcel to find neatly cut wads of old newspapers. He opened the second parcel. It was the same. He had been well and truly stung.

By the mid-1960s Ronnie Kray was planning a gangland federation in London, uniting all the criminal groups under one command, with himself as head. Yet he and Reg were still living at 178 Vallance Road, their parents' tiny two-up two-down cottage in the heart of Bethnal Green slumland. They were still psychologically unable to escape the white ghetto, despite their riches. But at least they were not ashamed of their origins. Over the years they invited home various celebrities, including the world boxing champions Joe Louis and Rocky Marciano, and Judy Garland, who sang a few numbers at the nearby Crown and Anchor pub after hours.

Every day a barber came to No. 178 to massage their hair with olive oil and surgical spirit. Every day more and more gangster clothes arrived. Ronnie had thirty suits – all from Savile Row or Woods of Kingsland Road, Dalston. He had fifty shirts, rarely wearing one twice, and a dark blue Al Capone coat, for he believed himself to be the reincarnation of the infamous mafioso, even though the latter had died when Ronnie was only thirteen. At night he washed his feet in a bowl of rosewater and milk. He and Reg turned 178 Vallance into Fort Vallance with a formidable arsenal of weaponry – choppers, machetes, knives, revolvers, a Luger automatic, a Mauser and sawn-off shotguns – which they stored beneath the floorboards.

In 1964 the Krays contacted the American Mafia. They had lengthy meetings at the London Hilton, on Park Lane, with Angelo Bruno, the head of a Philadelphia crime family, and Anthony 'Tony Ducks' Corallo, *capo* of the Luccheses, one of the powerful Mafia groups that dominated New York. On one of his visits Corallo offered Charlie Kray a 'small' gift as a gesture of good will from Thomas Lucchese, the godfather. Charlie told Corallo gifts weren't necessary, only friendship and cooperation. The mobster accordingly returned to New York with a suitcase containing $50,000.

In Peter Medak's film about the Krays the twins hand the Mafia a picture of their mum in exchange for the money. This did not happen in real life but it's a better story. After all, what could be more valuable than a framed picture of Violet Kray? The Mafia weren't sure what kind of screwballs they were up against. So to test the Krays' resolve they asked them to dispose of $250,000 worth of 'laundered bonds'. The Krays burnt the money, all counterfeit, in the dustbin at the back of No. 178.

To many in the East End the Krays were more than run-of-the-mill crooks. They were Robin Hood figures, handing large sums of money to poor families, supporting children's homes, protecting the local community. One of Ron's dreams was to open up a home for alcoholics on Cheshire Street, off Brick Lane, and he had his own original ideas as to how it would be run. When a drunk was first admitted he would be accommodated on the ground floor. He would rise to the first floor when his condition improved, and eventually move to the top floor, which would be comfortably furnished and carpeted, with a television and library. When he was cured he would be discharged. The home was never built, but it was probably enough that locals heard the scheme was being planned.

The myth perpetuated by the Krays' supporters was that the only people who suffered from their activities were other villains, those who had broken the unwritten East End underworld code of conduct. When the London chronicler Dan Farson explained this to the Cockney actor Arthur Mullard, and added that the Krays 'only killed their own kind', Mullard voiced the views of many when he responded in his inimitable fashion, 'Yus, 'ooman bein's.'

The Krays' callous disregard for the sanctity of human life was never more apparent than in the tragic story of Frank 'The Mad Axeman' Mitchell. A gigantic psychopathic simpleton, Mitchell was being held in Dartmoor prison until the Krays, needing a new henchman, decided to spring him a few weeks before Christmas 1966. They took him from Devon to London while reports of his escape dominated the news, and secreted him in a hideaway at 206a Barking Road, East Ham.

Mitchell didn't take too well to being treated like a caged animal, especially given that he expected to be paraded round the West End's leading nightspots and fêted by the Krays as an underworld hero. He was not placated by the call girl brought in to service him, and with the police on his trail and the tabloids describing him as 'Britain's most wanted man', he caught cabin fever, threatening to shoot the Krays if he was not allowed out. Ronnie decided Mitchell had to be 'eliminated'. On Christmas Eve the Krays' henchmen bundled the

Mad Axeman into a van and shot him dead while it was being driven along Barking Road. Mitchell's body was dumped in the sea off Newhaven – or was it? Rumours persist that the corpse was embedded in the wet concrete propping up Bow flyover.

By the mid-1960s the Krays had legitimate rivals – the cleverer, wiser, more ruthless Richardson brothers from across the water in Camberwell. The Krays were perturbed that their south London rivals were gaining a hold in the West End at their expense, making around £1,000 a week from a car-parking scam at London airport, were staging successful long firm scams, and becoming powerful abroad, thanks to their mining interests in South Africa.

When a Richardson gang member, Brian Mottram, opened a business on Hackney Road, less than a mile from the twins' headquarters, the Krays decided to push the south Londoners off their patch. Each member of the Kray firm was given a Richardson acolyte to follow, with Reggie Kray assigned Eddie Richardson and Ronnie Kray Charlie Richardson, the gang's leader. But there was one problem. None of the Kray gang knew what any of the Richardson gang (apart from Frankie Fraser) looked like. To compensate for this, members of the Kray firm began dropping in at Richardson haunts, where they would not look suspicious, such as the Astor Club in Mayfair. The Krays soon learned that the Richardsons were planning a raid on the Lion, a dingy, evil-looking public house run by the Krays in the heart of the Bethnal Green police 'no go' zone. As a pre-emptive strike they decided to attack the Richardsons in one of their favourite night spots, Mr Smith's club in Catford, south London.

The Catford fracas took place on 8 March 1966 and was particularly gruesome. A Kray acolyte, Richard Hart, was killed. The following day Ron, still foaming at the mouth at the news of Hart's demise, was in the Lion when he heard that the Richardsons' George Cornell was drinking in the Blind Beggar, Whitechapel – Kray territory. This, Ron explained, was 'a diabolical liberty'. He sought justice. 'Richard Hart had to be avenged. No one could kill a member of the Kray gang and expect to get away with it. Typical of the yobbo mentality of the man [Cornell]. Less than twenty-four hours after the Catford killing and here he was, drinking in a pub that was officially on our patch. It was as though he wanted to be shot.'

Cornell was sitting on a stool by the Blind Beggar's small U-shaped bar, drinking a light ale, when Ronnie Kray and an accomplice, Ian Barrie, entered. Cornell exclaimed what were to be his last words, 'Well, look who's here then', and, as Barrie fired a shot into the ceiling, Kray aimed his gun between Cornell's eyes and shot him dead.

There was little immediate response to Cornell's killing. Albie Woods, who had been drinking with the murdered man, cleared the pub of any incriminating glasses that might yield fingerprints, and the underworld code of 'not grassing' meant that both the barmaid and Woods claimed not to know the identity of the murderer – although, as Woods later pointed out, Cornell would probably not have wanted it any other way.

Kray himself felt invincible, returning to the pub some time after to order a pint of 'luger and lime'. He also began to tease Reg mercilessly about his 'lack of bottle'. Would Reg be able to offer a sacrificial victim? Reg chose as his target Jack 'The Hat' McVitie, a small-time villain who always wore a hat to hide his creeping hair loss. McVitie was a pathetic figure. One night in 1967 at the Tempo club by Highbury and Islington station he was watching Dorothy Squires, wife of Roger Moore, singing on stage when, noticing she was drunk, he rolled up to the stage and shouted out, 'That Roger Moore, what's he like in bed, then?' before dropping his trousers. Pandemonium. Word got back to the twins, who were not happy. Ronnie Kray was heard to say, 'To do that . . . to an entertainer of that calibre . . .'

Jack the Hat was already on a warning. He had already failed to obey a Kray order to kill an associate. Now he would have to be punished. On 28 October 1967 the twins' aide-de-camp Tony Lambrianou ferried Jack to a basement flat at 97 Evering Road, Stoke Newington, for a 'quiet word'. Jack was told there was going to be a party, but when he entered the room he found things were not swinging as he expected. 'Where's all the birds, where's all the booze?' asked the Hat.

Reggie responded by pointing a gun at McVitie's head. He fired, but the gun jammed. As McVitie tried to flee through the window his hat fell off. He was hauled back in and held down, so that he could not escape. Reg then picked up a carving knife and pushed it into McVitie's face below an eye. He also stabbed him in the throat with such force that the knife stuck to the wall and had to be wriggled around in McVitie's throat to be removed.

Once McVitie was dead the Krays were faced with the problem of disposing of the body. As it would not fit into the boot of their car it was placed upright on the back seat – Jack's hat firmly secured on his dead head – and driven on a long tortuous route through London to lose possible pursuers and confound potential witnesses, before being taken to a watery grave off the coast of Sussex.

Unbeknown to the Krays, Scotland Yard was building a watertight case against them, providing new identities for witnesses too frightened to speak and even convincing former allies to give evidence. In May 1968 the police staged a dawn swoop at their mum's new tower block flat in St Luke's and arrested the twins for various crimes, including the murders of Cornell and McVitie. A year later they received life sentences at the Old Bailey with the recommendation that they each serve thirty years.

Ronnie Kray never saw freedom again, dying behind bars in 1995. Reggie was released in 2000, but only when he was dying. Yet even from prison the Krays continued to exert a powerful hold on the London underworld through intimidation and contract beatings. The Krays' grand finales came towards the end of the twentieth century – their funerals at St Matthew's Bethnal Green. The first was that of Violet, the mother, in 1982, for which the Krays were let out of prison for the day handcuffed to enormous warders. Ronnie's funeral on 29 March 1995 was London's best attended since the death of Winston Churchill thirty years previously. His coffin was carried by four pallbearers – Johnny Nash, Freddie Foreman, Ginger Dennis and Charlie Kray – representing the four corners of the London gang-world. Reggie was present, handcuffed to a *woman* officer.

After the service the coffin, resting on a carriage decorated florally with the word 'Ron', was led by six black-plumed horses and twenty-five limousines around the local streets of his 'manor' and on to Chingford, where he was buried. In making its way to the cemetery the cortège of limousines crossed Bow flyover. Given that the procession had no need to take this route its inclusion perhaps indicated a nefarious association – the remains of the bones of one or two Kray victims in the cement propping up the roadway. Charlie Kray's funeral took place at St Matthew's on 19 April 2000 and Reg's on 11 October the same year. His was the least ostentatious and the only one not to feature a living Kray, of course.

There were many East End villains other than the Krays. After all, this is the land ruled by the profession of violence. The others though, could not compete on star quality, but some of them were nastier, more ruthless than the Krays. Particularly Freddie Foreman. Freddie had a nickname – Brown Bread Fred: 'Don't mess with Brown Bread Fred or you're dead.' Foreman was a hired assassin, the man who shot Frank 'The Mad Axeman' Mitchell for the Krays in 1966, as outlined above. He was also involved in another East End shooting, that of Ginger Marks, a villain who went out on the night of Friday 2 January 1965 and never came back.

Marks had gone to Bethnal Green to case a jeweller's with Jimmy Evans, a renowned safe-breaker, but he chose the wrong company that night, for Evans had been having an affair with Freddie Foreman's sister-in-law. Brown Bread Fred drove around the East End looking for Evans. Eventually he spotted him and Marks eating chips outside the Carpenter's Arms, a Kray-owned pub where the twins' mother, Violet, held court surrounded by over-dressed, bejewelled women sporting huge peroxide-bleached beehive hairdos every weekend in the 1960s.

Fred stopped the car, wound down the window and aimed his .38 revolver at Evans. The adulterous safe-breaker acted quickly. He grabbed Marks and used him as a human shield to ward off Foreman's bullets. Marks died instantly but Evans escaped, making his way to the Krays' nearby headquarters at 178 Vallance Road, where he was told that he could not be given any help. Foreman made off without the scalp of Evans, his intended victim, but with the corpse of Ginger Marks. What had happened to Marks, the world wondered? He had gone out for the night and simply 'disappeared'. The police knew that somebody – they didn't know who – had been shot outside the Carpenter's Arms. They also knew that the victim had been shot in the stomach, for they found a chip embedded in the wall of the pub.

Eventually detectives realized that the shooting had occurred around the same time that Marks disappeared. They searched 2,000 holiday caravans in Essex but found no leads. Marks was officially declared missing. Outlandish rumours spread: he had been thrown into the Thames near Staines with his legs encased in concrete; he had been dumped in a gravel pit in Kent; placed in the concrete pillars holding up Hammersmith flyover; buried in a Whitechapel bomb site. Someone claimed he had been tipped into a cement-mixer. One excellent theory described how a compliant undertaker had put Marks's corpse into an already filled coffin, as in the Sherlock Holmes story 'The Disappearance of Lady Frances Carfax'. In his book *Respect*, Foreman confessed to the murder, attributing his violent behaviour to the 'respect' that he craved 'at any cost'.

The jailing of the Krays in 1969 did not, surprisingly, lead to the end of East End crime. The killing continued, and this time it was hard to link the worst crimes to any particular gang, for there was no one powerful enough, charismatic enough, to assume the role of god-father. The 1970s murders were bizarre. At four o'clock in the morning of Friday 27 September 1974, only a few hours after the conclusion of the Jewish Day of Atonement, 69-year-old Alfie Cohen was found battered to death outside the Hole in the Wall kiosk on Commercial Road, Stepney, that he had run for forty years. Seven years previously his brother, Mike, had been beaten and robbed outside the stall, and had later died from his injuries. How incredible that the other brother should now become a victim too.

Alfie was well-known in the area. Taxi drivers, police officers, firemen, students, dockers and insomniacs would drop by at his stall for an early hours cup of tea. The murderers made off with just a few pounds, and the underworld was horrified. 'We will not rest until the guilty are brought to justice,' one villain, who lived on nearby Christian Street, told the local paper. 'We are all mucking in to try and find Alfie's murderers. We all respected him and this one time we'll be pleased to turn someone over to the law.'

Cohen's murder was outside the rules of East End gangland – although these rules had become unenforceable since the demise of the Kray firm – and two men were eventually caught. They were nobodies, low life on the make. It was brutal senseless murder. When police searched the kiosk for clues they found a total of £105,000 hidden under old boxes and stuffed into various corners, which the murderers had missed. What a strange and tragic story. Yet for those acquainted with the bizarre patterns that appear to govern the East End, patterns that may connect the medieval murder of Brother Martin at Holy Trinity Priory, the esoteric measurements used in creating the East End after the Fire, the Ratcliff Highway murders and Jack the Ripper's killing of Catherine Eddowes, Cohen's murder was particularly interesting. At his feet somebody, presumably the killers, had scattered two brass rings and some coins – just as Jack the Ripper had done at the feet of Annie Chapman in 1888. And coincidentally – or not – Cohen's kiosk stands 2,000 cubits (the length of the 'sacred measurement') from where Chapman was murdered.

## DIAL H FOR MURDER

Stranger still, from a criminal science point of view, was the story of the John Childs serial killings of the 1970s. At first it all seemed so simple. Terry Eve, a man who made teddy bears, fell out with his business partners, who decided to teach him a lesson. They bought a large butcher's mincing machine and installed it at 13 Dolphin House, Dolphin Lane, Poplar. Then they went to Eve's factory and strangled him with a piece of rope, put the body in their Jaguar, returned to Dolphin House and fed Eve into the machine. When it jammed they tried to dispose of the rest of the flesh down the lavatory. That also proved a problem, so they chopped him up and burned the corpse bit by bit in the flat over the course of twenty-four hours. They then placed the ashes in a plastic bag and scattered them over the Barking by-pass. That was how it came out in court.

Terry Pinfold and John Childs were convicted for Eve's murder. Childs, who lived at Dolphin House, soon began to fascinate the newspapers. To his neighbours he was 'Bruce', but to his mum he was Martin Jones. He decided to change his name when another man, who really was called John Childs, moved out of the same Poplar tower block. Jones took over his rent book and became John Childs. 'I thought he was a fairly normal bloke with a family,' said a neighbour. 'He owned a white Transit van.'

In fact Jones/Childs had a long criminal record, which stretched from petty theft to robbery, arson, burglary, attempted murder and real murder. His aim was to gain a place in Madame Tussaud's Chamber of Horrors. Next he targeted a business associate, Fred Sherwood, who ran a nursing home in Herne Bay. On 31 July 1978 Childs pretended to buy Sherwood's car, lured him to a bungalow and hit him with a hammer. Sherwood was finished off not by Childs, but by an associate, Harry 'Big H' MacKenny, the court heard.

Big H, all six foot four of him, was a qualified pilot, deep-sea diver and firearms expert, who ran a company making diving equipment in the same Dagenham factory where Childs worked. To family, friends and neighbours MacKenny was a 'loving and gentle giant', but there was a nastier side to him. Even the Krays were frightened of him, for he and Childs, the prosecution claimed, had set up a contract killings firm, 'Dial H for Murder'. Dial H offered its services to the mother of the fugitive peer Lord Lucan, offering to 'do' anyone who tried to harm or even find the missing peer. They approached the well-known racist Robert Relf, who was in prison for putting up a sign outside his house in Royal Leamington Spa stating he would sell only to white people, and asked him if he wanted any black people 'put away'. Relf declined their offer.

The court heard how a man called Thompson paid Dial H £2,000 to murder George Brett, a haulage contractor who had beaten him up. Childs, dressed as a City gent in a Homburg hat and carrying a furled umbrella, turned up at Brett's house on a Saturday morning early in 1975 claiming he wanted rid of a load. Brett drove Childs to the latter's factory in Dagenham. Also in the car was Brett's ten-year-old son, Terry. At the factory Childs gave Terry a teddy bear. It was a nice touch, even if it was probably from the murdered Eve's stock. An accomplice known to the court only as 'Mr B' then took Brett into another room and shot him in cold blood. Just to make sure that the son would not have to carry around with him for the rest of his life the horror of hearing the murder of his father Childs grabbed the boy and MacKenny shot him.

No one knew what had happened to Brett and his son, and all manner of fanciful rumours spread: that he was a police informer; that he knew too much about the location of a £400,000 bullion robbery for which his brother, John, was serving a fifteen-year sentence; even that he had stumbled across a gang that had taken over from the Krays as local underworld leaders. Childs later explained that he and MacKenny dismembered the bodies, placed them in sacks and spent the next twenty-four hours incinerating them in their living-room grate. Forensic scientists could not accept that bodies could be disposed of in such a fashion. To test out the story they got themselves an eleven-stone pig and burned it. It took them thirteen hours to eradicate the animal.

Childs began to drink more and dress strangely, like an undertaker, in a long dark overcoat and Homburg. While awaiting trial he went on hunger strike, eating only boiled sweets, in an attempt to gain a lighter sentence. It did not work. He received six life sentences. In 1998 he confessed to five more killings. Pinfold was jailed for 'procuring' MacKenny and Childs, the main prosecution witness, to murder Eve. MacKenny went down for four murders. He was not happy about his convictions, yelling at Mr Justice May, 'Straight people need protection from you', before turning to the jury and adding 'and from mongols and mugs like you'.

East End businessmen could now sleep more easily. The villains had been locked up. The story died. Dial H for Murder didn't enter the national consciousness alongside the exploits of the Krays and the Richardsons; there was no glamour attached. It was just a series of brutal and sickening murders. And that is how it stayed for nearly thirty years, until Pinfold and MacKenny appealed against their convictions and won. They were released in December 2003 and immediately sought suitable compensation. MacKenny, seventy-two years old, became the first prisoner serving a whole-life tariff to have his conviction quashed.

It turned out that the authorities had been a little too keen to nail Pinfold and MacKenny on the word of Childs who, according to a consultant forensic psychiatrist brought into examine the evidence, suffered from a severe anti-social personality disorder which made him an immensely plausible liar. Childs's evidence was 'worthless'. At the original trial it was Childs who, in being prosecuted for Eve's murder six years after the event, turned Queen's evidence on Pinfold and MacKenny.

Now some worrying circumstances surrounding Eve's murder came out. No murder weapon or corroborating witnesses had been found; there was no forensic evidence. In fact Childs's testimony was the prosecution's sole evidence that *any* of the six people had been murdered. And one other thing about Eve. There was no body, for Eve had not actually been killed. He was alive for years after his 'murder', living in west London under an assumed name – as police knew when the men were jailed.

# 14

# Rebirth?

The twenty-first century has arrived and the East End is London's most dynamic and progressive quarter. The Isle of Dogs is *the* prestige commerical location in London. Spitalfields is *the* Georgian village *par excellence*. Brick Lane is *the* most exciting street in Britain. How did it come to this?

Just as the Industrial Revolution created the monster that was the Victorian and twentieth-century East End, so the demise of heavy industry and long-established economic patterns has allowed a new East End to flourish. For centuries those moving upward within London society had moved west; to the new suburban estates of Mayfair (eighteenth century), Belgravia (Victorian times), Fulham and Putney (twentieth-century suburban sprawl). Now they often move east. The transfer of the newspaper groups from Fleet Street to the Isle of Dogs in the late 1980s led the way for other prestigious firms to move to what was London's forgotten island as recently as the 1970s. Well-paid professionals have colonized the smart new apartment blocks that now line the Thames east of Tower Bridge. The ex-Huguenot enclaves and earthy Victorian terraces around Spitalfields have recently become home to more artists than any other London neighbourhood.

In Docklands the great architect of this demographic revolution – remarkably – was the loathed and ridiculed figure of the 1980s Conservative prime minister Margaret Thatcher. While vast sections of British society became alienated from each other under her regime, so the story goes, those who shared the same entrepreneurial vision became richer, more powerful, more confident. In the Thatcherite dream the profits of the wealthy trickle down to the less fortunate, benefiting the entire community eventually. Which is exactly what has happened in the Isle of Dogs.

After the docks closed in the late 1960s the huge caverns of deep water, where tens of thousands of men had loaded and unloaded thousands of ships for more than 150 years, and the land alongside lay still, bereft of activity and people, with tumbledown warehouses, scraps of rotting metal and abandoned machinery littering the agoraphobic stretches shouting 'Awaiting Redevelopment'.

The dockside land was owned by public bodies – the Port of London Authority, Tower Hamlets council and, further east, Newham council, the latter two Labour-controlled. These public bodies were not geared towards making money. Their response to the dockland problem involved much wringing of hands and thumping of tables but little imagination.

The Tories found a solution. They created a hybrid public–private sector body – the London Docklands Development Corporation (LDDC) – composed of not just politicians, not just Labour politicians, whose acceptance of the invitation to join the body was met with taunts of 'class traitors', but businessmen who saw the potential of the derelict land.

The councils complained that the LDDC was undemocratic; that its members were appointed rather than elected, and were therefore not answerable to the public. They were right, but they had missed the point. If the revival of the East End had been left just to the politicians the land would still be rotting away. The LDDC set about its work. It outlined a vision, much mocked at the time, of a vibrant Isle of Dogs where aspiring professionals lived in apartment blocks of brick, rather than prefabricated slabs, or maybe in the renovated old dock warehouses, alongside the cleaned-up water; yachts and motor-boats would bob in docks previously filled with ivory-laden ships and lighters. Nearby would be offices geared to the new computer-based technology; modems and monitors rather than steam-hammers and capstans. Snaking through an area long notorious for its inaccessibility would be some form of hi-tech transport, which would connect the new commercial centre with the City.

Without the town halls in charge the various schemes prospered; even major setbacks – bankruptcies and temporary losses of confidence

– failed to stop the rise of the new docklands. By the end of the century the results were out. They were extraordinary. For the first time since the rebuilding of London after the Fire the East End got a good deal. The ghostly stacks of rotting industry around the docks were replaced by smartly appointed residential blocks – even tower slabs – aimed at those who wanted them: single people, City workers, professionals, rather than working-class families. Clever town houses set on three storeys, rather than maisonettes connected by the loathed 'streets in the sky', were built by old graving docks and marshalling yards. Within walking distance were the even more spectacular new head offices of major companies.

Through the new docklands weaves the *faux-naif* Docklands Light Railway. Now the most obscure Tower hamlets are connected by a labyrinth of lines serviced by ingenious driverless trains. The Docklands Light Railway meets the underground system at what used to be places to be avoided – Stratford, Canning Town, Millwall. Further east, alongside the deserted Royal Docks, the LDDC built an airport – London City – with fast links for small planes to major west European cities. An airport within easy reach of the City, an alternative to the holidaymakers' hell of Heathrow.

Standing triumphant over the new docklands at the north-western corner of the Isle of Dogs is Canary Wharf, a steel and granite city of immense precision and power. For much of the nineteenth and twentieth centuries the site was a landing quay between the West India Import and Export Docks, where bananas and tomatoes imported from the Canary Islands were taken off the boats. A two-storey warehouse was the only building on the site.

When the docks closed in 1980 Canary Wharf became derelict. It was revived following a meeting between two restaurateurs and the Credit Suisse First Boston bank held on a barge moored on the river nearby. They hired architects Skidmore, Owings and Merrill, creators of some of Chicago's and New York's most famous towers, to devise a new estate on the site, and brought in the Reichmann brothers, Canadian entrepreneurs, as developers.

Locals greeted the start of construction work in 1987 by dressing in funereal black and staging a mock procession in protest; they rejoiced at the collapse of the Reichmanns' Olympia and York company in 1992. Their antipathy was based more on class envy than reasoned argument: they feared that the new Isle of Dogs would attract a huge influx of well-paid middle-class professionals – what used to be called the bourgeoisie and is now disparagingly referred to as 'yuppies' – and that wine bars and coffee houses would fill the streets where for a hundred years men had bred racing pigeons and sucked on Woodbines hidden between their fingers.

The frustration of the threatened traditional island population with the new world rising around them manifested itself in the election of a councillor representing the proto-fascist British National Party (BNP) in Millwall in 1993. The BNP campaigned under the slogan 'Rights for Whites' in answer to the growing number of Bangladeshi immigrants moving into Tower Hamlets, which was ironic given that no local BNP supporter would have been able to trace their island heritage further back than the building of the docks in 1800. The BNP's success proved to be temporary, with little lasting effect on local life, which continued to change fast as new industrial units and waterside apartments replaced the redundant quays and dock-workers' cottages.

Meanwhile, the Canary Wharf scheme was rescued by a new consortium. By the mid-1990s it was growing apace. By the twenty-first century the results were apparent. Here stands Britain's tallest skyscraper – 1 Canada Square – surrounded by other lofty towers. They are visible from all over London, an occasional glimpse available walking along the genteel suburban streets of Muswell Hill or Norwood. Canary Wharf and Millwall are now home to major companies: Citigroup, Morgan Stanley Dean Witter, BZW, the Hongkong and Shanghai Bank. But their most remarkable catches have been the newspapers. The *Independent, Mirror* and *Telegraph* newspaper groups are now based on the island. The *Financial Times* and *Guardian* are printed nearby.

Fleet Street's move east was another product of the Tory government's ability to instil confidence in entrepreneurs, in particular the ambitious Australian newspaper magnate Rupert Murdoch. By the early 1980s Murdoch owned four of Britain's most successful newspapers – *The Times, Sunday Times, Sun* and *News of the World*.

He decided to build a new plant – secretly – in Wapping on land once part of London Docks. It would be run using new technology, without the traditional print unions. The plant, situated only a few yards from the site of the Ratcliff Highway murders of 1811, went up amid some of the most intense security ever seen in a British industrial plant. It was ringed with razor wire and a twelve-foot-high steel fence, monitored by searchlights and closed-circuit cameras. Computer equipment was smuggled in and installed in a room guarded by electronic security. Staff were warned to beware of car bombs and to check their vehicles carefully as they left work.

On Friday 24 January 1986 the first journalists were bussed in to the plant past the pickets and through the electronically controlled front gates. The pickets maintained their vigil throughout the winter. The fighting between protesters and police was savage and bloody. To protect themselves officers wore quasi-military uniforms. According to the Newham MP Ron Leighton, they used their truncheons 'not in self-defence but to batter, frighten and intimidate people . . . aiming their blows not to the body or legs, but the heads. I saw people penned in; they were not allowed to disperse and they were repeatedly charged. Words fail me to describe my feelings at what I saw.'

Many MPs wanted a public inquiry into alleged police violence outside the News International plant. Instead they got an internal police investigation, carried out by the Northamptonshire force, which spent two years scrutinizing photographs and videotapes, and taking thousands of statements. They were highly critical of the officers in charge of the Wapping operation. They found that there was no proper command and that the police operation on those nights was entirely out of control. They made charges against a number of police officers – charges of assault, perjury and conspiracy. Twenty-four officers were charged with criminal offences.

Interestingly the worst violence, which raged for a year, took place mostly on Wellclose Square, once the apex of the New Jerusalem as created by those who rebuilt London after the 1666 Fire, but by the 1980s an abandoned dystopia of utilitarian tower blocks and windswept clumps of grass, its mystical, if not its nefarious powers dormant.

Over on the Isle of Dogs the *Telegraph*'s relocation in the summer of 1987 was the most surprising. With the locale then barely reachable by public means of transport – the Docklands Light Railway was in its infancy – and the roads jammed, staff were brought in by water taxis. Those that made the transfer found themselves working in characterless, air-conditioned offices, where the windows could not be opened, an hour's journey from their Westminster and Soho haunts.

Yet here they have remained. The traditional working pattern of the newspaper, whereby refined journalists fluent in Horace and Virgil lounged on horsehair sofas in between tipples at Ye Olde Cheshire Cheese and El Vino's, is now as bygone as the thought of Canary Wharf being a repository for Atlantic island fruits.

But there are many complaints. Canary Wharf is 'unreal'. 'There is none of the fellowship of London EC4,' Alan Watkins, the veteran political columnist, noted in his 2001 book, *A Short Walk Down Fleet Street*. 'Canary Wharf now has a higher concentration of national newspapers than had been accommodated in Old Fleet Street,' but he added knowingly that 'separation on a vertical pattern creates isolation, which the inhabitants of tower blocks have long known but their architects have yet to learn'. To the *Observer*'s Nick Cohen Canary Wharf is at fault for being a 'gated work village . . . security guards around every corner and CCTV cameras on every wall'. Old-school island politicians such as Ted Johns, who led the humorous island UDI bid in the 1970s, railed against the way islanders were pushed out of the area during the building of Canary Wharf, much in the same way that those who lived in St Katharine's were mercilessly forced out in the early nineteenth century for the building of the docks.

The criticisms are valid. How can its resident journalists empathize with the public if they never meet them; how can they bear to work in an environment where every shop, bar and café is part of some ghastly chain, probably based in Seattle? Why should powerless people be forced out of their homes to fulfil the state's grand scheme? But then they remember the alternative: a dock of dirty water and a rusty crane. A lawless land cut off from the rest of the world, brutally run as private fiefdoms by extended families.

## THE NEW GEORGIANS

Although Spitalfields lost its silk industry early in the twentieth century, the area remained one of the liveliest, if also dirtiest, in London. At its northern end the long-running fruit and veg market brought good-natured chaos to the decaying Georgian streets. At its southern end the streets were dominated by the rag trade, born out of silk, which powered Petticoat Lane, London's best market for much of the century. By the end of the twentieth century Petticoat Lane had become an embarrassment to London. The Jewish food sellers, with their sweet plaited bread and pickled cucumbers, had given way to Cockney stallholders selling rubber burgers and inedible hot dogs. The high-quality tat sold by the Jews had been replaced by poor-quality rubbish sold by gentiles. The most inspired market traders had moved to Brick Lane and Columbia Road.

Throughout the last decades of the twentieth century Spitalfields Market was threatened with closure. Everyone knew it would go the way of Covent Garden, forced to a characterless suburb to accommodate the ever larger lorries bringing countryside produce to London. But people were also concerned with the future of the building. Would it be knocked down and replaced with an inappropriate granite and glass corporate block?

In 1992 Spitalfields Market closed, as expected. Remarkably the building was saved. It was turned into a flea market full of fascinating stalls selling exotic continental foods, cheap clothes, books and bric-à-brac. It attracts huge crowds every weekend. But its future remains precarious. The City gathers outside, casting an envious eye on the site. Prime real estate. In the early years of the twenty-first century Mammon won the first round, taking over part of the old market for offices. Few believe it will greet another century, and if Mammon consumes Spitalfields Market its march into Georgian Spitalfields will be unstoppable.

It is not only the City that threatens the character of the area. The worst single piece of architectural destruction in the East End in recent years has come courtesy of the public sector – Railtrack, London Underground, the Greater London Authority – who in 2002 combined to demolish, with consummate vandalism, one of London's greatest industrial sites, the Bishopsgate Goods Yard, a labyrinthine brick undercroft between Brick Lane and Shoreditch High Street, home to a remarkable diversity of stalls, in their zeal to upgrade the East London tube line. More such redevelopment and the reason for the area's popularity, which prompted the new line in the first place, will evaporate.

The changes in Spitalfields' various markets are negligible compared to the momentous transformation of Spitalfields as a residential area. During the early post-war decades Spitalfields' Georgian architecture was deemed passé. All around, the East End was being rid of eighteenth-century terraced houses with fanlights, panelling, mahogany features, ornamented staircases, carved doorframes, wooden floorboards and sash windows. Such houses that remained in Spitalfields were unlettable and unappealing to estate agents. Little repair work had been carried out on them for a hundred years.

When in the late 1970s old Spitalfields looked doomed a group of maverick historians squatted a stretch of properties in Elder Street as part of their campaign to preserve the area. They even managed to enlist the help of the poet laureate John Betjeman. Supporters began negotiating to buy the threatened properties. One of their number, Douglas Blain, targeted a row of houses in Elder Street and found himself dealing with a Polish landlord who used two surnames, Field and Galinsky, depending on whether he was buying or selling. Blain bought four terraced houses for £3,000 each. They were saved and are now worth more than £1 million each.

Within a decade Spitalfields' remaining Georgian infrastructure had been largely saved. The rotting houses of Fournier Street and its neighbours in the shadow of Hawksmoor's Christ Church were bought up by people willing and able to restore the original fittings. Future owners found themselves restrained from refurbishment by the strictest heritage regulations.

Of course there are detractors. They moan that a fake eighteenth-century theme park has sprung up in proletarian east London, that it is absurd that among the penniless Bangladeshis live these genteel learned architects, artists, designers . . . gay people. Then they are reminded of the alternative: the destruction of the last homogenous Georgian village in inner London and the further encroachment of the City.

## ANOTHER JERUSALEM

And then there's Brick Lane. For hundreds of years an industrious but nondescript side street, it is now the most celebrated road in Britain, holder of the crown held in the 1960s by King's Road and Carnaby Street, and in the 1970s by the Westway.

How do we explain the magic of Brick Lane? Is it enough to point to its chic, urban edginess, the barely interrupted stretches of brick terraced Victorian shops, the dazzling neon-lit curry houses with their excruciatingly annoying waiters quick to pounce on the hapless passer-by (£1 per customer they drag in); to the weekend flea and food market, particularly the whelk and kipper stall near Bacon Street; to the *two* twenty-four-hour beigel bakeries, the one patronized by the cognoscenti, the other avoided (those who have to ask which is which don't need to know the answer); to the coffee bars, owned by no chain, true heirs to the eighteenth-century Pall Mall houses as bastions of the New Enlightenment; to the country village tube station with its wooden floorboards, absence of ticket barriers and incongruous name: 'Shoreditch'; to the railway bridge where 'the National Front used to do battle with the fearless radicals of the Socialist Workers' Party every Sunday from closing time to opening time', according to Salman Rushdie in *The Satanic Verses*; to the handsome old brewery, with its gracious brick chimney and arches; to the ever-present ghosts of Jack the Ripper, Jack London, Bud Flanagan, Lew Grade, the Kray twins; to the metonymic book – *that* book: *Brick Lane*?

Do they completely explain Brick Lane's allure? Perhaps there is something else. Perhaps we can find it in terms of the one overriding theme that has governed the behaviour of the East End over the last 2,000 years. Perhaps Brick Lane's rise can be explained in mystical terms, using the tradition that dates back to the Romans' marking the territory on the eastern side of their city 'sacred', to the 'holy' murder of Brother Martin at Aldgate priory, to the building of Wren's New Jerusalem, with Wellclose Square in the East End as its apex, to the mysterious quasi-religious ephemera connected with the local Jack the Ripper murders.

Unusual announcements began to appear in the press in the late 1970s. They claimed that the Lord Maitreya had left the Himalayas and moved to London, to Brick Lane indeed, to live and work among the growing Bangladeshi population. The Maitreya is a Bodhisattva – an enlightened being intent on saving others. His supporters, led by the artist Benjamin Creme, explained that, as Christians await the return of Christ, as Muslims await the Imam Mahdi, Hindus a re-incarnation of Krishna, and the Jews the Messiah, those knowledge-able in mysticism will recognize that all those names refer to the same being – the Lord Maitreya – who manifested Himself 2,000 years ago in Palestine by overshadowing His disciple Jesus.

How would the public recognize the Maitreya, the curious asked? 'When Lord Maitreya appears, it will be as different beings to differ-ent people,' Creme has explained. 'He will appear as a man to a man, as a woman to a woman. He will appear as a white to a white, as a black to a black, as an Indian to an Indian.'

The Maitreya was spotted on Brick Lane in 1984 by a journalist, Patricia Pitchon. Dining in a curry house, she glanced up and saw 'a very tall man dressed entirely in white', who appeared to be gazing at her through the restaurant window. 'Initially I was blasted by a mar-vellous golden light as I tried to look at Him. I thought for a few moments that, inexplicably, I had gone blind, because my eyes were wide open, yet I could see nothing "out there". Instead, I saw the inte-rior of my head bathed in luminous gold.'

Gradually the media began to take an interest in this extraordinary unfolding story. On 31 July 1985 journalists from Britain's leading newspapers gathered at the Clifton curry house, 126 Brick Lane, to meet the Maitreya. It was a well-chosen site. Here just over 200 years previously the silk-weaver Samuel Best, a pauper who lived on bread, cheese and gin tinctured with rhubarb, announced himself as a prophet, chosen to lead the children of Israel back to Jerusalem.

The journalists waiting for the Maitreya whiled away the time by holding a lager-drinking contest. When no Maitreya appeared after an hour they continued to drink more lager. Eventually they left; disap-pointed and drunk. 'Once again, I am afraid God did not show,' wrote the *Guardian* Diary.

On 11 June 1988 the Maitreya *did* appear. But it was in Nairobi, Kenya, not Spitalfields, east London. The editor of the *Kenya Times* was impressed: 'I am convinced this was a miracle. I saw a bright star in the daytime. He had a light around His head and sparks came from His feet. He blessed the crowd in Swahili, muttered a Hebrew curse, and left in a car driven by a Mr Singh.'

The Maitreya has continued to appear throughout the East End – at local mosques and various curry houses – but only, it seems, to those who believe in Him. According to Creme, He continues to work His great deeds around the world from Brick Lane: helping to end the Cold War, break up the Soviet Union, reunify Germany, end apartheid in South Africa and preserve the endangered environment.

According to Buddhist lore, the Maitreya will appear 5,000 years after the death of Gautama. Given that the Gautama Buddha died in 483 BC the Maitreya's appearance in Brick Lane might be 2,500 years premature. Yet in October 2004 Creme announced, 'We do not have long to wait to see Him.' Nevertheless the world at large still awaits a positive, agreed sighting; in fact it awaits agreement that there is anything to wait for. Clerics at Christ Church Spitalfields, the Hawksmoor church that has stimulated visions of the East End for 300 years, have voiced their reservations. They have cited Matthew 24: 'For false Christs and false prophets will arise and mislead many.' It is too early to say whether they are right or whether the great day is to come. But at least Brick Lane and the East End are ready.

# Acknowledgements

Once again I must declare an immense debt to my agent Faith Evans and editor Margaret Bluman without whom this book would have been impossible and who were always at hand with advice and encouragement.

I would like to thank a number of people for all their help and guidance: Marian Walsh, Richard Aron, Clive Bettington, Celia Boggis, Judith Clute, Bela Cunha, Tessa Fry, Betty Glinert, David Grant, Cormach Moore, Martin Morris, John Naughton, Sheila Redclift, Tim Richard, Juliet Rose, Simon Rose, Sarah Shannon, David Stone, Lucie Sutherland, Andrea Vincenti, Danny Williams, Andrew at Rush Computers, the staff of the London Library, Louise Ball of Penguin and Jock McFadyen for the ingenious cover.

Many thanks to the staff of Tower Hamlets Archives, whose patience and attention to detail were invaluable.

A special thanks to Katy Walsh Glinert, who accompanied me so enthusiastically around the most obscure corners of the East End. Peter Golds provided me with a wonderful catalogue of stories and ideas. Last but not least I owe an incalculable debt to John Nicholson, who readily made available his endless store of extraordinary ideas and long out-of-print books.

# Bibliography

Adler, Herman, *The Baal Shem of London*, Berlin, 1903

Alderman, Geoffrey, *The Jewish Community in British Politics*, Clarendon, Oxford, 1983

Bermant, Chaim, *Point of Arrival*, Eyre Methuen, London, 1975

Berridge, V., 'East End Opium Dens and Narcotic Use in Britain', *London Journal* IV, 1978

Black, Gerry, *Jewish London: An Illustrated History*, Breedon Books, Derbyshire, 2003

Brandreth, Gyles, *The Funniest Man on Earth: The Story of Dan Leno*, Hamish Hamilton, London, 1977

Brown, R. Douglas, *The Port of London*, Terence Dalton, Suffolk, 1978

Burke, Thomas, *Limehouse Nights*, Grant Richards, London, 1921

Calder, Ritchie, *The Lesson of London*, Secker and Warburg, 1941

Calder-Marshall, Arthur, *The Enthusiast*, Faber and Faber, London, 1942

— *No Earthly Command*, Rupert Hart-Davis, London, 1957

Choo, Ng Kwee, *The Chinese in London*, Oxford University Press, London, 1968

Cross, Colin, *The Fascists in Britain*, Barrie and Rockcliff, London, 1961

Defoe, Daniel, *A Journal of the Plague Year 1665*, George Routledge and Sons, London, 1886

Eatwell, Roger, *Fascism, A History*, Chatto and Windus, London, 1995

Ellis, Peter Berresford, *The Great Fire of London: An Illustrated Account*, New English Library, London, 1976

Ellmers, Chris and Werner, Alex, *Dockland Life: A Pictorial History of London Docks 1860–1970*, Mainstream, London, 1991

Farson, Daniel, *Limehouse Days*, Michael Joseph, London, 1991

Fishman, William J., *East End Jewish Radicals*, Duckworth, London, 1975

— *East End 1888: A Year in the London Borough among the Labouring Poor*, Duckworth, London, 1988

Fitzgibbon, Constantine, *The Blitz*, Macdonald, London, 1970

Forman, Charlie, *Spitalfields: A Battle for Land*, Hilary Shipman, London, 1989

Freely, John, *The Lost Messiah: In Search of Sabbatai Zevi*, Penguin, London, 2001

Gilbert, Adrian, *The New Jerusalem*, Bantam Press, London, 2002

Greenwood, James, *The Seven Curses of London*, London, 1869

Harrisson, Thomas, *Living Through the Blitz*, Collins, London, 1976

Holmes, Colin, *Anti-Semitism in British Society 1876–1939*, Edward Arnold, London, 1979

Hostettler, Eve, *The Isle of Dogs: A Brief History Vol. 1 (1066–1918)*, Island History Trust, London, 2000

— *The Isle of Dogs: A Brief History Vol. 2 (The Twentieth Century)*, Island History Trust, London, 2002

James, P. D., and Critchley, T. A., *The Maul and the Pear Tree*, Constable, London, 1971

Katz, David S., *The Jews in the History of England 1485–1850*, Clarendon Press, Oxford, 1994

Knight, Stephen, *Jack the Ripper: The Final Solution*, Harrap, London, 1976

Linehan, Thomas P., *East London for Mosley*, Cass, London, 1996

Litvinoff, Emanuel, *Journey through a Small Planet,* Penguin, London, 1976

Llewellyn Smith, Sir Hubert, *The History of East London*, Macmillan, London, 1939

Lomas, Robert, *The Invisible College*, Headline, London, 2002

Lucas, Norman, *Britain's Gangland*, W. H. Allen, London, 1969

Mack, Joanna and Humphries, Steve, *The Making of Modern London 1939–45: London at War*, Sidgwick and Jackson, London, 1985

Merriman, Nick (ed.), *The Peopling of London*, Museum of London, London, 1993

Morton, H. V., *The Nights of London*, Methuen & Co., London, 1926

Morton, James, *East End Gangland*, Little, Brown, London, 2000

— *Gangland*, Little, Brown, London, 1992

Palmer, Alan, *The East End: Four Centuries of London Life*, John Murray, London, 1989

Piratin, Phil, *Our Flag Stays Red*, Lawrence and Wishart, London, 1948

Pudney, John, *London's Docks*, Thames & Hudson, London, 1975

Roth, Cecil, *Essays and Portraits in Anglo-Jewish History*, The Jewish Publication Society of America, Philadelphia, 1962

— *A History of the Jews in England*, Clarendon Press, Oxford, 1941

Rumbelow, Donald, *The Complete Jack the Ripper*, W. H. Allen, London, 1975

Samuel, Raphael, *East End Underworld, Chapters in the Life of Arthur Harding*, Routledge and Kegan Paul, 1981

Sinclair, Robert, *East London*, Robert Hale, London, 1960

Taylor, William, *This Bright Field*, Methuen, London, 2000

Thomas, Donald, *An Underworld at War*, John Murray, London, 2003

Thorogood, Horace, *East of Aldgate*, Allen & Unwin, London, 1935

Tinniswood, Adrian, *By Permission of Heaven*, Jonathan Cape, London, 2003

Van Ash, Cay and Rohmer, Elizabeth Sax, *Master of Villainy: A Biography of Sax Rohmer*, Tom Stacey, London, 1972

Webster, Nesta, *Secret Societies and Subversive Movements*, Boswell, London, 1924

# Index

'abbesses' 150
abbeys 7
'abbots' 151
Abiff, Hiram 94, 95
Aboukir, Battle of (1798) 215
Abridge 256
Adam 74, 118
Adam Smith Club 171
Adams, Polly 151
Adams, William 106
Addams, Jane 171
Adler, Dr Hermann 130
Admiralty 19
Admiralty Marshal 20
Agate Street school, Canning Town 232
alamodes 42
Albert Victor Christian Edward, Duke of Clarence (Prince Eddy) 90–93, 97, 245
*Albion* (cruiser) 219
Albright & Wilson, Canning Town 238
alchemy 71–4, 106
Aldgate 118
Aldgate East station 268
Aldgate police 141
Aldgate Pump 164
Alexander, Daniel 33
Alexander II, Tsar of Russia 122
Alexandra, Queen 91

Alexandra Palace 183
Alexandria library 71
Ali, Altab 268
Aliens Act (1906) 109, 144
Allen, Chesney 131
Alsop, Jane 151–2
Altab Ali Park 14
alum works 32
Amoy Place 116
Amsterdam 118, 119, 120, 126
anarchism 178–83
Anchor Brewery, Mile End 174
Ancient Monuments Act 201
Anderson, Constable 59–60
Anderson, Sir John 228
Anderson, Sir Robert 139
Anderson Shelters 228–9
Angel, Miriam 138
anglicization 129–30, 147
Anglo-Catholic movement 84
Antarctica 18
anti-Semitism 120, 133, 138, 139, 145, 146, 203–6, 212, 235–6, 259
Antwerp 36
*Arbeter Fraint* (Workers' Friend) 180, 182, 183, 187

Arbour Square police station 266
Archbishop of Canterbury 130, 177
Archer, Thomas 130
Archers public house, Osborn Street, Whitechapel 182–3
archery butts 41
*Architectural Review* 247
Arnold, Matthew 196
'Sonnet on East London' 51
Arnold Circus 161–2
Arnott, Jake: *The Long Firm* 274
Arsenal FC 224, 257
Artillery Lane 41
Ashkenazi Jews 120
Astor Club, Mayfair 278
atheism 178, 212
Atlantis 17
Attlee, Clement 195, 207, 257, 269
Auschwitz 267
Austin, William 62
Australia 20, 32, 35, 38, 146
Austrian Jews 144
*Avengers, The* (television series) 132

Back Lane (now Cable Street) 66

Bacon, John, Junior 44
Bacon Street 295
Baffin Island 17
Baker, Daniel: *A Certaine Warning for a Naked Heart* 6
Bakunin, Michael 183
Balfour, Arthur 143
Balfron Tower, Poplar 250, 251, 253
Bangladesh 263, 264
Bangladeshis/Bengalis 263–9, 290, 294, 296
Banglatown ix, 262–9
Bannister (colleague of John Palmer) 83
Baptists 45, 86
Barbican 41
Barents Sea 16
Barking, Essex 269
Barking by-pass 283
Barking Road, East Ham 277, 278
Barnardo, Thomas 170, 171–2, 269
Barnato, Barney (Barnett Isaacs) 131–2
Barnes 253
Barnett, Henrietta 170, 269
Barnett, Samuel 170, 269
Barrie, Ian 279
Bartlett, David 51
*London by Day and Night* 33
Bartlett, William Ashmead 174
Bas Tubes, Le, Isle of Dogs 191
Basildon, Essex 247
Batson (businessman) 215
Battle of Britain 229, 231, 247
Batty Street 138
Bauhaus 254
Bazalgette, Joseph 157

BBC ix, 90–91, 97, 132, 256
beak hunters 150
Beamish, Henry Hamilton 146
Beanse, Alice 226–7
Bearhind Lane, Bow 151
Beckman, Morris 260
Beckton, Essex 157
Beckton Gas Works 199, 230
Becontree 204
beer additives 153
Beerbohm, Max 169
Belgae 40
Belgian immigrants 40
Belgravia 287
Bell Lane, Spitalfields 121, 125, 129
Ben Akiva, Yossel 128
Ben Israel, Menasseh 119
Ben Truman brewery, Brick Lane 267
Bengalis *see* Bangladeshis/Bengalis
Bergson, Mina 70
Bergström, Erik 79–80
Berliner, Rabbi Shaul 78
Bermant, Chaim 139
Berner Street, off Commercial Road 88, 95, 98, 138
Berner Street International Workmen's Educational Club 138, 181
Besant, Annie 196–7
*The Laws of Population* 197
Bessarabians ix, 2, 133–5, 136, 182
Best, Samuel 296
Bethnal Green x, 13, 41, 43, 122, 148, 161, 168, 174, 207, 212, 229, 254, 256, 266, 267, 271, 281

Bethnal Green council 247, 249
Bethnal Green Road 49, 160
Bethnal Green tube station 205, 238
Betjeman, John 245, 294
Beveridge, William 171
Beverstein, Abraham ('Abraham Harris') 145
Bevin, Ernest 37
Bevis Marks synagogue, Aldgate 120
Bible
and Cromwell 118
'sacred' measurements of 10, 11–12
'Biff Boys' 203
Billingsgate fish market 73, 171
Billingsgate porters 28
Birkenhead, Lord 193
Birmingham 192
Bishop, John 160
Bishopsgate 40
Bishopsgate Goods Yard 294
bit fakers 150
Black Death ix, 2, 34, 153–4, 155
Black Ditch 155
'Blackchapel' 254
Blackshirts 206
Blackwall xiv, 14, 16, 108
Blackwall Dock 215
Blackwall Dockmaster 215
Blackwall Stairs 222
Blackwall Tunnel 251, 252
Blain, Douglas 294
Blair, Eric *see* Orwell, George
Blair, Tony 202
Blair Street, Poplar 107
Blake, William 79, 130
*Jerusalem* 10, 214

Blasker Walk (previously
Burrell's Wharf),
Millwall 218
Blind Beggar public
house, Whitechapel
173, 278, 279
Blitz 231, 236, 245
Bloom, Rebecca and
Morris 262
Bloom's Corner 262
Bloom's restaurant 262
Bloomsbury Group 130
Blue Coat Boy public
house, Norton Folgate
133
Blue Posts public house
(later Charlie Brown's)
221
Blue Star line 221
Board of Guardians for
the Relief of the Jewish
Poor 163
Board of Trade offices,
East India Dock Road
109
Bogard, Ikey ('Darky the
Coon') 133
Boleyn, Anne 40
Boleyn Ground stadium,
Upton Park ix
Bolshevism, Bolsheviks
187, 189, 190, 202,
212
bone-pickers 150
Booth, Catherine 173
Booth, William 84, 170,
172–4, 197
In Darkest England
and the Way Out
173–4
Borchalo district 189
Boston Transcript 113
bouncers 150
Bow x, 13, 86, 157, 166,
197, 198, 212, 228,
254
Bow Baths 199

Bow flyover 278, 280
Bow Road 198, 201
Bow Street magistrates 58
Bow Street Runners 61
'Boy I Love Is up in the
Gallery, The' 169
BP 224
Brady Street Dwellings,
Whitechapel 244–5
Brady youth club,
Hanbury Street 261–2
Bramley, Ted 235
Bran, a Celtic god
king 3
Brazil 86–7
Brett, George 284
Brett, John 284
brick kilns 41
Brick Lane ix, 41, 43, 45,
127, 132, 133, 141,
149, 181, 182, 206,
237, 261, 262, 265–9,
287, 293–7
Britannia public house,
Stepney 272
British and Foreign
Medicine Institution
83–4
British Brothers' League
142
British Communist Party
191–4
British Empire 14, 38,
128, 165, 217, 265
British League of
Ex–Servicemen 260–61
British National Party
259, 290
British Road Services 257
British Union of Fascists
(BUF) ix, 3, 179, 195,
203, 204, 207, 241,
259
British Vigilance Action
Committee 258–9
Britons, the (a London-
based society) 146

Britons Patriotic Society
258
Brockway, Fenner 209
Brodovich, Henry 136
Bromley Hall, Bow Road
(now Tower Hamlets
Registry Office) 198
Bromley-by-Bow x
Brooklyn Eagle 113
Broomfield Street, Poplar
107
brothels 133, 149, 162,
175–6, 245
Brotherhood Church,
Dalston 190
Brothers, Richard 71
Brown, Charlie 221
Brown, Charlie, Jnr
221
Brown and Lenox, Isle of
Dogs 216
Brunel, Isambard
Kingdom 217, 218
Bruno, Angelo 276
Brunswick Tavern,
Blackwall 108
Brunswick Theatre,
Wellclose Square 83
Brushfield Street,
Spitalfields 234
Bryant, Theodore 197
Bryant & May match-
makers, Bow 197, 238
Buckhurst Hill 256
Buck's Row, Whitechapel
(now Durward Street)
87, 94, 98
bug hunters 150
Bugsby's Marsh, Isle of
Dogs 221
Builder, The magazine
159
Bunch of Grapes public
house, Limehouse 107
Burdett Road 206
Burdett-Coutts, Angela
170, 174

Burke, Thomas 23, 112–13
*Limehouse Nights* 113
Burke, William 156
Burnett's works, Isle of Dogs 216
Burrell's firm, Isle of Dogs 257
Burrell's Wharf (now Blasker Walk), Millwall 218
buttoners 150
Byford, Harold 251
Byng (businessman) 215
Byron, George Gordon, Lord
'The Age of Bronze' 204
*Don Juan* 33
BZW 290

Cable Street (previously Back Street) 66, 103–4, 179, 245
battle of 207–11, 272
Cade, Jack 2, 177
Cagliostro (occultist) 76
Cahill, Thomas 65
Calder, Ritchie 232
calico-printing 13
'Call On' system 30–31, 34, 36, 39, 264
Camberwell 278
Cambridge Heath Road 49
Cambridge music hall, Commercial Street 166
Canada 17
Canada Square, Canary Wharf 290
Canary Wharf x, 213, 253, 289–92
Canning Town x, 107, 232, 238, 252, 254, 269, 289
Cannon Street Road 66, 104, 246
Canterbury 52

Canterbury music hall, Lambeth 166
Cantlie, James:
'Degeneration Amongst Londoners' (lecture) 51
Canton 100, 101
Cap Gris Nez, France 230
Cape Town 131
capitalism 178, 179
Capone, Al 276
Carleton, Billie 111
Carnaby Street 295
Carpenter's Arms public house 281
Casanova, Giacomo 76
Cassell's Pitch, Tar, Oil, Paint, Naptha and Varnish yard, Isle of Dogs 216
Catford 278
Cathay *see* China
Cathay Company 17
Catherine of Aragon 7
Catholics, and the Great Fire as punishment 7
Cat's Hole 25
Central Board of Health, Whitehall 156
Central Line 238
Central News Agency 88
Chancellor, Richard 16
Chang, Brilliant 112, 114
Chant, Mrs Ormiston 169
Chapman, Annie 87, 88, 91, 95, 98, 131, 137, 140, 141, 283
Charles I, King 7, 10, 31, 41, 77, 118
Charles II, King 2, 8, 41, 42, 119
Charlie Brown's pubs 221
Charrington, Frederick 170, 174–6
Chauliac, Guy de 154
Chauvet, Lewis 48, 49
Cheka 187–8
Chelsea 190, 253

Chenie sect 99
Cherubim Court 25
Cheshire Street, off Brick Lane 277
Chesterfield, Lord 82
Chi Ki 103
Chief Rabbi 126, 130, 139, 144, 179
Chigwell 256
Chigwell Row 256
Childs, John (Martin Jones) 283–6
Chin-Choo sect 99
China, search for 17
Chinatown ix, 110, 112–13, 115, 263
Chinese
and opium viii, 100–106
violence involving only the Chinese 99
destitute 99–100
sexual liaisons with white women 109–10
involved in British trade 128
Chingford 280
Chiswick, west London 240
Choat, Constable 184
cholera 2, 107, 155–7, 171
Christ Church Spitalfields 13, 45–6, 50, 165, 234, 245, 294, 297
Christian Street 282
Christian V, King of Denmark 12
Christianity vii, 10, 172, 196, 212
Church Lane, Commercial Road 123
Church of England 40, 45, 84, 130
Church Street (now Fournier Street) 44

Churchill, Sir Winston 37, 186, 187, 188, 202, 241, 265, 280
Cibber, Caius Gabriel 9, 12, 84, 86, 97
Citigroup 290
City Canal 215, 217
City Corporation 28
City of London vii, x, 44, 70, 236, 249, 256, 294
  narrow winding lanes of vii
  Romans build in 3
  Jews settle in 118, 120
City Road 61
Clapham 151
Clapton 147
Clark's café, Brick Lane 133
Clement VI, Pope 3
Cleveland Street, near Euston 90, 91, 92
Clifton curry house, Brick Lane 296
Club Row 44–5
Clyde shipyards 220, 224
Co-op shops 248
  coal-backers 30
  coal-heavers 53–4
  coal-whippers 30
coalition government 37
Cobb Street, off Petticoat Lane 272
Coborn, Charles 168
cocaine 111, 112
Cock and Neptune public house 82
codeine 101
Coffee House, Norris Street 265
Cohen, Alfie 282
Cohen, Mike 282
Cohen, Nick 292
Cohen, Rose 193, 194
Coldbath Fields prison 63, 65, 66, 68

Coldharbour, Isle of Dogs 215, 221
Coleridge, Samuel Taylor: 'Xanadu' 102
Collis Browne's Mixture 100
Colomb, Captain, MP 142
Colquhon, Patrick 20
Coltrane, Robbie 93
Columbia Market 174
Columbia Road 293
comet (1664) 5
Commercial Road 24, 35, 123, 124, 133, 138, 189, 206
Commercial Road, Stepney 282
Commercial Street 45, 124, 166, 180
Commercial Street police station 141
Commercial Tavern public house, Pennyfields 112
Commonwealth 8, 119
Communism, Communists 145, 188–91
  Battle of Cable Street 207–11
  congress (Whitechapel, 1907) 189–90, 195
Communist Party ix, 145
companies' porters 28
Connolly, Elizabeth 156
'Conquering and Bold Defiance, The' 48
conscription 144
Conservative government 288, 290
Constantinople 16, 120
containerization 38
convict hulks 20
Cook, Elizabeth (née Betts) 18
Cook, James 18

Cook, Thomas (travel firm) 163
'Coons, the' 133
Copeland, David 269
copperas 153
Corallo, Anthony 'Tony Ducks' 276
Cornell, George 278–9, 280
Cornhill 164
Cornwall 117
Cornwell, Patricia: Portrait of a Killer: Jack the Ripper – Case Closed 93
'corporatist' state 202
Corsica 76
costermongers 174
'countryside into the towns' concept 250–51
County Cork 174
County Hall 252
Court House, Wellclose Square 245
Courthorpe, Nathaniel 22
Covent Garden 61, 191, 293
Covent Garden Theatre 83
Coventry 50
Crazy Gang 131
Credit Suisse First Boston bank 289
Creechurch Lane synagogue 119
Creme, Benjamin 296, 297
crime 150–53
  river piracy viii, 20–21
  the great local growth industry 2
  dock workers 26–7
  in the Old Nichol 160
Criminal Bill (1911) 186
Criminologist, The 90
Crispin Street, Spitalfields 49

Cromwell, Oliver 7, 118, 119
Crook, Alice 91, 92, 93
Crook, Annie Elizabeth 91, 92, 245
Crossman, Richard 203
Crouch End 252
Crown and Anchor public house 276
Crown and Dolphin public house 70
Croydon, Surrey 229
Croydon airport 229
Cubitt, William 215–16
Cubitt Town x, 216, 222
Culpepper, Nicholas: *The Complete Herbal* 41, 73
Cunard line 221
curry houses 265
Custom House 73
Custom House stadium 222
Cuthbert, Tube 237
Cutler, Horace 252
Cutler Street, off Petticoat Lane 24
*Cutty Sark* 24

D-Day landing 38, 240, 241
Dacca 268
*Dad's Army* (television programme) 131
Dagenham, Essex 241, 284
*Daily Express* 112
*Daily Graphic* 158
*Daily Herald* 201, 232
*Daily Mail* 187
*Daily Telegraph* 1, 2
*Daily Worker* 194, 205, 235
Dalston, east London x, 130, 147, 190, 252, 260, 268

Dalston Lane police station 260
Damascus 85
Danes 3, 40
Daniels, Franny 272
Danish church, Wellclose Square 12, 84, 86, 97
Danish Embassy, Wellclose Square 245
Dark Entry 25
Dartmoor prison 33, 277
Davis, Eliza 121
Day of Atonement 127, 134, 141, 180–81, 182, 267, 282
Day of Judgement 140, 141
De Beers company 131
de Quincey, Thomas 63
*Confessions of an English Opium Eater* 101
'Murder Considered as One of the Fine Arts' 53
deal porters 29
Dee, John 17
Defence of the Realm Act (1914) 110
Delfont, Bernard, Baron (Boris Winogradsky) 132
Dennis, Ginger 280
Depp, Johnny 93, 138
'Deserters' Corner' 237
Dessau 254
Devil's Tavern, Wapping (later Prospect of Whitby) 32
Devonport, Lord 36
'Dial H for Murder' 284
Dial Square FC 224
*Dianella* 260
Dias, Bartolomeu 16
Dickens, Charles 32, 103, 174, 215

*The Mystery of Edwin Drood* 103, 104
*Oliver Twist* 121
*Our Mutual Friend* 107, 121
*The Uncommercial Traveller* 148
Dickens, Charles, Jnr: *Dictionary of London* 69, 104
diet 159, 222–3
disease 2, 153–7, 235
Disraeli, Benjamin: *Two Nations* 189
DNA testing 93
Dock Labour Scheme 39
Dock Road 246
Dock Street 208
Dock Strike (1889) 29, 34–6, 181
Dock Strike (1912) 187
dockers 26–7, 28–31, 34–7, 39
'docker's tanner' 34
Docklands 287
Docklands Light Railway 224, 289, 292
Dod Street 196
Dodd, Ralph 30
Dodd, Dr William 82
Dollis Hill 130
Dolphin House, Dolphin Lane, Poplar 283
Dolphin Square, Pimlico 260
Dolphin tavern 48
Donovan, Timothy 137
doodle-bugs 239–40
Doré, Gustave 165
Doree, George 52
Dorset Street, Spitalfields 89, 96, 98
Double 'R' club, Bow 272–3, 275
Downing Street 268
Doyle, Sir Arthur Conan 'The Disappearance of

Lady Frances Carfax' 282
'The Man with the Twisted Lip' 104, 113
Doyle, John 48, 49
dragsmen 151
Drake, Sir Francis 21
dredgermen viii, 21
Dreyfuss, Alfred 146
Driscoll, Sylvester 68
Drury Lane Theatre 83, 169
Duckham's Oil, Millwall 224
Duke's Place 75
Dundee Lodge, Freemasons 32
Dunstan, St, Bishop of London 14
Dunstan Houses, Stepney Green 182
Durward Street (previously Buck's Row) 94, 98
Dutch Jews 120, 126

Eagle, Solomon 5
East and West India Dock Company 27, 28
East End Communist Party 194, 234
East Ham x
East India Company ix, 21–2, 24, 46, 47, 99–100, 101
East India Dock 23–4, 27, 39, 107, 108, 192
East India Dock Company 24
East India Dock Road 31, 109, 221
East India House 47
East India Import Dock 38
East London Advertiser 225, 251

East London Antiquarian Society 171
East London Federation of Suffragettes 191, 198, 199
East London Observer 87–8, 136, 140
East London tube line 31, 294
Easter Spital sermons 41
Eastern Empire, Bow 166
Eastern Wanderers FC 224
Eastminster monastery 4
Eastwood, Clint 221
Eddowes, Catherine 4, 88, 89, 95, 98, 139, 274, 283
Eddy, Prince see Albert Victor Christian Edward, Duke of Clarence
Edict of Nantes 42
Edmonton 170
Edward, the Black Prince 107
Edward, Prince of Wales (later King Edward VIII, then Duke of Windsor) 108, 130, 219
Edward I, King 128
Edward III, King 107, 153
Edward VII, King 90, 91, 103
Eighth Army 238
El Alamein 238
El Vino's bar, Fleet Street 292
Elder Street, Spitalfields 43, 46, 51, 180, 294
Elen, Gus 168
Eliass, Gederts 186
Elijah, Ba'al Shem of Chelm 74
Elizabeth I, Queen 9, 21
Elul 140

Emin, Tracey 44
Empire Cinema, Mile End 273
English Board of Longitude 80
English Channel 38
English Civil War 11
English Friends of the 1905 Russian Revolution 190
English Heritage 249
entertainment 165–70
Epping 240
Epping Forest 76, 77, 78, 227–8
Eric Street, Mile End 271
Eskimos 17
Euston station 145, 233
evacuation 227–8, 233, 271
Evans, Jimmy 281
Evans-Gordon, Major William 142, 143
Eve, Terry 283, 284, 285–6
Eve Court, St Pancras 168–9
Evelyn, John 8, 9
Evening News 109
Everburning Lights of Trithemius 71
Evering Road, Stoke Newington 279
'Evil May Day' (1517) 2
'evil quarter-mile' 162
Exchange Buildings, Cutler Street 184
Execution Dock, Wapping 20, 32
'expropriation' 183–4
Ezekiel, Book of 46, 75

Falk, Chaim Jacob Samuel (the Ba'al Shem of London) 13, 71–8, 80, 82, 146, 245, 268
Farriner, Thomas 6–9

Farson, Daniel 221, 277
fascism 178, 194, 195, 201–12, 258–61, 265–9
Faulkner, Hugh 207–8
Federation of Suffragettes 198
Federation of Synagogues 182
Feigenbaum, Benjamin 181
Felixstowe, Suffolk 38
Fenchurch Street station 215
Fenian Barracks, Poplar 107
Fern Street, Poplar 107
Ferrari, Carlo 160
Festival of Britain (1951) 255
Fieldgate Street 190, 262
Fields, J. T. 103
Fiennes, Sir James 177
Fifty New Churches Act (1711) 45
*Financial Times* 290
First Commissioner of Works 201
First World War 36, 52, 108, 110, 130–31, 136, 144, 183, 186, 188, 199, 200, 202, 226
fish and chips 45
Fish Guano Company 107
Fish Street Hill 9
Fishman, Bill 189
Fitzrovians 130
Flanagan, Bud (Reuben Weintrop) 131, 295
Flanagan and Allen 131
Flanders 40, 202
Fleet Street 287, 290, 292
Fleming, Ian 250
Flemings 2
Flemish immigrants 40, 154
Fleur de Lys Street 43

Flower and Dean Street 162
Flower Observatory, Virginia 81
Fludd, Robert: *History of the Macrocosm and Microcosm* 77
flying the blue pigeon 151
flying bombs 239–42
Folkestone 218
food rationing 227, 242
Ford, Ford Madox: *Work* 162
Ford, Henry 136
Ford motor works, Dagenham 230, 238
Foreign Office 146
Foreman, Freddie 280, 281
*Respect* 282
Forest of Middlesex 16
Forester's Music Hall, Mile End 169
43 Group 259–61
Four Per Cent Industrial Dwellings Company 163
Fournier Street (previously Church Street) 44, 45, 50, 51, 127, 181, 267, 294
foxglove 153
Franco, General Francisco 207, 212, 265, 267
Frankish immigrants 40
Franklin, Benjamin 79
Fraser, Frankie 278
Fraternity of the Artillery 41
Free, Revd Richard 220
free love 178, 179
free trade 27
Freemasonry 10, 32, 71, 72, 76–7, 91–8, 139
French immigrants 2, 40
French Protestant churches 45, 46

French Revolution 146, 268
French silks 46, 47–8, 49
Frobisher, Martin 17
*From Hell* (film) 93–4, 95, 138
Fruit and Wool exchange, Brushfield Street, Spitalfields ('Mickey's Shelter') 234
Fu Manchu 114–15
Fulbourne Street 3
Fulham 287
Fung Wah 114
Furness line 221

Game, Sir Philip 207
Gandhi, Mahatma 157, 219
Gardiner's Corner 124
Gardstein, George *see* Mourrewitz, Poolka
Garford Street, Limehouse 111, 221
Garland, Judy 276
Garnet Street (previously New Gravel Lane) 59
Garthwaite, Anna Maria 43
Gautama Buddha 297
Gavin, Hector: *Sanitary Ramblings* 159
Gaza Strip 117
General Strike (1926) 191–3, 224
Gentile–Christian Front 259
*Gentleman's Magazine* 25, 46, 47, 75
'gentlemen dockers' 29
George III, King 47
George IV, King (as Prince Regent) 58
George V, King 192
George and Dragon public house, Ratcliff Highway 156

George public house,
Mile End 230
George Street,
Marylebone 265
Georgian Society 44
German community,
Poplar 108
German Jews 120, 126,
144
German restaurant,
Leman Street 183
Germany
Nazi 195, 211
invades Poland (1939)
211
Britain declares war on
212, 226
reunification 297
Gershon, Betsy 185
Gibberd, Frederick 244
Gilbert, Fred 168
Gilbert, Humphrey:
'Discourse of a
Discoverie for a new
passage to Cataia' 17
Gilbert and George 44
Ginsburg, Solomon 86–7
*A Wandering Jew in
Brazil* 87
Gladstone, William 197
Glastonbury 117
Gleeson family 227
Glengall, Countess of 216
Glengall Road (now Tiler
Road) 223, 224
Glengall Road bridge 257
Globe Town x
Glorious Revolution 120
Goering, *Reichsmarschall*
Hermann 230
Goldfinger, Erno 250,
251, 253
Goldsmid, Aaron 78
golems 70, 74
Goose and Gridiron Ale
House 77
Gorky, Maxim 189

Gostelo, Walter: *The
Coming of God in
Mercy, in Vengeance,
Beginning with Fire, to
Convert or Consume
all this so Sinful City* 6
Goulston Street,
Whitechapel 96, 125,
139
Gowen, James 56, 58, 59
Grade, Lew, Baron (Louis
Winogradsky) 132, 295
Grade, Michael 132
Graham, Aaron 58
Grant, Ted 208
Gravesend 36
Grays, Essex 247
Great Assembly Hall,
Mile End Road 175
Great Eastcheap 81
*Great Eastern* (previously
*Leviathan*) 218–19
Great Fire of London
(1666) vii, 6–9, 11, 75,
138, 289, 291
Great Seal of England 19,
77
Great Synagogue, Duke's
Place 75, 77, 78, 120
Greater London xiv
Greater London
Authority 293
Greater London Council
252
Greenwich 24, 121, 214,
216, 227
Greenwood, James:
*Music Hall Luminaries*
166–7
Greenwood Alley 43
Greville, Charles 158
Gropius, Walter 254
Groser, Father John 231
Groser, Red 192
Grove Road, Bow 239,
240
Grove Street, St George's

185
*Guardian* 290, 296
Gull, Sir William 91,
92–3, 93
Gun public house,
Coldharbour 221
Gun Street 178
Gunthorpe Street,
Aldgate 87
Guy's Hospital 91

Hackney, east London x
Hackney council 256
Hackney Marsh 13
Hackney Road 278
Hadrian's Wall 201
Hagmaier's pork butcher,
Poplar 108
Hainan Island 100
Hamburg 118, 122
Hamlyn, Paul 203
Hamm, Jeffrey 260, 261
Hampstead 250, 253
Hanbury Hall, Spitalfields
181
Hanbury Street,
Spitalfields 87, 95, 98,
131, 137, 141
Hardie, Keir 198
Harding, Arthur 133
Harding, Eleanor 235
Hare, William 156
Harkness, Margaret: *In
Darkest London* 164
Harley House, Bow 86
Harold Hill 204
Harrington, Bridget 59,
60
Harrington, Michael 62
Harrison, John 80
Harrison, John (a sail-
maker) 67, 68
*Harris's List of Covent
Garden Ladies* 71
Harrow Conservative
Party 202
Hart, Richard 278

Hart, Solomon 122
Hartley, Thomas, rector
of Winwick 79
hartshorn 153
Hastings, Warren 101
Hawaii 18
Hawkins and Tipson 258
Hawksmoor, Nicholas
viii, 12, 13, 44, 45, 84,
105, 106, 130, 152,
165, 294, 297
Haymarket 169
Haymarket Theatre, near
Piccadilly Circus 111
Head, Thomas 160
Heathrow airport 272,
289
heavy horsemen viii, 21
Hebrew Ladies'
Protective Society 123
Hebrew Socialist Union
(Agudah Hasozialistim
Chaverim) 178, 179
Helena, Empress 85
Helwys, Thomas: A Short
Declaration of the
Mystery of Iniquity 45
henbane 153
Heneage Street, off Brick
Lane 133
Henriques, Basil 210
Henry, Prince of Wales 17
Henry IV, King 12
Henry VII, King 40
Henry VIII, King 7, 41,
214
Hermetic Order of the
Golden Dawn, The 113
Hermetica 71
Herne Hill 113
heroin 101, 112
High Court 201
Highbury and Islington
station 279
Highbury Vale 164
Highpoint, Highgate
253

Highway, The (previously
Ratcliff Highway and
St George's Street)
69–70
Hills, Arnold 219–20
Hippocrates 6
Hiram's Lodge, Mitre
Square 96
Hitler, Adolf 194, 195,
201, 211, 212, 228,
232, 235, 238–9, 240,
259, 265, 267
Hockney, David: A
Bigger Splash 248
Hodge, Ivy 252
Hole in the Wall kiosk,
Commercial Road,
Stepney 282
Hollingshead, John 148,
149
Holloway prison 198,
201
Holloway Road 188
Hollybush Gardens, off
Bethnal Green Road 52
Holm, Ian 93
Holocaust denial 259
Holy Grail 117
Holy Trinity church 161
Holy Trinity Priory
Aldgate vii, 4, 95, 120,
283, 295
Home Office 233
Hongkong and Shanghai
Bank 290
Hooke, Robert 9
Hope Place, Limehouse
171
Hope-Kyd, David 143
'Horst Wessel Lied' 20
Hospital of the Blessed
Virgin Mary Without
Bishopsgate 2
Hospital of St Katharine
24–5
Houndsditch murders
183–5, 186–7

House of Commons 47,
50, 198
House of Lords 47, 142
housing 159–63, 263–4,
289
see also rebuilding of
the East End
Howard House, Church
Street (later Fournier
Street) 44
Hoxton 169, 249
Hubert, Robert 8, 138
Hudson, Henry 17, 18
Hudson Bay 18
Hughes brothers 93
Hughes Mansions,
Vallance Road 241
Huguenots 40–46, 125,
128, 149
Huish's road haulage firm
257
Hull House, Chicago 171
Hulme, Manchester 253
Hung League (Triads) 105
Hungerford Street, off
Commercial Road 35
Hwang–ti, Emperor 41
Hyde Park 35, 192
Hyndman, Henry 196

Ignatius of Llanthony,
Father 85–6
Ilford x, 25, 241
Illustrated London News
158–9
immigration
dockers support of
Powell (1968) 39
shapes the East End 40
Immigration Act (1981)
263
Immingham, Lincolnshire
38
Imperial Defence League
259
Incorporated Television
Company 132

Independent Labour
    Party 208, 209
*Independent* newspaper
    group 290
India, and opium 101
Industrial Revolution 1,
    50, 149, 243, 287
Ireland 174
Irish, the 34, 35, 46, 47,
    54, 107, 128, 129, 179,
    272
Irish potato famine
    (1840s) 34
Irongate Stairs 72, 123,
    132
Isaiah, Book of 86
*Iskra* (the Spark) revolu-
    tionary newspaper 189
Islanders' Public House
    223
Isle of Dogs (Stepney
    Marsh) 16, 22, 23, 70,
    107, 191, 213–25
    medieval 213
    its first building 213
    its name 213–14
    land reclaimed by
        Vanderdelf 214
    Millwall development
        214, 216, 217
    Coldharbour 215,
        221
    becomes hub of
        London industry
        (early nineteenth cen-
        tury) 213
    becomes an island 215
    city of burning light
        215–20
    population 215, 217
    Cubitt Town 216, 219,
        222
    housing 216, 225
    shipbuilding 217–20,
        224
    'city of desolation'
        220–25

pubs on the isle 221
and children 221–2
Mudchute 222
entertainment 222
diet 222–3
football 223–4
economic crisis 224
expansion of docks and
    commerce 224–5
Second World War 225
decline of 257–8
becomes home to
    Mammon and the
    media 213, 287–92
Isle House, Isle of Dogs
    215
Islington 71
Israel 259
Italian Fascist Party 203
Italian immigrants 2
Ivan the Terrible 16

Jack the Ripper vii, ix, 2,
    4, 87–98, 149, 161,
    162, 180, 245, 264,
    270, 274, 283, 295
    from hell 87–90
    the final solution 90–94
    the three Juwes 94–8
    Jacob the Ripper
        136–41
Jaffe, Rabbi David 74
James, St 44
James I, King 41, 45
James II, King (previously
    Duke of York) 8, 12,
    77, 82, 120
Jamme Masjid mosque,
    Brick Lane/Fournier
    Street 45, 127, 267
Jamrach's animal store,
    Ratcliff Highway 54–5
Jay, Revd Osborn 161
Jeffreys, Judge 32
Jelen, Samuel 210
Jerome, William 14
Jerusalem 12

Jesus Christ 79, 85, 117,
    119, 128, 173, 296
Jewell, Margaret 55–6,
    57, 58, 59
Jewish anarchists ix
Jewish Bakers' Union 145
Jewish Board of
    Guardians vii,
    123–4
*Jewish Chronicle* 140,
    144, 178–9
Jewish Furniture
    Workers' Union 145
Jewish ghetto ix, 2,
    124–7, 207, 264
'Jewish problem' 146
Jewish social club 3
Jewish Trunk and
    Pursemakers' Union
    183
Jews
    attacked by fascists in
        1930s 3
    Falk the *Ba'al Shem* of
        London 13, 71–8
    Hasidic 73
    and Jack the Ripper 96
    the invisible commu-
        nity 118–22
    arrival of the aliens viii,
        122–32
    pimps, fences and
        gangsters 132–6
    Jacob the Ripper
        136–41
    the Aliens Act 142–7
    and fascism 203–7
    Second World War
        235–6, 241
    *see also* anti-Semitism
Jews' Free School, Bell
    Lane, Spitalfields
    129–30
John of Gaunt 177
Johns, Ted 258, 292
Johnson, Dr Samuel 19,
    32–3, 82

Johnstone, John (opium den owner; previously Ah Sing) 104
Johnstone's London Commercial Directory 216
Jolly Sailors public house 57
Jolson, Al 36
Jones, Revd Harry 108
Jonson, Ben 214
Joseph, Keith, Baron 248
Joseph of Arimathea 117
Josephus 140
Joyce, William (Lord Haw Haw) 241
Jubela, Jubelo and Jubelum 94, 96
Jubilee Street club, Stepney 183, 187, 189
Juet, Robert 17
Jukes, Coulson and Co., Isle of Dogs 216
Jullien, Phillippe: Edouard VII 90
jury service 12

Kabbalah viii, 10, 11, 12, 70, 71, 73, 74, 76, 77, 78, 80, 245
Kalish, Zevi Hirsch 75
Kamenev, Lev 190, 193–4
Katz's shop, Brick Lane 261
Keeling House, Bethnal Green 249, 253
Kelly, John 95
Kelly, Mary 89, 90, 91, 95, 96, 98, 245
Kempton, Freda 112
Kensington 33
Kentucky club, Mile End Road 273–4
Kenya Times 296–7
Kew Gardens, Surrey 82
Keynes, J.M. 203

'Khaki General Election' (1918) 202
Kidd, Captain William 20
Kikal (owner, Odessa restaurant) 135
Kimberley 131
King, Bryan 152
'King, Mr' (of Limehouse) 114
King's Arms public house, New Gravel Lane (now Garnet Street) 59–60, 61, 64, 65, 66, 68, 69, 79
King's College, London 160
King's Cross 189
King's Road 295
Kingsland Road, Dalston 276
Knight, Stephen 92–3, 95, 96, 97
Jack the Ripper: The Final Solution 92
Knightsbridge 271
'Knockfergus' (Ratcliff) 54
Knox, Rawle 266–7
Knox, Rose 113–14
Krassin (Soviet ambassador to London) 195
Kray, Charles, Jnr 270, 271, 276, 280–81
Kray, Charles, Snr 237
Kray, May 270
Kray, Reginald 270, 272–5, 278–81
Kray, Ronald 221, 270–74, 276–80
Kray, Rose 270, 273
Kray, Violet 270, 276, 280, 281
Kray twins ix, 2, 135, 161, 241, 269–82, 284, 295
Krishna 296
Krupskaya, Nadezhda 188–9

Labour government 37, 201, 202
Labour Party
early days of ix, 200
'The Red Flag' 35
Mosley 202, 203
anti-death-penalty legislation 270
Lady Armstrong (ship) 34
Lahr, Charles 183
Lakeside shopping centre, Thurrock ix
Lambeth 166
Lambrianou, Tony 279
Lamentations, Book of 9
lampblack 29–30
Lancet journal 125
Langes, Charles Pierre Paul Savalette de 76
Langham Hotel, Portland Place 104
Lansbury, Daisy 199
Lansbury, George 189, 190, 198, 199, 200, 201, 203, 255, 269
Lansbury's Bulletin 192
Lansbury estate, Poplar 254–5
Lascars 99, 103, 105, 221, 263
Lasdun, Sir Denys 249, 251, 253
Last Supper 117
laudanum 101
Lax, Revd W. H. 109
Le Corbusier 246, 248, 254
Lea River x, 13, 16, 40, 107, 200, 219
Leadenhall Street 101, 164
League of Christian Reformers 259
'Leather Apron' (John Pizer) 137
Lee, Jimmy 'Cannonball' 270

Leeson, Benjamin 133
Leeson, Detective
    Sergeant 185–6
Leghorn (Livorno) 118
Leigh, Mike 207
Leighton, Ron, MP 291
Leman Street 183, 208
Leman Street police
    station 137, 209
Lenin, Vladimir 186,
    188–90, 191, 212
Leno, Dan (George
    Galvin) 168–9
Leutha, dogs of 214
*Leviathan* (later *Great
    Eastern*) 217–18
Levy, Elias 77–8
Lewey, mayor of Stepney
    228
Lewis, Kid 203
Lewis, Wyndham 130
Lewis's store, Liverpool
    218
Leyton x
Leytonstone x
Liberal government 144,
    186
Liberal–Conservative
    coalition 202
Liberty of Norton Folgate
    44
Lieberman, Aaron
    178–80, 182
light horsemen 21
Limehouse x, 13–14, 16,
    61, 99, 100, 102, 103,
    105, 106–7, 109–15,
    151, 209, 263
Limehouse Causeway
    105, 111, 112, 114,
    115, 116
Lin Tse-hsü, Imperial
    Commissioner 101
Lion public house,
    Bethnal Green 278
Lipski, Israel 138–9
Lithuanian Jews 126, 180

'Little Blitz' 239
Little Parliament 118
Litvinoff, Maxim 190,
    195
Liverpool 36, 218
    Roman Catholic
        Cathedral 255
Liverpool, Lord 203
Liverpool Street station
    189, 233
Lloyd, Marie (Matilda
    Victoria Wood) 168,
    169–70
Llyndin lake 117
    fort 54
lodging-houses 149, 162
Lombard, Revd B. S.
    145–6
London
    rebuilt after Great Fire
        9–13, 97, 98
    as a port 15, 22–8
    docks blitzed in Second
        World War 37–8
    becomes centre of the
        financial world 126
London, Jack 1, 163–5,
    295
    *The People of the
        Abyss* 163, 190
London, Tilbury and
    Southend Railway
    Company 28
London and St
    Katharine's Docks
    Company 28
London Bridge 60, 72,
    74, 177
London Chest Hospital,
    Bethnal Green 266
London City Airport ix,
    278, 289
London County Council
    200–201, 211, 246,
    247
London Docklands
    Development

Corporation (LDDC)
    288
London Docks 23, 27,
    33, 39, 69, 290
London Hilton, Park
    Lane 276
London Hospital 135,
    136, 156, 166, 171,
    207, 240
London Society for
    Promoting Christianity
    Among the Jews 122,
    127
London Street,
    Limehouse 106
London Underground
    293
London Vegetarian
    Society 219
London Working Men's
    Association 50
Long Grove asylum 273
'long lights' 43
Lord Chancellor 12, 19,
    77
Lord Rodney's Head pub-
    lic house, Whitechapel
    Road 207
Lord's cricket ground 242
Los 214
Loughton 256
Louis, Joe 276
Louis XVI, King of
    France 76
Louis Philippe Joseph,
    Duc d'Orléans 76
Louis-Philippe, King of
    the French 76
Lovatt, Lord 73
Low Ping You, Ada 111
Lowder, Revd Charles 84,
    85, 86
Lubetkin, Berthold 253
Lucan, Lord 284
Lucchese, Thomas 276
Lucchese family 276
Ludgate Hill 25

Luftwaffe 229, 230, 241
lumpers viii, 21
Lusk, George 89
lustrings 42
Luxemburg, Rosa 189
Lyons 92

Macclesfield 50
McCoy, Charlie 'Kid'
    (Max Moses) 134, 136
MacDonald, James
    Ramsay 190, 201
Machzikei Hadas
    V'Shomrei Shabbas
    127
Mcintosh estate, Poplar
    107
McKenna, Edward 141
MacKenny, Harry 'Big H'
    284, 285
Maconochies firm 222–3
McVitie, Jack 'The Hat'
    279–80
Madagascar 146
Madame Tussaud's
    Chamber of Horrors
    284
Mafia 276–7
Mahdi, Imam 296
Mahomet, Dean 265
Maitreya, Lord 295–6
Manchester 45, 192, 198,
    220, 253
Manchester Guardian 137
Manhattan, New York 22
Manitoba 172
Manning, Cardinal 35
Mansell Street 179
Marble Arch 49
Marciano, Rocky 276
Mare Street, Hackney
    271
Marine Police
    Establishment 22
Marine Square (later
    Wellclose Square)
    12–13

Mark Lane station 208
Marks, Ginger 281–2
Marks and Spencer 203
Marks' delicatessen,
    Wentworth Street 261
Marlborough, Wiltshire
    64
Marr, Celia 55, 58, 59,
    63, 64, 66, 67, 69, 152
Marr, Timothy 55, 56,
    58, 59, 62, 63, 64, 66,
    67, 69, 152
Marranos 118, 119
Marseilles 248
Marshalsea prison,
    Southwark 20
Martin, Brother 4, 283,
    295
Martin, Terry 272
Marx, Eleanor 196
Marx, Joseph 185, 186
Marx, Karl 193, 196
Mary, Queen (as Princess
    Mary of Teck) 52
Mary Tudor 7–8
Marylebone 71
Masonic Rite of
    Philalethes ('Searchers
    after Truth') 76
Massacre of St
    Bartholomew (1572)
    40, 42
Masterman, Charles 186
match girls' strike (1888)
    34, 181, 196–7, 238
Matilda, Queen 24
Matthew, St, gospel of
    297
Matthew T. Shaw & Co.
    Ltd 224–5
Maurice, Revd F. D. 196
Maxse, Leo 146
Maxwell, Robert 132
May, Mr Justice 285
Mayfair 7, 221, 287
Mayhew, Henry 30,
    33–4

Mayo, Dr 82
Meath Road, West Ham
    231
Medak, Peter 276
Merceron, Joseph 160
Merchant, John 40
Meridian line 107
Merrick, John (the
    Elephant Man) 166
Merson, Billy 36
Methodists 49–50, 71,
    86, 127
Metropolitan Board of
    Works 157
Metropolitan Police 69,
    135, 160, 183, 184,
    207
Meux's Brewery 24
midden men 150
Middlesex Street 125
Midland & Scottish
    Railway 222
Mies van der Rohe,
    Ludwig 246
Mile End x, 6, 18, 122,
    177, 206, 229, 230,
    244
Mile End Road 166, 175,
    210, 273
Mile End Waste 270
Militant Tendency 208,
    268
Millennium Dome 221
Millwall xiv, 214, 216,
    217, 218, 230, 289,
    290
Millwall Dock 39, 217,
    257
Millwall Dock and Canal
    Company 217
Millwall FC 223
Milton, John: Samson
    Agonistes 12
Ming Street 116
Minister's House, Church
    Street (later Fournier
    Street) 44

Ministry of Information, Senate House, Bloomsbury 232
Minories monastery 4
Mint, the 73
*Mirror* newspaper group 290
Mitchell, Frank 'The Mad Axeman' 277–8, 281
mitochondrial DNA (mtDNA) 93
Mitre Square, Aldgate 4, 88, 95–6, 98, 139
Mitre Street, Aldgate 274
Molotov, Vyacheslav 37, 195
monasteries vii, 7, 84
Money Bag Alley 25
monkey suckers viii, 21
Montague, Samuel, MP 180, 182
Montgomery, Bernard Law, Viscount 240
Monument, Fish Street Hill 9, 12
Mooney, George 230–31
Moore, Roger 279
Moorfields 8
Morgan Stanley Dean Witter 290
*Morning Chronicle* 99
morphine 101
Morris, William 196
Morrison, Arthur 149, 158, 162, 164
    *A Child of the Jago* 161
    *Tales of Mean Streets* 1, 161
Morton's firm 222, 223
Moscheles, Felix 190
Moscow 188
*Moscow Daily News* 193
Moses, Max *see* McCoy, Charlie 'Kid'
Mosley, Oswald 179, 202–4, 206–12, 239, 258–61, 267, 269, 272

Mosley Memorandum 202–3
Mottram, Brian 278
Mount of Olives 12
Mountjoy, Christopher 41
Mourrewitz, Poolka ('George Gardstein') 184–5, 187
Mr Smith's club, Catford 278
Mudchute 222
mudlarks viii, 21
Mulberry Street, Whitechapel 137
Mullard, Arthur 277
multum 153
Murder (Abolition of Death Penalty) Act (1965) 270
Murdoch, Rupert 290–91
Murray, John 56
Muscovy Company 16
music hall ix, 166–70
Mussolini, Benito 201–2, 212, 258, 265, 267
Muswell Hill 290
Myddelton Square, Islington 12

Nairobi, Kenya 296–7
Napoleon Bonaparte 54
Narrow Street, Limehouse 106
Nash, Johnny 280
Nashe, Thomas and Jonson, Ben: *The Isle of Dogs* 214
National Amalgamated Stevedores' and Dockers' Union ('the Blues') 37
National Day of Fasting and Prayer (March 1832) 157
National Front ix, 265–6, 267–8, 295

National Health Service 171, 256
National Old Age Pensions Association 231
*National Review* 146
National Sailors' and Firemen's Union 109
national socialism 211
National Society for the Prevention of Cruelty to Children 174
National Theatre, South Bank 249
National Union of Railwaymen 193
National Union of Women's Suffrage Societies 198
National Union of Working Classes 157
nationalism 178, 258, 261, 268
Nelson, Admiral Horatio, Lord 84, 215
Nelson Street, Mile End 175
Netley, William 91, 92, 93
Neuhoff, Theodor von 76
Neuve Eglise, Fournier Street/Brick Lane 127
New Church 81
New Cross station 227
New Enlightenment 295
New Gravel Lane (now Garnet Street) 59, 61, 62, 63, 64, 69
New Jerusalem vii, 10, 245, 291, 295
New Model Army 118
New Order Group 258
New Party 203
New Road 142, 262
*New Statesman* 232
New Testament 71
New York 276

New Zealand 108
Newcastle Arms public house, Isle of Dogs 221
Newfoundland 17, 18
Newgate prison 45, 138, 160
Newham council 288
News International 291
*News of the World* 290
Newton, John 19
'Nice Quiet Day, A' 68, 167
Nichols, Mary Ann ('Polly') 87, 91, 94–5, 136, 140
Nightingale, Florence 157
nihilism 178
Nilus, Sergei 146
Ningpo 100
'No Popery' riots (1859) 152
Noah 80
nonconformism 45
Norfolk, Duke of 2
Norman, Henry, MP 143
Norman Conquest 118
Normans 3, 15, 40
North Greenwich station 224
North Quay 29
North Street, Poplar 109
North-east Passage, search for 16
North-west Passage 16–17, 18
Northamptonshire police force 291
Norton Folgate 44, 46, 133
Norwood 290
Notting Hill 261
Numbers, Book of 11
nut galls 153
nux vomica 153
Nyasa, Lake 219

*Observer* 266, 292

Odessa restaurant, Stepney 135
Odessans 135–6
Ofili, Chris 44
Old Bailey 187, 280
Old Bethnal Green Road 207
Old Ford xiv, 107
Old Ford Road 191, 199
Old Gravel Lane, Shadwell 84
Old Montague Street 181
Old Nichol ix, 158–62, 254
Old Nichol gang 160–61
Old Nichol Street 158, 159
Old Testament viii, 10, 71, 118
Olivier, Dr Charles P. 81
Olney, George 55, 56
Omega studios 130
Operation Sealion (*Unternehmen Seelöwe*) 229
opium viii, 100–106, 110–11
Order of the Sons of St George 259
Orr, Mrs 63–4
Orwell, George (Eric Blair) 115–16, 163, 164, 168, 232, 241
*1984* 243
*Down and Out in Paris and London* 116
Osborn Street, Whitechapel 183
Ossie (a forger) 275
Otley, Roi 246
Oval cricket ground 242

Pacific Ocean 18
Paddington station 233
'Paki-bashing' 266
Palace of Westminster 157

Pale of Settlement 147
Pall Mall 295
Palmer, John 83
Pankhurst, Christabel 198
Pankhurst, Emmeline 198, 199
Pankhurst, Sylvia 198, 199
Pantomime Police 21
Paragon Theatre of Varieties, Mile End Road 166
Paris 188
Park Lane 131
Parliamentarians 7
Pas de Calais 240, 242
*Passport to Pimlico* (film) 258
Paton, Revd W. W. 231
Payne, Violet 112
Pear Tree Alley 66
Pear Tree Tavern 62–4, 66, 67, 68
Peel, Sir Robert 160
Peking 110
penny gaffes 166
Pennyfields 111, 112, 116
People's Charter 50
People's Palace, Mile End Road 142, 229
People's Russian Information Bureau 191
Pepys, Samuel 120, 214
Perceval, Spencer 67
'Perkoff' (leader of Bessarabians) 134, 135
Peters, Jacob 184, 187–8
Peterson, John 62
Peto, Samuel Morton 27
Petrov (bookshop owner) 189
Petrovsky, Max 193
Petticoat Lane 121, 125–6, 241, 261, 293

Pharmacy Acts (1868 and 1908) 110
philanthropists ix, 170–76
Phillips, Watts: *The Wild Tribes of London* 34, 69, 121–2
'Philosopher's Stone' 72
Philpot Street 135
Phoenicians 117
Phoney War 212, 229
'phossy jaw' 197
Piatkow, Peter ('Peter the Painter') 184, 185, 186
Piccadilly Circus 112, 260
Pie Corner, Smithfield 7
Pierhead, Wapping 33
Pillory Lane 25
Pimlico 258
pimps 132–3
Pinfold, Terry 283, 285
Piratin, Phil 195, 234, 261
Pitchon, Patricia 296
Pitt, William, the Younger 23
Pizer, John ('Leather Apron') 137
Plague (1665) ix, 2, 5–6, 7, 11, 119, 154–5, 226
Plaistow Marshes 27
Plato 17
Plumstead 157
pogroms (1881) viii, 122
Poland, Germany invades (1939) 211
Polish Jews 126
*Polisher Yidl, Der* (the Little Polish Jew) 180
poll-tax rebels (1381) 2
Pollitt, Harry 194
Pool of London 55, 106
Poolaroone island 22
Poor Jews' Temporary Shelter 123, 129
Poor Law Guardians 200
Pope, the

effigy burnt after Great Fire 8–9
Huguenot hatred of 43
and the plague 154
Poplar x, 14, 29, 99, 102, 106, 107, 115, 124, 156, 166, 200–201, 215, 230, 254, 263, 283
Poplar council 247, 257
Poplar High Street 108
Poplar Labour Party 200
Poplar Town Hall 192
popularism 200–201
Port of London 38, 150, 265
Port of London Authority (PLA) 36, 39, 222, 235, 288
portage brotherhoods 28
Portland 218
Portugal, and colonies 21
Portuguese Jews 126
Post Office Tower, Fitzrovia 253
Potsdam conference (1945) 188
Poultenay, Sir John 215
Pound, Ezra 131
Powell, Enoch 39
Prague 93
prefabs 243–4
Prescot Street 72, 74
press gangs 19, 84, 107
Price (businessman) 215
Prince, John 13
Prince of Denmark tavern 166
Princes (now Princelet) Street 43
Princes Square 13, 81
Princess Music Hall, Leeds 169
Prospect of Whitby pub, Wapping 32
prostitution 149, 160, 162, 246

protection racketeers 211
Protestants
and the Great Fire as punishment 7–8
Huguenot silk weavers 40, 42, 51
education 129
*Protocols of the Meetings of the Learned Elders of Zion* (Nilus) 146
Proudhon, Pierre 183
Public Order Act 211
Pudding Lane 6, 7, 8, 9
Pugh (a carpenter) 58
pure-pickers 150
Puritans 118
Purity Party 169
Putney 287

Quakers 5
Quatuor Coronati Masonic Lodge, No. 2076 96
Queenhithe 15
Queen's Theatre, Poplar 166
Quersitanus 71
Quilter Street 207

racism 258, 264, 265–6, 268, 284
Ragged Schools Union 174
Railtrack 293
Railway Tavern, Garford Road/West India Dock Road (Charlie Brown's) 113–14, 221
Ralegh, Sir Walter 17
Ranelagh Road, West Ham 231
rat-catchers 25
Ratcliff 14, 16, 22, 54, 99, 119
Ratcliff Cross 17
Ratcliff Highway 84, 156, 206, 442

Ratcliff Highway *cont.*
  becomes London's
    most violent road 53
  history of 54
  degeneration of 54
  fire of 1794 54
  'Knockfergus' nick-
    name 54
  Jamrach's animal store
    54–5
  subsequent names 69
Ratcliff Highway murders
  (1811) ix, 2, 53–70,
  96, 283, 291
  murder of the Marrs
    55–9, 152
  false leads 57–9
  murder of the
    Williamsons 59–61
  arrest at the Pear Tree
    Tavern 61–4
  John Williams: mur-
    derer or martyr?
    64–7
  killers on the loose?
    67–9
Ratcliff Stairs 15–16
Read, John Kingsley 268
rebuilding of the East End
  Orwell on life in the
    East End (late 1940s)
    243
  prefabs built 243–4
  lack of public debate
    244
  needless destruction
    244–5
  a machine for living in
    246–54
  from our house to
    Bauhaus 254–8
Red Cow (now the Town
  of Ramsgate) pub,
  Wapping 32
'Red Flag, The' 35
'Red Friday' (31 July
  1925) 192

Redman, Joseph 85
Regal snooker club, Eric
  Street, Mile End 271
Regent's Park 25
Reichmann brothers
  289–90
Relf, Robert 284
Representation of the
  People Act (1918) 199
Revelations, Book of 6, 71
Rhodes, Cecil 131
Ribbentrop, Joachim von
  259
Rice, William 63
Richard II, King 177
Richardson, Charlie 271,
  278
Richardson, Eddie 278
Richardson brothers 274,
  278
Richter (a German sailor)
  64
Ridley Road market,
  Dalston 260
Ritchie, J. Ewing: *Days
  and Nights in London*
  162
Ritter (a Polish Jew) 139
river piracy viii, 20–21
river police 22–3
Robin Hood Gardens,
  Poplar 251–2
Robsahm (friend of
  Swedenborg) 79
Rocker, Rudolf 182–3,
  187
rocket attack 238–42
rogue auctioneers 151
Rohmer, Sax (Arthur
  Stansfield Ward) 112,
  113–15
  *The Drums of Fu
    Manchu* 115
  *Emperor Fu Manchu*
    115
  *The Mystery of Dr Fu-
    Manchu* 115

*The Shadow of Fu
  Manchu* 115
roll-on/roll-off ferries 38
Roman Road 212
Romans 40, 140, 295
  Tower Hill left as
    sacred territory vii, 3
Romford, Essex x,
  269
Romford Market ix
Rommel, Erwin 238
Ronan Point tragedy,
  Canning Town (1968)
  252–3
Rook Street, Poplar 107
Rookery 25
Rose, Harry 259
Rose, Mrs (an East End
  madam) 175–6
Rosenberg, Isaac 130–31,
  142
Rosicrucians 113
Ross, Revd D. 142
Ross, Sammy 272
Rotherhithe 33
Rothschild, Lord 129,
  142, 143, 163, 182
Rothschild Dwellings 163
Rothschild family 132,
  203
Rotterdam 36, 38, 229
Rouen 118
Roughneck 209
Roundabout Tavern 53
Royal Academy of Arts
  44
Royal Air Force (RAF)
  229
Royal Albert Dock 27, 28
Royal Command
  Performances 170
royal commission on the
  coal industry (1925–6)
  191, 192
Royal Docks 289
Royal Institute of British
  Architects 251

Royal Leamington Spa 284
Royal Mint Street 209
Royal Society vii, 8, 9, 10, 84
'royals' 31
Royalty Theatre, Wellclose Square 83
Rumanian café, Settles Street/Commercial Road 133, 135
Rumanian Jews 126
Rumbelow, Donald: *Jack the Ripper: The Complete Casebook* 92
Rushdie, Salman: *The Satanic Verses* 295
Russell's yard, Millwall 217, 219
Russia *see* Soviet Union
Russian Jews 120, 126, 145
Russian Revolution (1917) 3, 145, 186, 187, 188, 190, 193, 194, 195, 225

'sacred geometry' 11
Saffron Hill 1
St Anne church, Limehouse 106
St Bartholomew-the-Great Gatehouse 8
St Botolph's churchyard, Aldgate 5
St Dunstan and All Saints church, Stepney (Church of the High Seas) 14
St Dunstan in the East church 11, 12, 105
St Dunstan in the West church, Fleet Street 11
St George's district 148, 207, 261
St George's Street (previously Ratcliff Highway; later The Highway) 69
St George's Turnpike 66
St George's Vestry 142
St George's Watch House 66
St George's-in-the-East church 13, 61, 152
St James's 221
St Jude's church, Whitechapel 170
St Katharine's district 12, 15, 292
St Katharine's Dock 17, 24–6, 27, 38, 39, 83
St Katharine's Dock Company 24
St Katharine's Hospital monastery 4
St Leonard's Street, Poplar 107
St Luke's 280
St Magnus Martyr church 73
St Mary Graces abbey 12
St Mary Matfellon church 14
St Mary Spital Cross 41
St Mary Spital priory and hospital 40, 41
St Mary Woolnoth church 13
St Matthew, Gospel of 87
St Matthew's church, Bethnal Green 280, 281
St Paul's Cathedral xiii, 10, 11, 12, 14, 25
St Paul's church, Shadwell 54, 61
St Peter's church, Old Gravel Lane, Shadwell 84
St Petersburg 188
St Petersburg Soviet strike 189
St Saviour and the Cross's mission hall and chapel of ease 84–5, 97
St Saviour's church 91, 97
St Saviour's Infirmary, Euston 97
Saladin 85
Salisbury, Lord 91, 142
Salmon and Ball public house, Bethnal Green 49, 203, 260
Salmon Lane, Limehouse 106
Salomons, Alderman 121
Salvation Army 84, 165, 173, 183, 197
Samuel, Harry 143
Samuel, Herbert 145
San Francisco 110
Sandys, Duncan 240
Sandys Row 262
Saunders Ness Road 216
Savile, Sir Henry 42
Savoy hotel, Strand 234
Savoy palace, Strand 177
Saxons 40
Scales, Lucy 151
Scales, Margaret 151
scarlet-dyeing 13
Schewzik's Russian Vapour Baths, Brick Lane 123
Schwartz, Israel 138
Scotland Yard 280
Scots Guards 186
scuffle hunters 21
Seal of Solomon (Star of David) 72, 98
Second World War ix, 14, 37–8, 116, 120, 201, 212, 225, 226–42
Britain declares war on Germany (1939) 212, 226
food rationing 227, 242
evacuation 227–8, 233, 271

Second World War
*cont.*
    shelters 228–9,
        233–6
    first German bomb-
        ing of London area
        (June 1940) 229
    first East End attack
        (24 August 1940)
        229
    the East End alight
        230–33
    deep-shelter mentality
        233–6
    the myth of the Blitz
        236–8
    rocket attack 238–42
    information sup-
        pressed 232, 240
    end of the war 242
*Secrets and Lies* (film)
    207
*selichos* 140
Sephardic Jews 120
Settles Street 133, 135,
    262
Seven Sisters Road 191
Seven Stars public house,
    Brick Lane 267
Seven Years War
    (1756–63) 47
Sevenoaks, Kent 227
sewer system 157
Shackleton, Ernest 109
Shacklewell 261
Shadwell x, 15, 18, 31,
    60, 103, 124, 272
Shadwell barracks 99
Shadwell workhouse 155
Shaftesbury, Lord 171
Shakespeare, William 41
sharpers 151
Shaw, Jack 209–10
Shaw, Stanley 142
'She Sits among Her
    Cabbages and Peas'
    170

Shelby, Norman *see*
    McCoy, Charlie 'Kid'
Shelley, Mary:
    *Frankenstein* 74
Sherwood, Fred 284
Ship Alley 83
Shipping Federation 35
'Shobbos Goy' 127
shofulmen 151
Shoreditch 41, 162, 249
Shoreditch council 247
Shoreditch High Street
    294
Shoreditch station 295
Shovel Alley 25
show trials, Soviet
    (1930s) 190, 193
Sickert, Joseph 90–92,
    93, 97
Sickert, Walter 90, 91,
    92, 93
Sidney Street siege (1911)
    185–7
Sieff, Israel 203
silk weaving ix, 13,
    40–52, 158
Silvertown x, 199
Simon, John 209
Sims, George R.: *In
    Limehouse and the Isle
    of Dogs* 220
Singer, Isaac Bashevis
    *The Golem* 74
    *The Manor* 177–8
Sir Charles Price and Co.,
    Isle of Dogs 216
Six Keys of Eudoxus 71
'Skeleton Army' 173
Skidmore, Owings and
    Merrill 289
Slade School of Art 130
slavery 19, 25
smallpox 19
Smith, Emma 161
Smith, Revd George
    Charles (Bosun Smith)
    84

Smith, Marmaduke 44
Smithfield 7, 8
Smithson, Peter and
    Alison 251–2
Snow, John 157
Snowdon's, Isle of Dogs
    225
Social Democratic
    Federation 196
socialism, socialists 178,
    180, 188, 190, 195–6,
    200, 201, 255
Socialist League 196
Socialist Workers' Party
    268, 295
Society for the Protection
    of Ancient Buildings 44
Society of the Holy Cross
    85, 152
Soho 271, 292
Sokolow, William 184
Solomon, King 117
Solomons, Ikey 121
Sotheby's auctioneers,
    London 81
South Africa 131, 133,
    278, 297
Southcott, Joanna 71
Southwark Cathedral 97
Soviet Union
    Hitler attacks (1941)
        195
    becomes an ally against
        the Nazis 238
    break-up of 297
Soviet–German non-
    aggression treaty
    (1939) 195, 235
Spain
    and colonies 21
    war with (1656) 119
'Spaniard That Blighted
    My Life, The' 36
Spanish Armada (1588)
    21
Spanish Civil War 207
Spanish Inquisition 118

Spanish Jews 126
*Sparrers Can't Sing* (film) 273
*Spearhead* newspaper 267
Special Constabulary 192
Spencer House, St James's Place 132
spice routes 22
Spital Square 44
Spitalfields ix, x, 13, 40–41, 42, 124, 148–9, 233, 241, 244, 247, 263, 264, 265, 268, 287, 293–4
Spitalfields Fair 41
Spitalfields Great Synagogue, Brick Lane/Fournier Street (later Jamme Masjid mosque) 181, 182, 267
Spitalfields market 44, 178, 293
Spitalfields Riots 46–9
Spitalfields Weavers' Act (1773) 49
Spot, Jack 209, 211, 272
'spotted fever' 235
Spring-heeled Jack 2, 151–2
Squires, Dorothy 279
Squirries Street, off Bethnal Green Road 204
Stalin, Joseph (previously Dzugashvili) 188, 189–90, 193, 235, 265
Stamford Hill 147
Star Inn, Fish Street Hill 7
Star Street 35
Stead, W. T. 138
Steamship public house, Poplar 108
steamships 23
Stean Street, Dalston 270
Stephen, King 24
Stephens Smith and Co. 257–8

Stepney x, 1, 5, 6, 14, 22, 99, 129, 130, 131, 133, 135, 149, 163, 172, 175, 194, 195, 206, 207, 231, 236, 237, 243, 247, 256, 261, 263
Stepney Causeway 172
Stepney council 247
Stepney Fields 53
Stepney Green 3, 125, 182
Stepney Marsh *see* Isle of Dogs
Stepney station 164
stevedores 29, 34, 53
*stiebels* (home-based synagogues) 126–7, 130
Stillwell, Kitty 59, 60
Stoke Newington police station 260
Stop At Nothing mob *see* Bessarabians
Stowell, Thomas 90
Strand xiii
Strangers' Home for Asiatics, Africans and South Sea Islanders, West India Dock Road 100
Stratford x, 289
'street in the sky' concept 250, 289
Stride, Elizabeth 88, 91, 95, 98, 138, 139
suffragettism 178, 198–9
sugarmen 29
suicide 65–7, 68–9
*Sun* 290
Sun Tavern Fields 54
*Sunday Night at the London Palladium* (television programme) 132
*Sunday Times* 290
Svaars, Fritz 185, 186
Swaffer, Hannen: 'The Cockney is Bloody but Unbowed' 232–3

sweatshops 124, 127, 145, 149, 181, 259
Swedenborg, Emanuel 13, 79–81, 82
Swedish Academy of Sciences 80
Swedish church, Princes Square 81
Sweet Apple Court 43
Sylhet 263
Syracuse, Sicily 180

Tabram, Martha 87, 140
tacklehouse porters 28
tailors' strike (1889) 181
tailors' strike (1906) 183
tailors' strike (1912) 187
tallymen 29
Tasel Close 41
Tawney, Richard 171
taxation 12, 82, 177
tea clippers 24
Teddington, Middlesex 36
*Telegraph* newspaper group 290, 291–2
Telford, Thomas 25
Temperance Society 174
Temple Bar 12
Temple of Solomon 94, 95
Tempo club, Highbury 279
Terminus Café, Mile End Road 275
Thames Ironworks 219–20, 224
Thames River
river piracy viii, 20–21
sailors bring debauchery to the East End viii–ix
a boundary of the East End x, 13
brings immigrants to London viii
convict hulks in 20
Thames water 30

Thames River *cont.*
  flooding of Wapping 31
  bureaucratic confusion
    36
  tidal 36
  and Great Seal of
    England 77
  floating corpses 107
  and Joseph of
    Arimathea 117
  MPs take action after
    summer of 1858 157
  and the Isle of Dogs
    213, 214, 216, 219,
    227, 230
  in the Second World
    War 230, 231, 242
Thames Street 7
Thames Tunnel 33
Thatcher, Margaret,
  Baroness 268, 287
'third way' 202
Three Bells public house
  70
Three Colt Street,
  Limehouse 106
*Thunderbirds* (television
  series) 132
Thurlow, Lord 77
Thurrock ix
ticket porters 28
Tiger Bay 149
Tilbury 27–8
Tilbury goods depot,
  Gower's Walk, off
  Commercial Road
  235–6
Tiler Road (previously
  Glengall Road) 223
Tillett, Ben 36
*Times, The* 57, 111, 139,
  141, 197, 290
tin traders 117
Titian: *Portrait of
  Isabella d'Este in Red*
  77
Tokmak, Ukraine 132

Tollington Park, Stroud
  Green 178
Tooke (businessman) 215
toshers 21, 150
Tottenham Hotspur FC
  230
Tours 92
Tower Bridge 215, 287
Tower Green 40
Tower Hamlets 289, 290
Tower Hamlets council
  244–5, 249, 258, 288
Tower Hill 19, 210
  location of vii
  hallowed status vii, 3
  union rallies 36
  scaffold 73
  linked with Blackwall
    Dock 215
Tower House, Stepney
  193–4
Tower Liberty 73, 82
Tower of London 15, 32,
  54, 73, 82
  built by Normans 3
  the ravens 3
  Richard II hides in 177
  stormed by Cade and
    his men 177
Town of Ramsgate pub,
  Wapping (previously
  Red Cow) 32
Toynbee Hall, Spitalfields
  170–71, 193
Toynbee Shakespeare
  Club 171
trade
  growth dominated by
    East India Company
    ix, 21–2
  river-borne 14
trade unions 34, 48, 145,
  181, 183, 192, 197
Trades Union Congress
  (TUC) 192, 193
  General Council 193
traffic congestion 246

Transport and General
  Workers' Union
  (TGWU) ('the Whites')
  37
Transylvania 147
Tredegar Square, Bow 245
Tree of Life 11
Trellick Tower, North
  Kensington 250
Tremlett, George 251
Treves, Dr Frederick 166
Triads 105
tribes of London, ancient
  vii, 3
Trotsky, Leon (Lev
  Bronstein) 188, 189,
  190, 191, 194
True Cross 85
Tubbs, Ralph: *Living in
  Cities* 247
Turner, J. M. W. 32
Turner (the Williamsons'
  lodger) 60–61, 62, 64
Turner Street, off
  Commercial Road 152
'Two Lovely Black Eyes'
  168
Tyburn 8, 49
Tyndall, John 267–8
Tyne shipyards 220

Union Movement 259,
  260
Union of British Freedom
  258
*Unité d'habitation* 248
United Synagogue 130
Unwin, Mr (coroner) 65
Upper North Road pri-
  mary school, Poplar
  108
Uppsala Cathedral 81
Upton, Essex 76
Upton Park ix, 230

V1 rockets (doodle-bugs)
  239–40

V2 rockets 240–41
V3 rockets 242
Vallance Road, Bethnal
    Green 237, 241, 270,
    273, 276, 281
Valline, John 48, 49
Vanderdelf, Cornelius 31,
    214
Vanuatu 18
VE Day 242
Vegetarian Cycling and
    Athletic Club 219
velvets 42–3
Vermilloe, Mr and Mrs
    63
vibrio 155
Victoria, Queen 44, 91,
    101, 174
Victoria, Vesta 167
Victoria and Albert
    Museum, South
    Kensington 43
Victoria Dock 27
Victoria Dock Company
    27
Victoria Park x, 199,
    205, 210, 211, 226,
    231, 260
Victoria Street 103
Vigilance Committee 169
Violenia, Emmanuel 137

Wade's Arms public
    house, Jeremiah Street,
    Poplar 35
Waeppa, Saxon chieftain
    31
Wainer, Lieb 180
'Waiting at the Church'
    167
Walloon refugees 52
Walthamstow 25, 241
Walworth 1
Wanstead 31, 256
Wapping x, 15, 20, 23,
    31–4, 55, 59, 60, 117,
    290, 291

Wapping High Street 31,
    32, 33
Wapping New Stairs 22
Wapping on the Woze 32
Ward, Nathaniel 82
Warner, Benjamin 52
Warren, Sir Charles 96
Waterford, Henry,
    Marquis of 152
Waterloo, Battle of
    (1815) 203
Waterloo Barracks,
    Tower of London 271
Watkins, Alan: A Short
    Walk Down Fleet
    Street 292
Watney Street 31, 264
Watney Streeters 135,
    272
Watt, James 23
Weige brothers 108
Weintrop, Reuben ('Bud
    Flanagan') 131
Weishaupt, Adam 183
Welfare State 171
Wellclose Square (previ-
    ously Marine Square)
    66, 74–5, 166, 295
the East End's first
    planned estate viii
a centre of intrigue viii,
    ix, 13
Falk's villa 74, 77, 268
Swedenborg lives in 79
special municipal privi-
    leges 82
theatres and music hall
    83
shops 83–4
social decline 86
and Jack the Ripper 97,
    98
Danish history 97
needless destruction in
    245
and News International
    291

Wellington, Arthur
    Wellesley, 1st Duke of
    203
Wells, Charles Deville
    168
Wembley 261
Wensley, Detective
    Inspector 185–6
Wentworth Model
    Buildings 264
Wentworth Street 261
Wesley, John 49–50, 127
West End 204, 232, 278
West Ham xiv, 198, 231,
    256
West Ham United FC ix,
    220, 230
West India Company 23
West India Dock 23, 27,
    34, 215, 230
West India Dock
    Company 23
West India Dock Road,
    Limehouse 100, 116,
    221
West India Import and
    Export Docks 289
West Indian immigrants
    266
Westminster 292
Westminster, Duke of 131
Westway 295
Westwood's iron and steel
    works, Millwall 225
White, Arnold 142
'White Cockade, The'
    35
White Horse Lane,
    Stepney 210
White Rose public house,
    Ratcliff Highway 61,
    140
Whitechapel x, 1, 5, 6,
    14, 75, 97, 124, 129,
    133, 135, 136, 139,
    149, 157, 162, 170,
    173, 177, 179, 190,

Whitechapel *cont.*
194, 206, 247, 261,
263, 271
Whitechapel High Street
125, 262
Whitechapel public
library 193
Whitechapel Road 3, 5,
125, 166, 207
Whitechapel station 94,
185, 210, 259
Whitechapel Vigilance
Committee 89
Whiteread, Rachael 44
'Who Do You Think
You're Kidding, Mr
Hitler?' 131
Wigram, Robert 24
Wilde, Oscar: *The Picture
of Dorian Gray* 104
Wilhelm II, Kaiser 183
Wilkes Street 43
Willesden 252
William I, King 118
William III, King
(William of Orange)
32, 42, 120
Williams, Councillor 143
Williams, John 62–7, 68,
69, 70
Williams, Kathleen 239
Williamson, Elizabeth
59–62, 64, 65, 67, 69

Williamson, John 59, 60,
61, 64, 65, 67
Willoughby, Sir Hugh 16
Wilton's music hall,
Wellclose Square 83,
85–6, 166–7, 245
Winchevsky, Morris 180,
182
windmills 214, 216
Windsor, Barbara 273
Windsor, Duchess of 219
Windsor, Duke of *see*
Edward, Prince of
Wales
Wingate, General Orde
259
Winter of Discontent
(1978–9) 268
Women's Social and
Political Union (WSPU)
198, 199
Woods, Albie 279
Woods of Kingsland
Road, Dalston 276
Woolwich Arsenal 224
Workers' Education
Association 171, 193
Wormwood Scrubs 210,
260
Wren, Sir Christopher 12,
45, 82
rebuilding of London
vii, 8, 9–13, 295

use of religious rite in
calculations vii,
10–12
Wright, Thomas: *Some
Habits and Customs of
the Working Classes*
220
Wyngarde, Peter 184

Yarrow's, Cubitt Town
219, 224
Ye Olde Cheshire Cheese,
Fleet Street 292
Yeo, Alfred 200
Yiddish 127–8
York Minster public
house, Philpot Street
135

Zechariah 11
Zetland Hall, Mansell
Street 179
Zevi, Shabbatai 119–20
Ziaur, President 268
*Zielraum* 230
Ziggy's café, Cobb Street
272
Zinoviev, Grigori 190,
193–4
Zionism 143, 178, 259
Zionist Federation 143